MOPED ARMY

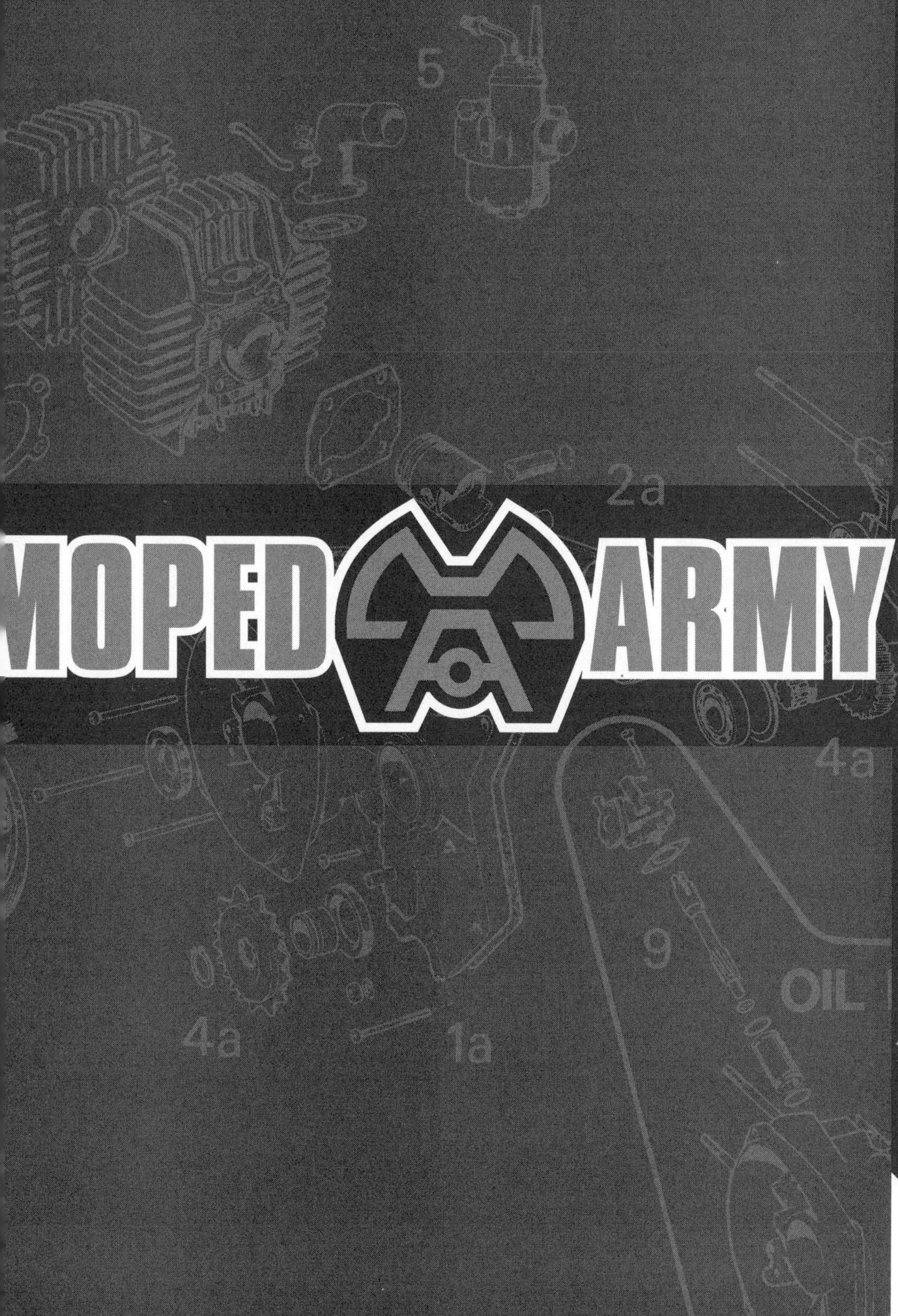
5
2a
4a
9
OIL
4a
1a

MOPED ARMY (SECOND PRINTING, JUNE 2008)
Published by CAFE DIGITAL STUDIOS
P.O. Box 51595, Kalamazoo, Michigan 49005 USA

 Printed in the USA at Malloy Printing, Ann Arbor, MI
ISBN-10# 0-9768565-4-9 ISBN-13# 978-0-9768565-4-2

Other books by Paul Sizer from CAFE DIGITAL STUDIOS:

LITTLE WHITE MOUSE OMNIBUS: THE COMPLETE SERIES
ISBN-10 # 0-9768565-5-7 ISBN-13 # 978-0-9768565-5-9 (CDC-007)

B.P.M. (Beats Per Minute)
ISBN-10# 0-9768565-6-5 ISBN-13# 978-0-9768565-6-6 (CDC-008)

Visit our online store at www.paulsizer.com for **LITTLE WHITE MOUSE, B.P.M.** and **MOPED ARMY** downloads, color galleries, books and merchandise.

PAUL SIZER:
story_analog/digital art_fx_graphics

MOPED ⬡ ARMY

with

DANIEL ROBERT KASTNER, SIMON KING:
technical data_inspiration

JANE IRWIN:
data entry_tweaking_tech input_support

book_interface_design/cover_illustrations/coloring:
PAUL SIZER/Cafe Digital Studios

author_photography:
DOUGLAS NEAL

PAVING THE FUTURE

WHY PAUL SIZER SPENT TWO YEARS DRAWING MOPEDS...

From mice to mopeds, I'm slowly working my way through the alphabet.

When I decided to try my hand at doing a graphic novel start-to-finish, I had some fears and questions, mostly about my ability to keep focus on such a big (for me, at least) undertaking. LITTLE WHITE MOUSE served as my training wheels, and gave me the confidence to plow ahead and give myself a new set of requirements and challenges for my next project. Once again, real life proved the most fertile of areas to dig for ideas. The Moped Army snuck up on me, slapped me upside the head and became my new focus.

Truthfully, I felt some apprehension about approaching the Moped Army and asking if they'd mind if I took their story and threw it 272 years into the future. Not because they were scary, but because I wasn't sure I was . . . cool enough to do the job right. That fear was chucked out the window the minute I asked them. The members of the Moped Army love what they do, and they do it because they love it. Not for huge financial gains, not for getting tons of fear and respect (although they do have that), not for making their lives care-free and easy. The Moped Army work damn hard to do what they love. Just like comic creators. What a coincidence.

So haul ass and hit the pavement running. You're about to ride through an amazing and weird world that's hard, dark, strange and yet very familiar. I've done my best to fill it with an assortment of people who would never be put together in a million years, and who yet absolutely belong together. I also put a lot of high speed, breakneck, kickass, hi-tech/lo-tech, two-stroke action to make sure you didn't fall asleep. It's not just the destination, it's also the ride. Make it count.

–PAUL SIZER, Kalamazoo, August 2005

SPECIAL THANKS:

- To **Dan**, **Simon** and ALL members of the **MOPED ARMY** for the support, energy and love I've gotten on this project before it even came out! You are the inspiration behind all this craziness. Hope you dig it the most!
- To my Beta readers (**Trisha Lynn Sebastian, Dan Traeger, Tony Isabella, Kevin King, Tim O'Shea** and **Johanna Draper Carlson**) for being my third and fourth eyes on this project.
- To **Kito Jumanne-Marshall** for being my photo reference model for Simone. If I've made her half as beautiful as you, I've done my job!
- To every moped rider on Earth who's purchased a MOPED ARMY patch from me over the past year. Piece by piece, you've helped this project come together, and joined the fashion elite in the process.
- To all the retailers, online reporters and reviewers who've gotten behind this book.
- To all my fans, who have been infinitely patient. Hope it was worth the wait!

- Finally, to **Jane Irwin**, for being my muse, my proofreader, my typist, my critic, my editor, my butt-kicker, my distraction and my focus, but most for being my wife and partner, in art and in life. Thank you for everything. We make a pretty good team . . .

TWO STROKES OF GENIUS

THE BRAINS BEHIND THE REAL MOPED ARMY

SIMON KING

I've watched the growth of the Moped Army from a unique and interesting viewpoint. I might have helped kick-start it into an organized form but the makings of this group were already bubbling just below the surface. For the first few years we foraged for knowledge, parts, and other people interested in these strange and forgotten machines. Despite being fun, convenient, and economical most of America gave up on the moped decades ago after only a few short years of popularity. Our small group of friends hoped to bring the moped back.

To my surprise small pockets of people throughout the nation shared our idea. Through our website we met moped fans everywhere who were banding together to fill the streets with these two-stroke wonders. The information and parts are a little less rare now but the enthusiasm for mopeds keeps growing. The Moped Army is much more than the vehicles, introducing people across the country and catalyzing friendships that might never have otherwise existed. At this point there's no question about the future of mopeds because this swarm will continue to grow.

CONTACT: simon@mopedarmy.com

DANIEL ROBERT KASTNER

The Moped Army for me started out as unbridled youth. Being bored in a small college town, and wanting some adventure. Its humble beginnings of three guys sitting around in a coffee shop never prepared me for where it is now. Tons of people stretched across the US and Canada, all with an obsession for everything moped. I am a bit overwhelmed at times with the idea that so much grew out of our small obscure group.

The Moped Army is still in its infancy. It is hard to imagine, but I think that only in the last 2 years or so has the ball really started moving. We keep adding branches, and those branches keep adding members. It is like a snowball that is rolling out of Kalamazoo that will end on the doorstop of every major city, and many minor ones. At the core of this will be people having fun, mashing peds, meeting up, racing, and just tearing ass from one hangout to another.

CONTACT: dan@mopedarmy.com

MOPED ARMY founders (l-r)
Daniel Robert Kastner and Simon King.

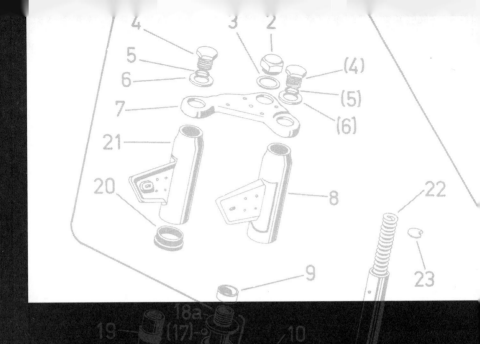
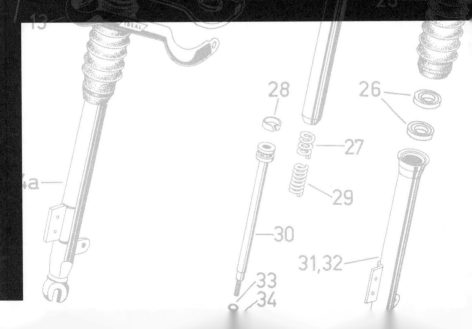

BOLT HARBOR A.D. 2277
WELCOME TO THE FUTURE...

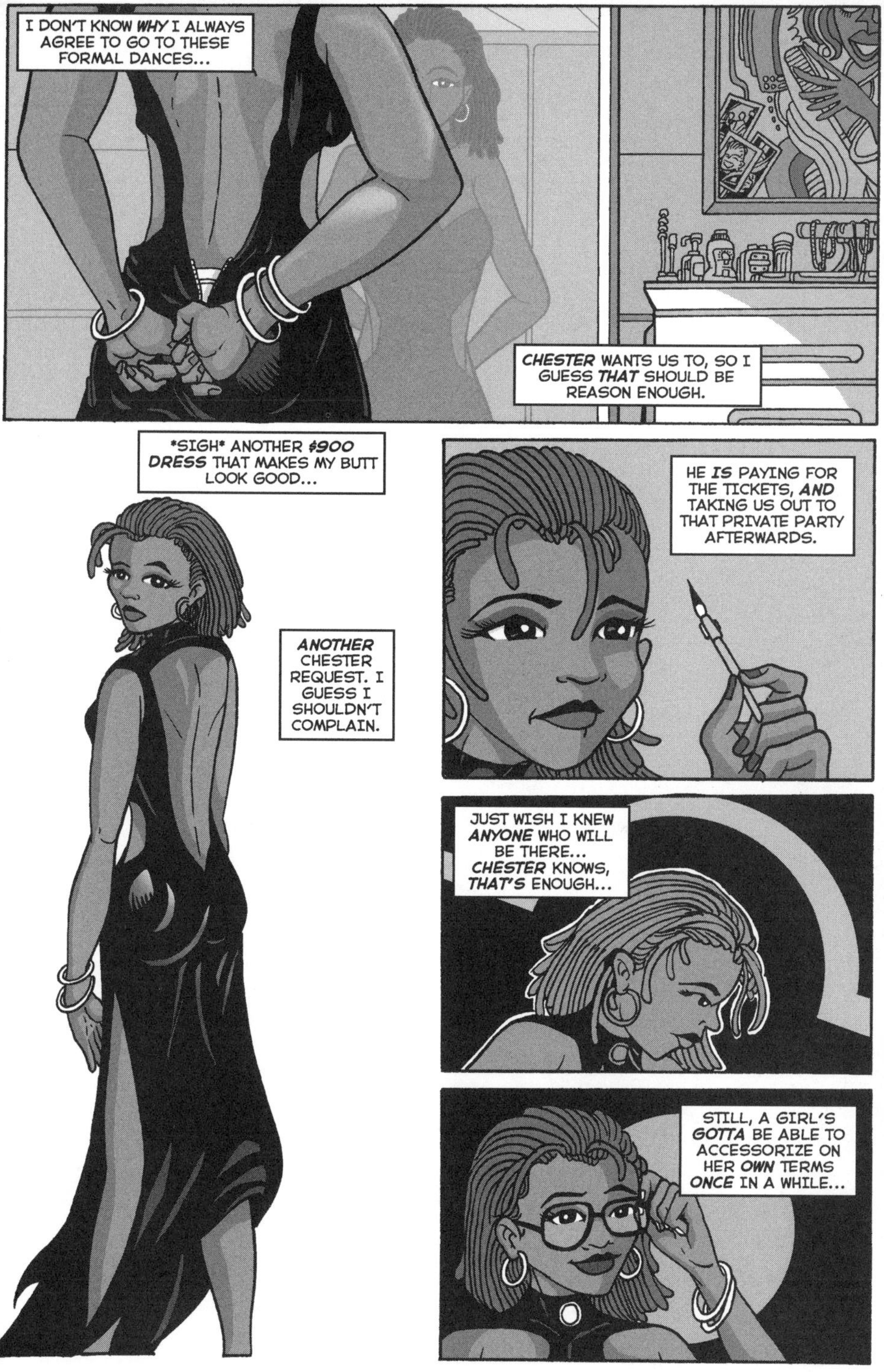
I DON'T KNOW WHY I ALWAYS AGREE TO GO TO THESE FORMAL DANCES...
CHESTER WANTS US TO, SO I GUESS THAT SHOULD BE REASON ENOUGH.
SIGH ANOTHER $900 DRESS THAT MAKES MY BUTT LOOK GOOD...
ANOTHER CHESTER REQUEST. I GUESS I SHOULDN'T COMPLAIN.
HE IS PAYING FOR THE TICKETS, AND TAKING US OUT TO THAT PRIVATE PARTY AFTERWARDS.
JUST WISH I KNEW ANYONE WHO WILL BE THERE... CHESTER KNOWS, THAT'S ENOUGH...
STILL, A GIRL'S GOTTA BE ABLE TO ACCESSORIZE ON HER OWN TERMS ONCE IN A WHILE...

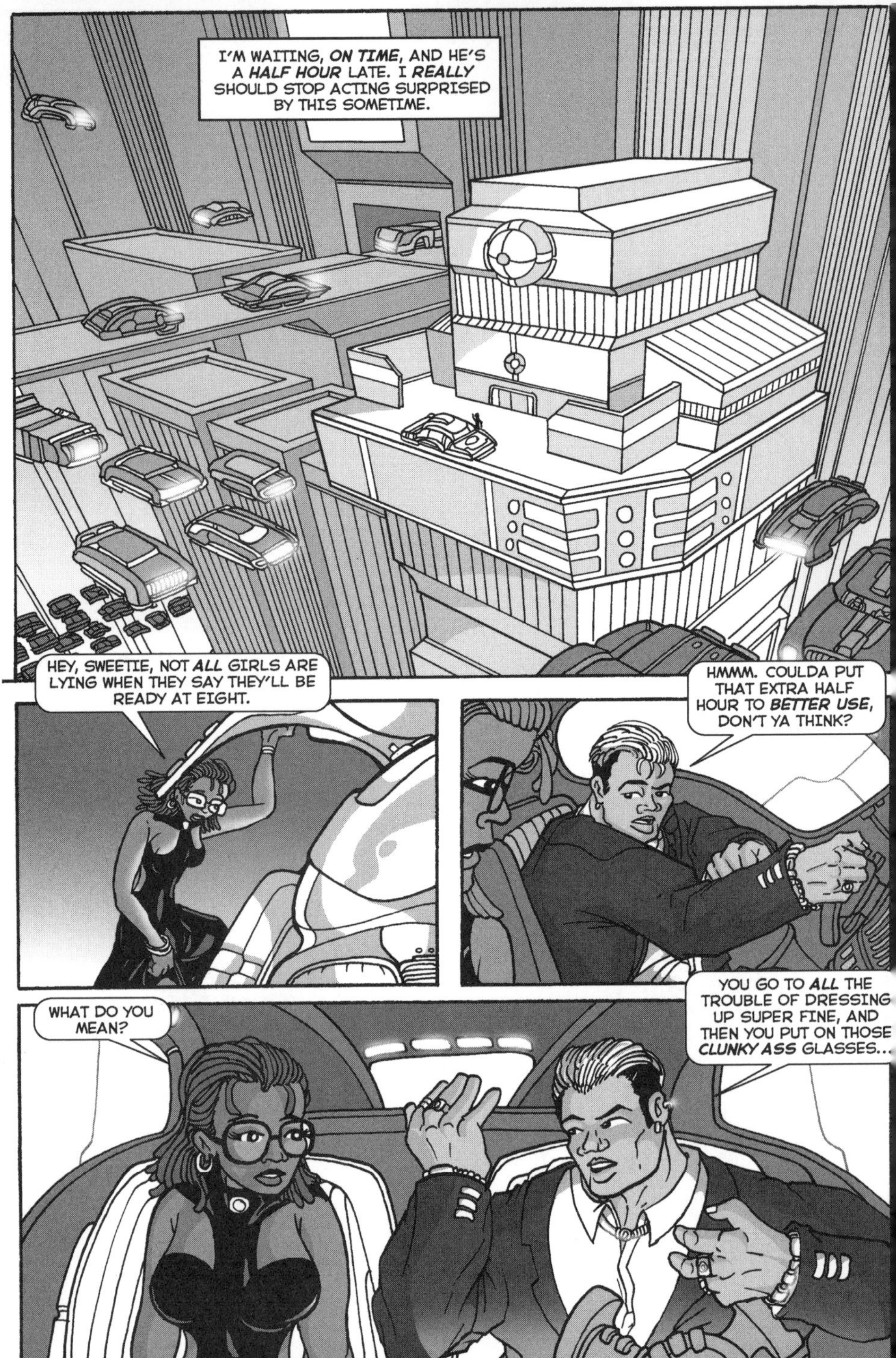
I'M WAITING, ON TIME, AND HE'S A HALF HOUR LATE. I REALLY SHOULD STOP ACTING SURPRISED BY THIS SOMETIME.
HEY, SWEETIE, NOT ALL GIRLS ARE LYING WHEN THEY SAY THEY'LL BE READY AT EIGHT.
HMMM. COULDA PUT THAT EXTRA HALF HOUR TO BETTER USE, DON'T YA THINK?
WHAT DO YOU MEAN?
YOU GO TO ALL THE TROUBLE OF DRESSING UP SUPER FINE, AND THEN YOU PUT ON THOSE CLUNKY ASS GLASSES...

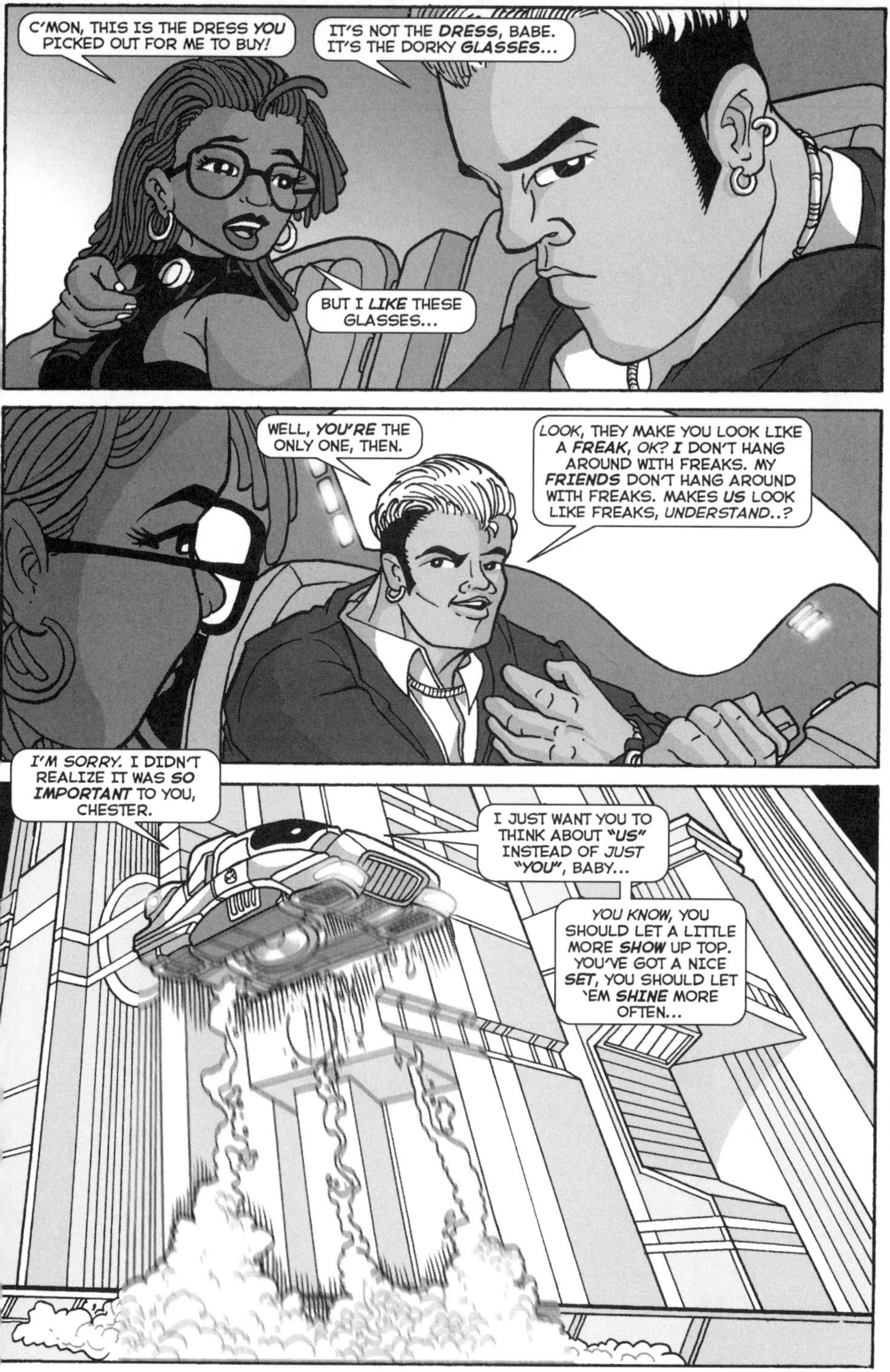
C'MON, THIS IS THE DRESS *YOU* PICKED OUT FOR ME TO BUY!
IT'S NOT THE ***DRESS***, BABE. IT'S THE DORKY ***GLASSES***...
BUT I ***LIKE*** THESE GLASSES...
WELL, ***YOU'RE*** THE ONLY ONE, THEN.
LOOK, THEY MAKE YOU LOOK LIKE A ***FREAK***, *OK?* ***I*** DON'T HANG AROUND WITH FREAKS. MY ***FRIENDS*** DON'T HANG AROUND WITH FREAKS. MAKES ***US*** LOOK LIKE FREAKS, *UNDERSTAND..?*
I'M SORRY. I DIDN'T REALIZE IT WAS ***SO IMPORTANT*** TO YOU, CHESTER.
I JUST WANT YOU TO THINK ABOUT ***"US"*** INSTEAD OF *JUST* ***"YOU"***, BABY...
YOU KNOW, YOU SHOULD LET A LITTLE MORE ***SHOW*** UP TOP. YOU'VE GOT A NICE ***SET***, YOU SHOULD LET 'EM ***SHINE*** MORE OFTEN...

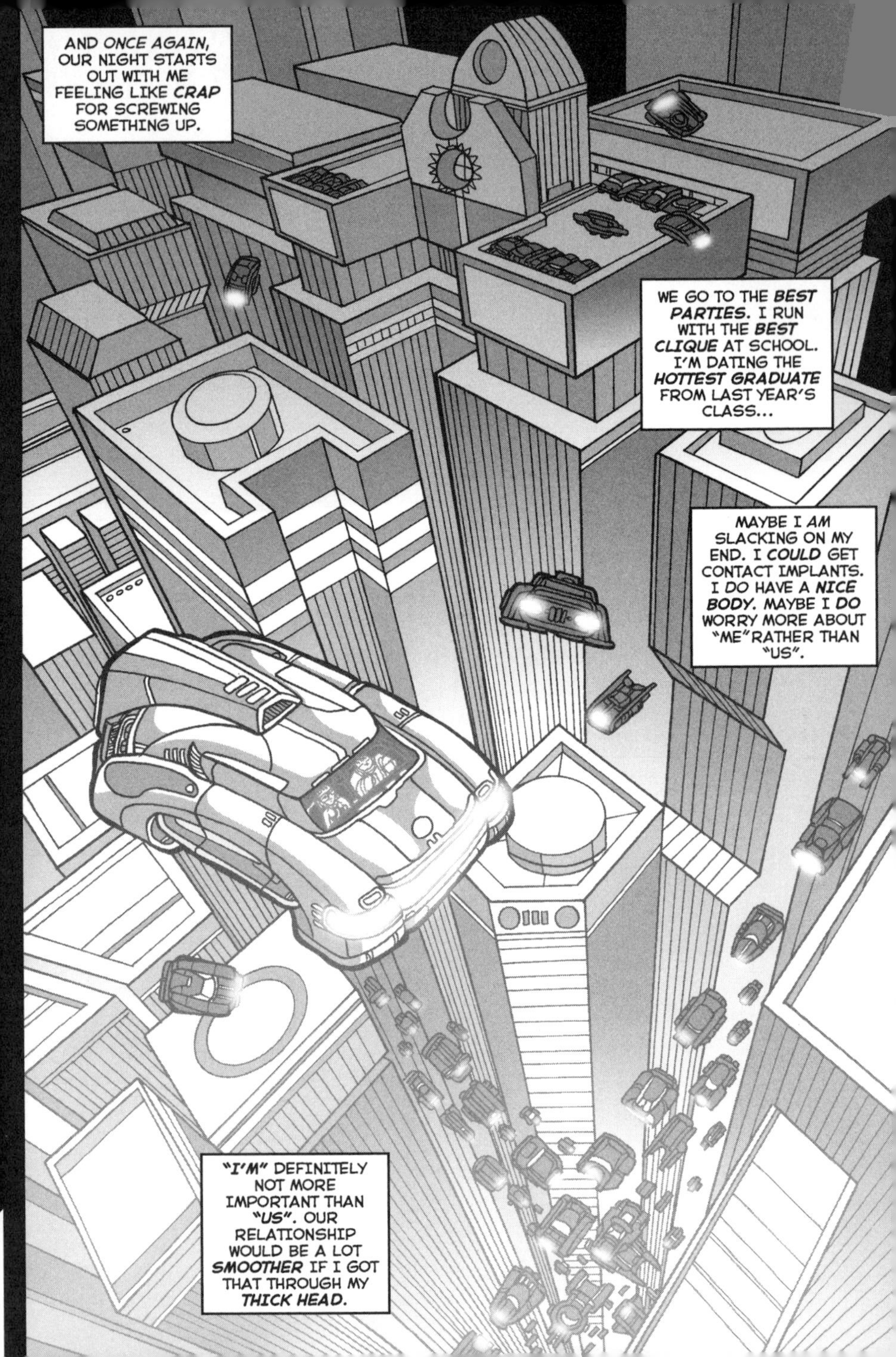
AND *ONCE AGAIN*, OUR NIGHT STARTS OUT WITH ME FEELING LIKE ***CRAP*** FOR SCREWING SOMETHING UP.
WE GO TO THE ***BEST PARTIES***. I RUN WITH THE ***BEST CLIQUE*** AT SCHOOL. I'M DATING THE ***HOTTEST GRADUATE*** FROM LAST YEAR'S CLASS...
MAYBE I *AM* SLACKING ON MY END. I ***COULD*** GET CONTACT IMPLANTS. I *DO* HAVE A ***NICE BODY***. MAYBE I ***DO*** WORRY MORE ABOUT "ME" RATHER THAN "US".
"I'M" DEFINITELY NOT MORE IMPORTANT THAN ***"US"***. OUR RELATIONSHIP WOULD BE A LOT ***SMOOTHER*** IF I GOT THAT THROUGH MY ***THICK HEAD***.

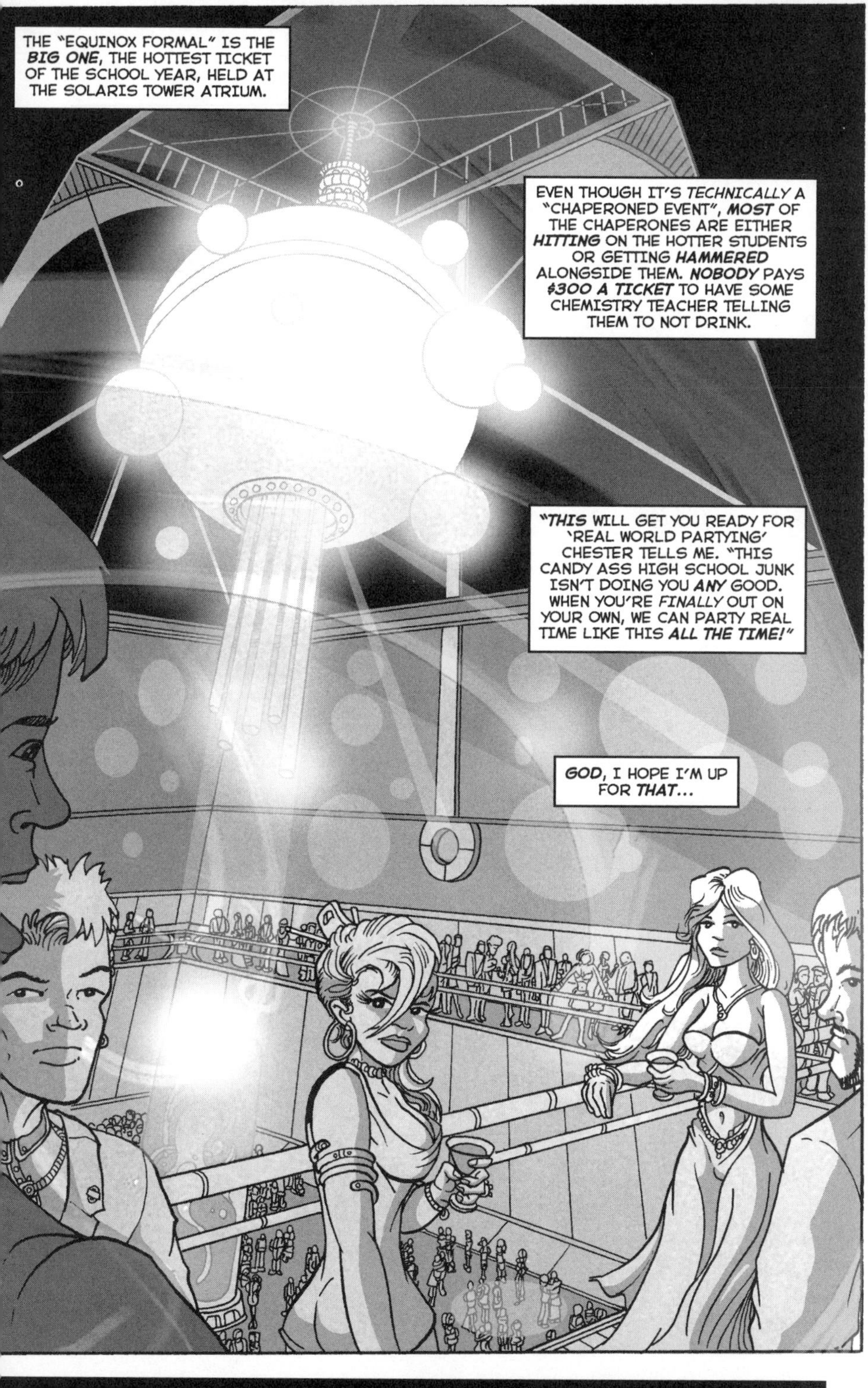
THE "EQUINOX FORMAL" IS THE *BIG ONE*, THE HOTTEST TICKET OF THE SCHOOL YEAR, HELD AT THE SOLARIS TOWER ATRIUM.
EVEN THOUGH IT'S *TECHNICALLY* A "CHAPERONED EVENT", ***MOST*** OF THE CHAPERONES ARE EITHER ***HITTING*** ON THE HOTTER STUDENTS OR GETTING ***HAMMERED*** ALONGSIDE THEM. ***NOBODY*** PAYS ***$300 A TICKET*** TO HAVE SOME CHEMISTRY TEACHER TELLING THEM TO NOT DRINK.
"***THIS*** WILL GET YOU READY FOR 'REAL WORLD PARTYING'" CHESTER TELLS ME. "THIS CANDY ASS HIGH SCHOOL JUNK ISN'T DOING YOU ***ANY*** GOOD. WHEN YOU'RE *FINALLY* OUT ON YOUR OWN, WE CAN PARTY REAL TIME LIKE THIS ***ALL THE TIME!***"
GOD, I HOPE I'M UP FOR ***THAT***...

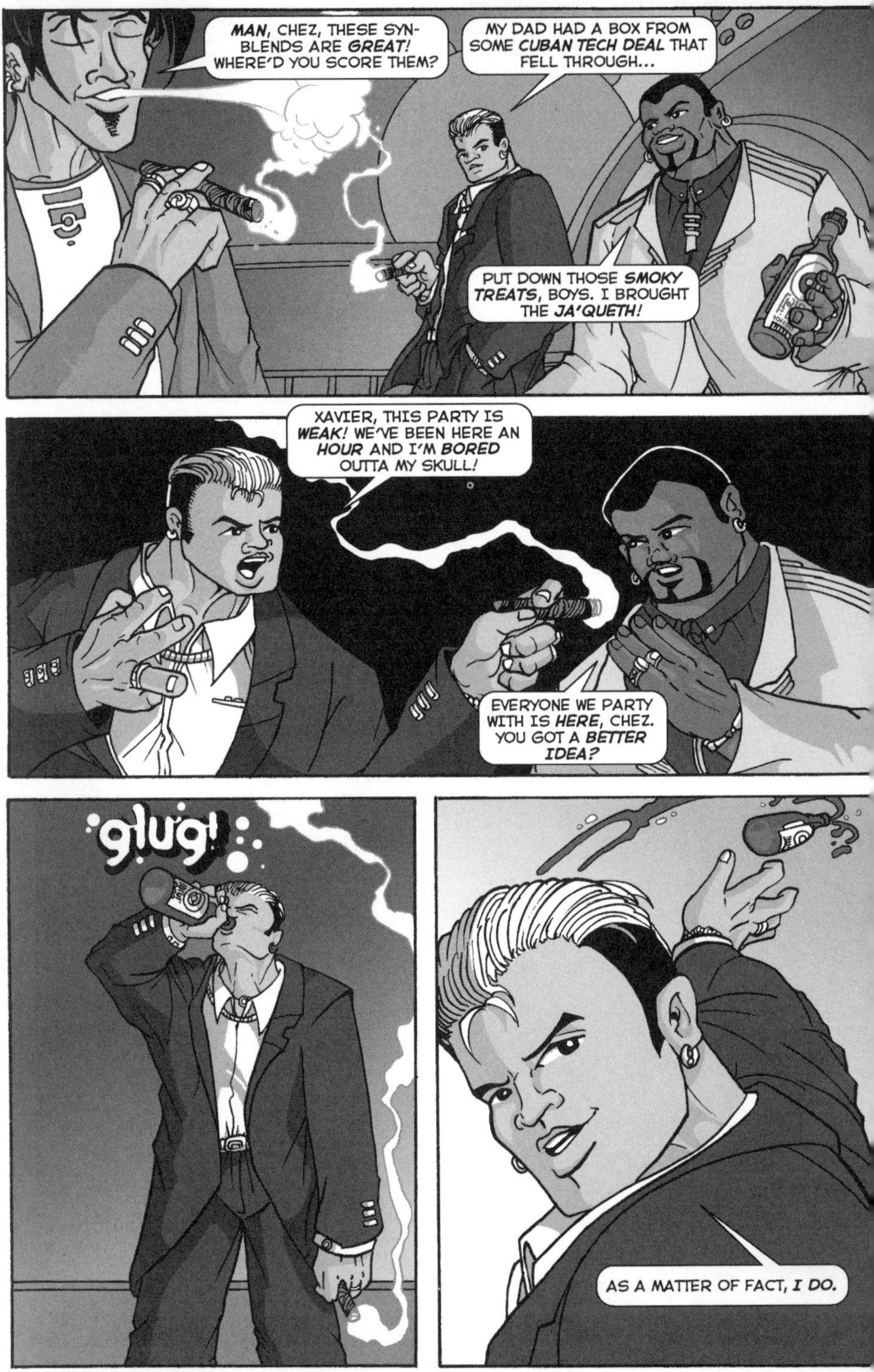
MAN, CHEZ, THESE SYN-BLENDS ARE GREAT! WHERE'D YOU SCORE THEM?
MY DAD HAD A BOX FROM SOME CUBAN TECH DEAL THAT FELL THROUGH...
PUT DOWN THOSE SMOKY TREATS, BOYS. I BROUGHT THE JA'QUETH!
XAVIER, THIS PARTY IS WEAK! WE'VE BEEN HERE AN HOUR AND I'M BORED OUTTA MY SKULL!
EVERYONE WE PARTY WITH IS HERE, CHEZ. YOU GOT A BETTER IDEA?
glug!
AS A MATTER OF FACT, I DO.

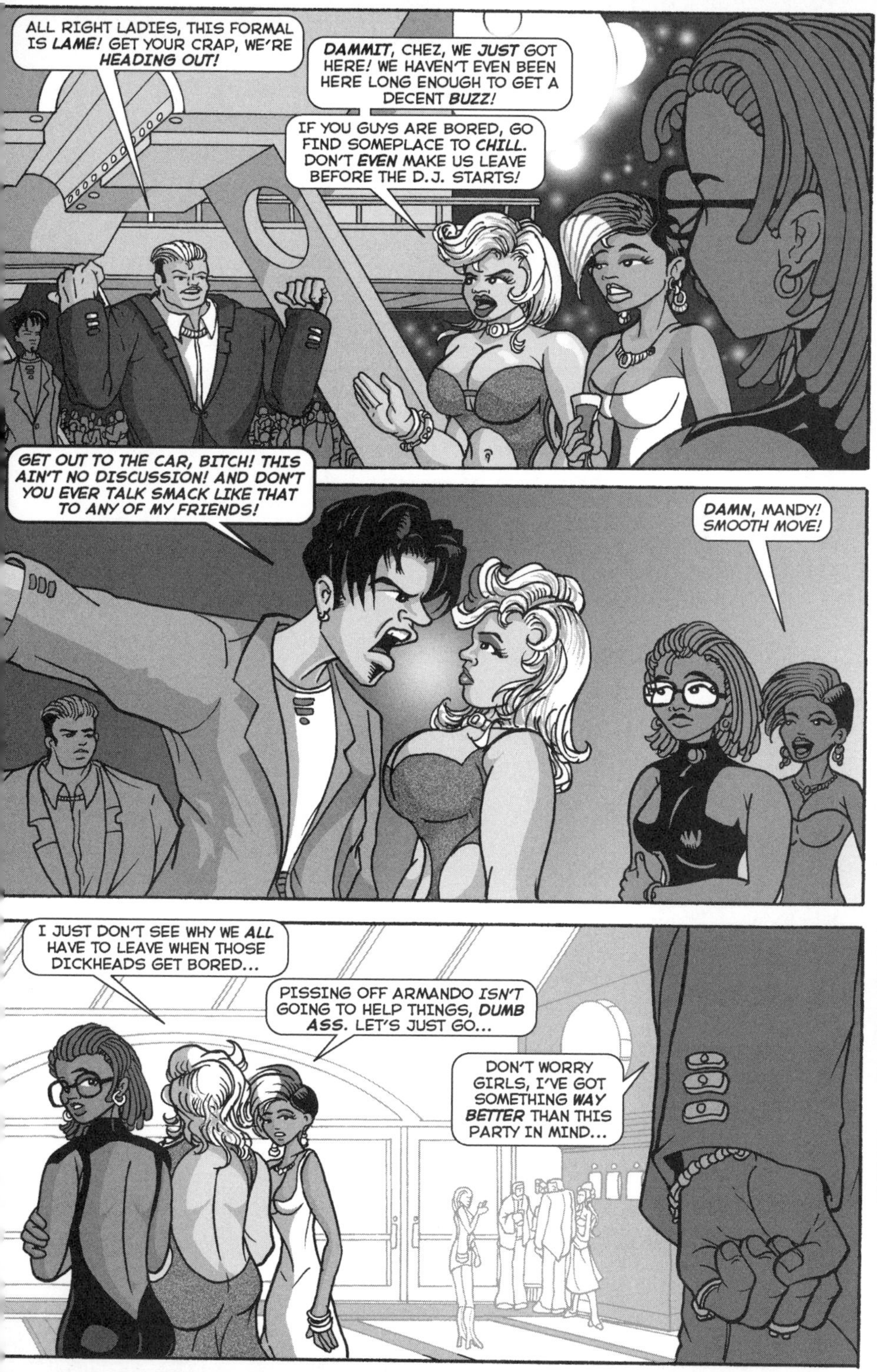
ALL RIGHT LADIES, THIS FORMAL IS LAME! GET YOUR CRAP, WE'RE HEADING OUT!
DAMMIT, CHEZ, WE JUST GOT HERE! WE HAVEN'T EVEN BEEN HERE LONG ENOUGH TO GET A DECENT BUZZ!
IF YOU GUYS ARE BORED, GO FIND SOMEPLACE TO CHILL. DON'T EVEN MAKE US LEAVE BEFORE THE D.J. STARTS!
GET OUT TO THE CAR, BITCH! THIS AIN'T NO DISCUSSION! AND DON'T YOU EVER TALK SMACK LIKE THAT TO ANY OF MY FRIENDS!
DAMN, MANDY! SMOOTH MOVE!
I JUST DON'T SEE WHY WE ALL HAVE TO LEAVE WHEN THOSE DICKHEADS GET BORED...
PISSING OFF ARMANDO ISN'T GOING TO HELP THINGS, DUMB ASS. LET'S JUST GO...
DON'T WORRY GIRLS, I'VE GOT SOMETHING WAY BETTER THAN THIS PARTY IN MIND...

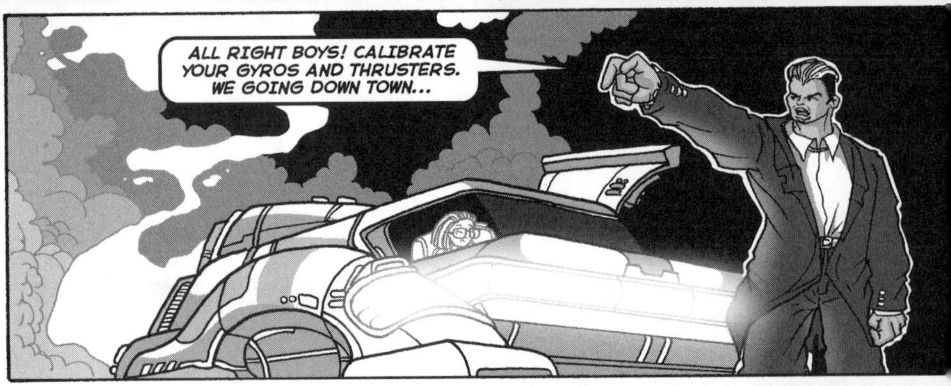
ALL RIGHT BOYS! CALIBRATE YOUR GYROS AND THRUSTERS. WE GOING DOWN TOWN...

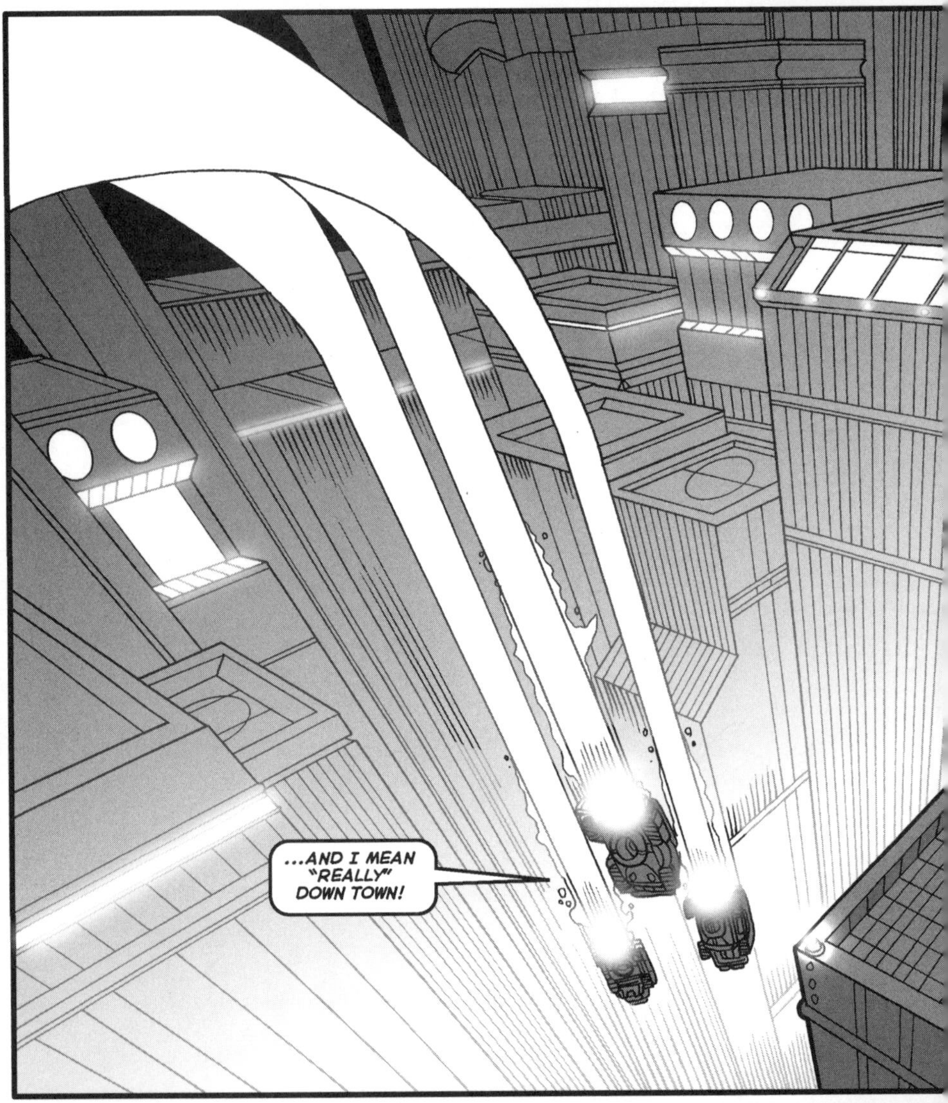
...AND I MEAN "REALLY" DOWN TOWN!

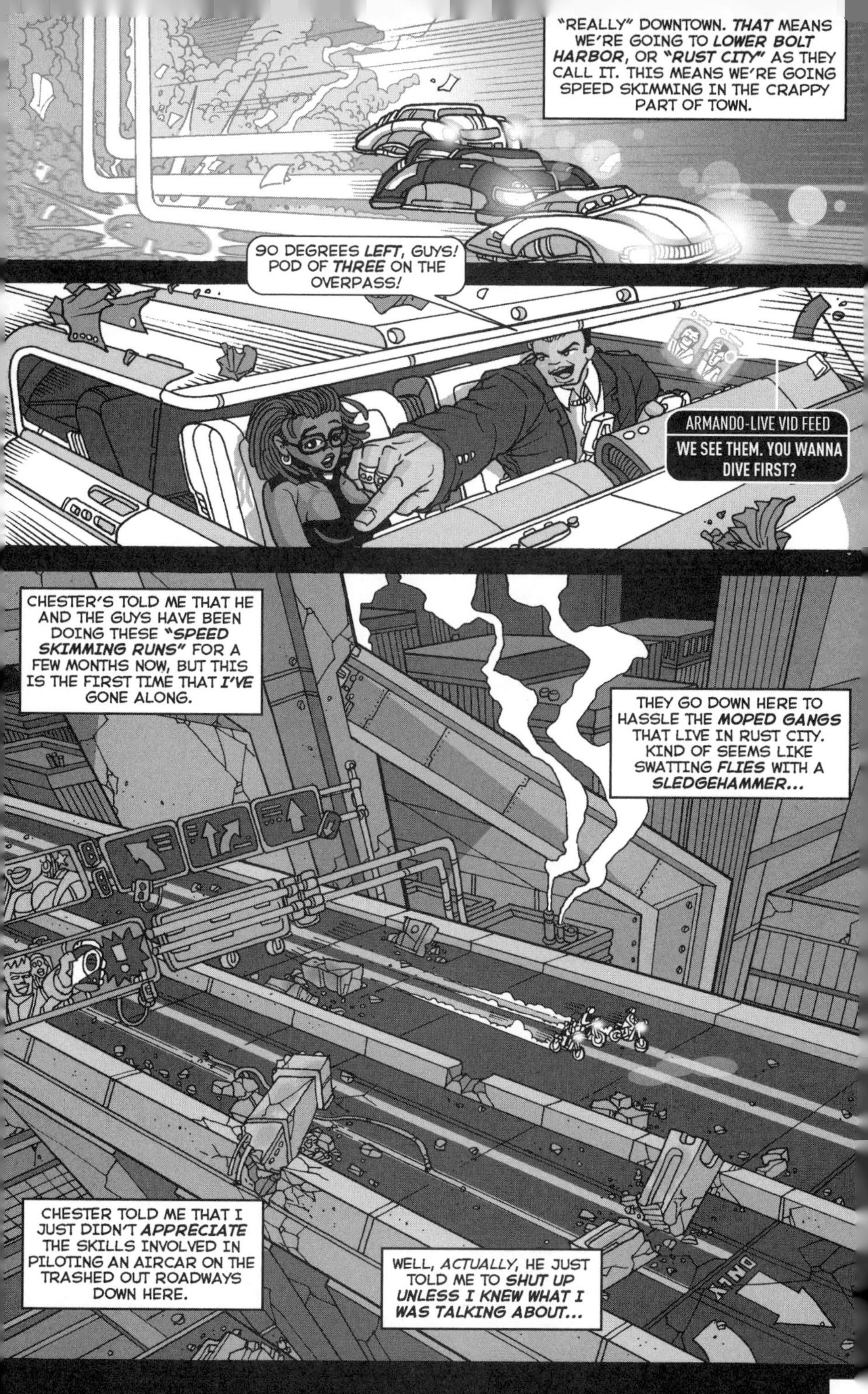
"REALLY" DOWNTOWN. THAT MEANS WE'RE GOING TO LOWER BOLT HARBOR, OR "RUST CITY" AS THEY CALL IT. THIS MEANS WE'RE GOING SPEED SKIMMING IN THE CRAPPY PART OF TOWN.
90 DEGREES LEFT, GUYS! POD OF THREE ON THE OVERPASS!
ARMANDO-LIVE VID FEED
WE SEE THEM. YOU WANNA DIVE FIRST?
CHESTER'S TOLD ME THAT HE AND THE GUYS HAVE BEEN DOING THESE "SPEED SKIMMING RUNS" FOR A FEW MONTHS NOW, BUT THIS IS THE FIRST TIME THAT I'VE GONE ALONG.
THEY GO DOWN HERE TO HASSLE THE MOPED GANGS THAT LIVE IN RUST CITY. KIND OF SEEMS LIKE SWATTING FLIES WITH A SLEDGEHAMMER...
CHESTER TOLD ME THAT I JUST DIDN'T APPRECIATE THE SKILLS INVOLVED IN PILOTING AN AIRCAR ON THE TRASHED OUT ROADWAYS DOWN HERE.
WELL, ACTUALLY, HE JUST TOLD ME TO SHUT UP UNLESS I KNEW WHAT I WAS TALKING ABOUT...

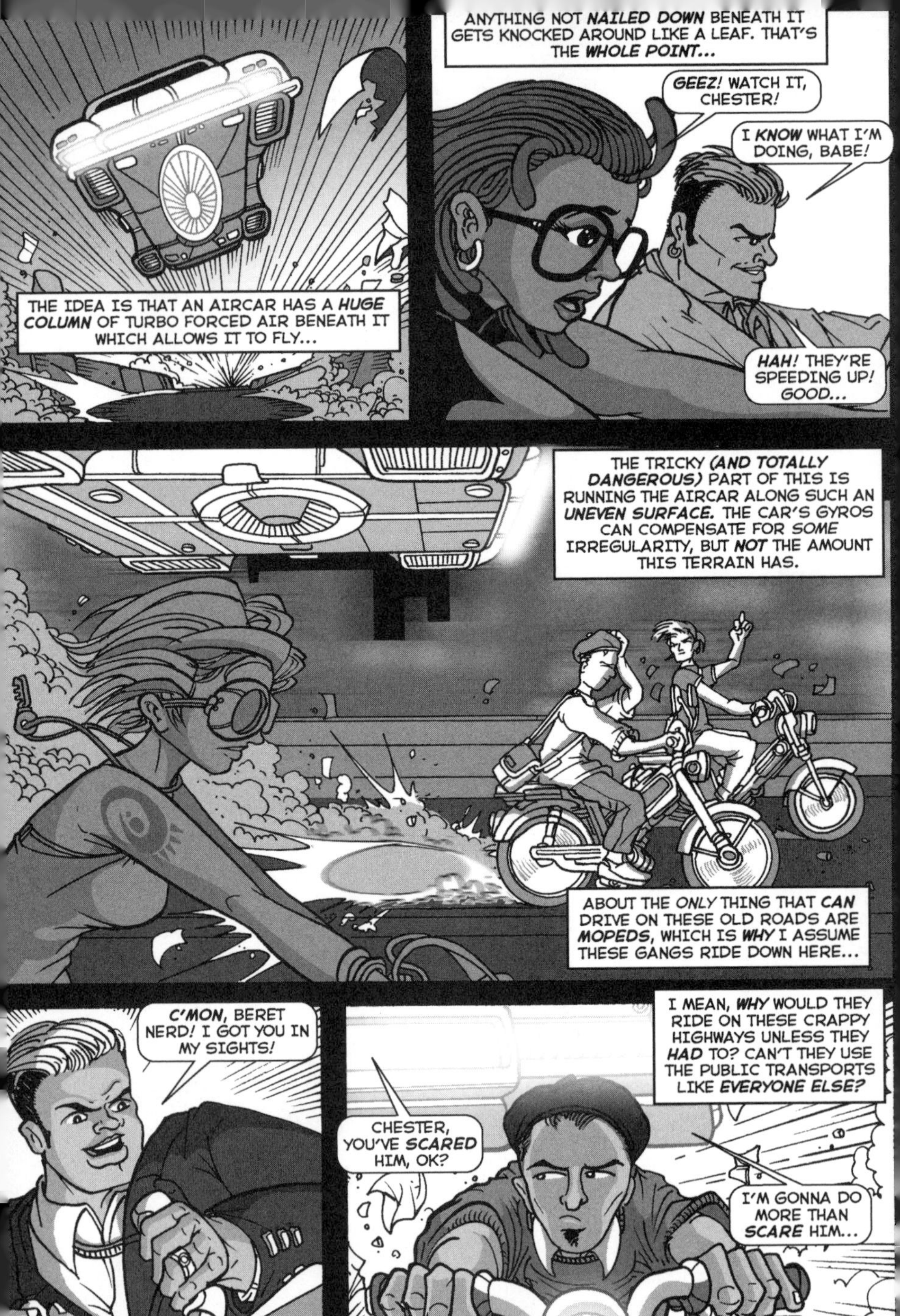

THE IDEA IS THAT AN AIRCAR HAS A *HUGE COLUMN* OF TURBO FORCED AIR BENEATH IT WHICH ALLOWS IT TO FLY...
ANYTHING NOT *NAILED DOWN* BENEATH IT GETS KNOCKED AROUND LIKE A LEAF. THAT'S THE *WHOLE POINT...*
GEEZ! WATCH IT, CHESTER!
I *KNOW* WHAT I'M DOING, BABE!
HAH! THEY'RE SPEEDING UP! GOOD...
THE TRICKY *(AND TOTALLY DANGEROUS)* PART OF THIS IS RUNNING THE AIRCAR ALONG SUCH AN *UNEVEN SURFACE.* THE CAR'S GYROS CAN COMPENSATE FOR *SOME* IRREGULARITY, BUT *NOT* THE AMOUNT THIS TERRAIN HAS.
ABOUT THE *ONLY* THING THAT *CAN* DRIVE ON THESE OLD ROADS ARE *MOPEDS,* WHICH IS *WHY* I ASSUME THESE GANGS RIDE DOWN HERE...
C'MON, BERET NERD! I GOT YOU IN MY SIGHTS!
I MEAN, *WHY* WOULD THEY RIDE ON THESE CRAPPY HIGHWAYS UNLESS THEY *HAD* TO? CAN'T THEY USE THE PUBLIC TRANSPORTS LIKE *EVERYONE ELSE?*
CHESTER, YOU'VE *SCARED* HIM, OK?
I'M GONNA DO MORE THAN *SCARE* HIM...

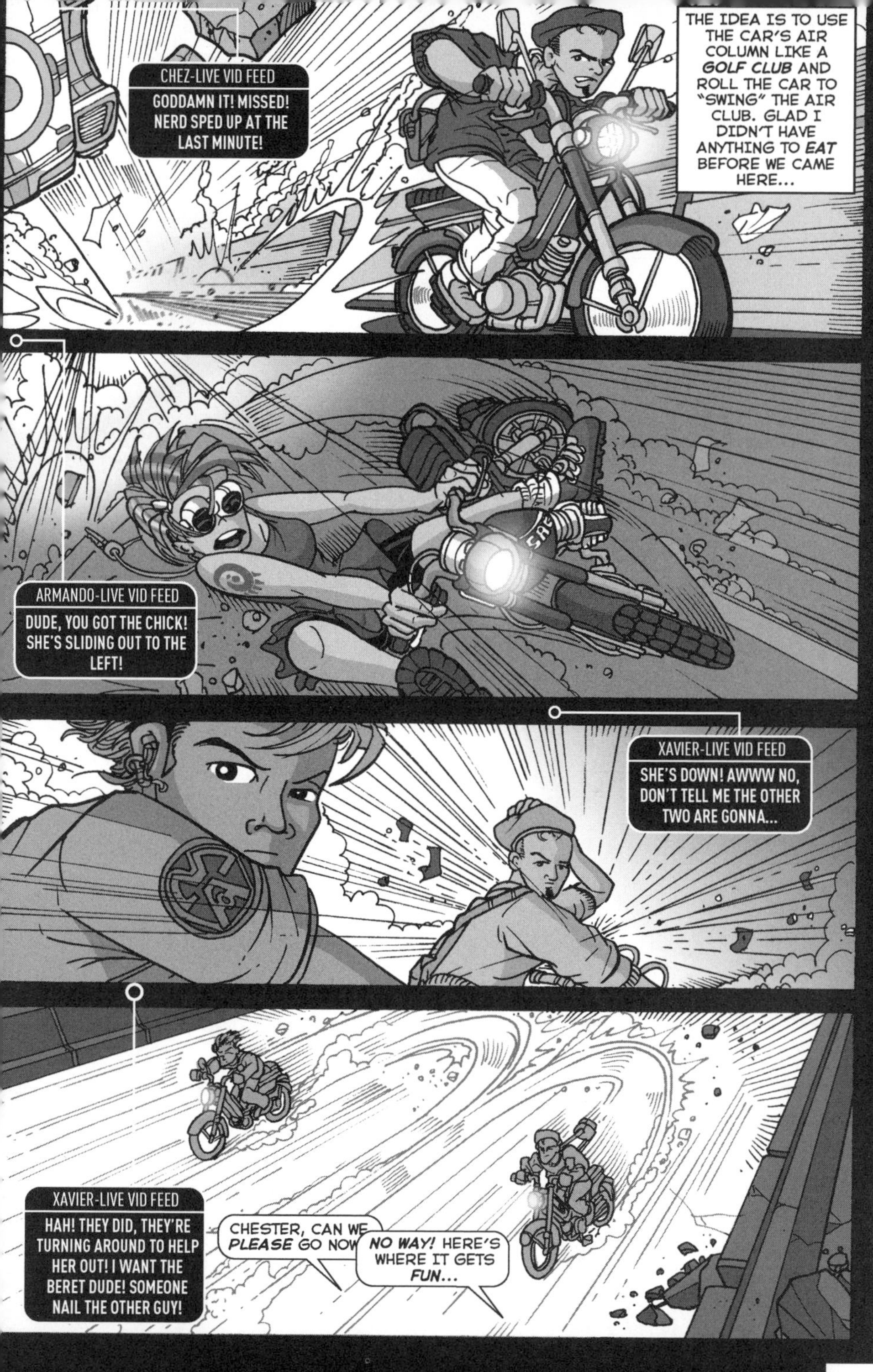
CHEZ-LIVE VID FEED
GODDAMN IT! MISSED! NERD SPED UP AT THE LAST MINUTE!
THE IDEA IS TO USE THE CAR'S AIR COLUMN LIKE A *GOLF CLUB* AND ROLL THE CAR TO "SWING" THE AIR CLUB. GLAD I DIDN'T HAVE ANYTHING TO *EAT* BEFORE WE CAME HERE...
ARMANDO-LIVE VID FEED
DUDE, YOU GOT THE CHICK! SHE'S SLIDING OUT TO THE LEFT!
XAVIER-LIVE VID FEED
SHE'S DOWN! AWWW NO, DON'T TELL ME THE OTHER TWO ARE GONNA...
XAVIER-LIVE VID FEED
HAH! THEY DID, THEY'RE TURNING AROUND TO HELP HER OUT! I WANT THE BERET DUDE! SOMEONE NAIL THE OTHER GUY!
CHESTER, CAN WE *PLEASE* GO NOW
NO WAY! HERE'S WHERE IT GETS *FUN*...

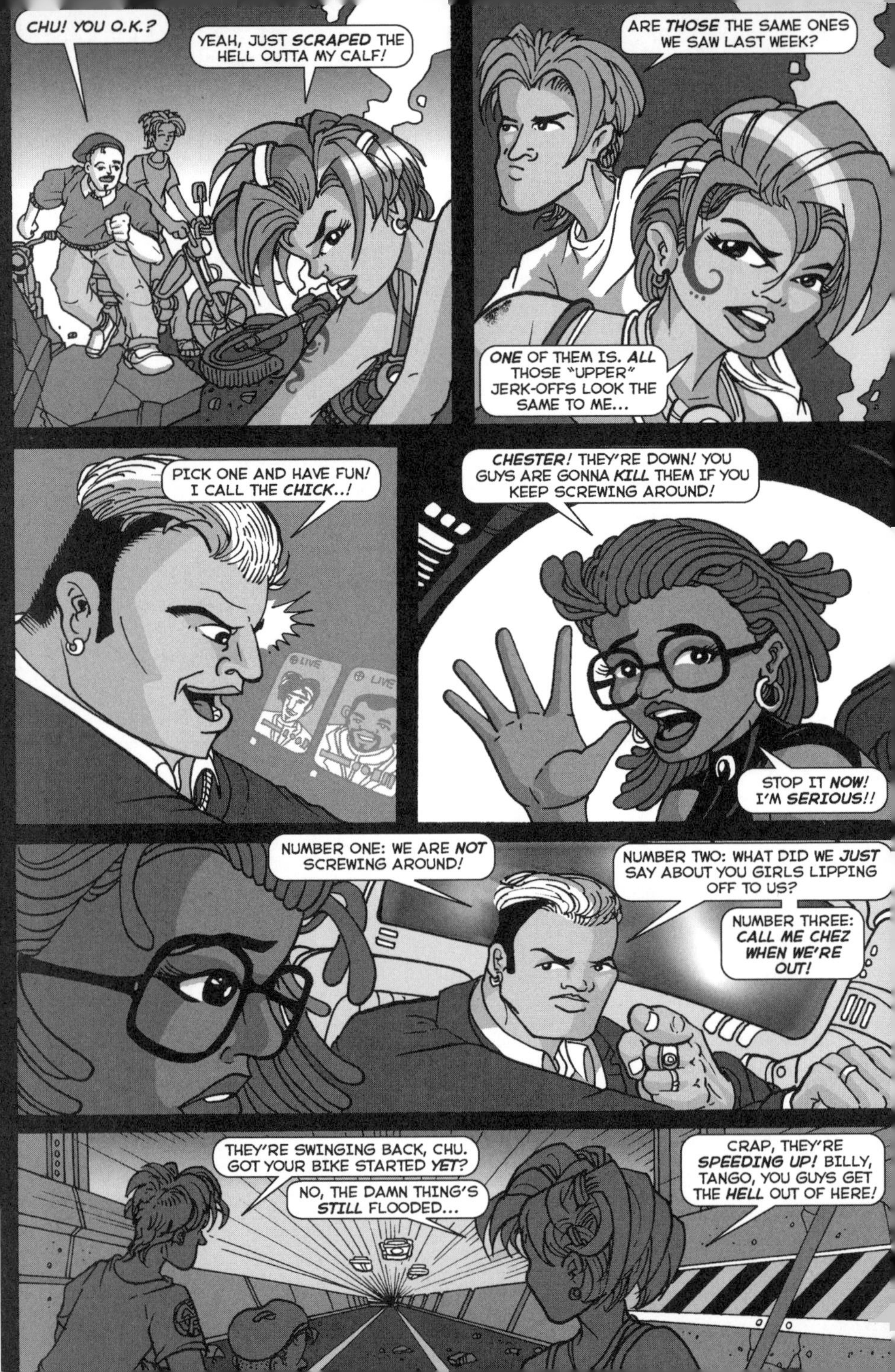
CHU! YOU O.K.?
YEAH, JUST SCRAPED THE HELL OUTTA MY CALF!
ARE THOSE THE SAME ONES WE SAW LAST WEEK?
ONE OF THEM IS. ALL THOSE "UPPER" JERK-OFFS LOOK THE SAME TO ME...
PICK ONE AND HAVE FUN! I CALL THE CHICK..!
LIVE
LIVE
CHESTER! THEY'RE DOWN! YOU GUYS ARE GONNA KILL THEM IF YOU KEEP SCREWING AROUND!
STOP IT NOW! I'M SERIOUS!!
NUMBER ONE: WE ARE NOT SCREWING AROUND!
NUMBER TWO: WHAT DID WE JUST SAY ABOUT YOU GIRLS LIPPING OFF TO US?
NUMBER THREE: CALL ME CHEZ WHEN WE'RE OUT!
THEY'RE SWINGING BACK, CHU. GOT YOUR BIKE STARTED YET?
NO, THE DAMN THING'S STILL FLOODED...
CRAP, THEY'RE SPEEDING UP! BILLY, TANGO, YOU GUYS GET THE HELL OUT OF HERE!

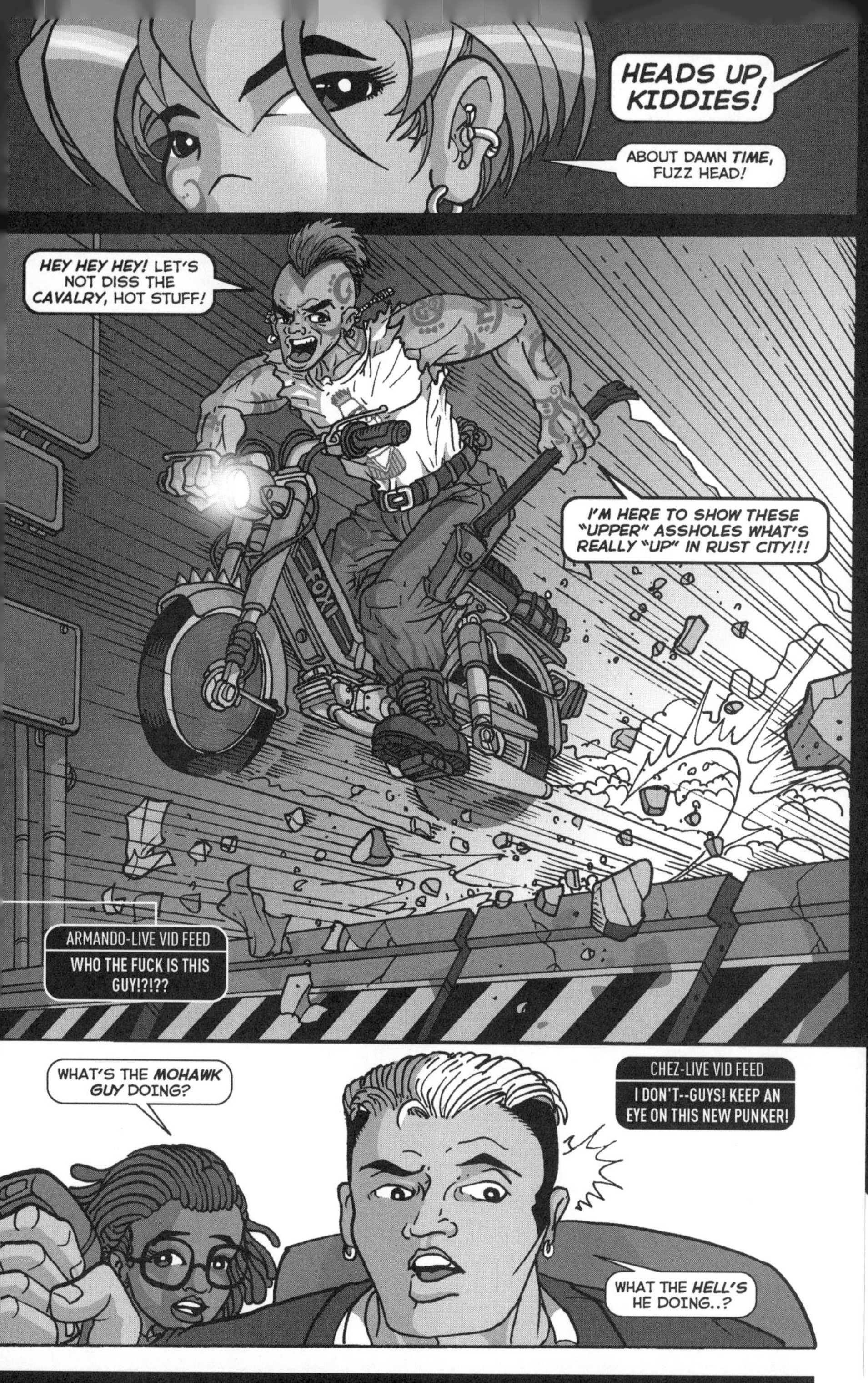
HEADS UP, KIDDIES!
ABOUT DAMN TIME, FUZZ HEAD!
HEY HEY HEY! LET'S NOT DISS THE CAVALRY, HOT STUFF!
I'M HERE TO SHOW THESE "UPPER" ASSHOLES WHAT'S REALLY "UP" IN RUST CITY!!!
ARMANDO-LIVE VID FEED
WHO THE FUCK IS THIS GUY!?!??
WHAT'S THE MOHAWK GUY DOING?
CHEZ-LIVE VID FEED
I DON'T--GUYS! KEEP AN EYE ON THIS NEW PUNKER!
WHAT THE HELL'S HE DOING..?

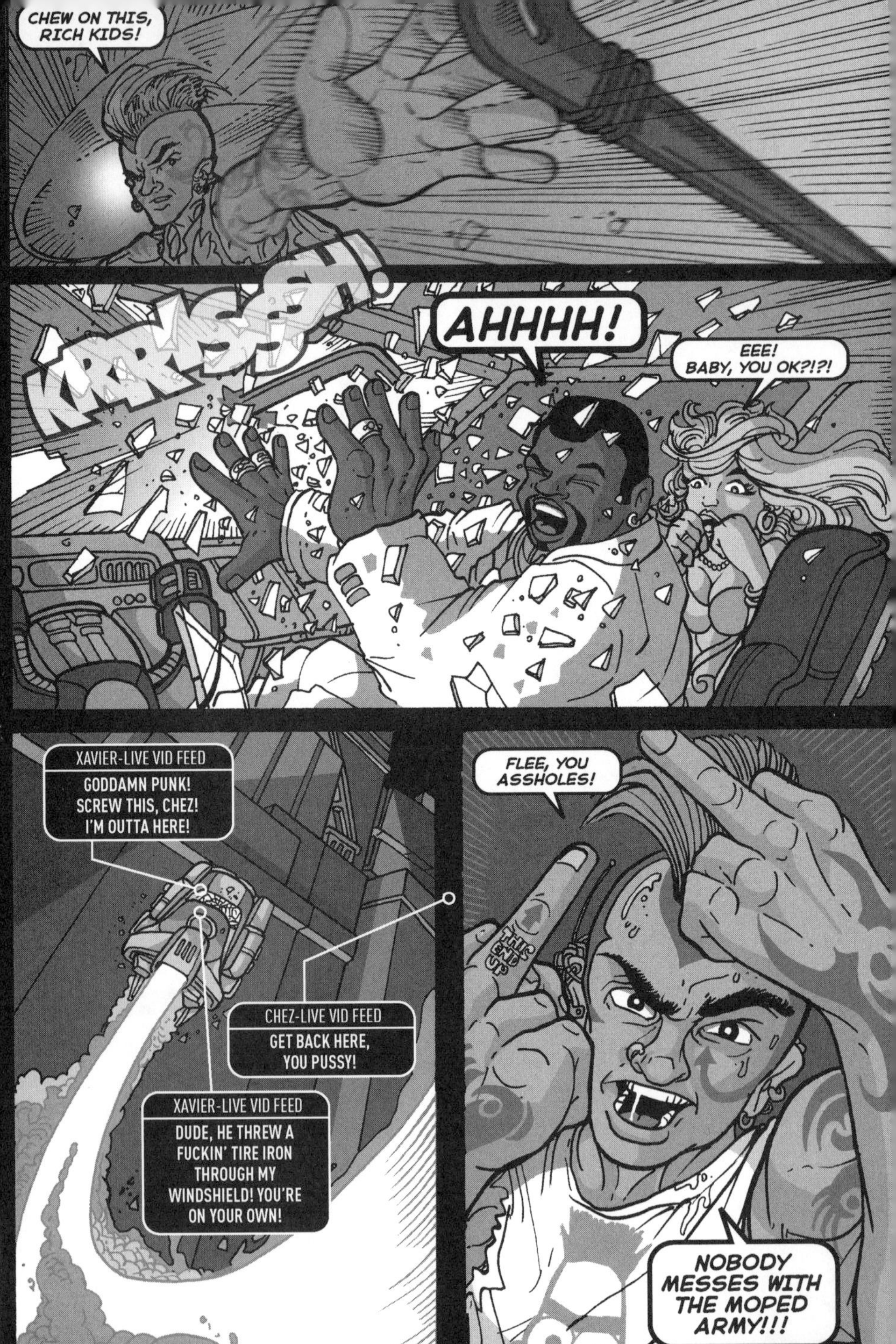
CHEW ON THIS, RICH KIDS!
AHHHH!
EEE! BABY, YOU OK?!?!
XAVIER-LIVE VID FEED
GODDAMN PUNK! SCREW THIS, CHEZ! I'M OUTTA HERE!
CHEZ-LIVE VID FEED
GET BACK HERE, YOU PUSSY!
XAVIER-LIVE VID FEED
DUDE, HE THREW A FUCKIN' TIRE IRON THROUGH MY WINDSHIELD! YOU'RE ON YOUR OWN!
FLEE, YOU ASSHOLES!
NOBODY MESSES WITH THE MOPED ARMY!!!

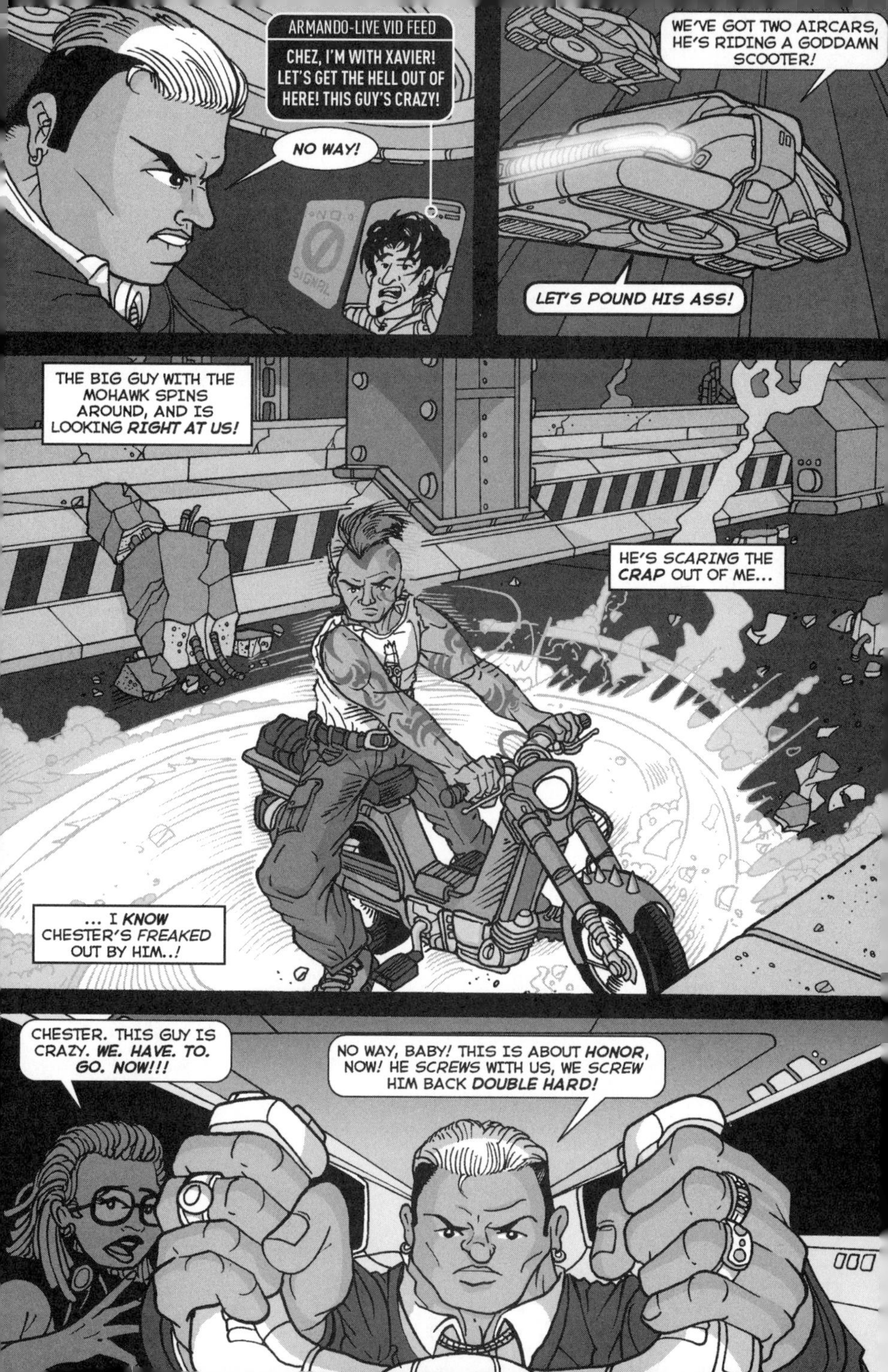
ARMANDO-LIVE VID FEED
CHEZ, I'M WITH XAVIER! LET'S GET THE HELL OUT OF HERE! THIS GUY'S CRAZY!
NO WAY!
NO SIGNAL
WE'VE GOT TWO AIRCARS, HE'S RIDING A GODDAMN SCOOTER!
LET'S POUND HIS ASS!
THE BIG GUY WITH THE MOHAWK SPINS AROUND, AND IS LOOKING *RIGHT AT US!*
HE'S *SCARING* THE ***CRAP*** OUT OF ME...
... I ***KNOW*** CHESTER'S *FREAKED* OUT BY HIM..!
CHESTER. THIS GUY IS CRAZY. ***WE. HAVE. TO. GO. NOW!!!***
NO WAY, BABY! THIS IS ABOUT ***HONOR***, NOW! HE *SCREWS* WITH US, WE *SCREW* HIM BACK ***DOUBLE HARD!***

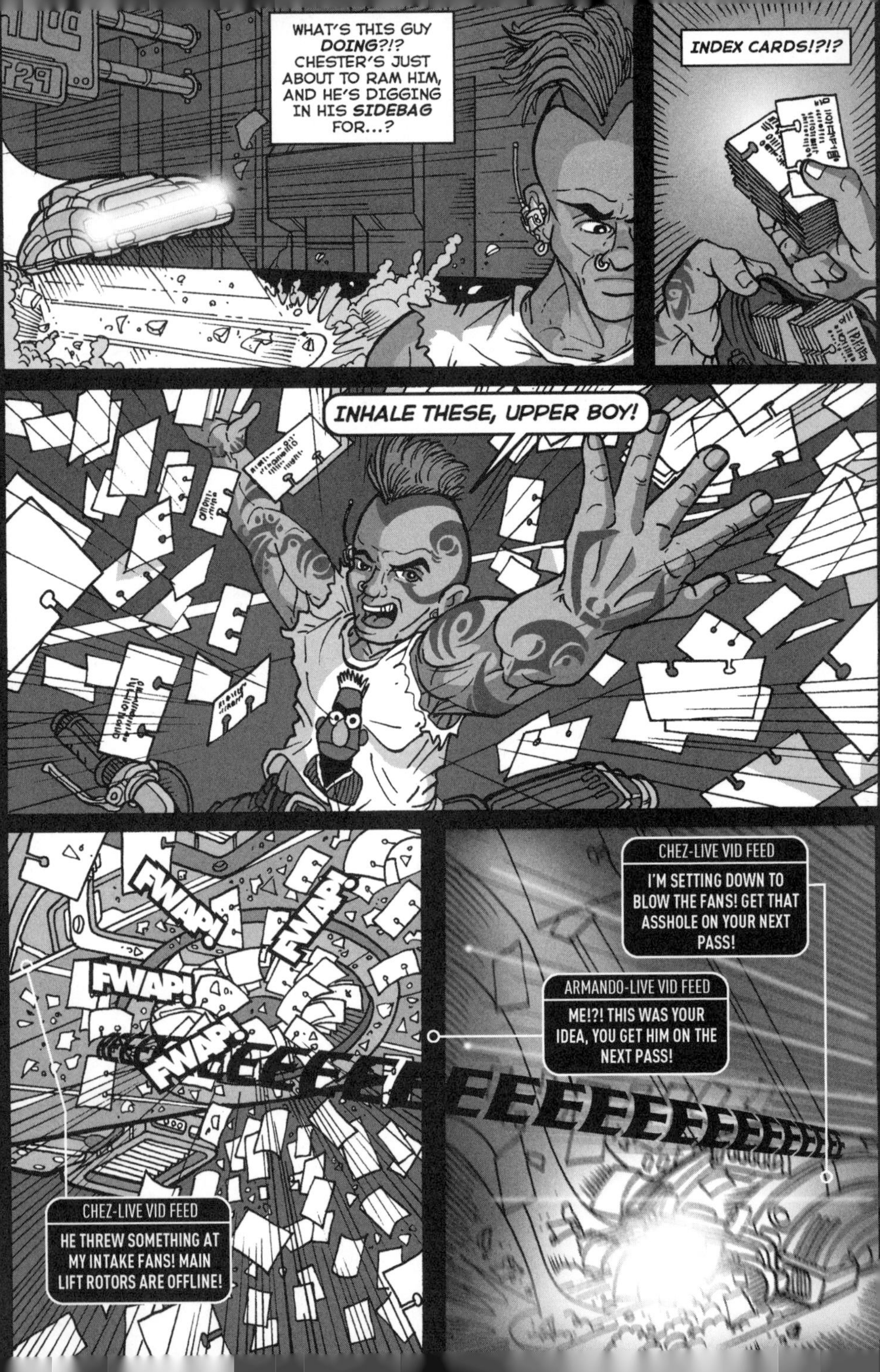
WHAT'S THIS GUY DOING?!? CHESTER'S JUST ABOUT TO RAM HIM, AND HE'S DIGGING IN HIS SIDEBAG FOR...?
INDEX CARDS!?!?
INHALE THESE, UPPER BOY!
FWAP!
FWAP!
FWAP!
FWAP!
CHEZ-LIVE VID FEED
HE THREW SOMETHING AT MY INTAKE FANS! MAIN LIFT ROTORS ARE OFFLINE!
CHEZ-LIVE VID FEED
I'M SETTING DOWN TO BLOW THE FANS! GET THAT ASSHOLE ON YOUR NEXT PASS!
ARMANDO-LIVE VID FEED
ME!?! THIS WAS YOUR IDEA, YOU GET HIM ON THE NEXT PASS!
EEEEEEEEEEEEEEEEEEE

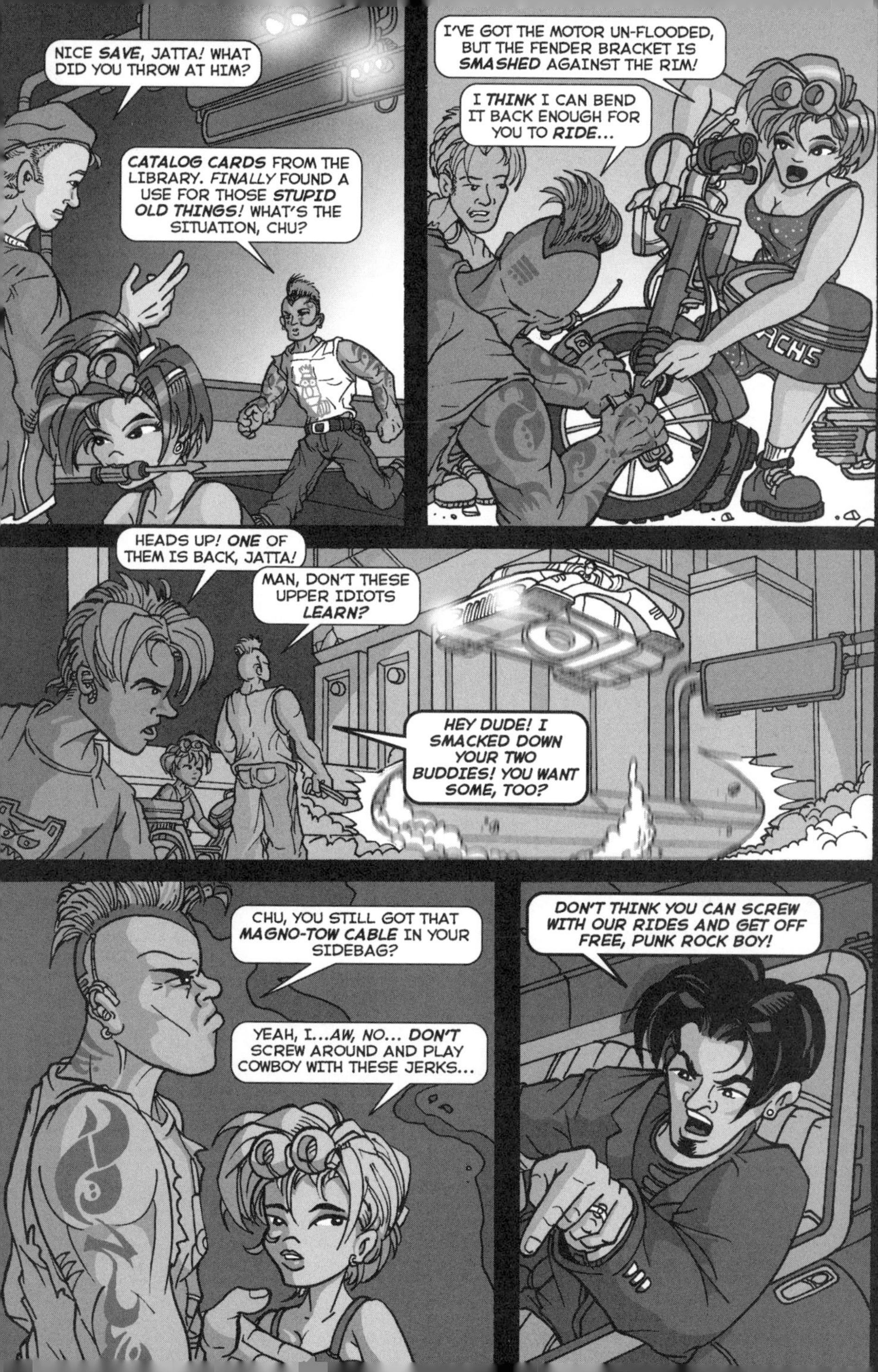
NICE SAVE, JATTA! WHAT DID YOU THROW AT HIM?
CATALOG CARDS FROM THE LIBRARY. FINALLY FOUND A USE FOR THOSE STUPID OLD THINGS! WHAT'S THE SITUATION, CHU?
I'VE GOT THE MOTOR UN-FLOODED, BUT THE FENDER BRACKET IS SMASHED AGAINST THE RIM!
I THINK I CAN BEND IT BACK ENOUGH FOR YOU TO RIDE...
HEADS UP! ONE OF THEM IS BACK, JATTA!
MAN, DON'T THESE UPPER IDIOTS LEARN?
HEY DUDE! I SMACKED DOWN YOUR TWO BUDDIES! YOU WANT SOME, TOO?
CHU, YOU STILL GOT THAT MAGNO-TOW CABLE IN YOUR SIDEBAG?
YEAH, I...AW, NO... DON'T SCREW AROUND AND PLAY COWBOY WITH THESE JERKS...
DON'T THINK YOU CAN SCREW WITH OUR RIDES AND GET OFF FREE, PUNK ROCK BOY!

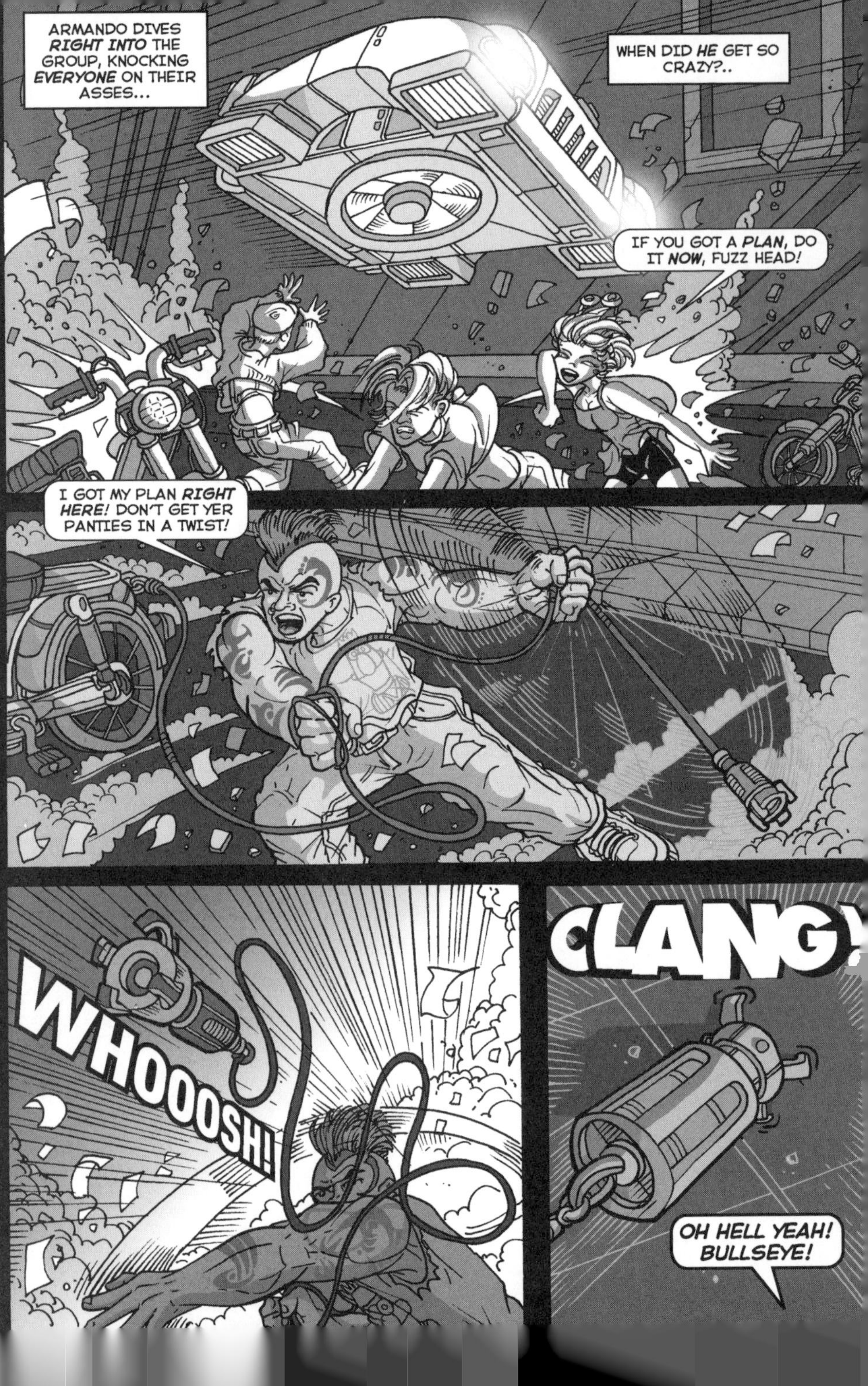
ARMANDO DIVES RIGHT INTO THE GROUP, KNOCKING EVERYONE ON THEIR ASSES...
WHEN DID HE GET SO CRAZY?..
IF YOU GOT A PLAN, DO IT NOW, FUZZ HEAD!
I GOT MY PLAN RIGHT HERE! DON'T GET YER PANTIES IN A TWIST!
WHOOOOSH!
CLANG!
OH HELL YEAH! BULLSEYE!

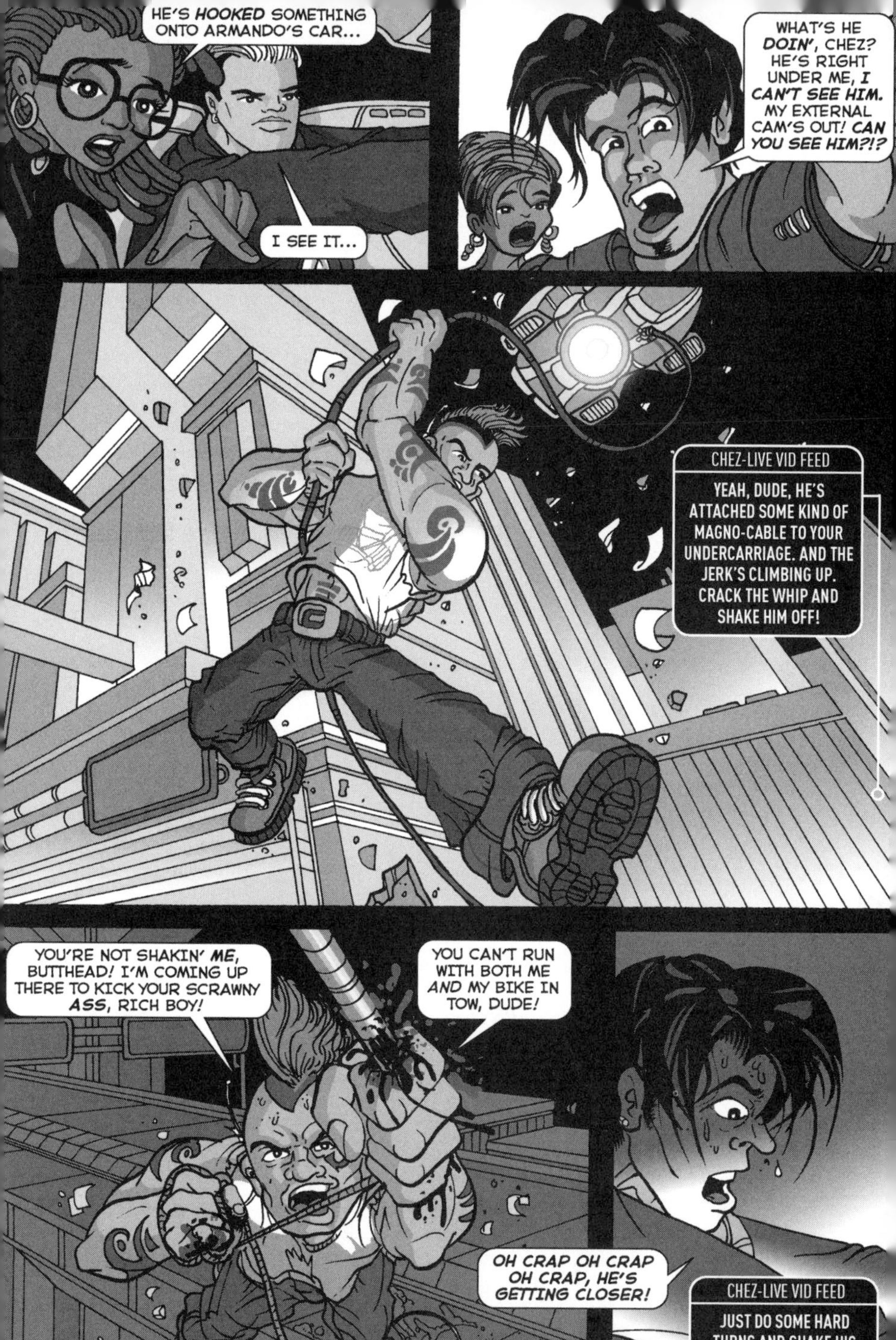
HE'S HOOKED SOMETHING ONTO ARMANDO'S CAR...
I SEE IT...
WHAT'S HE DOIN', CHEZ? HE'S RIGHT UNDER ME, I CAN'T SEE HIM. MY EXTERNAL CAM'S OUT! CAN YOU SEE HIM?!?
CHEZ-LIVE VID FEED
YEAH, DUDE, HE'S ATTACHED SOME KIND OF MAGNO-CABLE TO YOUR UNDERCARRIAGE. AND THE JERK'S CLIMBING UP. CRACK THE WHIP AND SHAKE HIM OFF!
YOU'RE NOT SHAKIN' ME, BUTTHEAD! I'M COMING UP THERE TO KICK YOUR SCRAWNY ASS, RICH BOY!
YOU CAN'T RUN WITH BOTH ME AND MY BIKE IN TOW, DUDE!
OH CRAP OH CRAP OH CRAP, HE'S GETTING CLOSER!
CHEZ-LIVE VID FEED
JUST DO SOME HARD TURNS AND SHAKE HIS DUMB ASS, MAN!

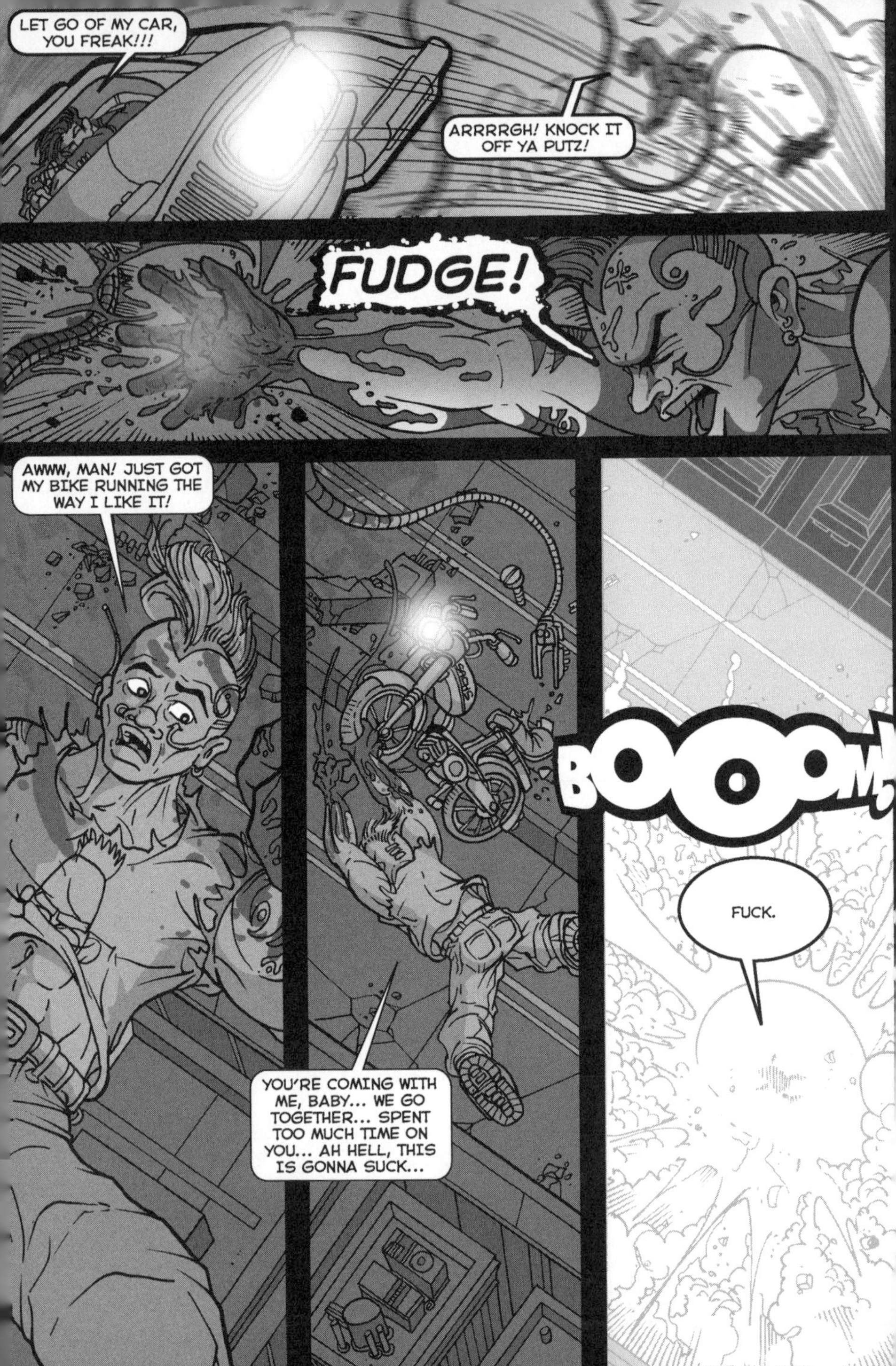
LET GO OF MY CAR, YOU FREAK!!!
ARRRRGH! KNOCK IT OFF YA PUTZ!
FUDGE!
AWWW, MAN! JUST GOT MY BIKE RUNNING THE WAY I LIKE IT!
YOU'RE COMING WITH ME, BABY... WE GO TOGETHER... SPENT TOO MUCH TIME ON YOU... AH HELL, THIS IS GONNA SUCK...
BOOOOM!
FUCK.

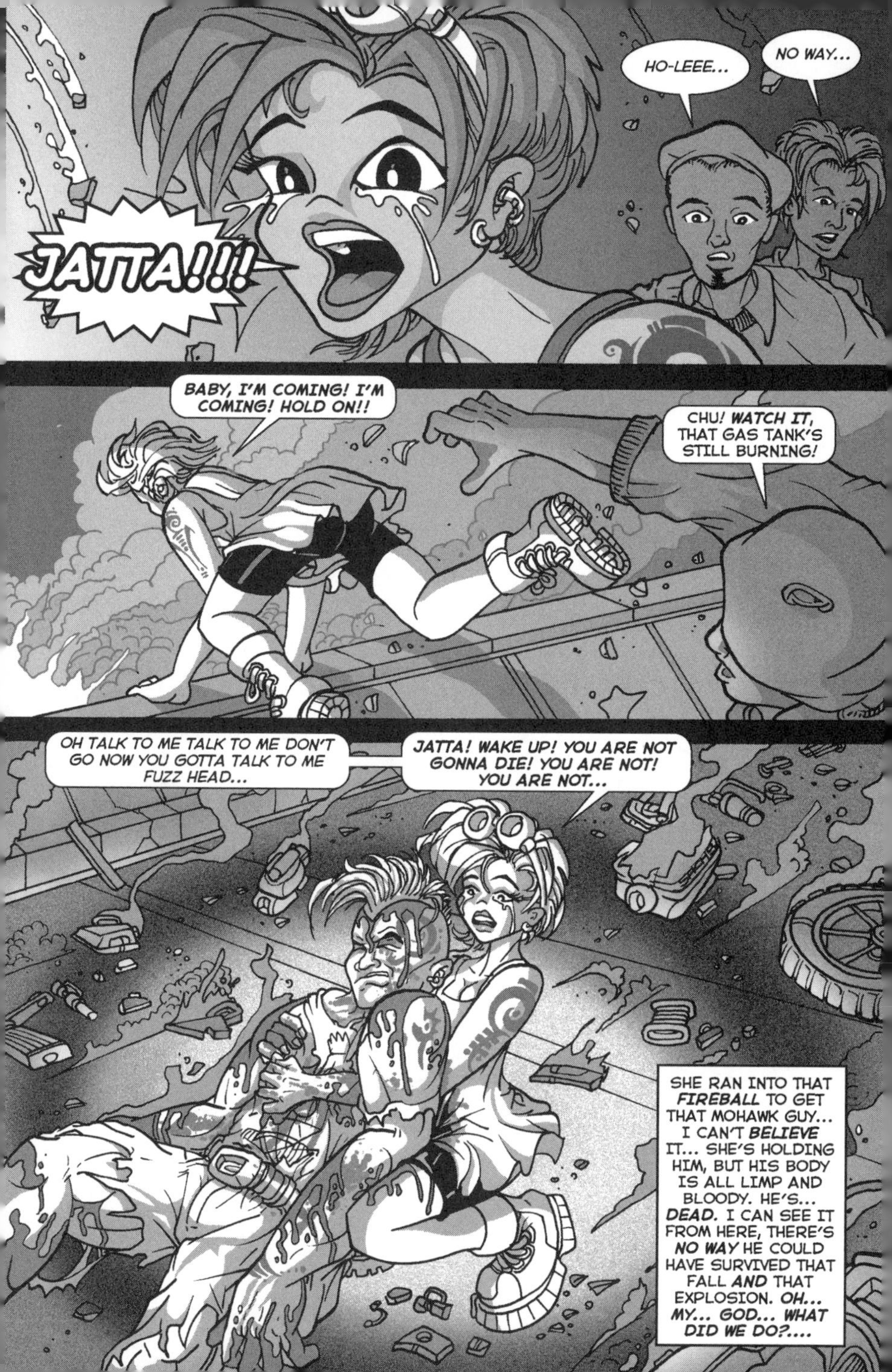
HO-LEEE...
NO WAY...
JATTA!!!!
BABY, I'M COMING! I'M COMING! HOLD ON!!
CHU! WATCH IT, THAT GAS TANK'S STILL BURNING!
OH TALK TO ME TALK TO ME DON'T GO NOW YOU GOTTA TALK TO ME FUZZ HEAD...
JATTA! WAKE UP! YOU ARE NOT GONNA DIE! YOU ARE NOT! YOU ARE NOT...
SHE RAN INTO THAT FIREBALL TO GET THAT MOHAWK GUY... I CAN'T BELIEVE IT... SHE'S HOLDING HIM, BUT HIS BODY IS ALL LIMP AND BLOODY. HE'S... DEAD. I CAN SEE IT FROM HERE, THERE'S NO WAY HE COULD HAVE SURVIVED THAT FALL AND THAT EXPLOSION. OH... MY... GOD... WHAT DID WE DO?....

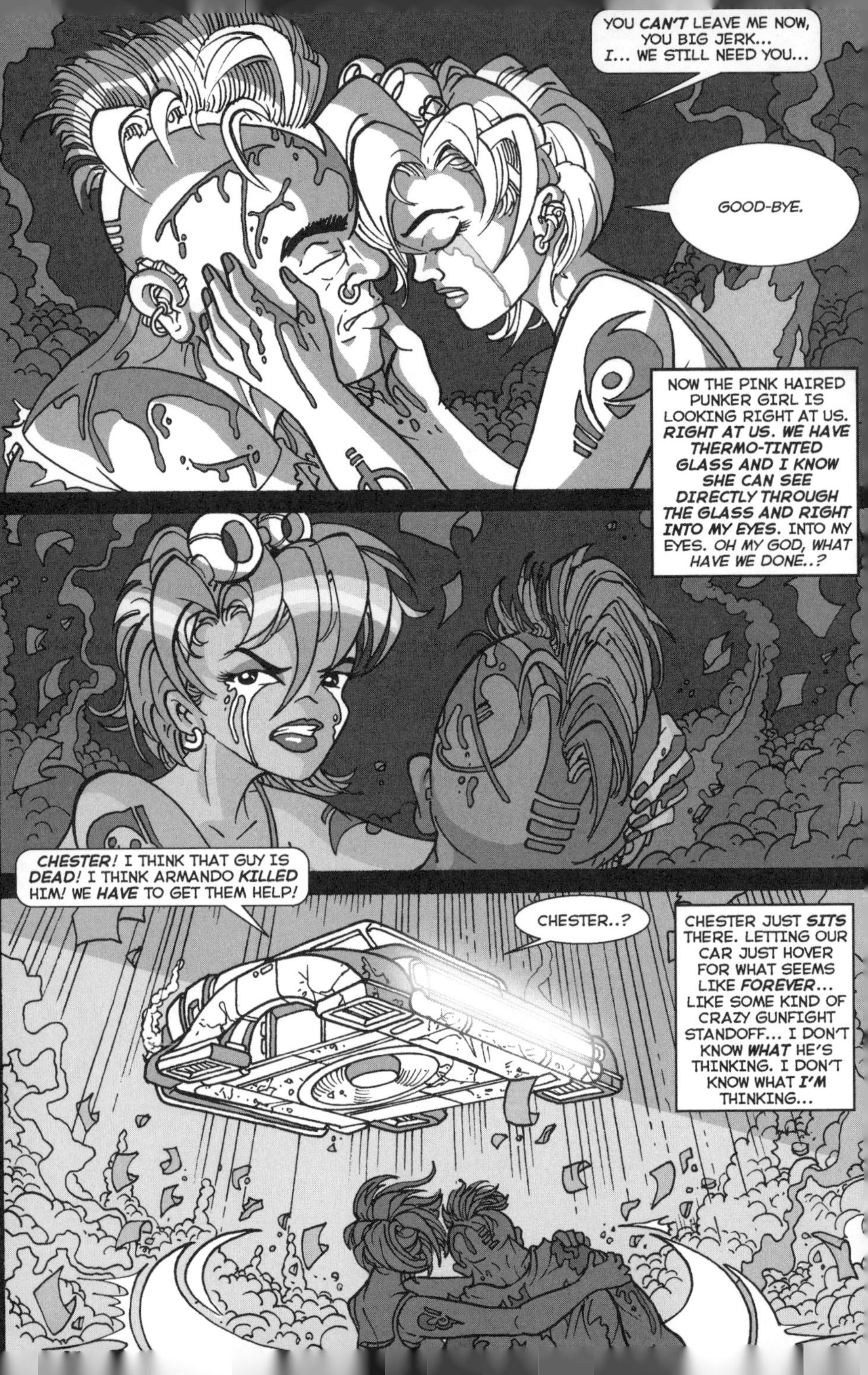

YOU CAN'T LEAVE ME NOW, YOU BIG JERK... I... WE STILL NEED YOU...
GOOD-BYE.
NOW THE PINK HAIRED PUNKER GIRL IS LOOKING RIGHT AT US. RIGHT AT US. WE HAVE THERMO-TINTED GLASS AND I KNOW SHE CAN SEE DIRECTLY THROUGH THE GLASS AND RIGHT INTO MY EYES. INTO MY EYES. OH MY GOD, WHAT HAVE WE DONE..?
CHESTER! I THINK THAT GUY IS DEAD! I THINK ARMANDO KILLED HIM! WE HAVE TO GET THEM HELP!
CHESTER..?
CHESTER JUST SITS THERE. LETTING OUR CAR JUST HOVER FOR WHAT SEEMS LIKE FOREVER... LIKE SOME KIND OF CRAZY GUNFIGHT STANDOFF... I DON'T KNOW WHAT HE'S THINKING. I DON'T KNOW WHAT I'M THINKING...

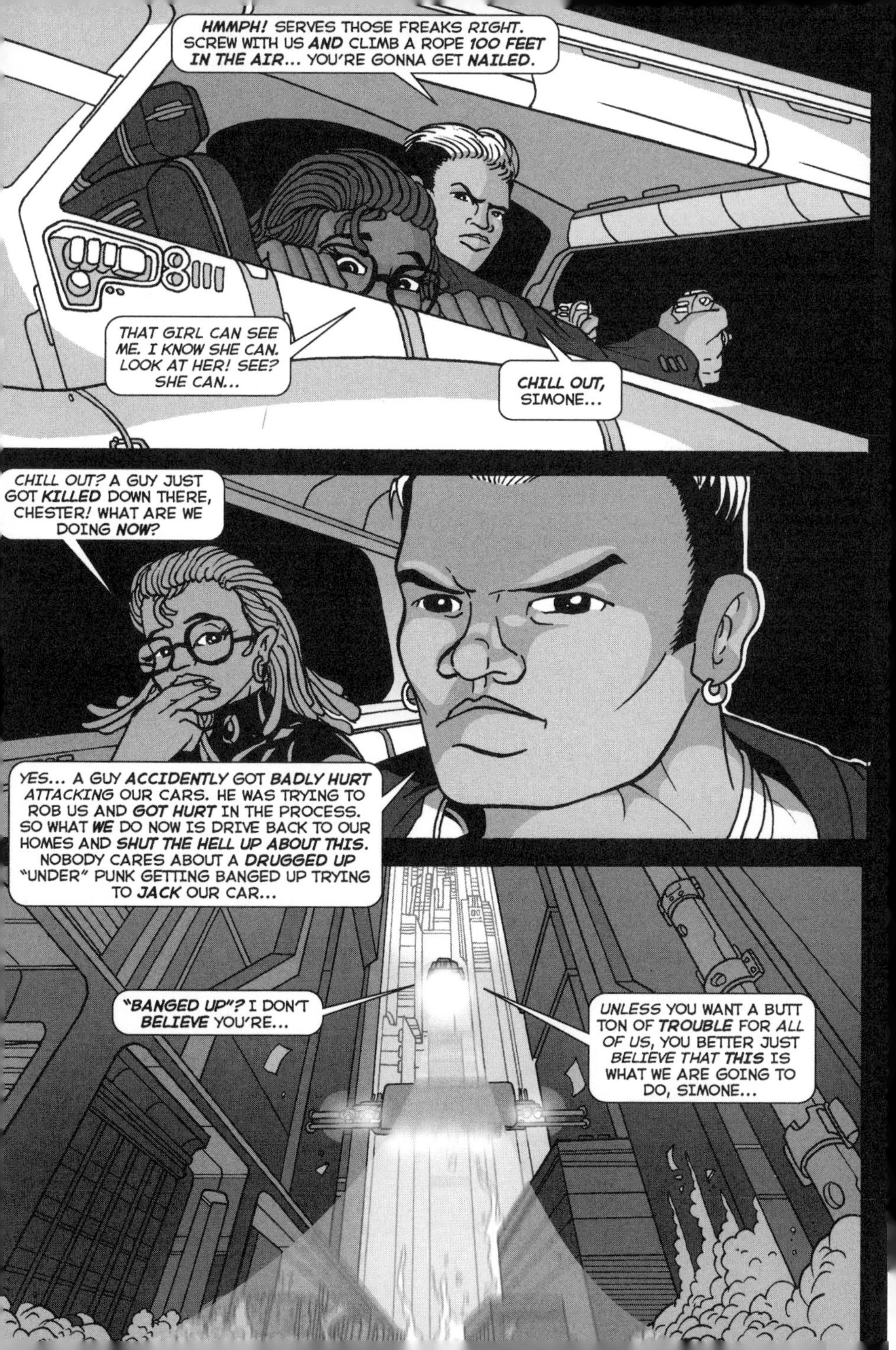
HMMPH! SERVES THOSE FREAKS RIGHT. SCREW WITH US AND CLIMB A ROPE 100 FEET IN THE AIR... YOU'RE GONNA GET NAILED.
THAT GIRL CAN SEE ME. I KNOW SHE CAN. LOOK AT HER! SEE? SHE CAN...
CHILL OUT, SIMONE...
CHILL OUT? A GUY JUST GOT KILLED DOWN THERE, CHESTER! WHAT ARE WE DOING NOW?
YES... A GUY ACCIDENTLY GOT BADLY HURT ATTACKING OUR CARS. HE WAS TRYING TO ROB US AND GOT HURT IN THE PROCESS. SO WHAT WE DO NOW IS DRIVE BACK TO OUR HOMES AND SHUT THE HELL UP ABOUT THIS. NOBODY CARES ABOUT A DRUGGED UP "UNDER" PUNK GETTING BANGED UP TRYING TO JACK OUR CAR...
"BANGED UP"? I DON'T BELIEVE YOU'RE...
UNLESS YOU WANT A BUTT TON OF TROUBLE FOR ALL OF US, YOU BETTER JUST BELIEVE THAT THIS IS WHAT WE ARE GOING TO DO, SIMONE...

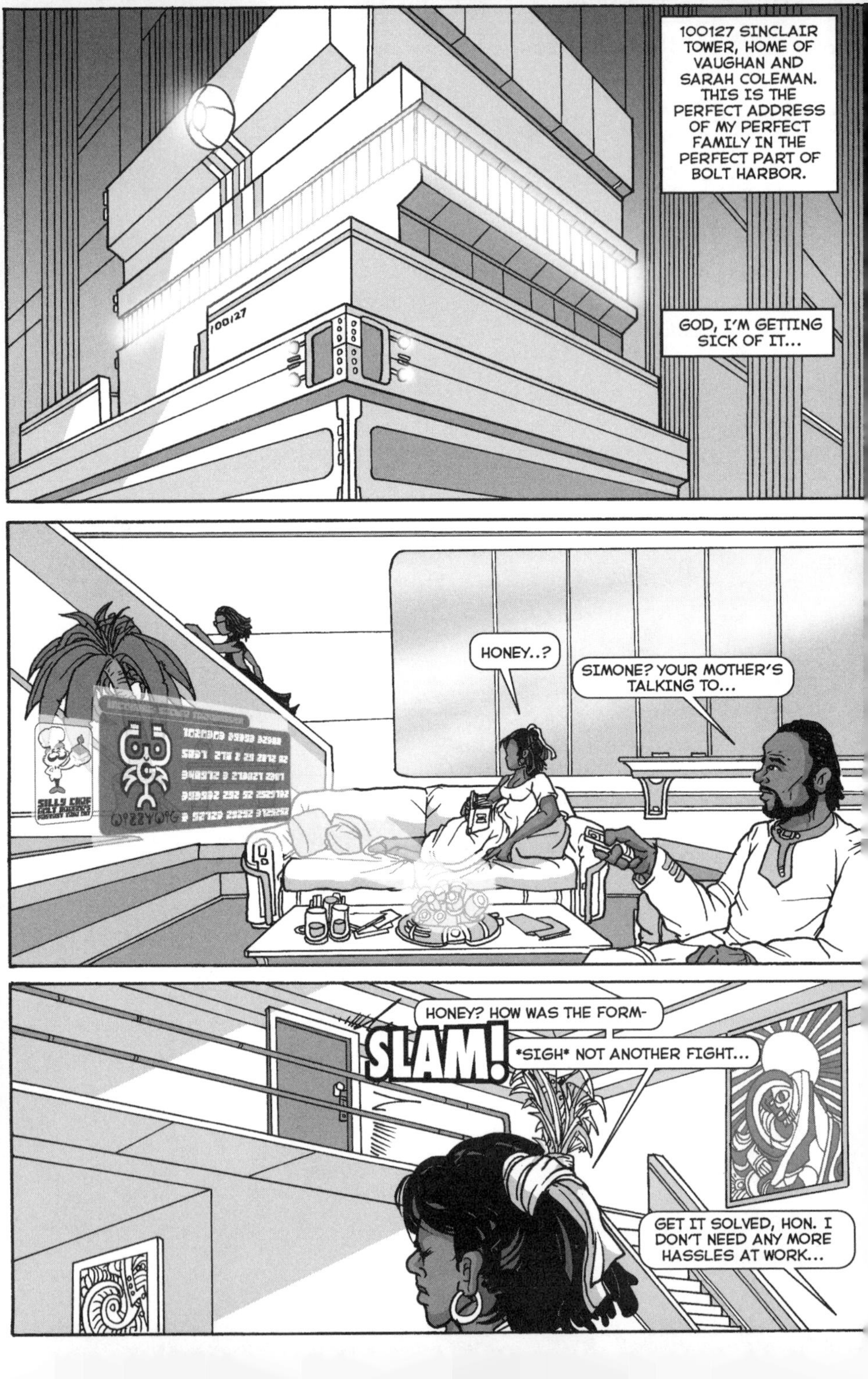
100127 SINCLAIR TOWER, HOME OF VAUGHAN AND SARAH COLEMAN. THIS IS THE PERFECT ADDRESS OF MY PERFECT FAMILY IN THE PERFECT PART OF BOLT HARBOR.
100127
GOD, I'M GETTING SICK OF IT...
HONEY..?
SIMONE? YOUR MOTHER'S TALKING TO...
HONEY? HOW WAS THE FORM-
SLAM!
SIGH NOT ANOTHER FIGHT...
GET IT SOLVED, HON. I DON'T NEED ANY MORE HASSLES AT WORK...

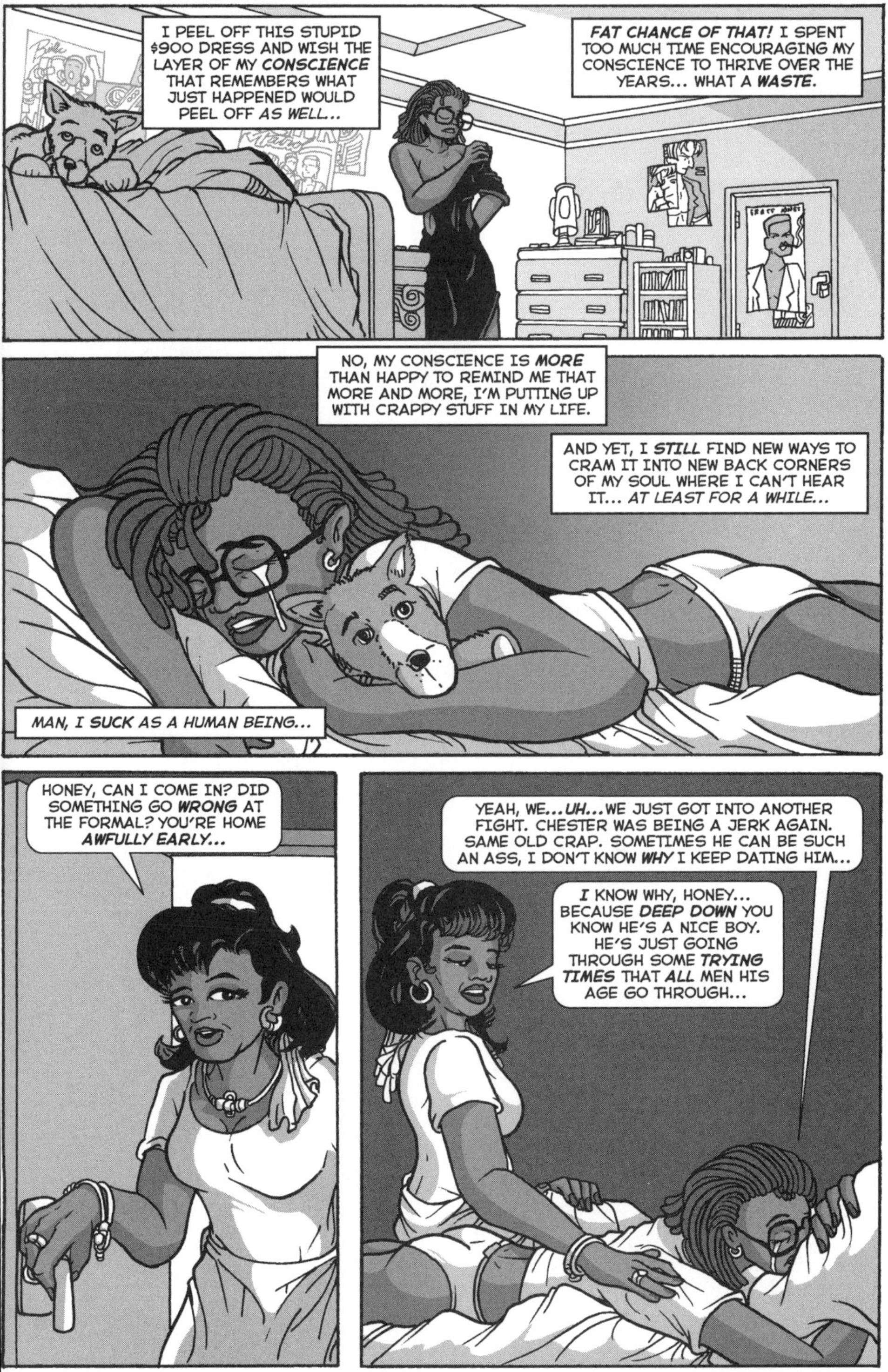
I PEEL OFF THIS STUPID $900 DRESS AND WISH THE LAYER OF MY CONSCIENCE THAT REMEMBERS WHAT JUST HAPPENED WOULD PEEL OFF AS WELL...
FAT CHANCE OF THAT! I SPENT TOO MUCH TIME ENCOURAGING MY CONSCIENCE TO THRIVE OVER THE YEARS... WHAT A WASTE.
NO, MY CONSCIENCE IS MORE THAN HAPPY TO REMIND ME THAT MORE AND MORE, I'M PUTTING UP WITH CRAPPY STUFF IN MY LIFE.
AND YET, I STILL FIND NEW WAYS TO CRAM IT INTO NEW BACK CORNERS OF MY SOUL WHERE I CAN'T HEAR IT... AT LEAST FOR A WHILE...
MAN, I SUCK AS A HUMAN BEING...
HONEY, CAN I COME IN? DID SOMETHING GO WRONG AT THE FORMAL? YOU'RE HOME AWFULLY EARLY...
YEAH, WE...UH...WE JUST GOT INTO ANOTHER FIGHT. CHESTER WAS BEING A JERK AGAIN. SAME OLD CRAP. SOMETIMES HE CAN BE SUCH AN ASS, I DON'T KNOW WHY I KEEP DATING HIM...
I KNOW WHY, HONEY... BECAUSE DEEP DOWN YOU KNOW HE'S A NICE BOY. HE'S JUST GOING THROUGH SOME TRYING TIMES THAT ALL MEN HIS AGE GO THROUGH...

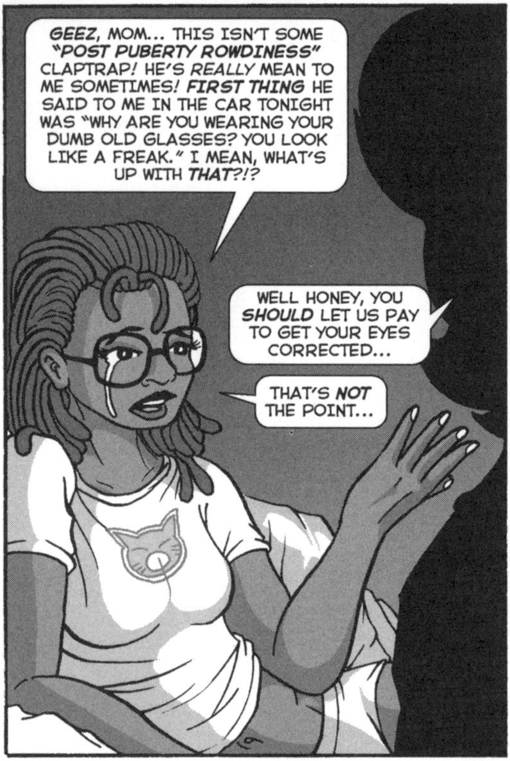
GEEZ, MOM... THIS ISN'T SOME "POST PUBERTY ROWDINESS" CLAPTRAP! HE'S REALLY MEAN TO ME SOMETIMES! FIRST THING HE SAID TO ME IN THE CAR TONIGHT WAS "WHY ARE YOU WEARING YOUR DUMB OLD GLASSES? YOU LOOK LIKE A FREAK." I MEAN, WHAT'S UP WITH THAT?!?
WELL HONEY, YOU SHOULD LET US PAY TO GET YOUR EYES CORRECTED...
THAT'S NOT THE POINT...

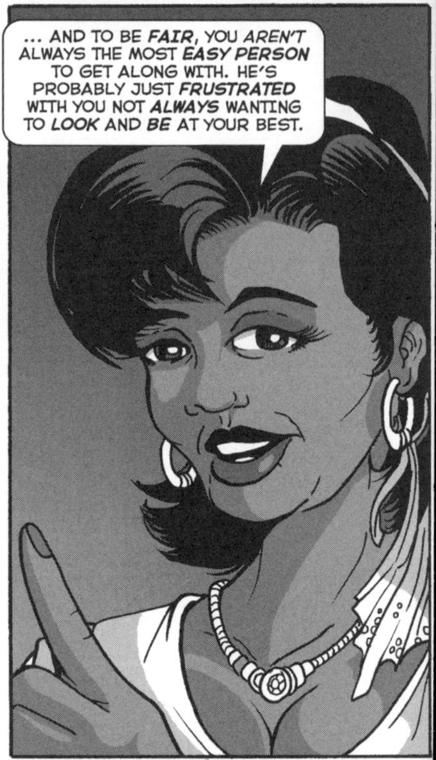
... AND TO BE FAIR, YOU AREN'T ALWAYS THE MOST EASY PERSON TO GET ALONG WITH. HE'S PROBABLY JUST FRUSTRATED WITH YOU NOT ALWAYS WANTING TO LOOK AND BE AT YOUR BEST.

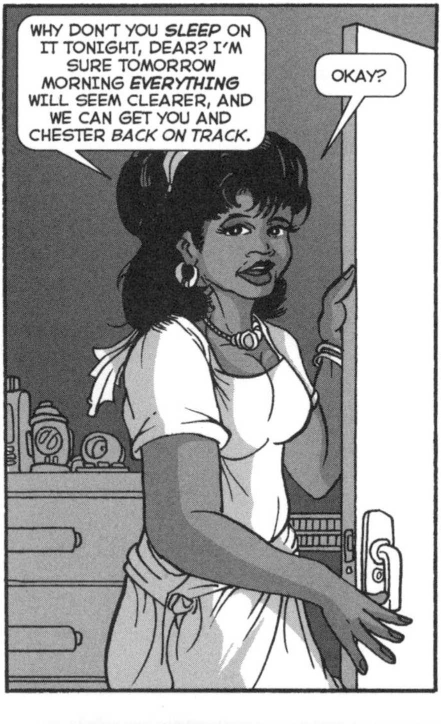
WHY DON'T YOU SLEEP ON IT TONIGHT, DEAR? I'M SURE TOMORROW MORNING EVERYTHING WILL SEEM CLEARER, AND WE CAN GET YOU AND CHESTER BACK ON TRACK.
OKAY?

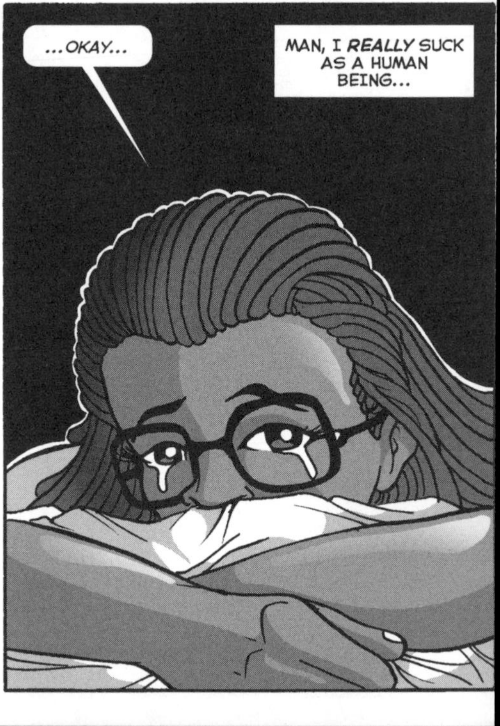
...OKAY...
MAN, I REALLY SUCK AS A HUMAN BEING...

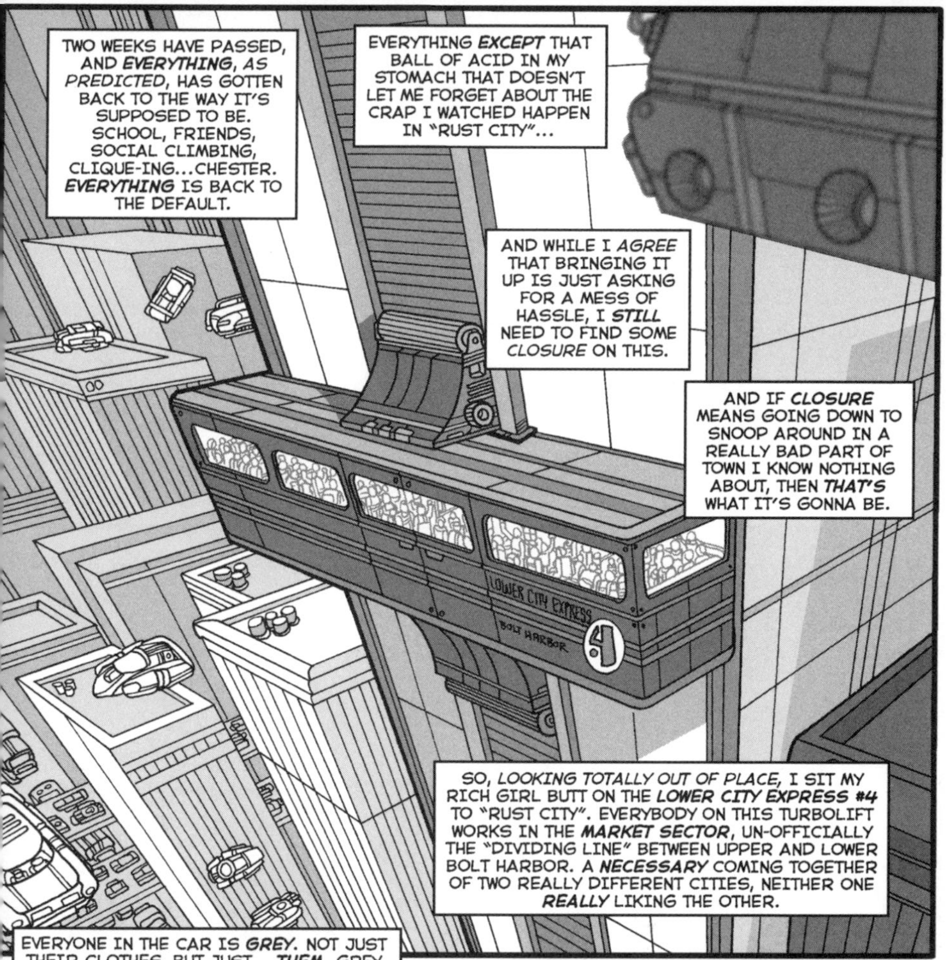
TWO WEEKS HAVE PASSED, AND *EVERYTHING*, AS *PREDICTED*, HAS GOTTEN BACK TO THE WAY IT'S SUPPOSED TO BE. SCHOOL, FRIENDS, SOCIAL CLIMBING, CLIQUE-ING...CHESTER. *EVERYTHING* IS BACK TO THE DEFAULT.
EVERYTHING *EXCEPT* THAT BALL OF ACID IN MY STOMACH THAT DOESN'T LET ME FORGET ABOUT THE CRAP I WATCHED HAPPEN IN "RUST CITY"...
AND WHILE I *AGREE* THAT BRINGING IT UP IS JUST ASKING FOR A MESS OF HASSLE, I *STILL* NEED TO FIND SOME *CLOSURE* ON THIS.
AND IF *CLOSURE* MEANS GOING DOWN TO SNOOP AROUND IN A REALLY BAD PART OF TOWN I KNOW NOTHING ABOUT, THEN *THAT'S* WHAT IT'S GONNA BE.
LOWER CITY EXPRESS
BOLT HARBOR
4
SO, *LOOKING TOTALLY OUT OF PLACE*, I SIT MY RICH GIRL BUTT ON THE *LOWER CITY EXPRESS #4* TO "RUST CITY". EVERYBODY ON THIS TURBOLIFT WORKS IN THE *MARKET SECTOR*, UN-OFFICIALLY THE "DIVIDING LINE" BETWEEN UPPER AND LOWER BOLT HARBOR. A *NECESSARY* COMING TOGETHER OF TWO REALLY DIFFERENT CITIES, NEITHER ONE *REALLY* LIKING THE OTHER.

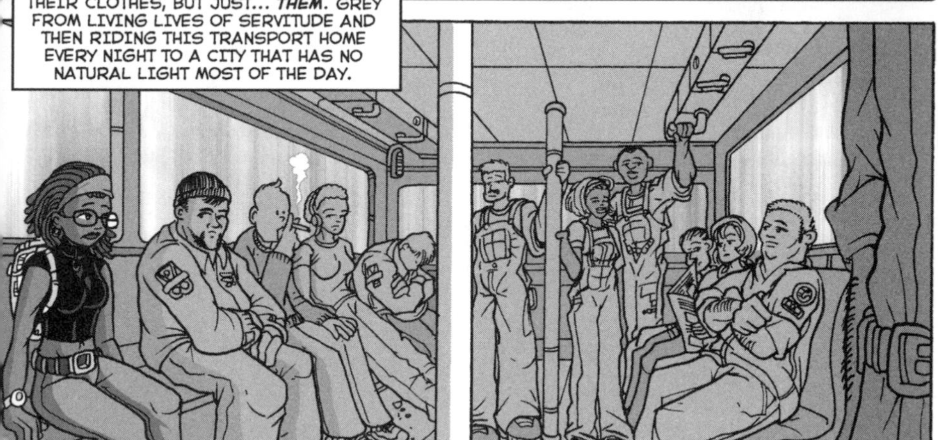
EVERYONE IN THE CAR IS *GREY*. NOT JUST THEIR CLOTHES, BUT JUST... *THEM*. GREY FROM LIVING LIVES OF SERVITUDE AND THEN RIDING THIS TRANSPORT HOME EVERY NIGHT TO A CITY THAT HAS NO NATURAL LIGHT MOST OF THE DAY.
I *SHOULDN'T* HAVE WORN MY EXPENSIVE BOOTS. *DEAD GIVEAWAY.*

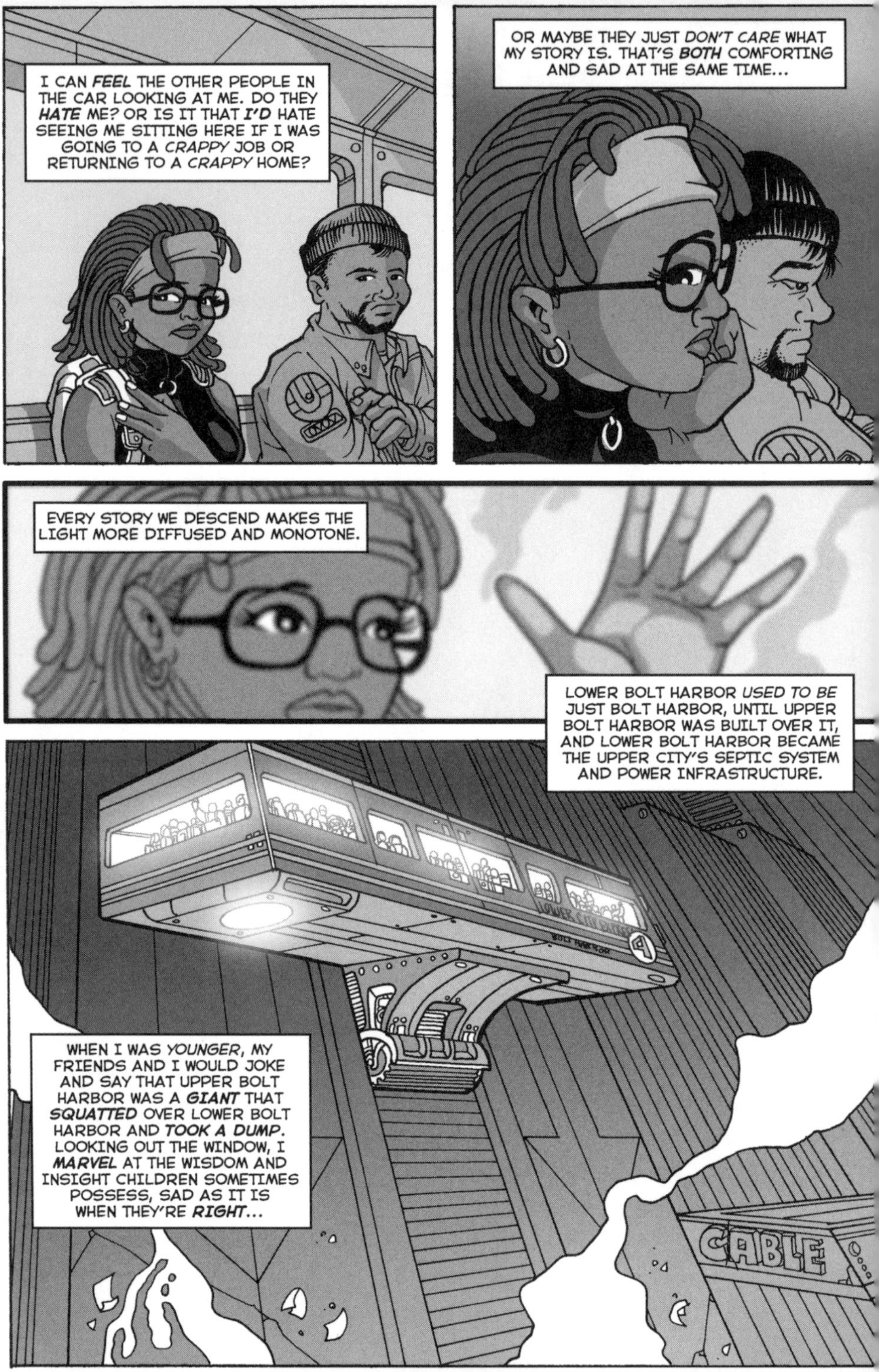
I CAN FEEL THE OTHER PEOPLE IN THE CAR LOOKING AT ME. DO THEY HATE ME? OR IS IT THAT I'D HATE SEEING ME SITTING HERE IF I WAS GOING TO A CRAPPY JOB OR RETURNING TO A CRAPPY HOME?
OR MAYBE THEY JUST DON'T CARE WHAT MY STORY IS. THAT'S BOTH COMFORTING AND SAD AT THE SAME TIME...
EVERY STORY WE DESCEND MAKES THE LIGHT MORE DIFFUSED AND MONOTONE.
LOWER BOLT HARBOR USED TO BE JUST BOLT HARBOR, UNTIL UPPER BOLT HARBOR WAS BUILT OVER IT, AND LOWER BOLT HARBOR BECAME THE UPPER CITY'S SEPTIC SYSTEM AND POWER INFRASTRUCTURE.
WHEN I WAS YOUNGER, MY FRIENDS AND I WOULD JOKE AND SAY THAT UPPER BOLT HARBOR WAS A GIANT THAT SQUATTED OVER LOWER BOLT HARBOR AND TOOK A DUMP. LOOKING OUT THE WINDOW, I MARVEL AT THE WISDOM AND INSIGHT CHILDREN SOMETIMES POSSESS, SAD AS IT IS WHEN THEY'RE RIGHT...
CABLE

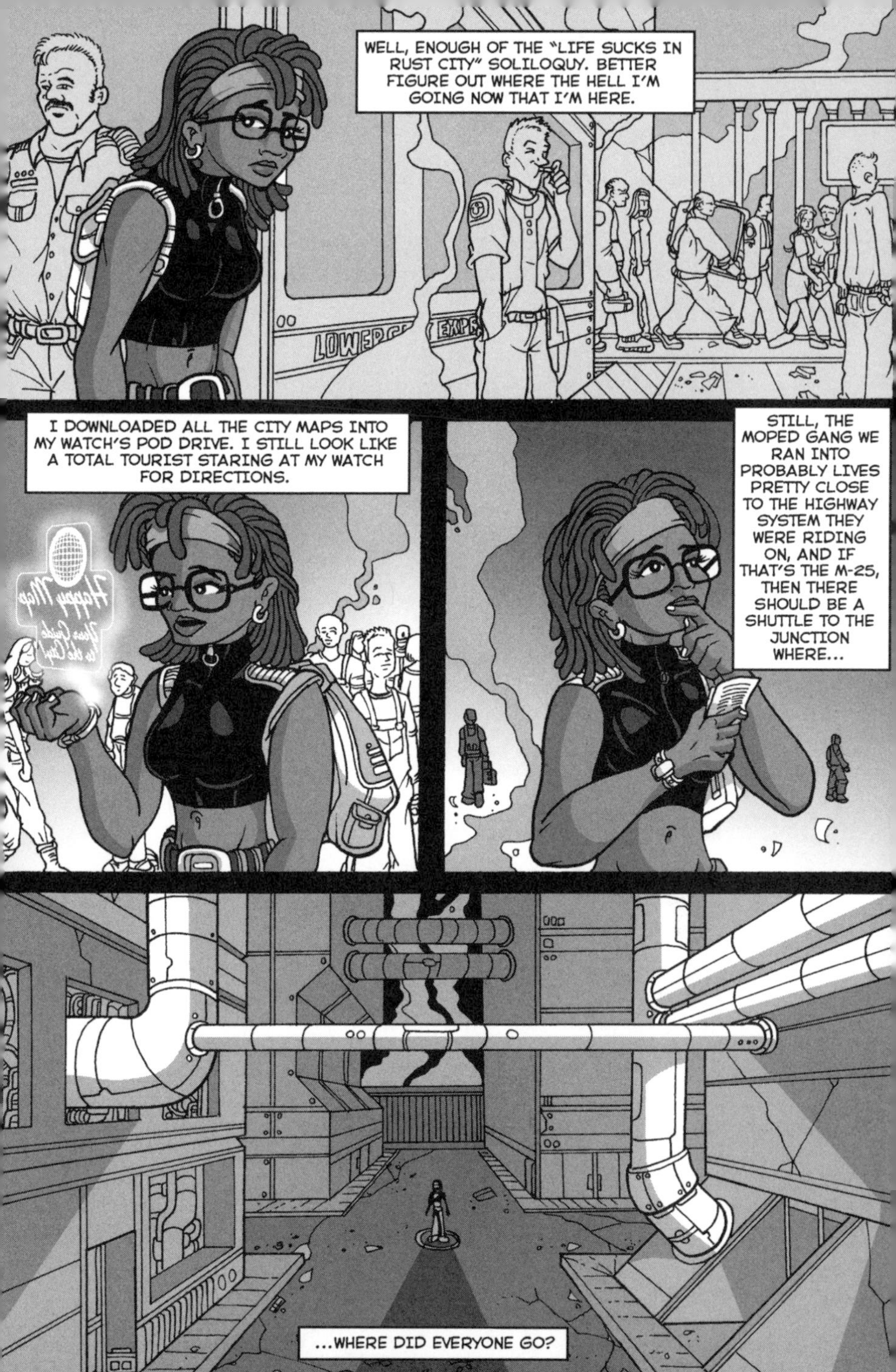
WELL, ENOUGH OF THE "LIFE SUCKS IN RUST CITY" SOLILOQUY. BETTER FIGURE OUT WHERE THE HELL I'M GOING NOW THAT I'M HERE.
I DOWNLOADED ALL THE CITY MAPS INTO MY WATCH'S POD DRIVE. I STILL LOOK LIKE A TOTAL TOURIST STARING AT MY WATCH FOR DIRECTIONS.
Happy Map
Your Guide to the City!
STILL, THE MOPED GANG WE RAN INTO PROBABLY LIVES PRETTY CLOSE TO THE HIGHWAY SYSTEM THEY WERE RIDING ON, AND IF THAT'S THE M-25, THEN THERE SHOULD BE A SHUTTLE TO THE JUNCTION WHERE...
...WHERE DID EVERYONE GO?

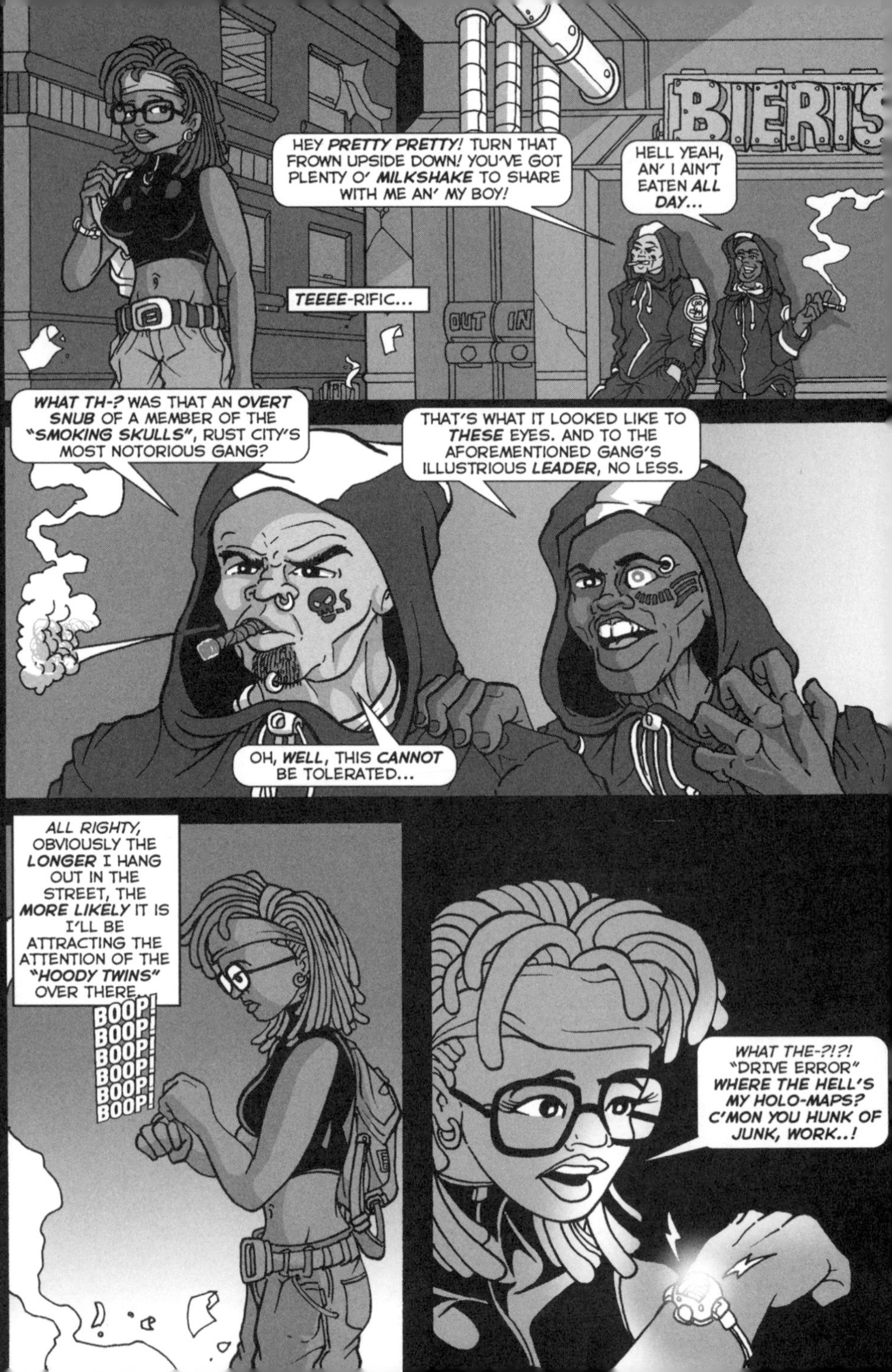

HEY PRETTY PRETTY! TURN THAT FROWN UPSIDE DOWN! YOU'VE GOT PLENTY O' MILKSHAKE TO SHARE WITH ME AN' MY BOY!
HELL YEAH, AN' I AIN'T EATEN ALL DAY...
TEEEE-RIFIC...
BIERI'S
OUT
IN
WHAT TH-? WAS THAT AN OVERT SNUB OF A MEMBER OF THE "SMOKING SKULLS", RUST CITY'S MOST NOTORIOUS GANG?
THAT'S WHAT IT LOOKED LIKE TO THESE EYES. AND TO THE AFOREMENTIONED GANG'S ILLUSTRIOUS LEADER, NO LESS.
OH, WELL, THIS CANNOT BE TOLERATED...
ALL RIGHTY, OBVIOUSLY THE LONGER I HANG OUT IN THE STREET, THE MORE LIKELY IT IS I'LL BE ATTRACTING THE ATTENTION OF THE "HOODY TWINS" OVER THERE...
BOOP! BOOP! BOOP! BOOP! BOOP! BOOP!
WHAT THE-?!?! "DRIVE ERROR" WHERE THE HELL'S MY HOLO-MAPS? C'MON YOU HUNK OF JUNK, WORK..!

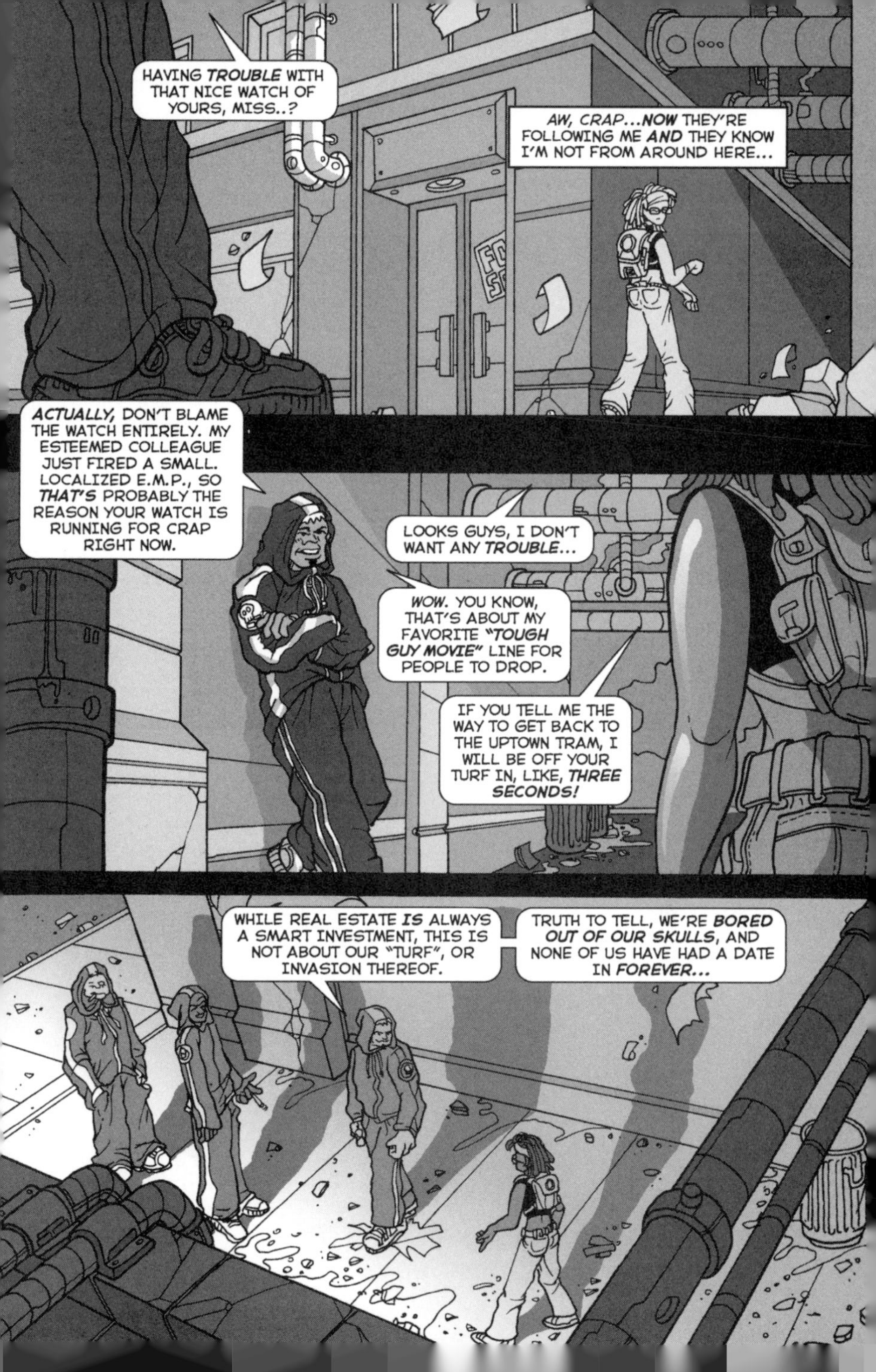
HAVING TROUBLE WITH THAT NICE WATCH OF YOURS, MISS..?
AW, CRAP...NOW THEY'RE FOLLOWING ME AND THEY KNOW I'M NOT FROM AROUND HERE...
ACTUALLY, DON'T BLAME THE WATCH ENTIRELY. MY ESTEEMED COLLEAGUE JUST FIRED A SMALL. LOCALIZED E.M.P., SO THAT'S PROBABLY THE REASON YOUR WATCH IS RUNNING FOR CRAP RIGHT NOW.
LOOKS GUYS, I DON'T WANT ANY TROUBLE...
WOW. YOU KNOW, THAT'S ABOUT MY FAVORITE "TOUGH GUY MOVIE" LINE FOR PEOPLE TO DROP.
IF YOU TELL ME THE WAY TO GET BACK TO THE UPTOWN TRAM, I WILL BE OFF YOUR TURF IN, LIKE, THREE SECONDS!
WHILE REAL ESTATE IS ALWAYS A SMART INVESTMENT, THIS IS NOT ABOUT OUR "TURF", OR INVASION THEREOF.
TRUTH TO TELL, WE'RE BORED OUT OF OUR SKULLS, AND NONE OF US HAVE HAD A DATE IN FOREVER...

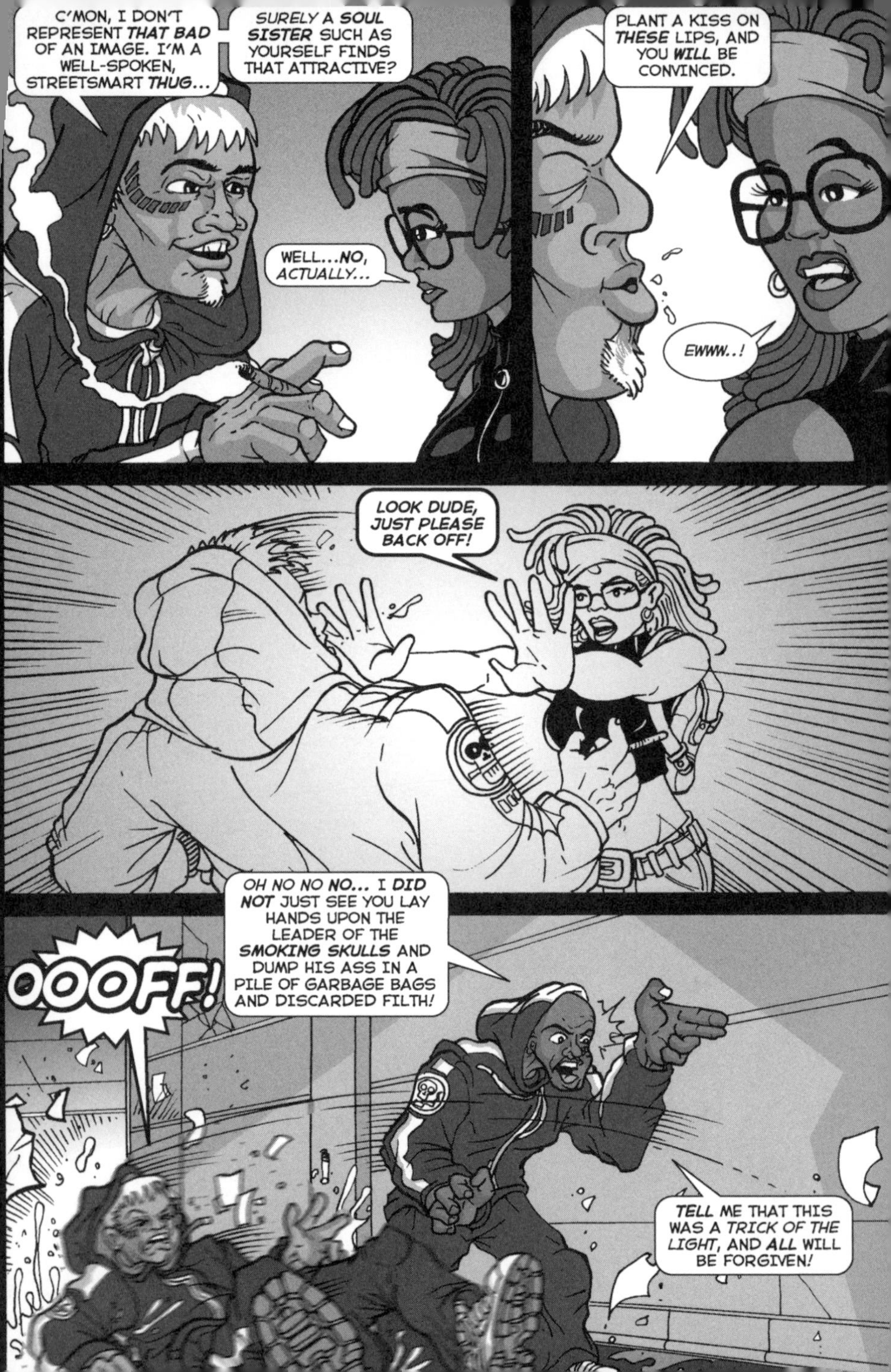
C'MON, I DON'T REPRESENT THAT BAD OF AN IMAGE. I'M A WELL-SPOKEN, STREETSMART THUG...
SURELY A SOUL SISTER SUCH AS YOURSELF FINDS THAT ATTRACTIVE?
WELL...NO, ACTUALLY...
PLANT A KISS ON THESE LIPS, AND YOU WILL BE CONVINCED.
EWWW..!
LOOK DUDE, JUST PLEASE BACK OFF!
OOOFF!
OH NO NO NO... I DID NOT JUST SEE YOU LAY HANDS UPON THE LEADER OF THE SMOKING SKULLS AND DUMP HIS ASS IN A PILE OF GARBAGE BAGS AND DISCARDED FILTH!
TELL ME THAT THIS WAS A TRICK OF THE LIGHT, AND ALL WILL BE FORGIVEN!

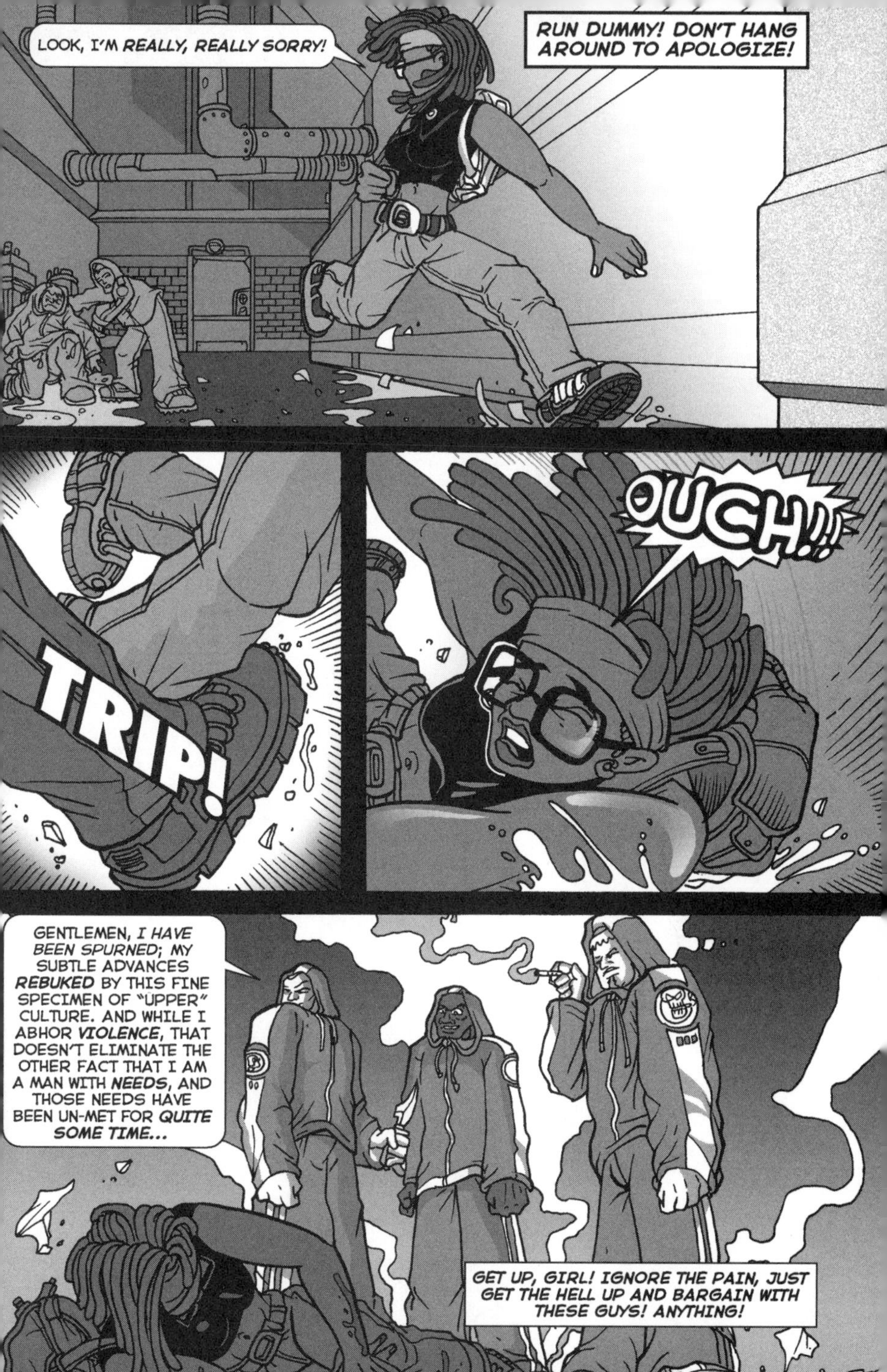
LOOK, I'M REALLY, REALLY SORRY!
RUN DUMMY! DON'T HANG AROUND TO APOLOGIZE!
TRIP!
OUCH!!!
GENTLEMEN, I HAVE BEEN SPURNED; MY SUBTLE ADVANCES REBUKED BY THIS FINE SPECIMEN OF "UPPER" CULTURE. AND WHILE I ABHOR VIOLENCE, THAT DOESN'T ELIMINATE THE OTHER FACT THAT I AM A MAN WITH NEEDS, AND THOSE NEEDS HAVE BEEN UN-MET FOR QUITE SOME TIME...
GET UP, GIRL! IGNORE THE PAIN, JUST GET THE HELL UP AND BARGAIN WITH THESE GUYS! ANYTHING!

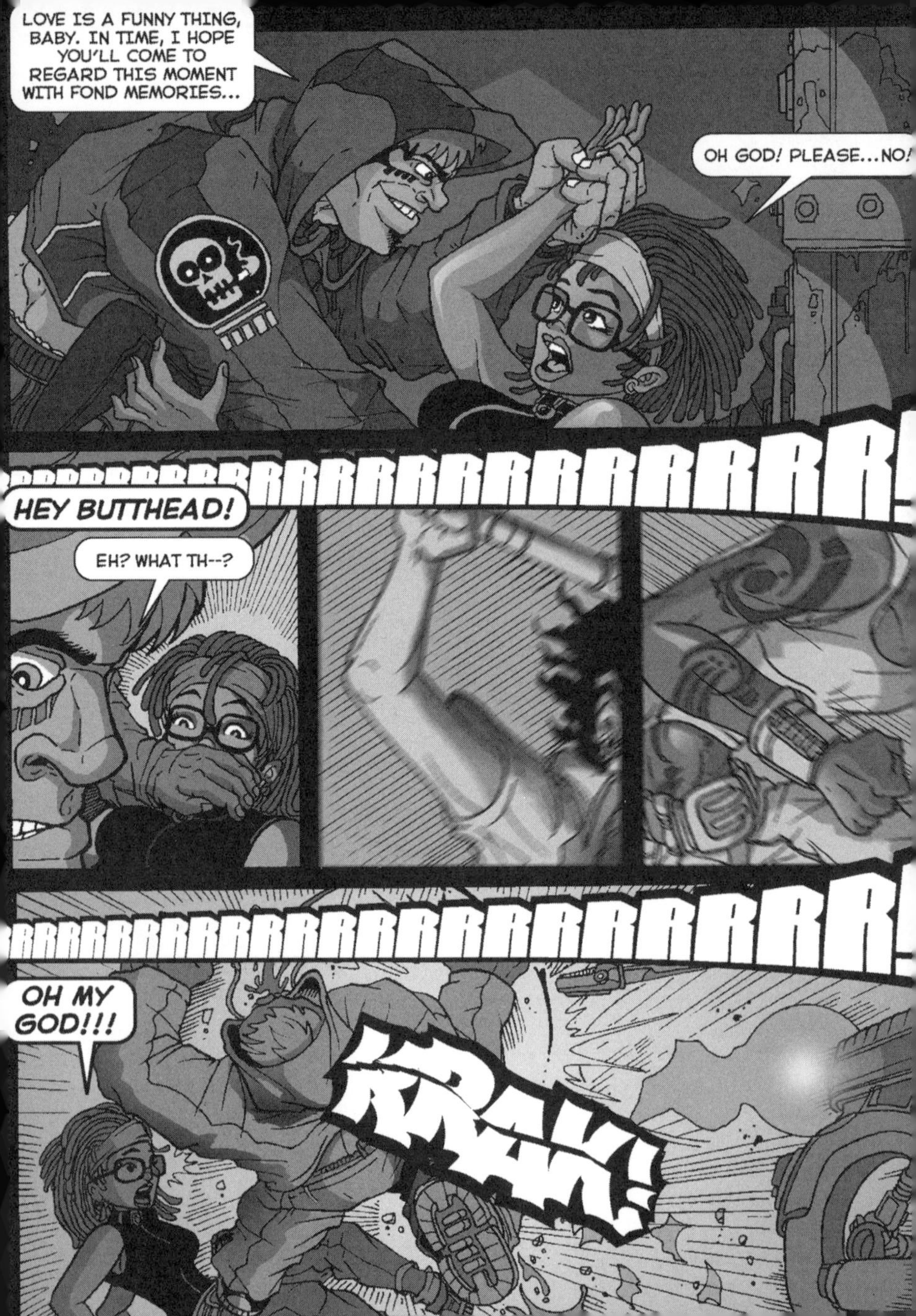

LOVE IS A FUNNY THING, BABY. IN TIME, I HOPE YOU'LL COME TO REGARD THIS MOMENT WITH FOND MEMORIES...
OH GOD! PLEASE...NO!
RRRRRRRRRRRRRRRRRRRRRR!
HEY BUTTHEAD!
EH? WHAT TH--?
RRRRRRRRRRRRRRRRRRRRRRR!
OH MY GOD!!!
KRAK!

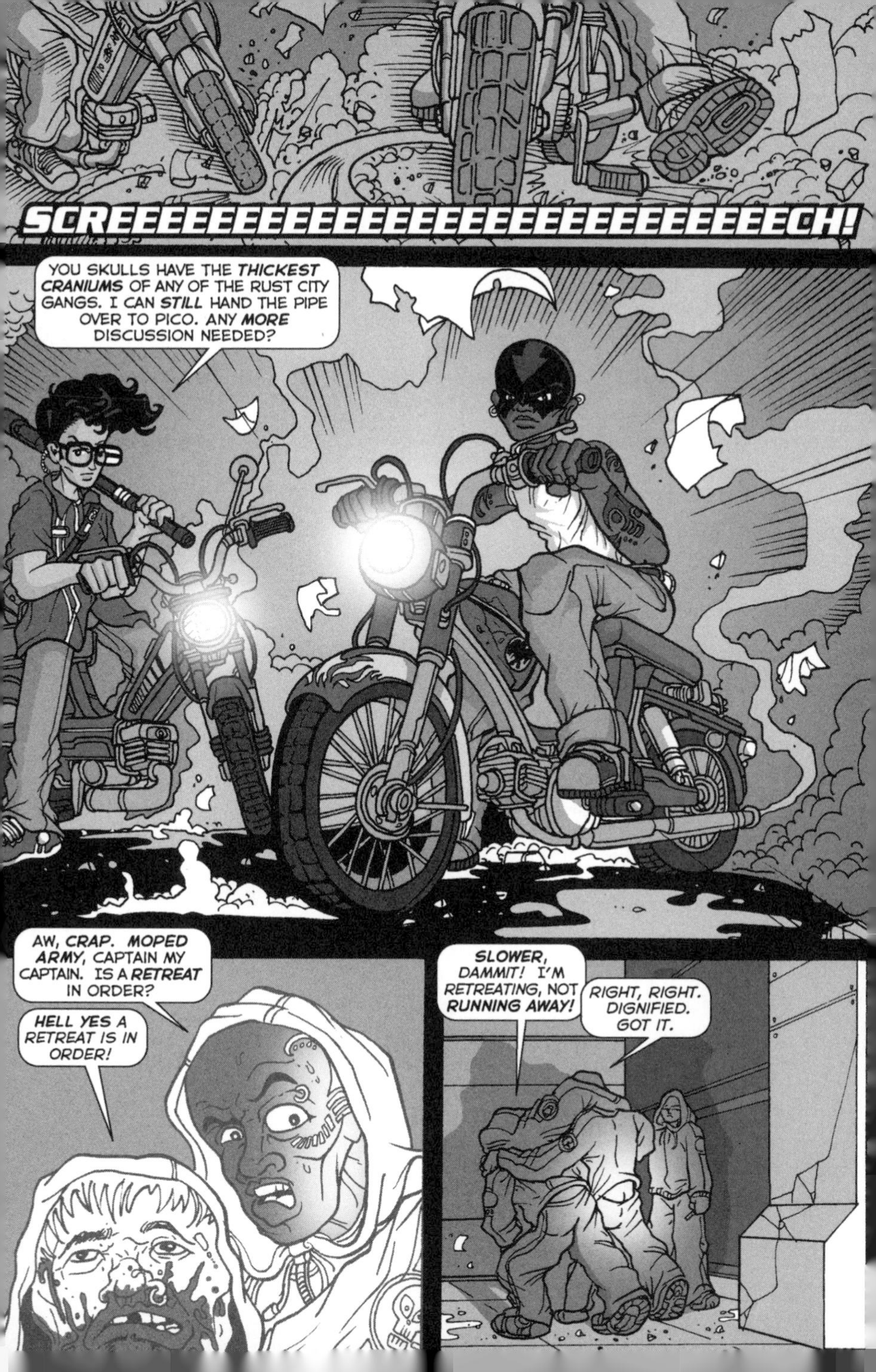
SCREEEEEEEEEEEEEEEEEEEEEEEEEEEEEEEECH!
YOU SKULLS HAVE THE THICKEST CRANIUMS OF ANY OF THE RUST CITY GANGS. I CAN STILL HAND THE PIPE OVER TO PICO. ANY MORE DISCUSSION NEEDED?
AW, CRAP. MOPED ARMY, CAPTAIN MY CAPTAIN. IS A RETREAT IN ORDER?
HELL YES A RETREAT IS IN ORDER!
SLOWER, DAMMIT! I'M RETREATING, NOT RUNNING AWAY!
RIGHT, RIGHT. DIGNIFIED. GOT IT.

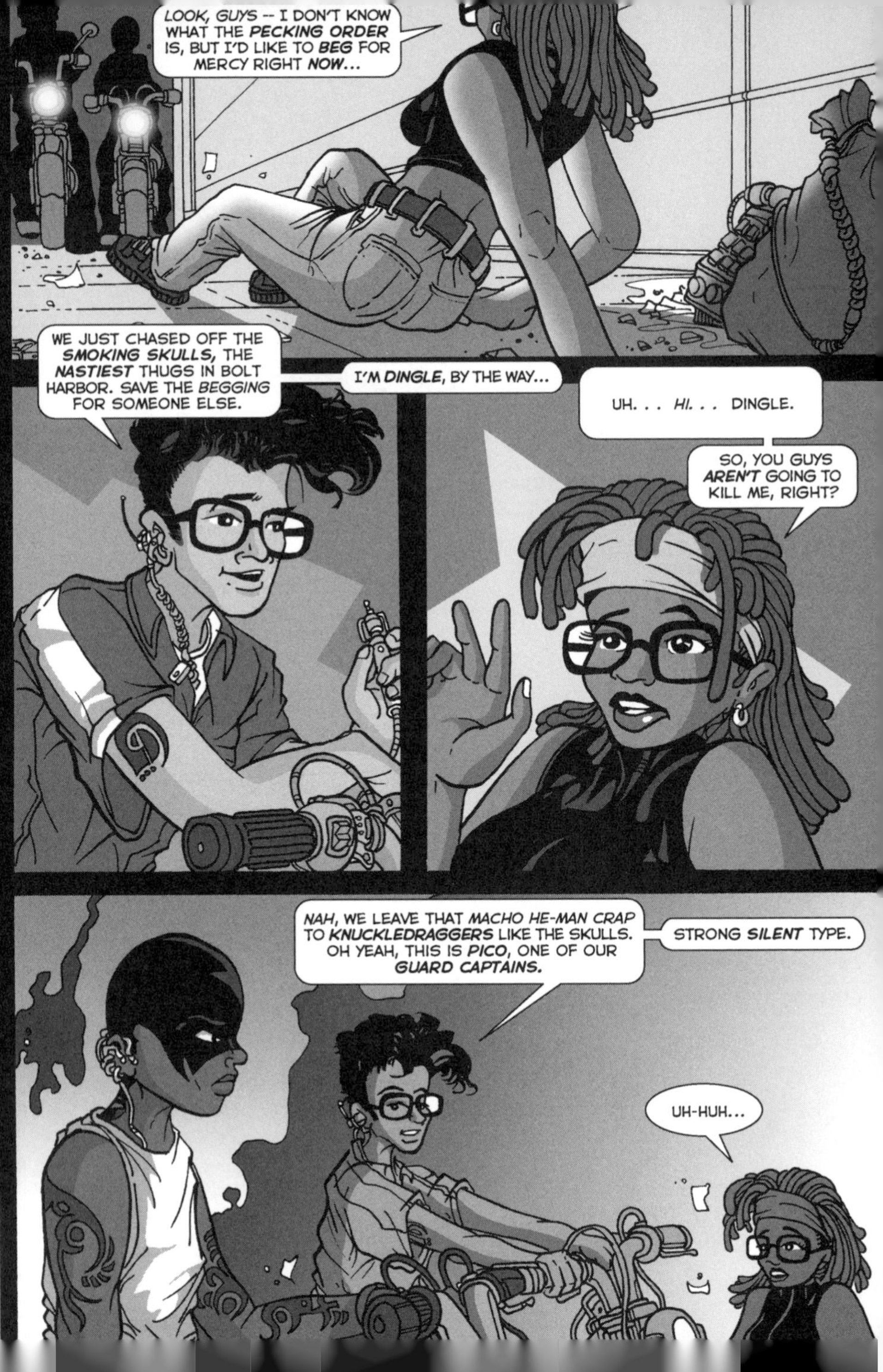
LOOK, GUYS -- I DON'T KNOW WHAT THE PECKING ORDER IS, BUT I'D LIKE TO BEG FOR MERCY RIGHT NOW...
WE JUST CHASED OFF THE SMOKING SKULLS, THE NASTIEST THUGS IN BOLT HARBOR. SAVE THE BEGGING FOR SOMEONE ELSE.
I'M DINGLE, BY THE WAY...
UH. . . HI. . . DINGLE.
SO, YOU GUYS AREN'T GOING TO KILL ME, RIGHT?
NAH, WE LEAVE THAT MACHO HE-MAN CRAP TO KNUCKLEDRAGGERS LIKE THE SKULLS. OH YEAH, THIS IS PICO, ONE OF OUR GUARD CAPTAINS.
STRONG SILENT TYPE.
UH-HUH...

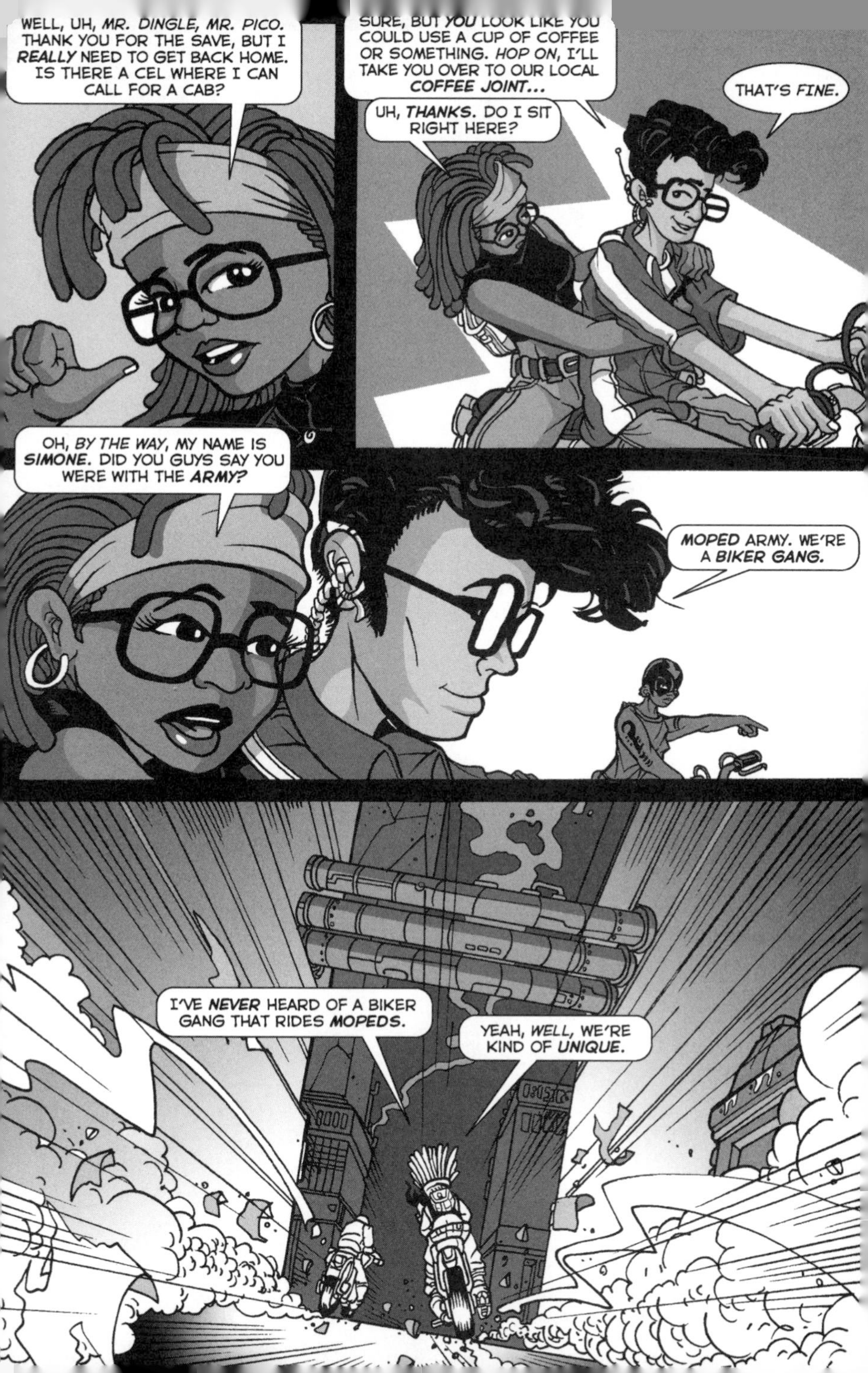
WELL, UH, *MR. DINGLE, MR. PICO.* THANK YOU FOR THE SAVE, BUT I *REALLY* NEED TO GET BACK HOME. IS THERE A CEL WHERE I CAN CALL FOR A CAB?
SURE, BUT *YOU* LOOK LIKE YOU COULD USE A CUP OF COFFEE OR SOMETHING. *HOP ON*, I'LL TAKE YOU OVER TO OUR LOCAL *COFFEE JOINT...*
UH, *THANKS*. DO I SIT RIGHT HERE?
THAT'S *FINE*.
OH, *BY THE WAY*, MY NAME IS *SIMONE*. DID YOU GUYS SAY YOU WERE WITH THE *ARMY?*
MOPED ARMY. WE'RE A *BIKER GANG.*
I'VE *NEVER* HEARD OF A BIKER GANG THAT RIDES *MOPEDS*.
YEAH, *WELL*, WE'RE KIND OF *UNIQUE*.

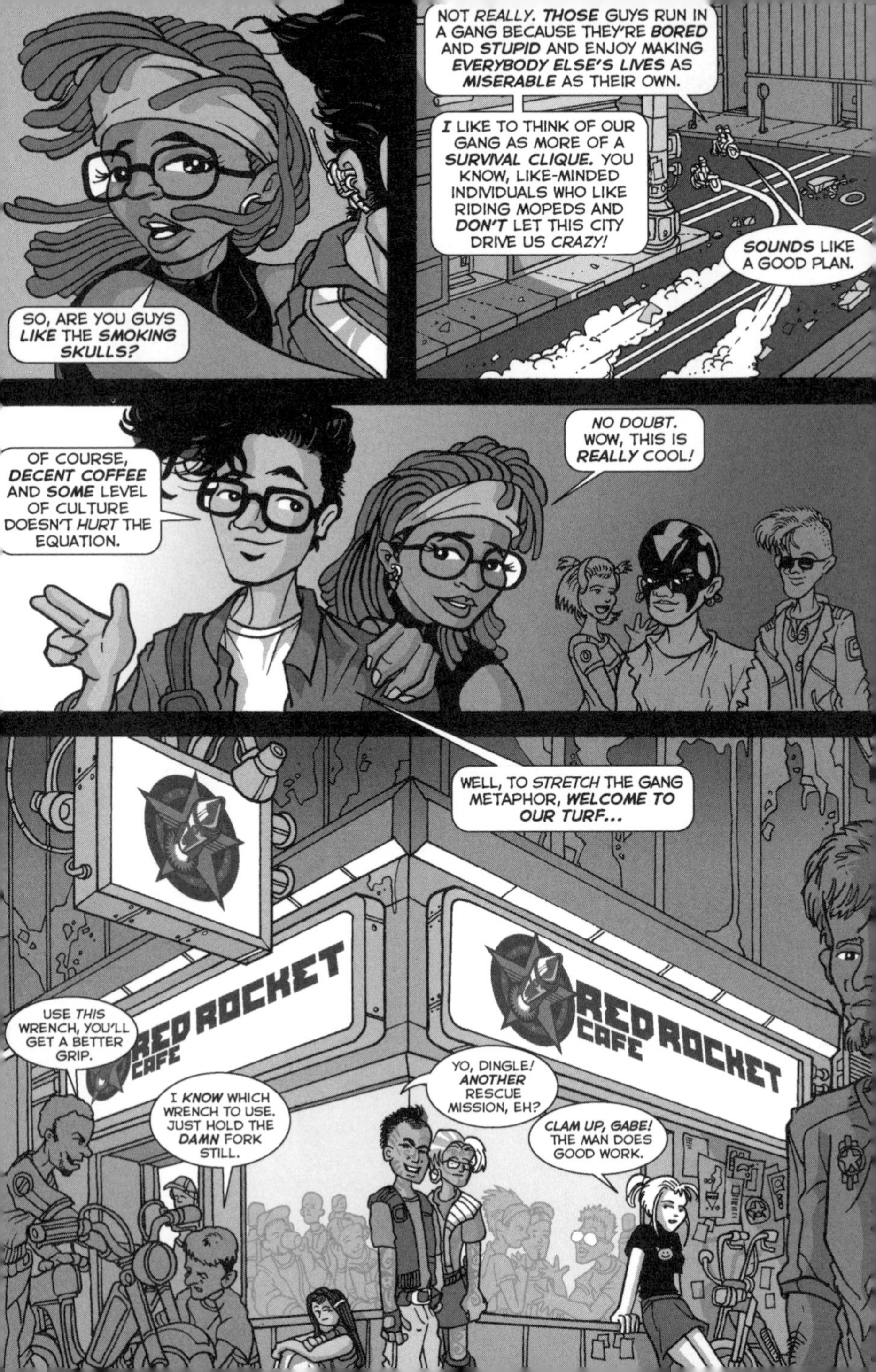

SO, ARE YOU GUYS LIKE THE SMOKING SKULLS?
NOT REALLY. THOSE GUYS RUN IN A GANG BECAUSE THEY'RE BORED AND STUPID AND ENJOY MAKING EVERYBODY ELSE'S LIVES AS MISERABLE AS THEIR OWN.
I LIKE TO THINK OF OUR GANG AS MORE OF A SURVIVAL CLIQUE. YOU KNOW, LIKE-MINDED INDIVIDUALS WHO LIKE RIDING MOPEDS AND DON'T LET THIS CITY DRIVE US CRAZY!
SOUNDS LIKE A GOOD PLAN.
OF COURSE, DECENT COFFEE AND SOME LEVEL OF CULTURE DOESN'T HURT THE EQUATION.
NO DOUBT. WOW, THIS IS REALLY COOL!
WELL, TO STRETCH THE GANG METAPHOR, WELCOME TO OUR TURF...
RED ROCKET CAFE
USE THIS WRENCH, YOU'LL GET A BETTER GRIP.
I KNOW WHICH WRENCH TO USE. JUST HOLD THE DAMN FORK STILL.
YO, DINGLE! ANOTHER RESCUE MISSION, EH?
CLAM UP, GABE! THE MAN DOES GOOD WORK.
RED ROCKET CAFE

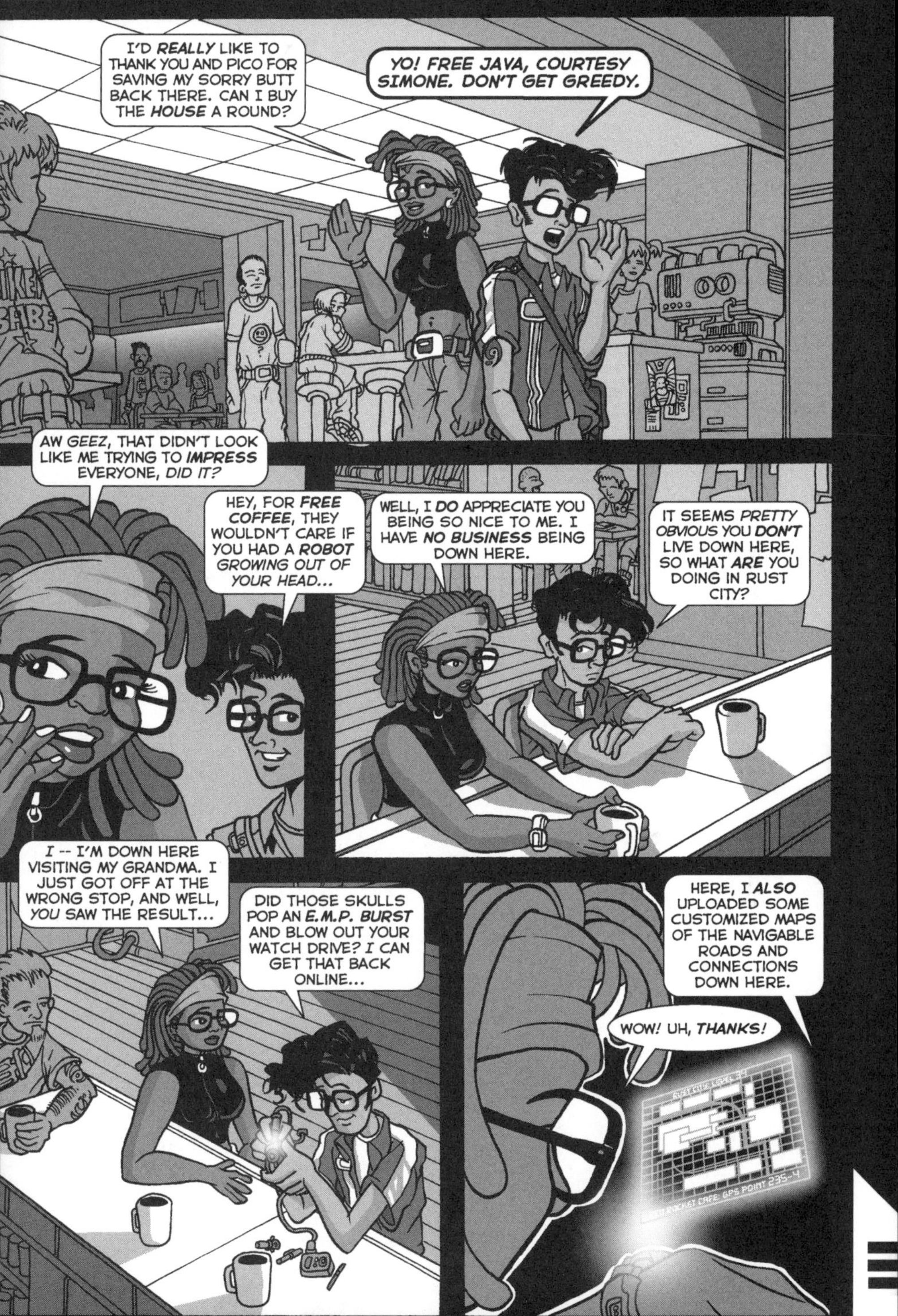
I'D REALLY LIKE TO THANK YOU AND PICO FOR SAVING MY SORRY BUTT BACK THERE. CAN I BUY THE HOUSE A ROUND?
YO! FREE JAVA, COURTESY SIMONE. DON'T GET GREEDY.
AW GEEZ, THAT DIDN'T LOOK LIKE ME TRYING TO IMPRESS EVERYONE, DID IT?
HEY, FOR FREE COFFEE, THEY WOULDN'T CARE IF YOU HAD A ROBOT GROWING OUT OF YOUR HEAD...
WELL, I DO APPRECIATE YOU BEING SO NICE TO ME. I HAVE NO BUSINESS BEING DOWN HERE.
IT SEEMS PRETTY OBVIOUS YOU DON'T LIVE DOWN HERE, SO WHAT ARE YOU DOING IN RUST CITY?
I -- I'M DOWN HERE VISITING MY GRANDMA. I JUST GOT OFF AT THE WRONG STOP, AND WELL, YOU SAW THE RESULT...
DID THOSE SKULLS POP AN E.M.P. BURST AND BLOW OUT YOUR WATCH DRIVE? I CAN GET THAT BACK ONLINE...
HERE, I ALSO UPLOADED SOME CUSTOMIZED MAPS OF THE NAVIGABLE ROADS AND CONNECTIONS DOWN HERE.
WOW! UH, THANKS!

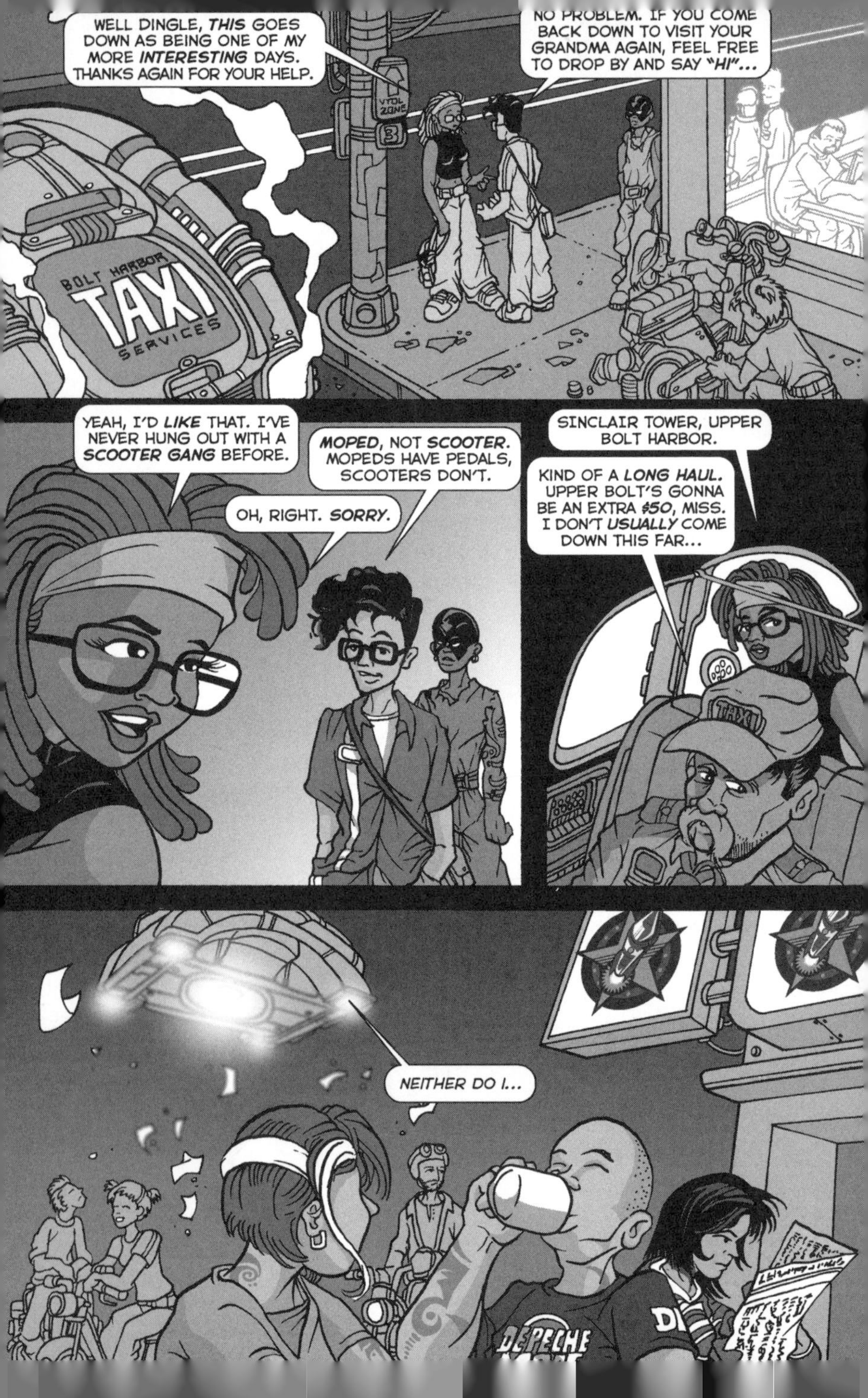
WELL DINGLE, *THIS* GOES DOWN AS BEING ONE OF MY MORE *INTERESTING* DAYS. THANKS AGAIN FOR YOUR HELP.
NO PROBLEM. IF YOU COME BACK DOWN TO VISIT YOUR GRANDMA AGAIN, FEEL FREE TO DROP BY AND SAY *"HI"*...
VTOL ZONE 3
BOLT HARBOR TAXI SERVICES
YEAH, I'D *LIKE* THAT. I'VE NEVER HUNG OUT WITH A *SCOOTER GANG* BEFORE.
MOPED, NOT *SCOOTER*. MOPEDS HAVE PEDALS, SCOOTERS DON'T.
OH, RIGHT. *SORRY*.
SINCLAIR TOWER, UPPER BOLT HARBOR.
KIND OF A *LONG HAUL*. UPPER BOLT'S GONNA BE AN EXTRA *$50*, MISS. I DON'T *USUALLY* COME DOWN THIS FAR...
NEITHER DO I...

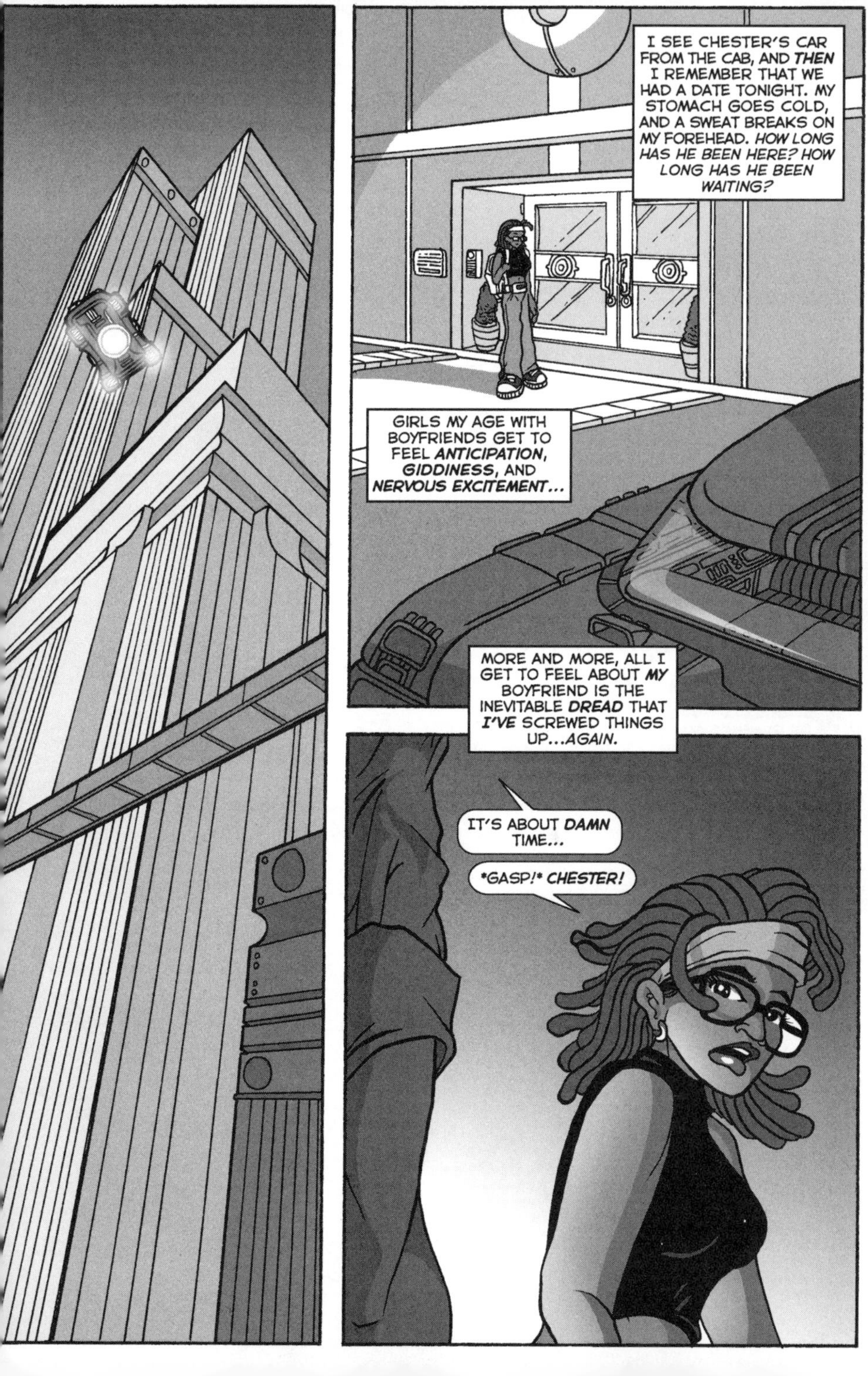
I SEE CHESTER'S CAR FROM THE CAB, AND THEN I REMEMBER THAT WE HAD A DATE TONIGHT. MY STOMACH GOES COLD, AND A SWEAT BREAKS ON MY FOREHEAD. HOW LONG HAS HE BEEN HERE? HOW LONG HAS HE BEEN WAITING?
GIRLS MY AGE WITH BOYFRIENDS GET TO FEEL ANTICIPATION, GIDDINESS, AND NERVOUS EXCITEMENT...
MORE AND MORE, ALL I GET TO FEEL ABOUT MY BOYFRIEND IS THE INEVITABLE DREAD THAT I'VE SCREWED THINGS UP...AGAIN.
IT'S ABOUT DAMN TIME...
GASP! CHESTER!

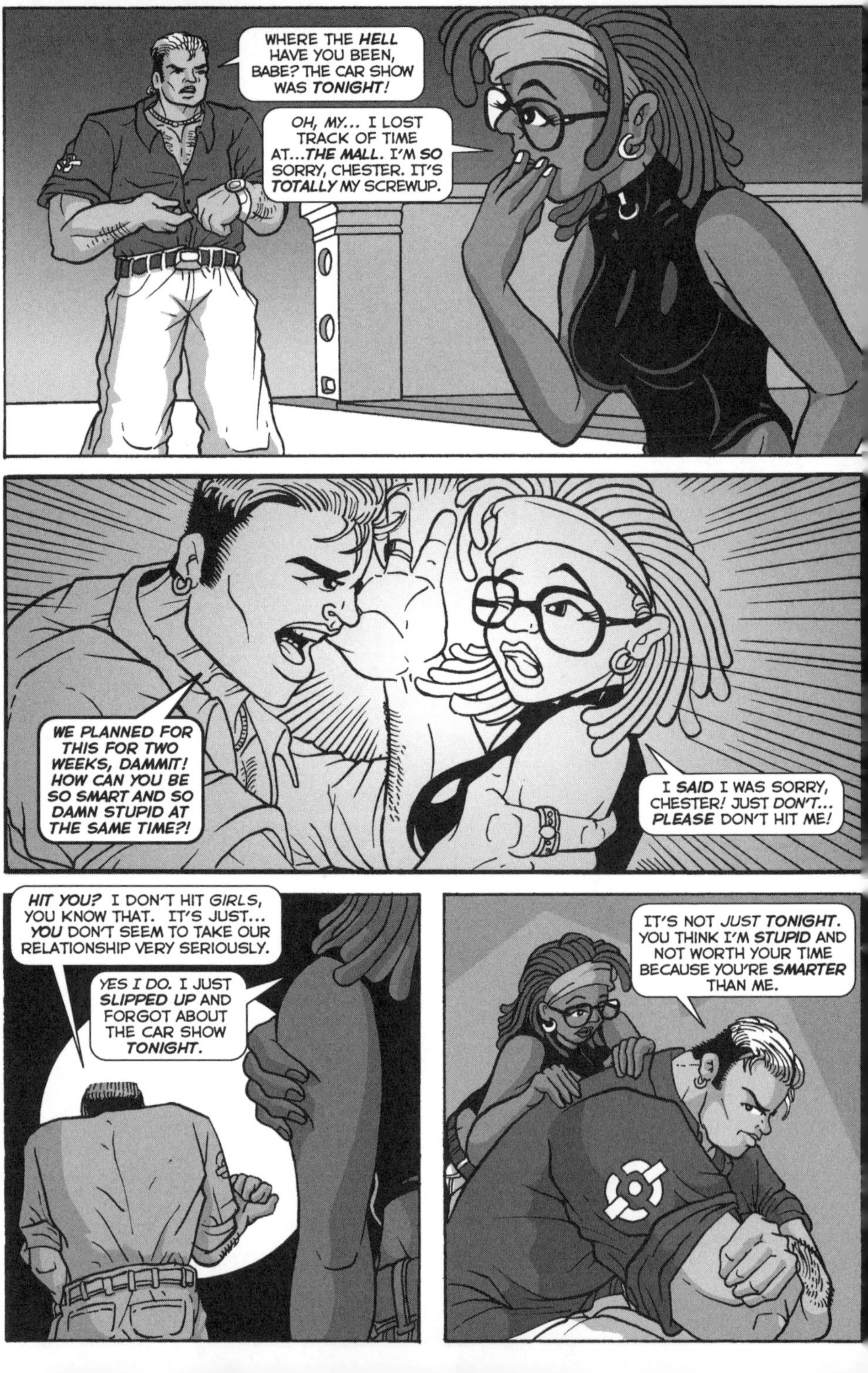
WHERE THE HELL HAVE YOU BEEN, BABE? THE CAR SHOW WAS TONIGHT!
OH, MY... I LOST TRACK OF TIME AT...THE MALL. I'M SO SORRY, CHESTER. IT'S TOTALLY MY SCREWUP.
WE PLANNED FOR THIS FOR TWO WEEKS, DAMMIT! HOW CAN YOU BE SO SMART AND SO DAMN STUPID AT THE SAME TIME?!
I SAID I WAS SORRY, CHESTER! JUST DON'T... PLEASE DON'T HIT ME!
HIT YOU? I DON'T HIT GIRLS, YOU KNOW THAT. IT'S JUST... YOU DON'T SEEM TO TAKE OUR RELATIONSHIP VERY SERIOUSLY.
YES I DO. I JUST SLIPPED UP AND FORGOT ABOUT THE CAR SHOW TONIGHT.
IT'S NOT JUST TONIGHT. YOU THINK I'M STUPID AND NOT WORTH YOUR TIME BECAUSE YOU'RE SMARTER THAN ME.

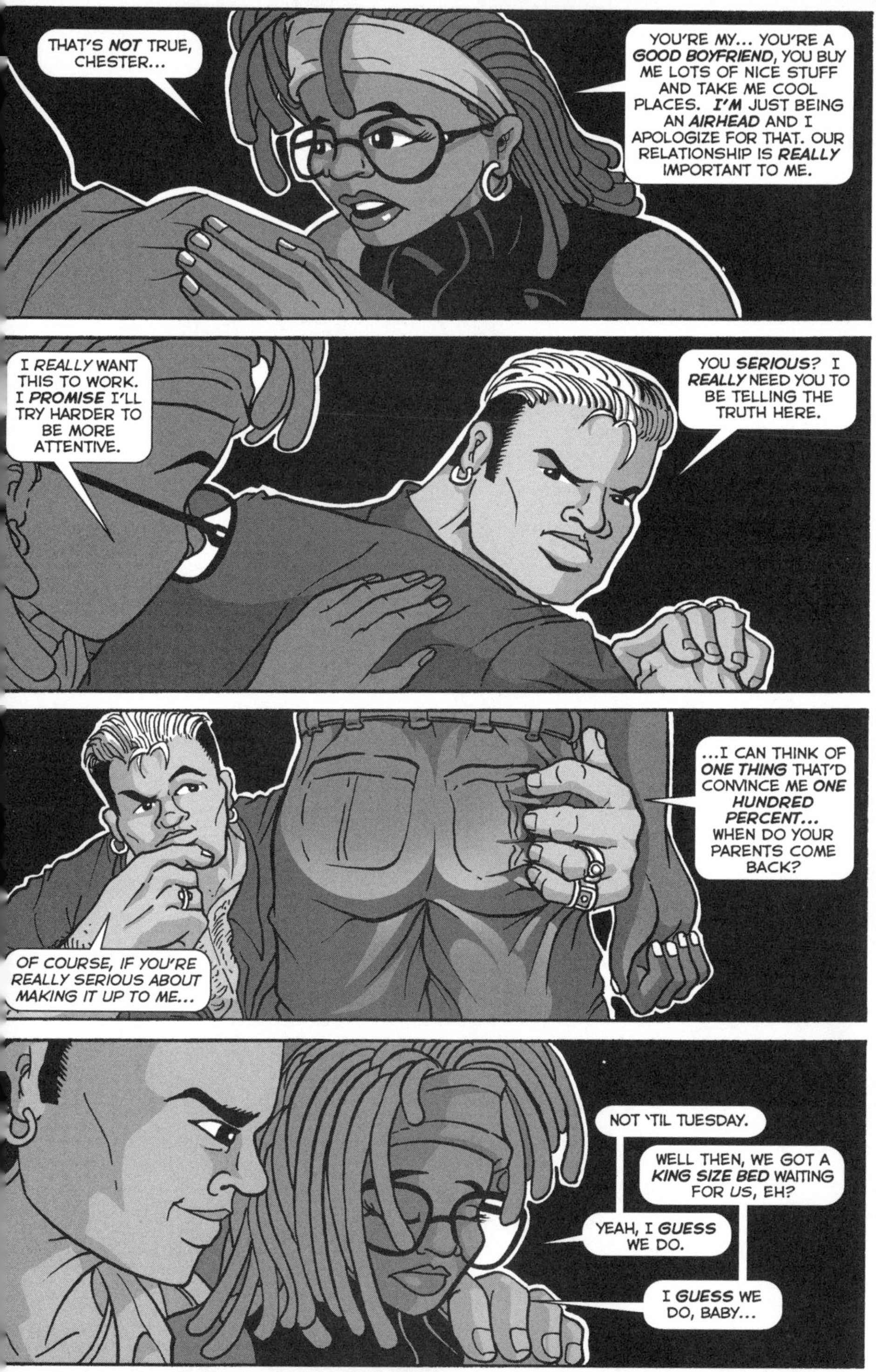
THAT'S *NOT* TRUE, CHESTER...
YOU'RE MY... YOU'RE A *GOOD BOYFRIEND*, YOU BUY ME LOTS OF NICE STUFF AND TAKE ME COOL PLACES. *I'M* JUST BEING AN *AIRHEAD* AND I APOLOGIZE FOR THAT. OUR RELATIONSHIP IS *REALLY* IMPORTANT TO ME.
I *REALLY* WANT THIS TO WORK. I *PROMISE* I'LL TRY HARDER TO BE MORE ATTENTIVE.
YOU *SERIOUS*? I *REALLY* NEED YOU TO BE TELLING THE TRUTH HERE.
...I CAN THINK OF *ONE THING* THAT'D CONVINCE ME *ONE HUNDRED PERCENT...* WHEN DO YOUR PARENTS COME BACK?
OF COURSE, IF YOU'RE REALLY SERIOUS ABOUT MAKING IT UP TO ME...
NOT 'TIL TUESDAY.
WELL THEN, WE GOT A *KING SIZE BED* WAITING FOR *US*, EH?
YEAH, I *GUESS* WE DO.
I *GUESS* WE DO, BABY...

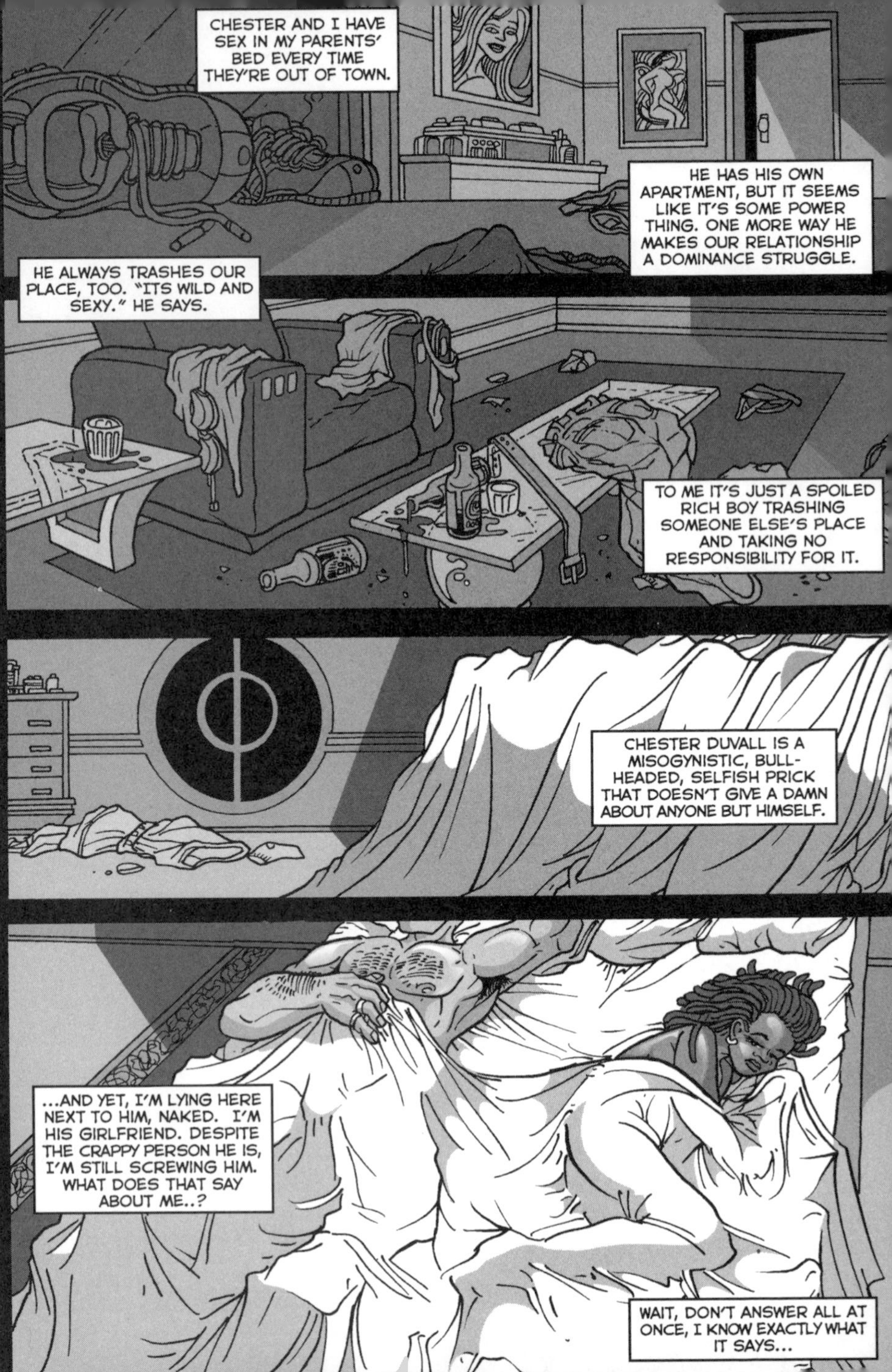
CHESTER AND I HAVE SEX IN MY PARENTS' BED EVERY TIME THEY'RE OUT OF TOWN.
HE HAS HIS OWN APARTMENT, BUT IT SEEMS LIKE IT'S SOME POWER THING. ONE MORE WAY HE MAKES OUR RELATIONSHIP A DOMINANCE STRUGGLE.
HE ALWAYS TRASHES OUR PLACE, TOO. "ITS WILD AND SEXY." HE SAYS.
TO ME IT'S JUST A SPOILED RICH BOY TRASHING SOMEONE ELSE'S PLACE AND TAKING NO RESPONSIBILITY FOR IT.
CHESTER DUVALL IS A MISOGYNISTIC, BULL-HEADED, SELFISH PRICK THAT DOESN'T GIVE A DAMN ABOUT ANYONE BUT HIMSELF.
...AND YET, I'M LYING HERE NEXT TO HIM, NAKED. I'M HIS GIRLFRIEND. DESPITE THE CRAPPY PERSON HE IS, I'M STILL SCREWING HIM. WHAT DOES THAT SAY ABOUT ME..?
WAIT, DON'T ANSWER ALL AT ONCE, I KNOW EXACTLY WHAT IT SAYS...

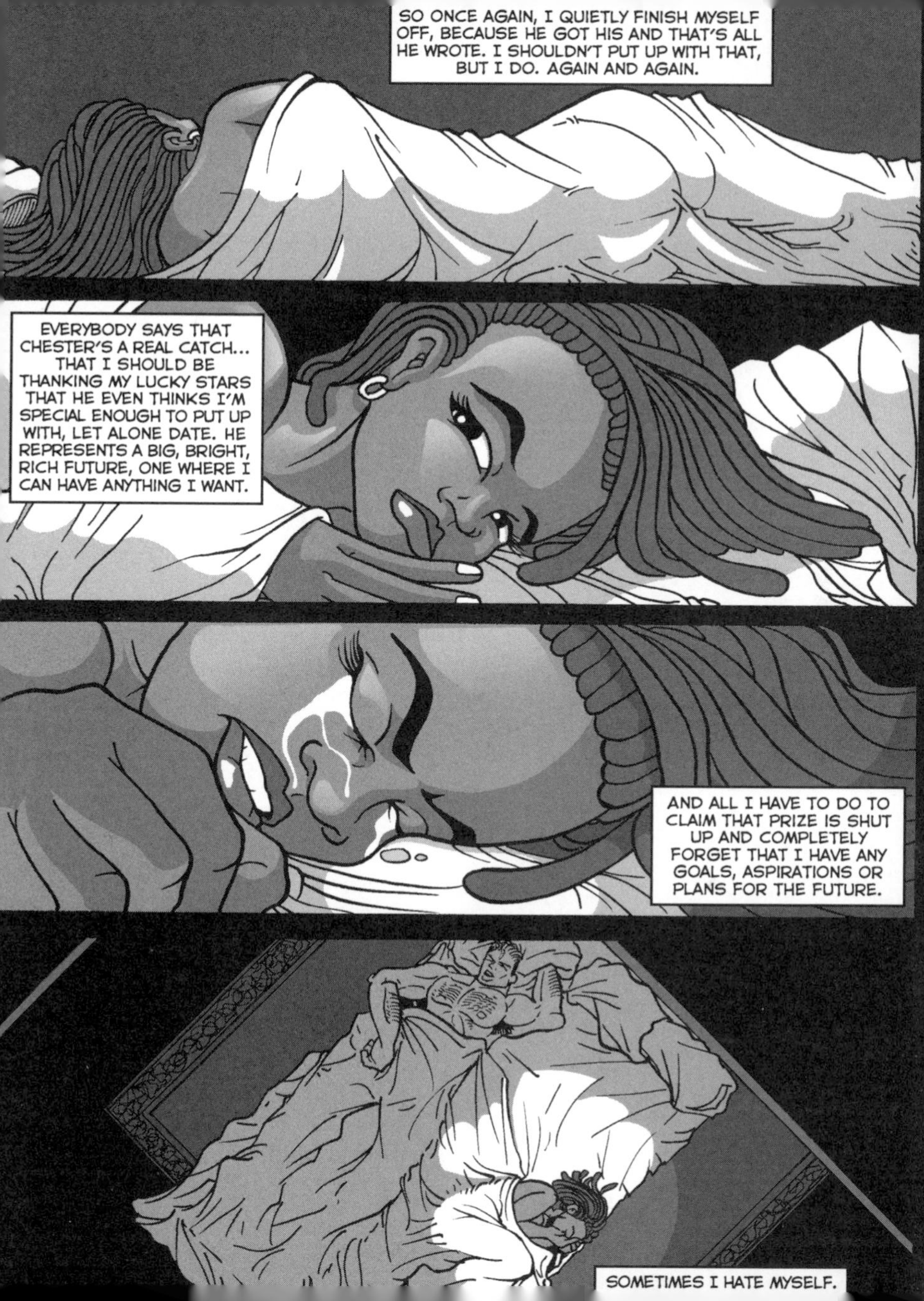
SO ONCE AGAIN, I QUIETLY FINISH MYSELF OFF, BECAUSE HE GOT HIS AND THAT'S ALL HE WROTE. I SHOULDN'T PUT UP WITH THAT, BUT I DO. AGAIN AND AGAIN.
EVERYBODY SAYS THAT CHESTER'S A REAL CATCH... THAT I SHOULD BE THANKING MY LUCKY STARS THAT HE EVEN THINKS I'M SPECIAL ENOUGH TO PUT UP WITH, LET ALONE DATE. HE REPRESENTS A BIG, BRIGHT, RICH FUTURE, ONE WHERE I CAN HAVE ANYTHING I WANT.
AND ALL I HAVE TO DO TO CLAIM THAT PRIZE IS SHUT UP AND COMPLETELY FORGET THAT I HAVE ANY GOALS, ASPIRATIONS OR PLANS FOR THE FUTURE.
SOMETIMES I HATE MYSELF.

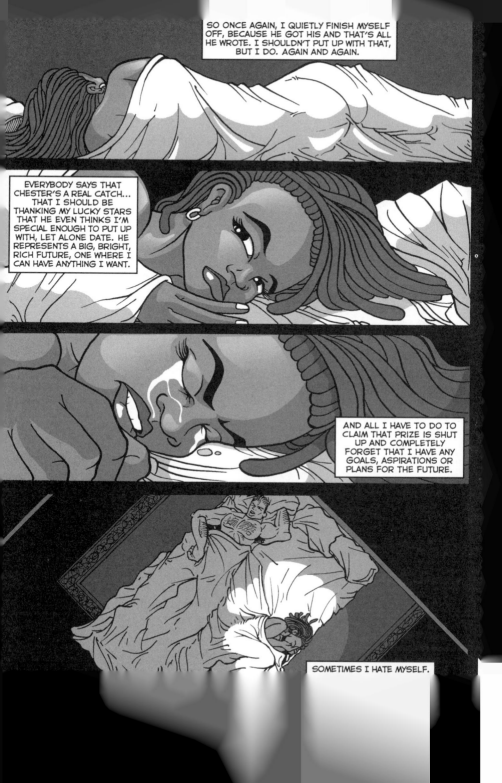

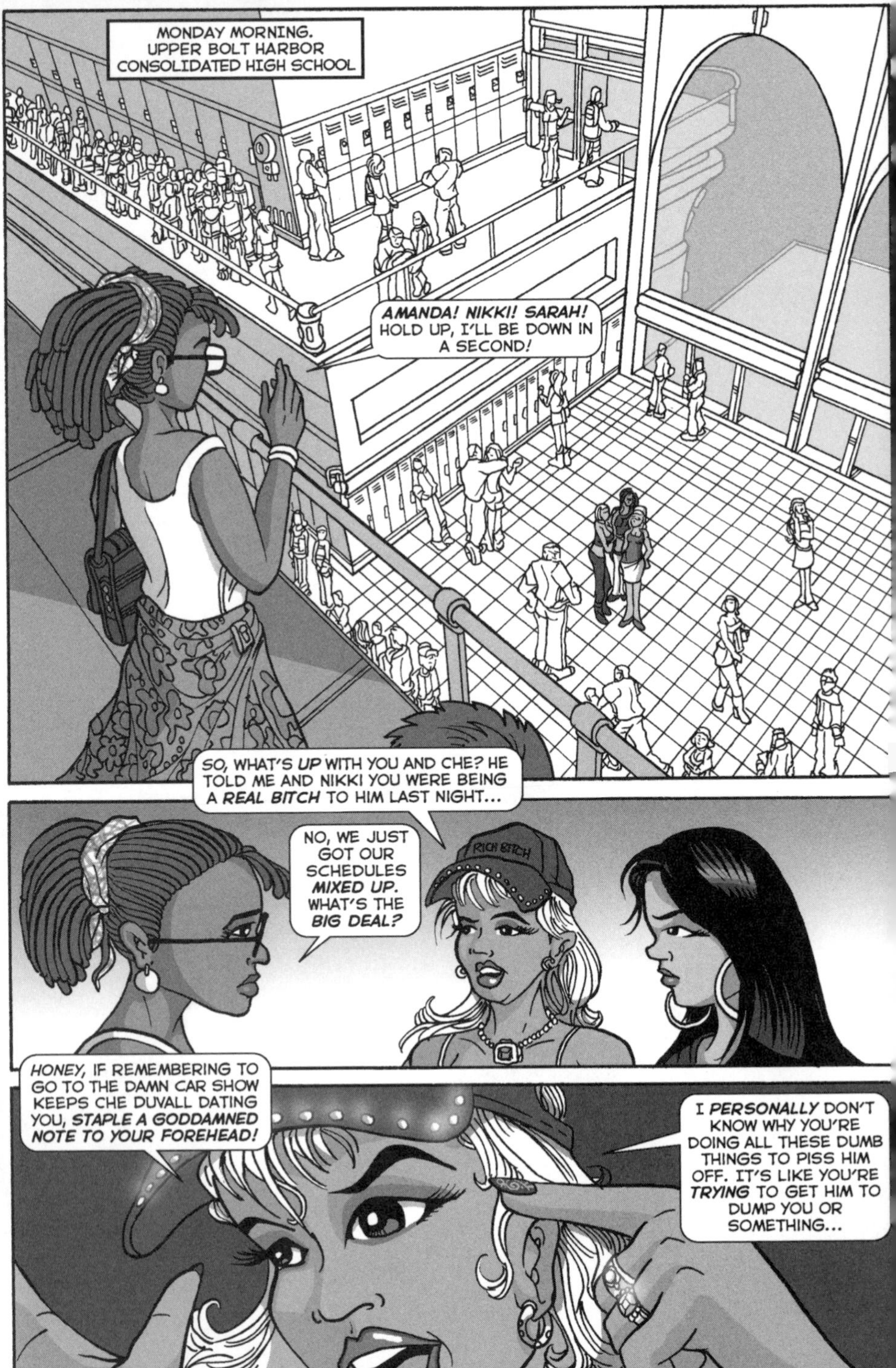
MONDAY MORNING. UPPER BOLT HARBOR CONSOLIDATED HIGH SCHOOL
AMANDA! NIKKI! SARAH! HOLD UP, I'LL BE DOWN IN A SECOND!
SO, WHAT'S UP WITH YOU AND CHE? HE TOLD ME AND NIKKI YOU WERE BEING A REAL BITCH TO HIM LAST NIGHT...
NO, WE JUST GOT OUR SCHEDULES MIXED UP. WHAT'S THE BIG DEAL?
RICH BITCH
HONEY, IF REMEMBERING TO GO TO THE DAMN CAR SHOW KEEPS CHE DUVALL DATING YOU, STAPLE A GODDAMNED NOTE TO YOUR FOREHEAD!
I PERSONALLY DON'T KNOW WHY YOU'RE DOING ALL THESE DUMB THINGS TO PISS HIM OFF. IT'S LIKE YOU'RE TRYING TO GET HIM TO DUMP YOU OR SOMETHING...

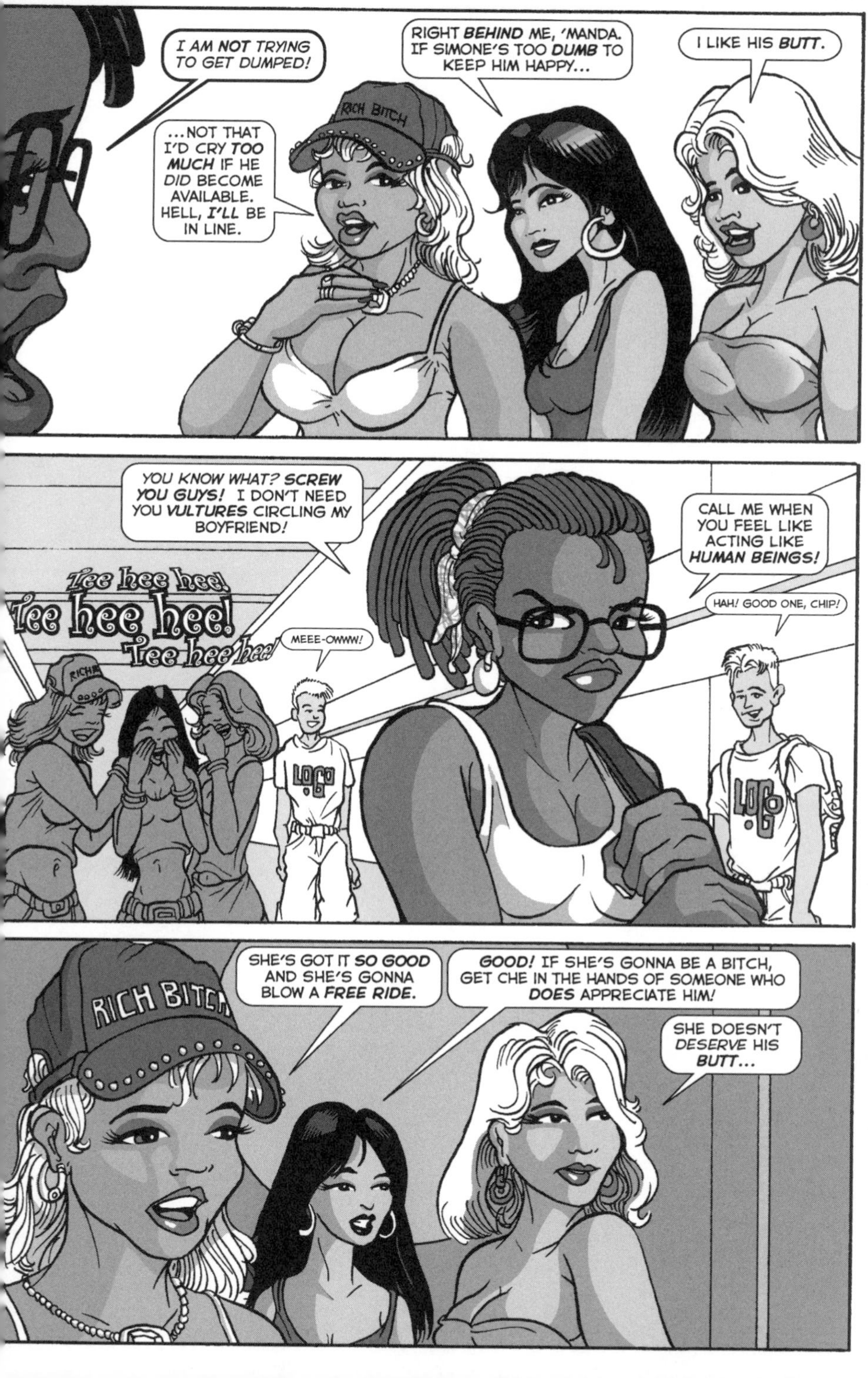
I AM NOT TRYING TO GET DUMPED!
RICH BITCH
...NOT THAT I'D CRY TOO MUCH IF HE DID BECOME AVAILABLE. HELL, I'LL BE IN LINE.
RIGHT BEHIND ME, 'MANDA. IF SIMONE'S TOO DUMB TO KEEP HIM HAPPY...
I LIKE HIS BUTT.
YOU KNOW WHAT? SCREW YOU GUYS! I DON'T NEED YOU VULTURES CIRCLING MY BOYFRIEND!
Tee hee hee!
Tee hee hee!
Tee hee hee!
MEEE-OWWW!
CALL ME WHEN YOU FEEL LIKE ACTING LIKE HUMAN BEINGS!
HAH! GOOD ONE, CHIP!
RICH BITCH
SHE'S GOT IT SO GOOD AND SHE'S GONNA BLOW A FREE RIDE.
GOOD! IF SHE'S GONNA BE A BITCH, GET CHE IN THE HANDS OF SOMEONE WHO DOES APPRECIATE HIM!
SHE DOESN'T DESERVE HIS BUTT...

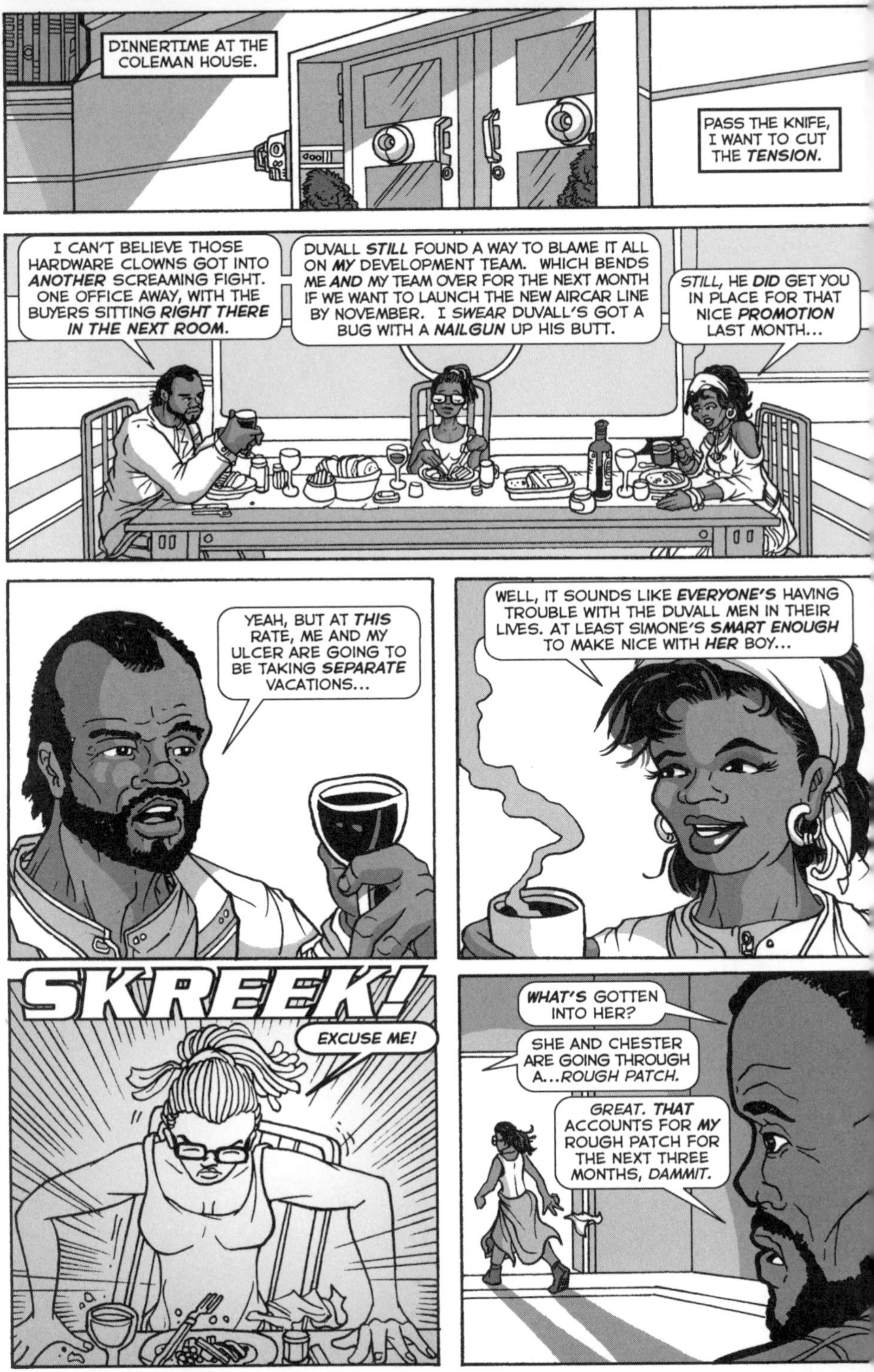
DINNERTIME AT THE COLEMAN HOUSE.
PASS THE KNIFE, I WANT TO CUT THE *TENSION.*
I CAN'T BELIEVE THOSE HARDWARE CLOWNS GOT INTO *ANOTHER* SCREAMING FIGHT. ONE OFFICE AWAY, WITH THE BUYERS SITTING *RIGHT THERE IN THE NEXT ROOM.*
DUVALL *STILL* FOUND A WAY TO BLAME IT ALL ON *MY* DEVELOPMENT TEAM. WHICH BENDS ME *AND* MY TEAM OVER FOR THE NEXT MONTH IF WE WANT TO LAUNCH THE NEW AIRCAR LINE BY NOVEMBER. I *SWEAR* DUVALL'S GOT A BUG WITH A *NAILGUN* UP HIS BUTT.
STILL, HE *DID* GET YOU IN PLACE FOR THAT NICE *PROMOTION* LAST MONTH...
YEAH, BUT AT *THIS* RATE, ME AND MY ULCER ARE GOING TO BE TAKING *SEPARATE* VACATIONS...
WELL, IT SOUNDS LIKE *EVERYONE'S* HAVING TROUBLE WITH THE DUVALL MEN IN THEIR LIVES. AT LEAST SIMONE'S *SMART ENOUGH* TO MAKE NICE WITH *HER* BOY...
SKREEK!
EXCUSE ME!
WHAT'S GOTTEN INTO HER?
SHE AND CHESTER ARE GOING THROUGH A...*ROUGH PATCH.*
GREAT. THAT ACCOUNTS FOR *MY* ROUGH PATCH FOR THE NEXT THREE MONTHS, *DAMMIT.*

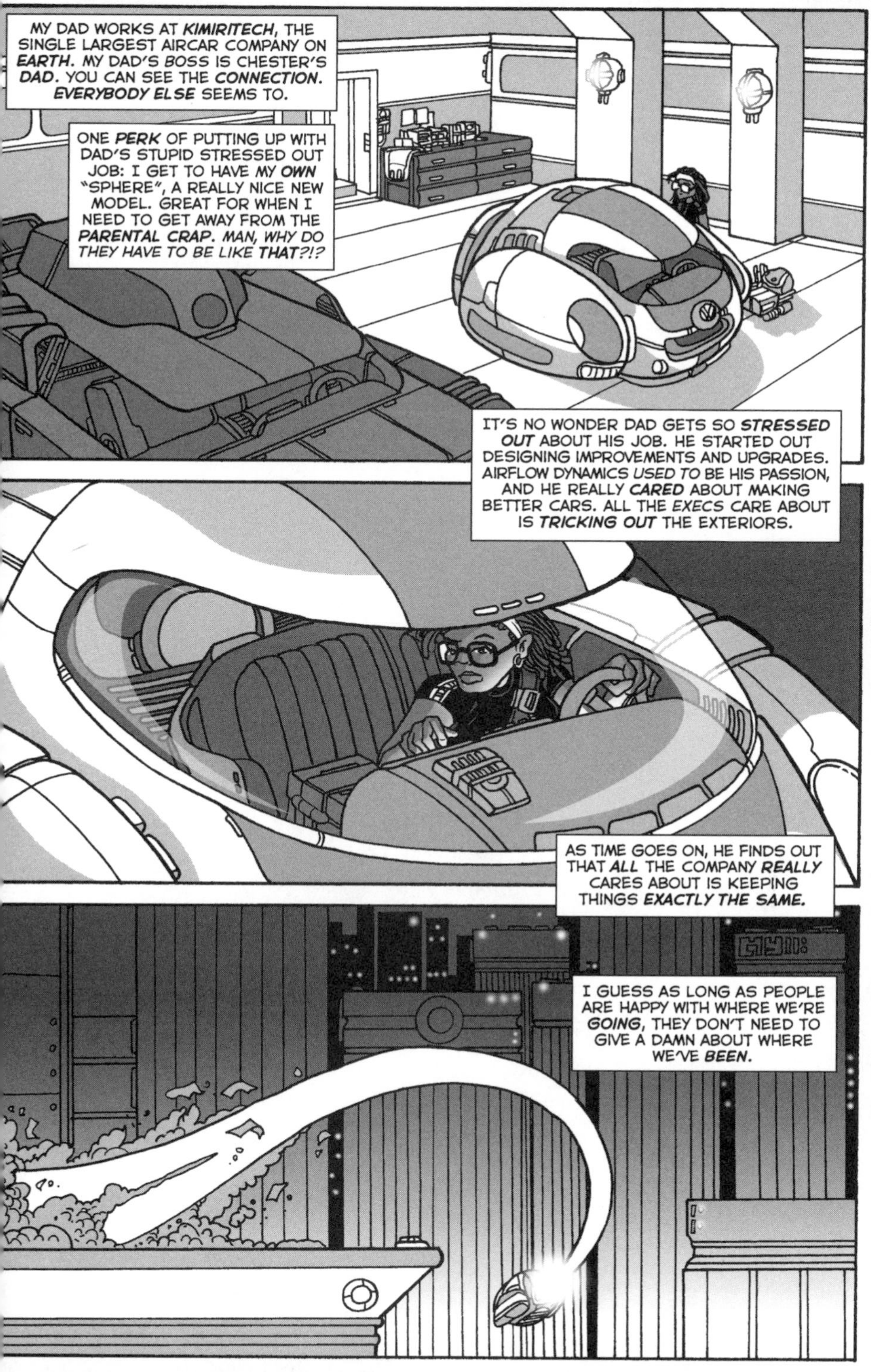
MY DAD WORKS AT KIMIRITECH, THE SINGLE LARGEST AIRCAR COMPANY ON EARTH. MY DAD'S BOSS IS CHESTER'S DAD. YOU CAN SEE THE CONNECTION. EVERYBODY ELSE SEEMS TO.
ONE PERK OF PUTTING UP WITH DAD'S STUPID STRESSED OUT JOB: I GET TO HAVE MY OWN "SPHERE", A REALLY NICE NEW MODEL. GREAT FOR WHEN I NEED TO GET AWAY FROM THE PARENTAL CRAP. MAN, WHY DO THEY HAVE TO BE LIKE THAT?!?
IT'S NO WONDER DAD GETS SO STRESSED OUT ABOUT HIS JOB. HE STARTED OUT DESIGNING IMPROVEMENTS AND UPGRADES. AIRFLOW DYNAMICS USED TO BE HIS PASSION, AND HE REALLY CARED ABOUT MAKING BETTER CARS. ALL THE EXECS CARE ABOUT IS TRICKING OUT THE EXTERIORS.
AS TIME GOES ON, HE FINDS OUT THAT ALL THE COMPANY REALLY CARES ABOUT IS KEEPING THINGS EXACTLY THE SAME.
I GUESS AS LONG AS PEOPLE ARE HAPPY WITH WHERE WE'RE GOING, THEY DON'T NEED TO GIVE A DAMN ABOUT WHERE WE'VE BEEN.

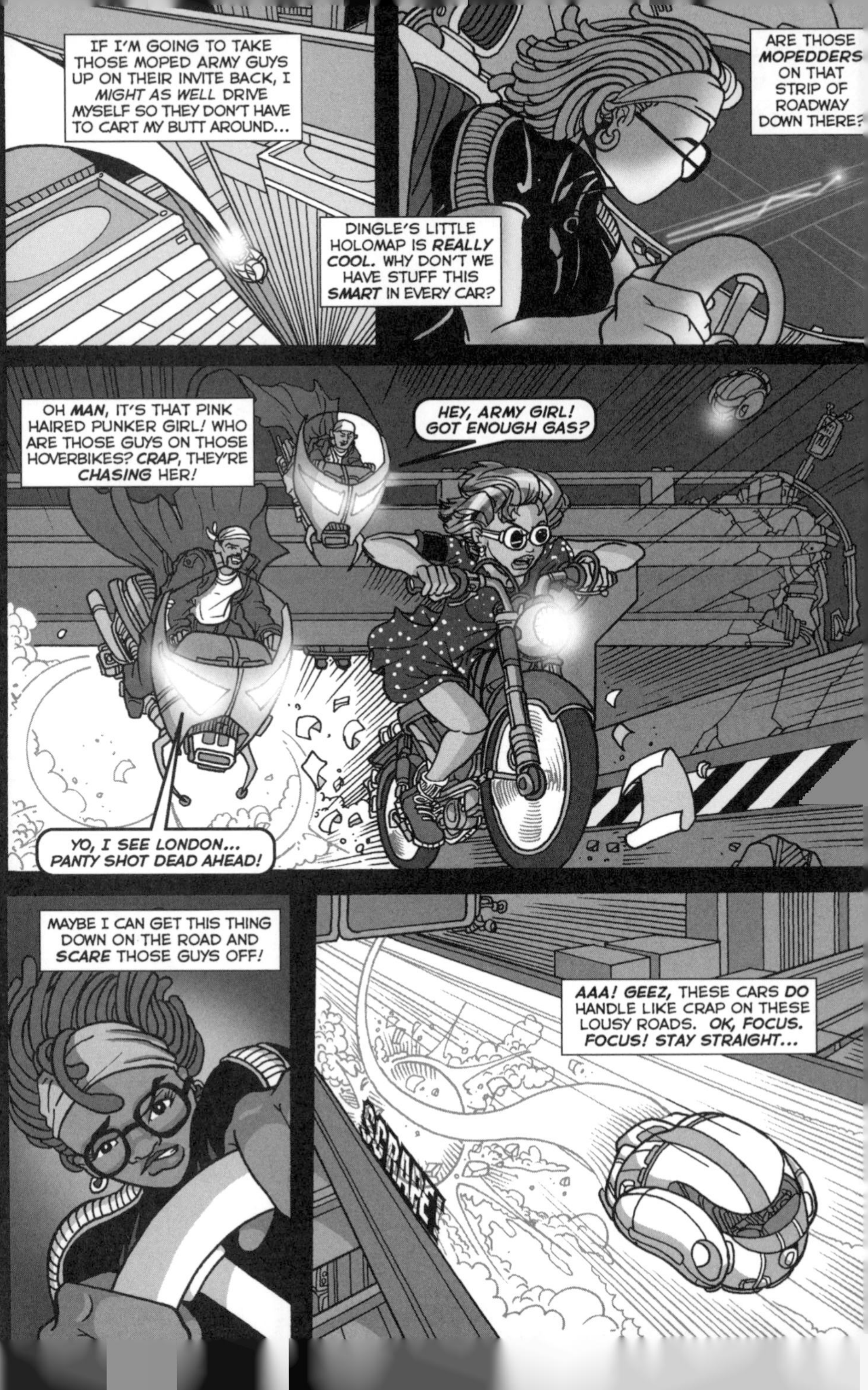
IF I'M GOING TO TAKE THOSE MOPED ARMY GUYS UP ON THEIR INVITE BACK, I *MIGHT AS WELL* DRIVE MYSELF SO THEY DON'T HAVE TO CART MY BUTT AROUND...
ARE THOSE *MOPEDDERS* ON THAT STRIP OF ROADWAY DOWN THERE?
DINGLE'S LITTLE HOLOMAP IS *REALLY COOL.* WHY DON'T WE HAVE STUFF THIS *SMART* IN EVERY CAR?
OH *MAN*, IT'S THAT PINK HAIRED PUNKER GIRL! WHO ARE THOSE GUYS ON THOSE HOVERBIKES? *CRAP*, THEY'RE *CHASING* HER!
HEY, ARMY GIRL! GOT ENOUGH GAS?
YO, I SEE LONDON... PANTY SHOT DEAD AHEAD!
MAYBE I CAN GET THIS THING DOWN ON THE ROAD AND *SCARE* THOSE GUYS OFF!
AAA! GEEZ, THESE CARS *DO* HANDLE LIKE CRAP ON THESE LOUSY ROADS. *OK, FOCUS. FOCUS! STAY STRAIGHT...*
SCRAPE!

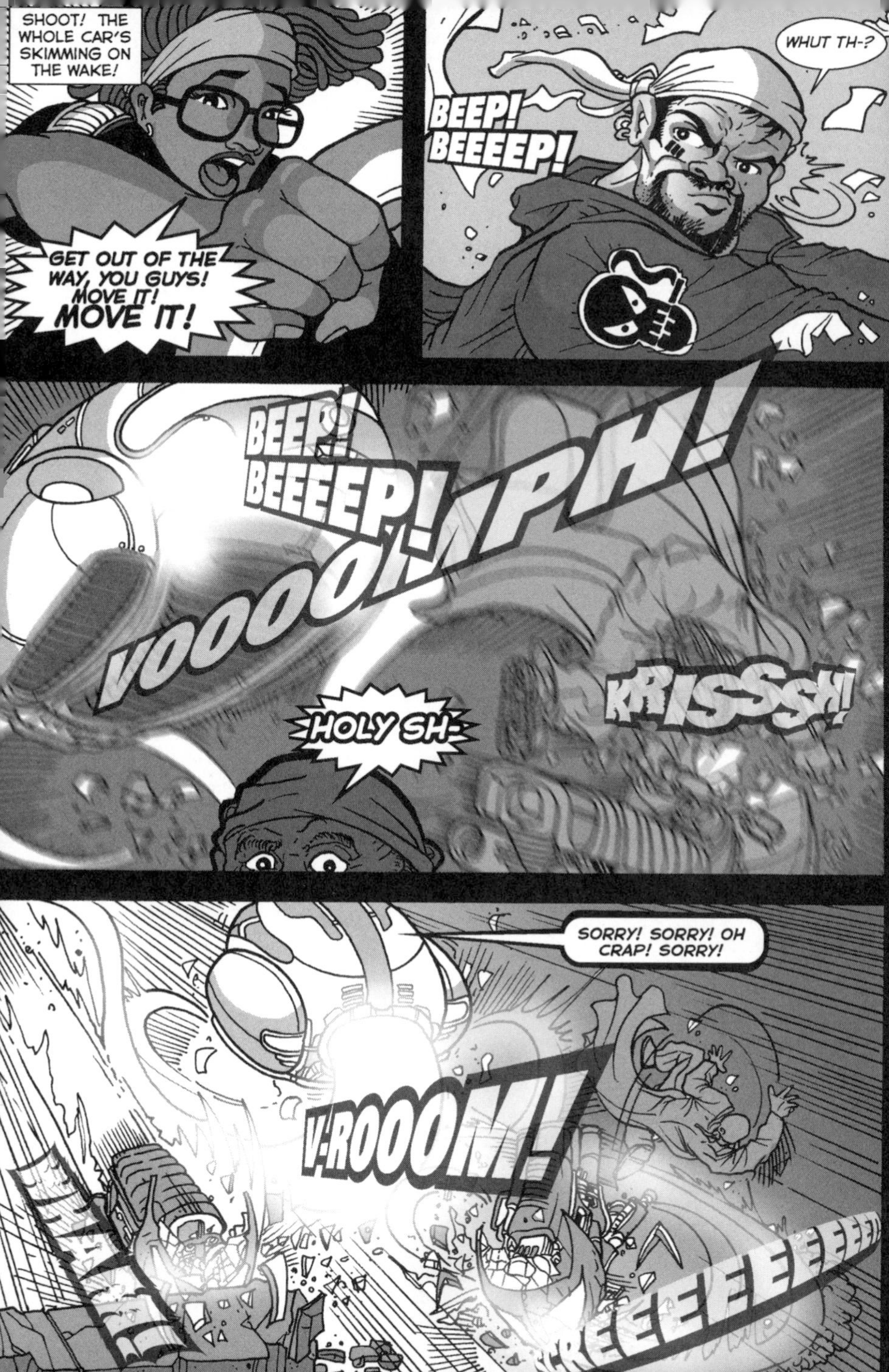
SHOOT! THE WHOLE CAR'S SKIMMING ON THE WAKE!
GET OUT OF THE WAY, YOU GUYS! MOVE IT! MOVE IT!
BEEP! BEEEEP!
WHUT TH-?
BEEP! BEEEEP!
KRISSSH!
HOLY SH-
SORRY! SORRY! OH CRAP! SORRY!
V-ROOOM!

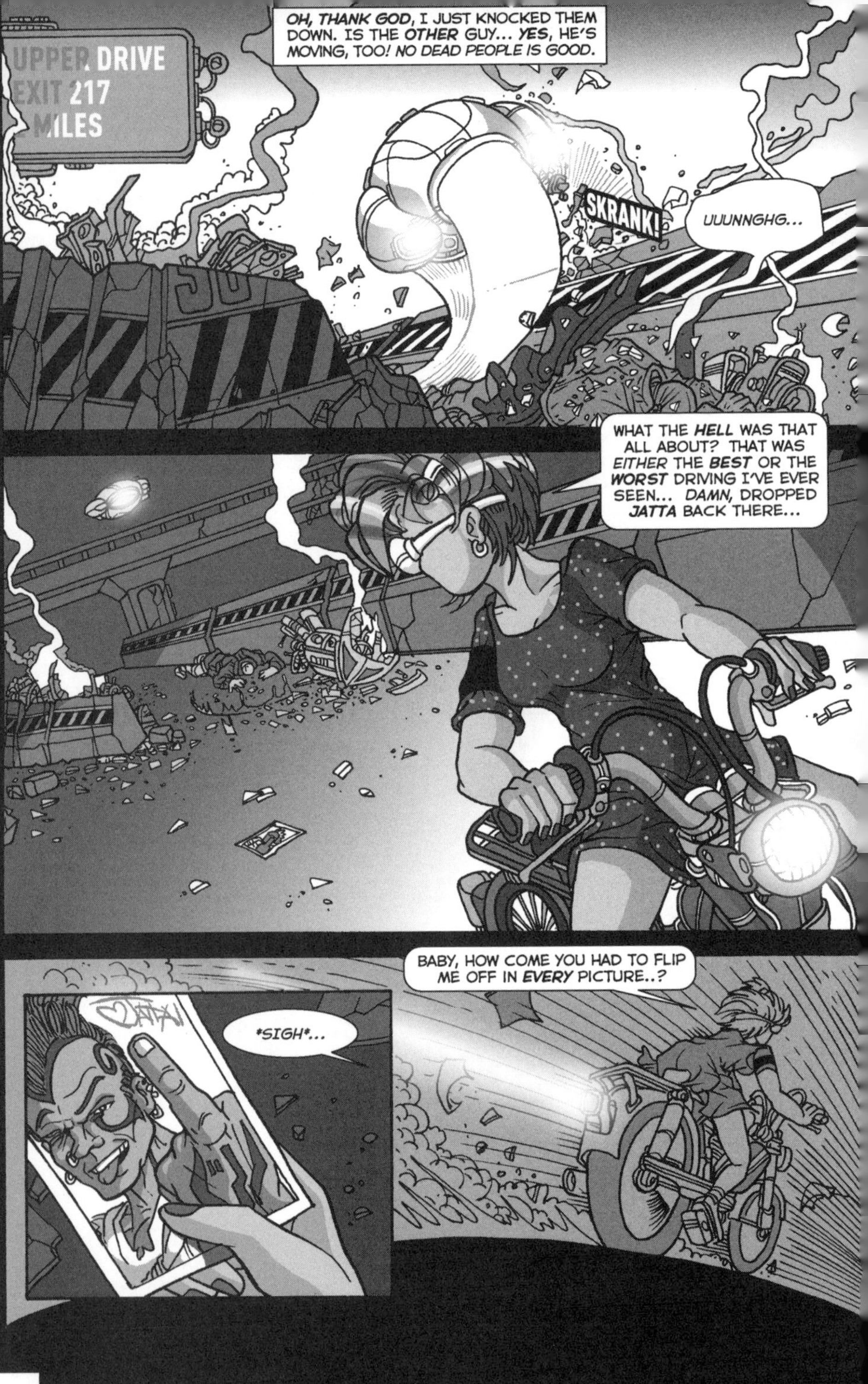
UPPER DRIVE
EXIT 217
MILES
OH, THANK GOD, I JUST KNOCKED THEM DOWN. IS THE OTHER GUY... YES, HE'S MOVING, TOO! NO DEAD PEOPLE IS GOOD.
SKRANK!
UUUNNGHG...
WHAT THE HELL WAS THAT ALL ABOUT? THAT WAS EITHER THE BEST OR THE WORST DRIVING I'VE EVER SEEN... DAMN, DROPPED JATTA BACK THERE...
SIGH...
BABY, HOW COME YOU HAD TO FLIP ME OFF IN EVERY PICTURE..?

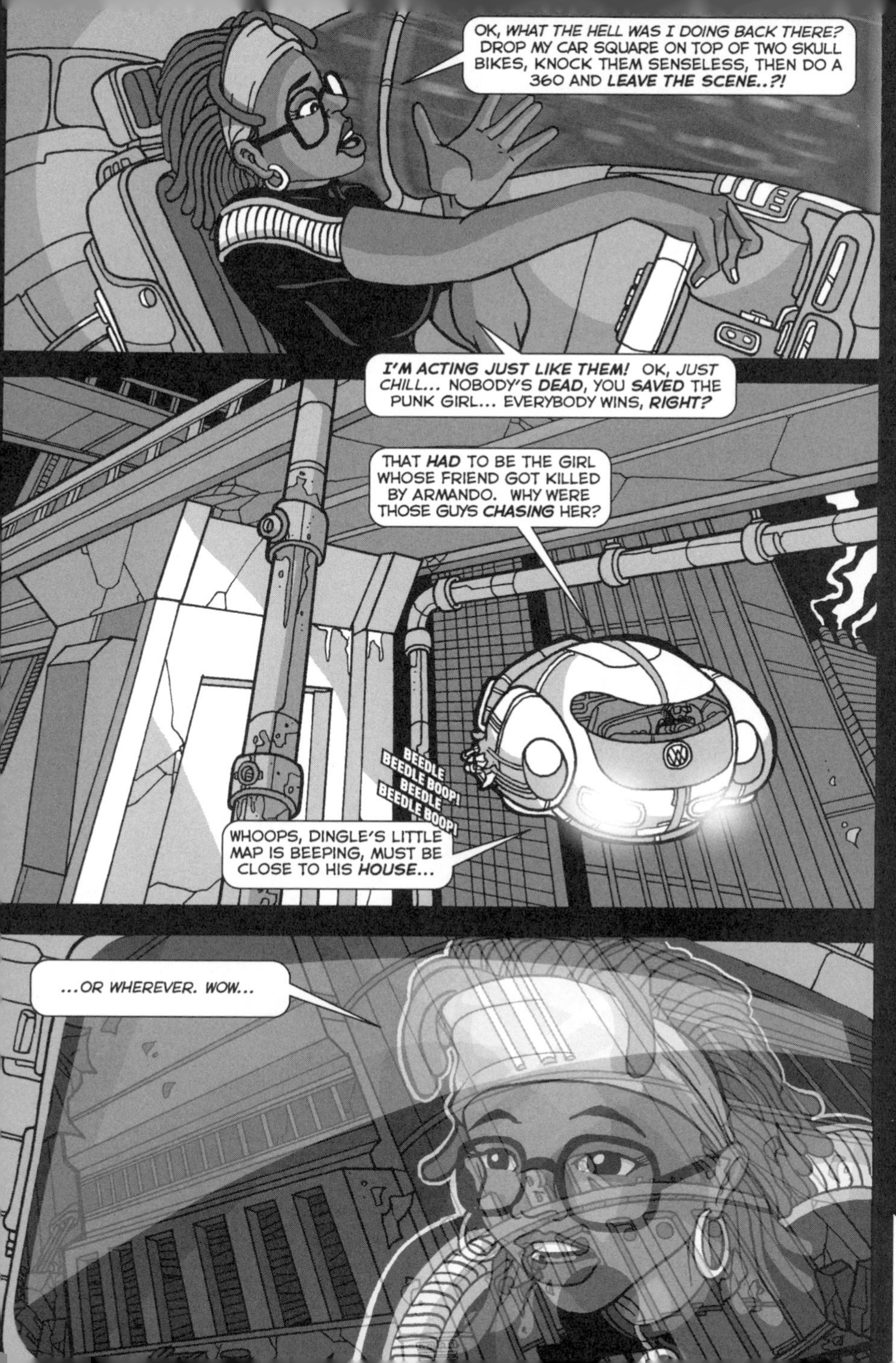
OK, WHAT THE HELL WAS I DOING BACK THERE? DROP MY CAR SQUARE ON TOP OF TWO SKULL BIKES, KNOCK THEM SENSELESS, THEN DO A 360 AND LEAVE THE SCENE..?!
I'M ACTING JUST LIKE THEM! OK, JUST CHILL... NOBODY'S DEAD, YOU SAVED THE PUNK GIRL... EVERYBODY WINS, RIGHT?
THAT HAD TO BE THE GIRL WHOSE FRIEND GOT KILLED BY ARMANDO. WHY WERE THOSE GUYS CHASING HER?
BEEDLE BEEDLE BOOP! BEEDLE BEEDLE BOOP!
WHOOPS, DINGLE'S LITTLE MAP IS BEEPING, MUST BE CLOSE TO HIS HOUSE...
...OR WHEREVER. WOW...

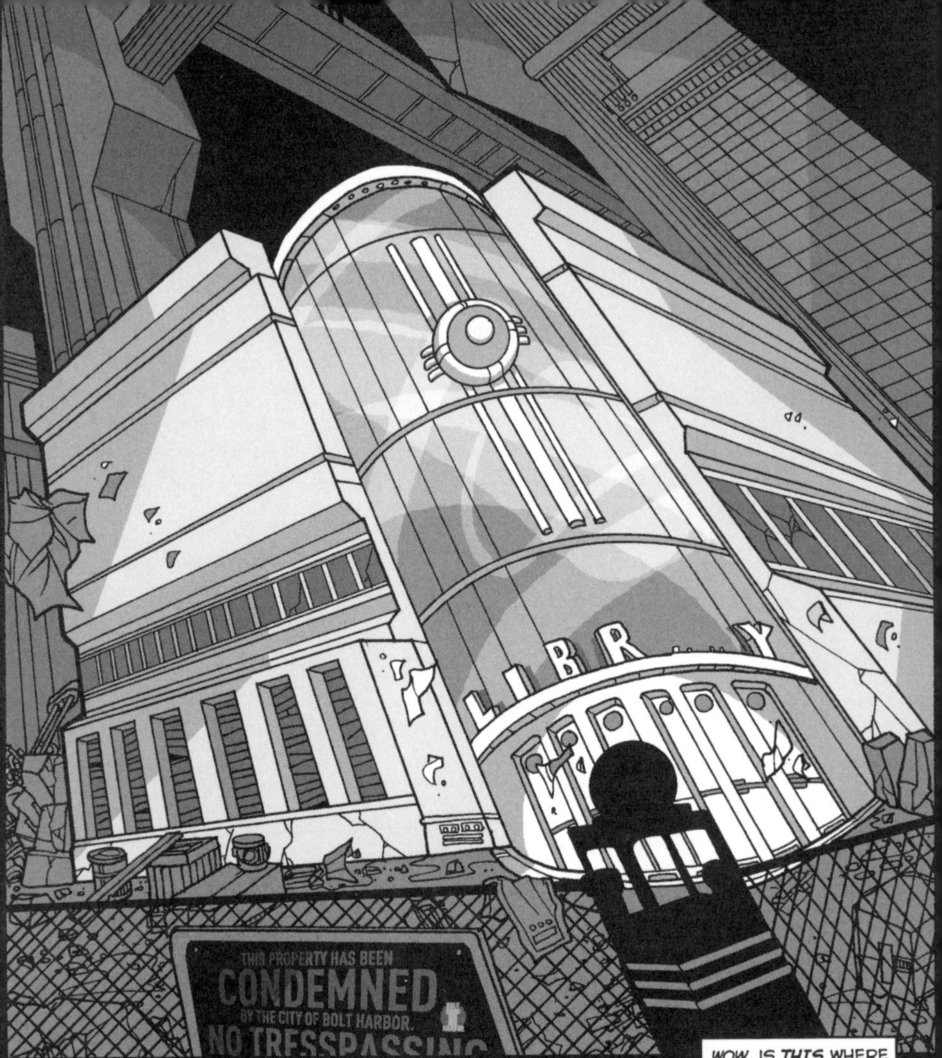
THIS PROPERTY HAS BEEN
CONDEMNED
BY THE CITY OF BOLT HARBOR.
NO TRESSPASSING

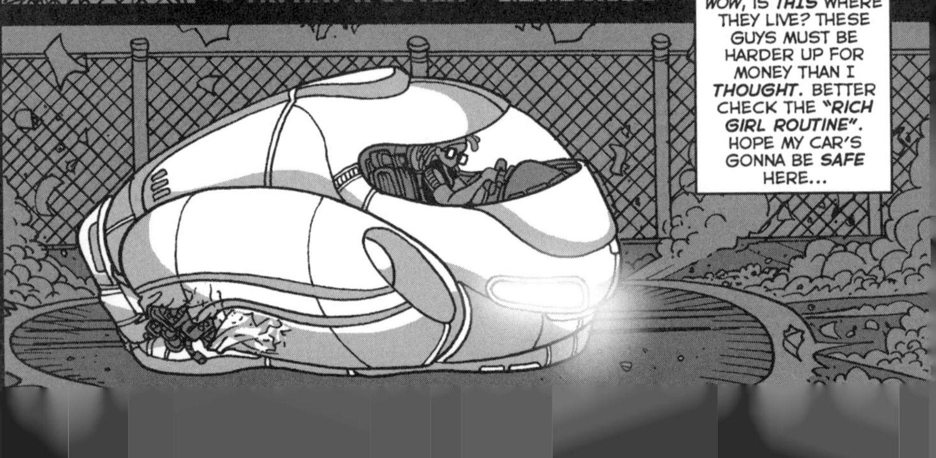
WOW, IS ***THIS*** WHERE THEY LIVE? THESE GUYS MUST BE HARDER UP FOR MONEY THAN I ***THOUGHT***. BETTER CHECK THE ***"RICH GIRL ROUTINE"***. HOPE MY CAR'S GONNA BE ***SAFE*** HERE...

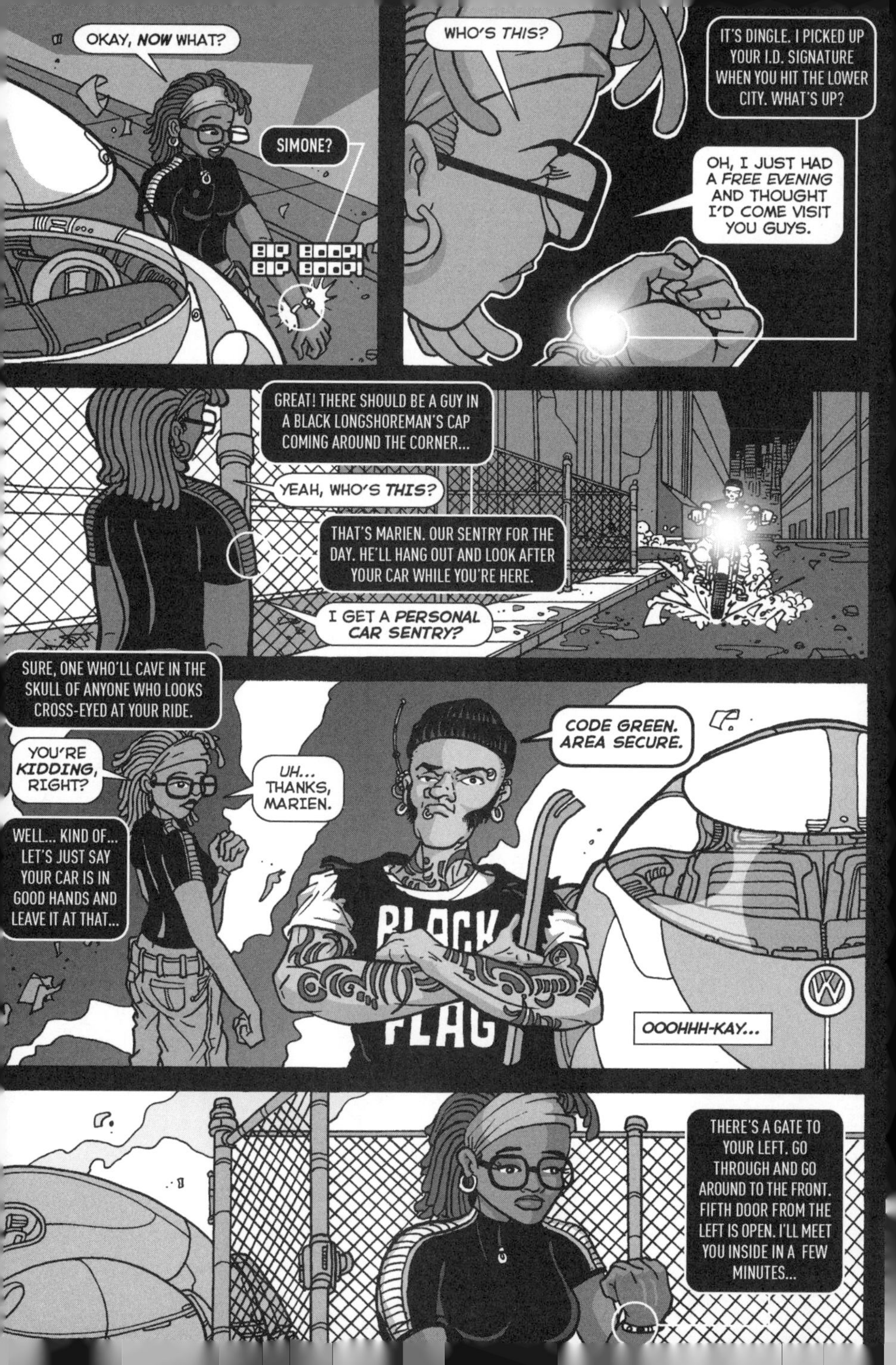
OKAY, NOW WHAT?
SIMONE?
BIP BOOP! BIP BOOP!
WHO'S THIS?
IT'S DINGLE. I PICKED UP YOUR I.D. SIGNATURE WHEN YOU HIT THE LOWER CITY. WHAT'S UP?
OH, I JUST HAD A FREE EVENING AND THOUGHT I'D COME VISIT YOU GUYS.
GREAT! THERE SHOULD BE A GUY IN A BLACK LONGSHOREMAN'S CAP COMING AROUND THE CORNER...
YEAH, WHO'S THIS?
THAT'S MARIEN. OUR SENTRY FOR THE DAY. HE'LL HANG OUT AND LOOK AFTER YOUR CAR WHILE YOU'RE HERE.
I GET A PERSONAL CAR SENTRY?
SURE, ONE WHO'LL CAVE IN THE SKULL OF ANYONE WHO LOOKS CROSS-EYED AT YOUR RIDE.
YOU'RE KIDDING, RIGHT?
WELL... KIND OF... LET'S JUST SAY YOUR CAR IS IN GOOD HANDS AND LEAVE IT AT THAT...
UH... THANKS, MARIEN.
CODE GREEN. AREA SECURE.
BLACK FLAG
OOOHHH-KAY...
THERE'S A GATE TO YOUR LEFT. GO THROUGH AND GO AROUND TO THE FRONT. FIFTH DOOR FROM THE LEFT IS OPEN. I'LL MEET YOU INSIDE IN A FEW MINUTES...

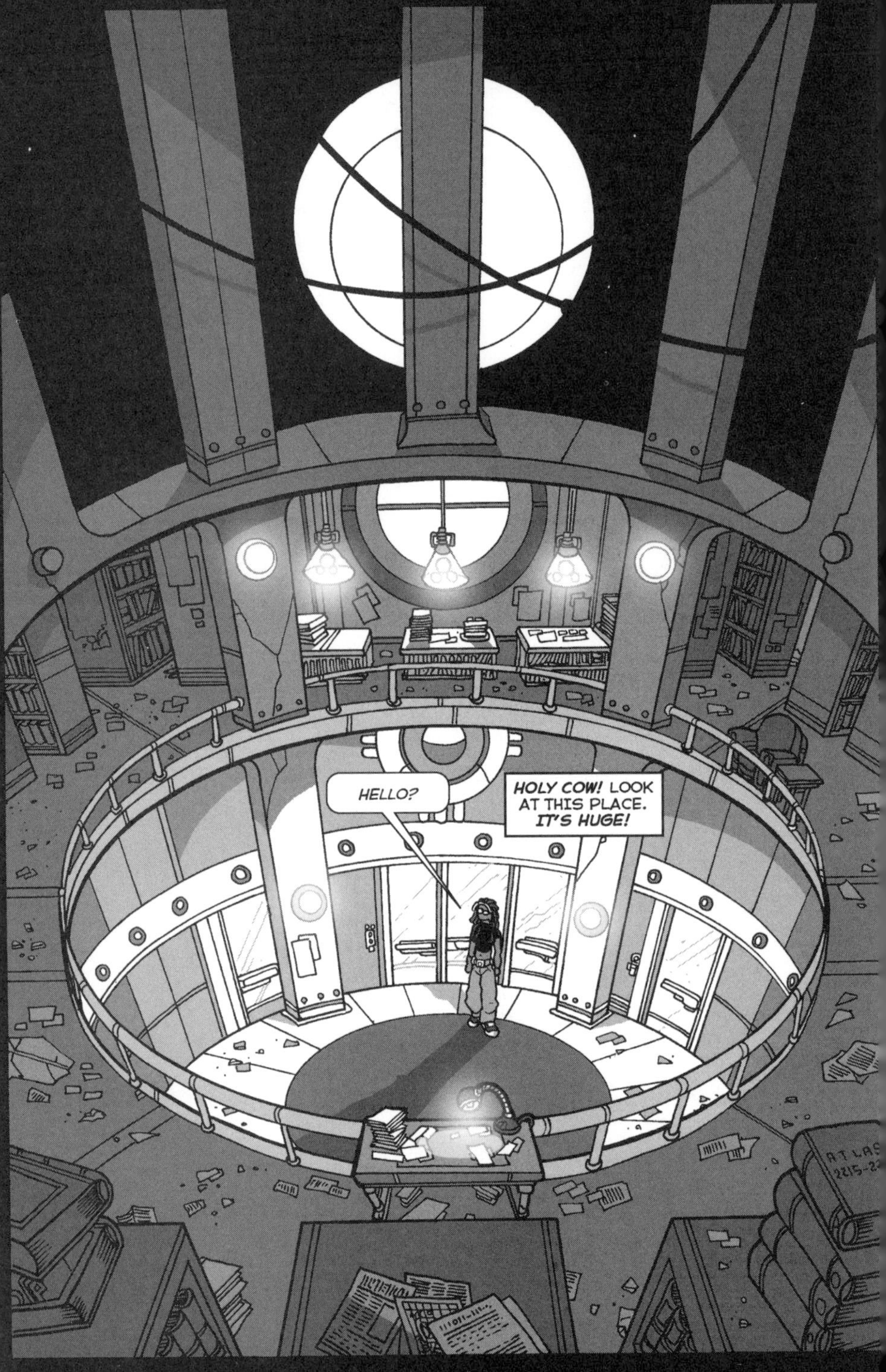
HELLO?
HOLY COW! LOOK AT THIS PLACE. IT'S HUGE!

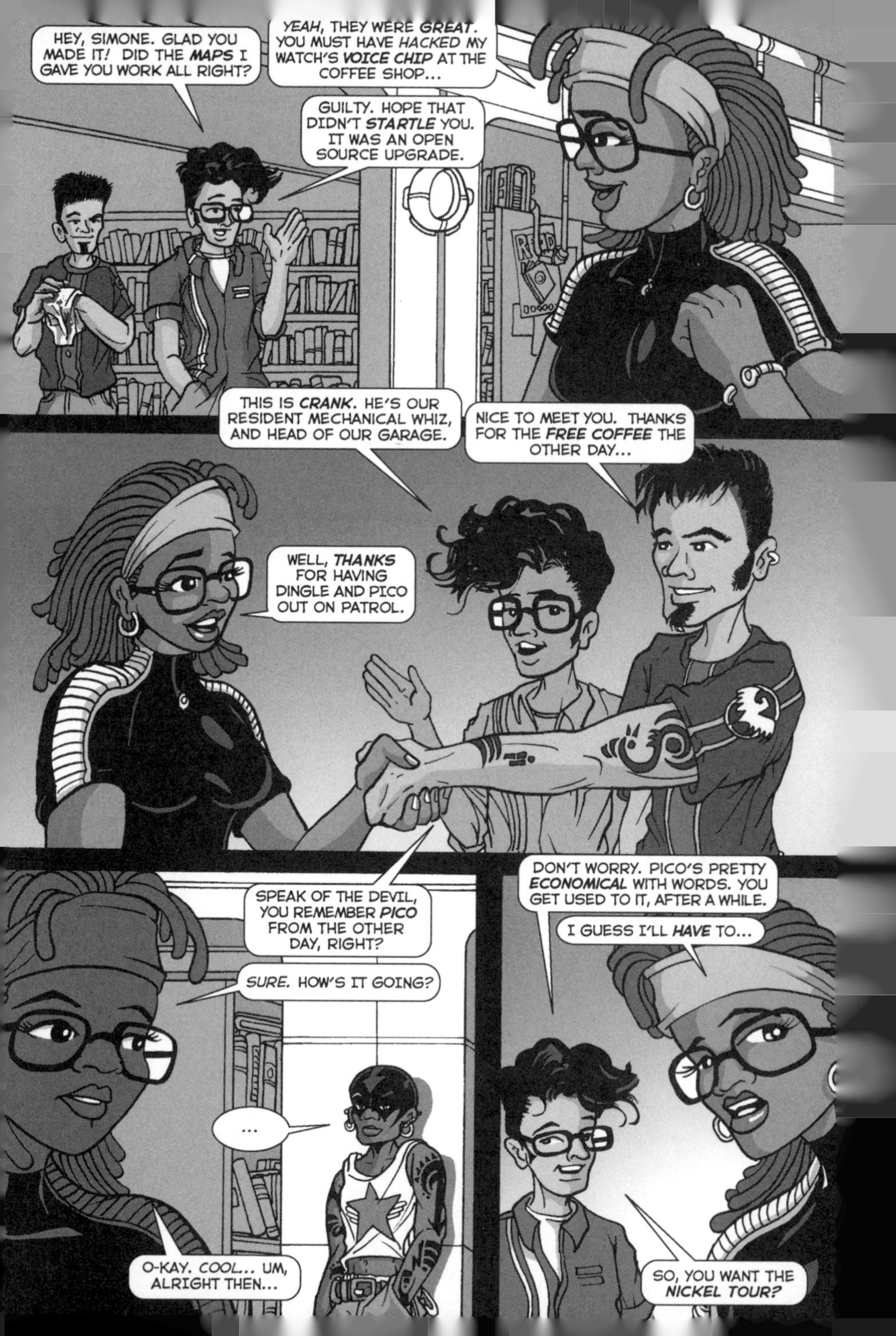
HEY, SIMONE. GLAD YOU MADE IT! DID THE *MAPS* I GAVE YOU WORK ALL RIGHT?
YEAH, THEY WERE *GREAT*. YOU MUST HAVE *HACKED* MY WATCH'S *VOICE CHIP* AT THE COFFEE SHOP...
GUILTY. HOPE THAT DIDN'T *STARTLE* YOU. IT WAS AN OPEN SOURCE UPGRADE.
THIS IS *CRANK*. HE'S OUR RESIDENT MECHANICAL WHIZ, AND HEAD OF OUR GARAGE.
NICE TO MEET YOU. THANKS FOR THE *FREE COFFEE* THE OTHER DAY...
WELL, *THANKS* FOR HAVING DINGLE AND PICO OUT ON PATROL.
SPEAK OF THE DEVIL, YOU REMEMBER *PICO* FROM THE OTHER DAY, RIGHT?
SURE. HOW'S IT GOING?
...
O-KAY. *COOL*... UM, ALRIGHT THEN...
DON'T WORRY. PICO'S PRETTY *ECONOMICAL* WITH WORDS. YOU GET USED TO IT, AFTER A WHILE.
I GUESS I'LL *HAVE* TO...
SO, YOU WANT THE *NICKEL TOUR?*

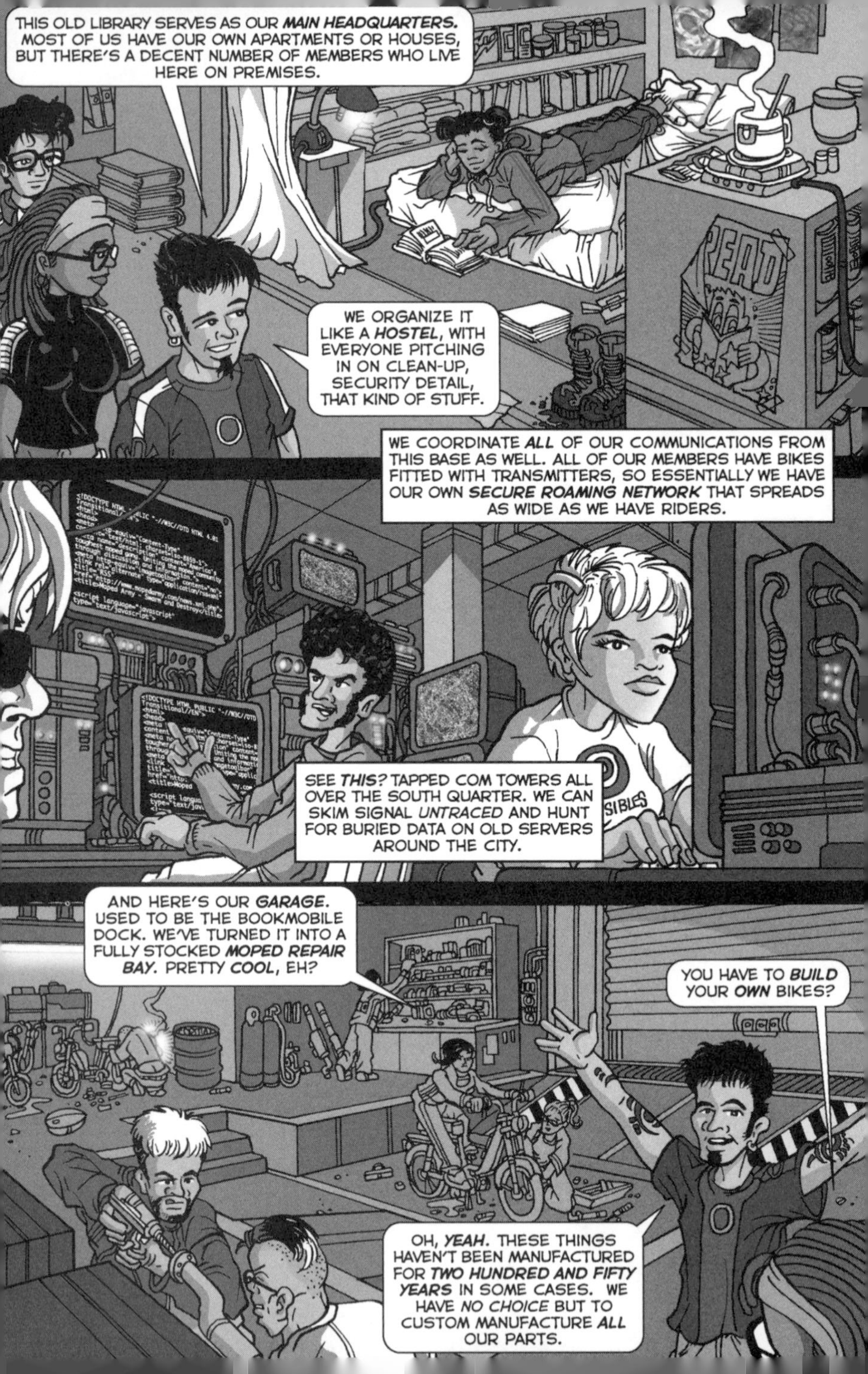

THIS OLD LIBRARY SERVES AS OUR *MAIN HEADQUARTERS.* MOST OF US HAVE OUR OWN APARTMENTS OR HOUSES, BUT THERE'S A DECENT NUMBER OF MEMBERS WHO LIVE HERE ON PREMISES.
WE ORGANIZE IT LIKE A *HOSTEL*, WITH EVERYONE PITCHING IN ON CLEAN-UP, SECURITY DETAIL, THAT KIND OF STUFF.
WE COORDINATE *ALL* OF OUR COMMUNICATIONS FROM THIS BASE AS WELL. ALL OF OUR MEMBERS HAVE BIKES FITTED WITH TRANSMITTERS, SO ESSENTIALLY WE HAVE OUR OWN *SECURE ROAMING NETWORK* THAT SPREADS AS WIDE AS WE HAVE RIDERS.
SEE *THIS?* TAPPED COM TOWERS ALL OVER THE SOUTH QUARTER. WE CAN SKIM SIGNAL *UNTRACED* AND HUNT FOR BURIED DATA ON OLD SERVERS AROUND THE CITY.
AND HERE'S OUR *GARAGE*. USED TO BE THE BOOKMOBILE DOCK. WE'VE TURNED IT INTO A FULLY STOCKED *MOPED REPAIR BAY*. PRETTY *COOL*, EH?
YOU HAVE TO *BUILD* YOUR *OWN* BIKES?
OH, *YEAH*. THESE THINGS HAVEN'T BEEN MANUFACTURED FOR *TWO HUNDRED AND FIFTY YEARS* IN SOME CASES. WE HAVE *NO CHOICE* BUT TO CUSTOM MANUFACTURE *ALL* OUR PARTS.

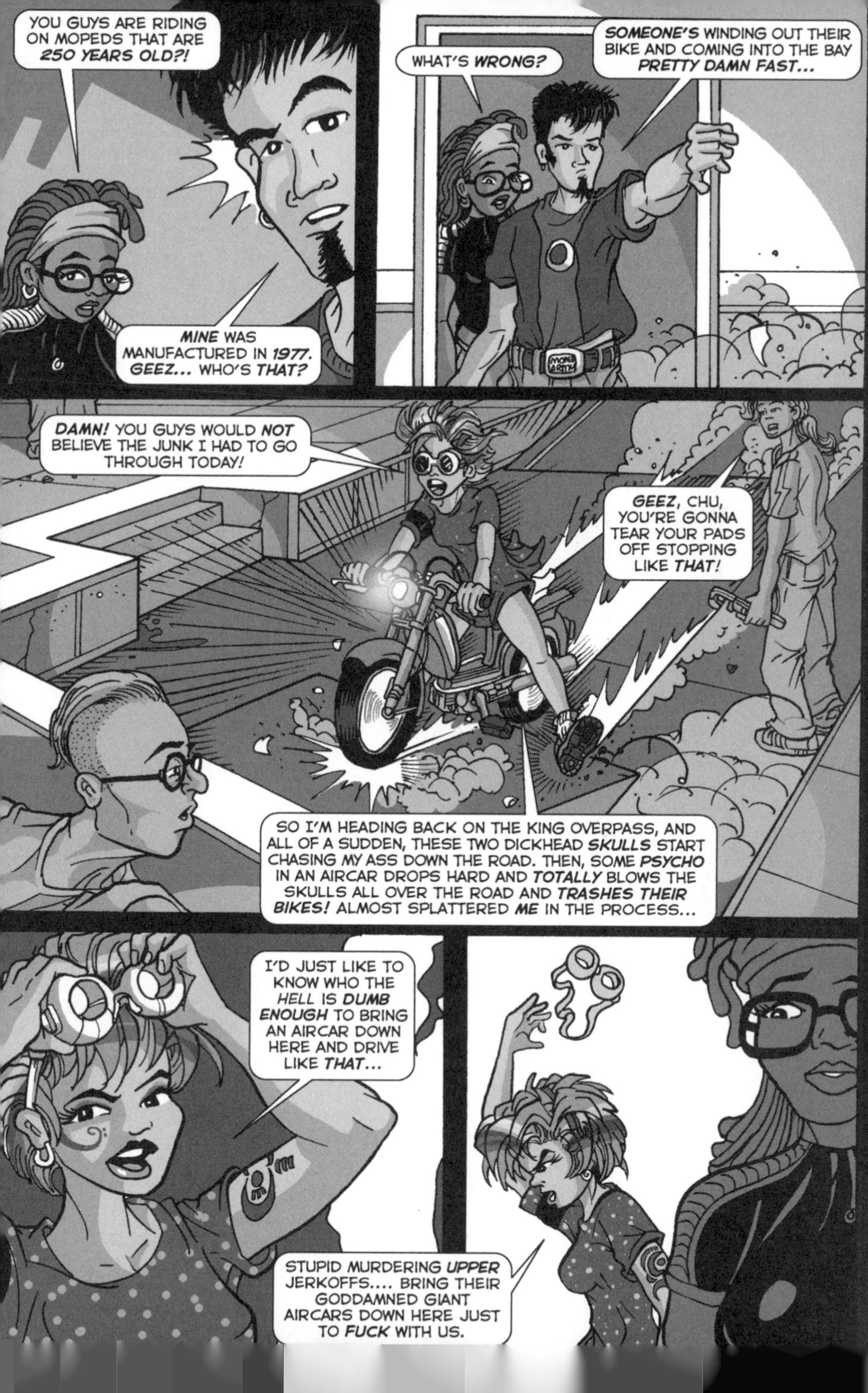
YOU GUYS ARE RIDING ON MOPEDS THAT ARE 250 YEARS OLD?!
MINE WAS MANUFACTURED IN 1977. GEEZ... WHO'S THAT?
WHAT'S WRONG?
SOMEONE'S WINDING OUT THEIR BIKE AND COMING INTO THE BAY PRETTY DAMN FAST...
DAMN! YOU GUYS WOULD NOT BELIEVE THE JUNK I HAD TO GO THROUGH TODAY!
GEEZ, CHU, YOU'RE GONNA TEAR YOUR PADS OFF STOPPING LIKE THAT!
SO I'M HEADING BACK ON THE KING OVERPASS, AND ALL OF A SUDDEN, THESE TWO DICKHEAD SKULLS START CHASING MY ASS DOWN THE ROAD. THEN, SOME PSYCHO IN AN AIRCAR DROPS HARD AND TOTALLY BLOWS THE SKULLS ALL OVER THE ROAD AND TRASHES THEIR BIKES! ALMOST SPLATTERED ME IN THE PROCESS...
I'D JUST LIKE TO KNOW WHO THE HELL IS DUMB ENOUGH TO BRING AN AIRCAR DOWN HERE AND DRIVE LIKE THAT...
STUPID MURDERING UPPER JERKOFFS.... BRING THEIR GODDAMNED GIANT AIRCARS DOWN HERE JUST TO FUCK WITH US.

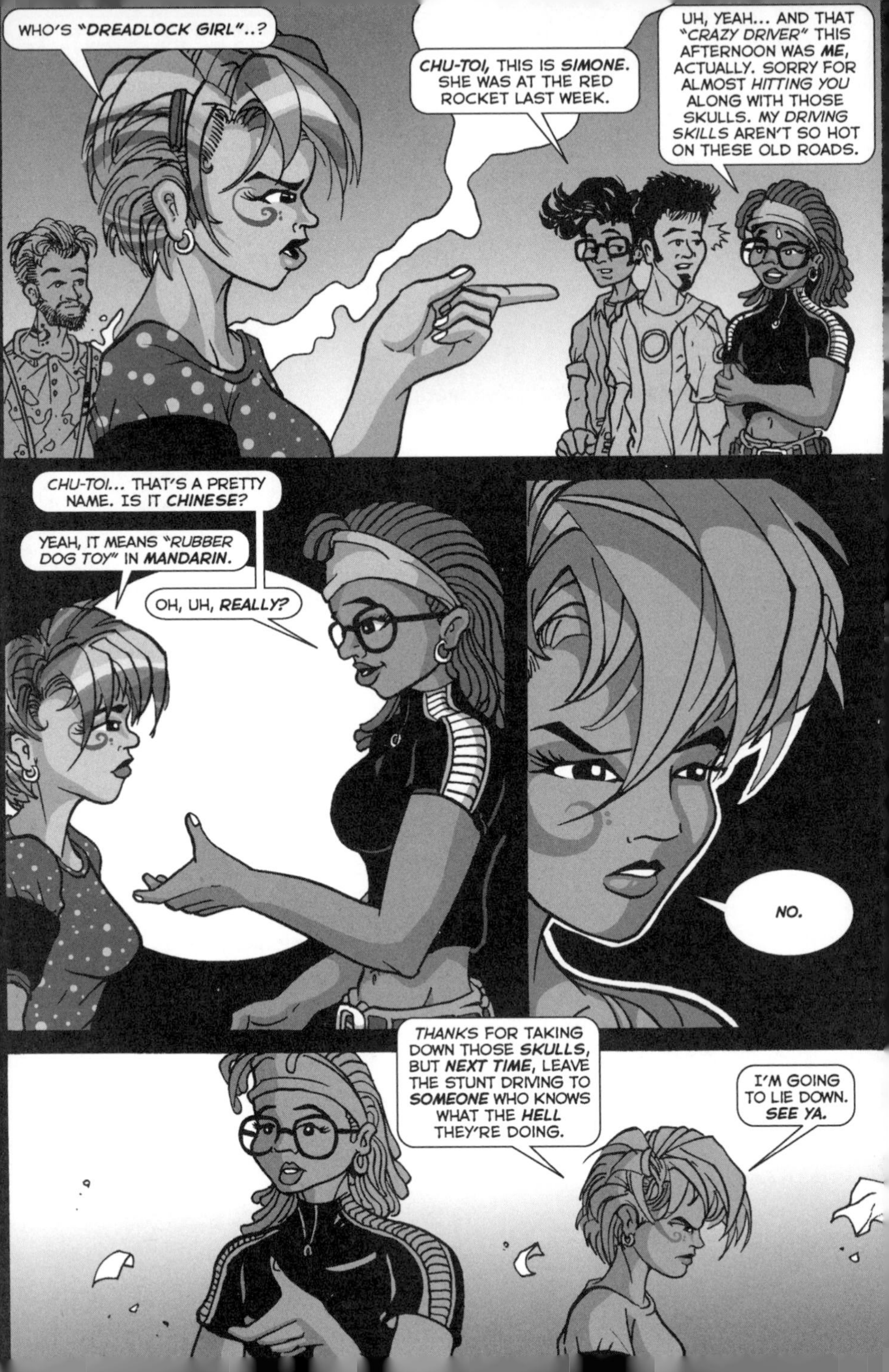
WHO'S "DREADLOCK GIRL"..?
CHU-TOI, THIS IS SIMONE. SHE WAS AT THE RED ROCKET LAST WEEK.
UH, YEAH... AND THAT "CRAZY DRIVER" THIS AFTERNOON WAS ME, ACTUALLY. SORRY FOR ALMOST HITTING YOU ALONG WITH THOSE SKULLS. MY DRIVING SKILLS AREN'T SO HOT ON THESE OLD ROADS.
CHU-TOI... THAT'S A PRETTY NAME. IS IT CHINESE?
YEAH, IT MEANS "RUBBER DOG TOY" IN MANDARIN.
OH, UH, REALLY?
NO.
THANKS FOR TAKING DOWN THOSE SKULLS, BUT NEXT TIME, LEAVE THE STUNT DRIVING TO SOMEONE WHO KNOWS WHAT THE HELL THEY'RE DOING.
I'M GOING TO LIE DOWN. SEE YA.

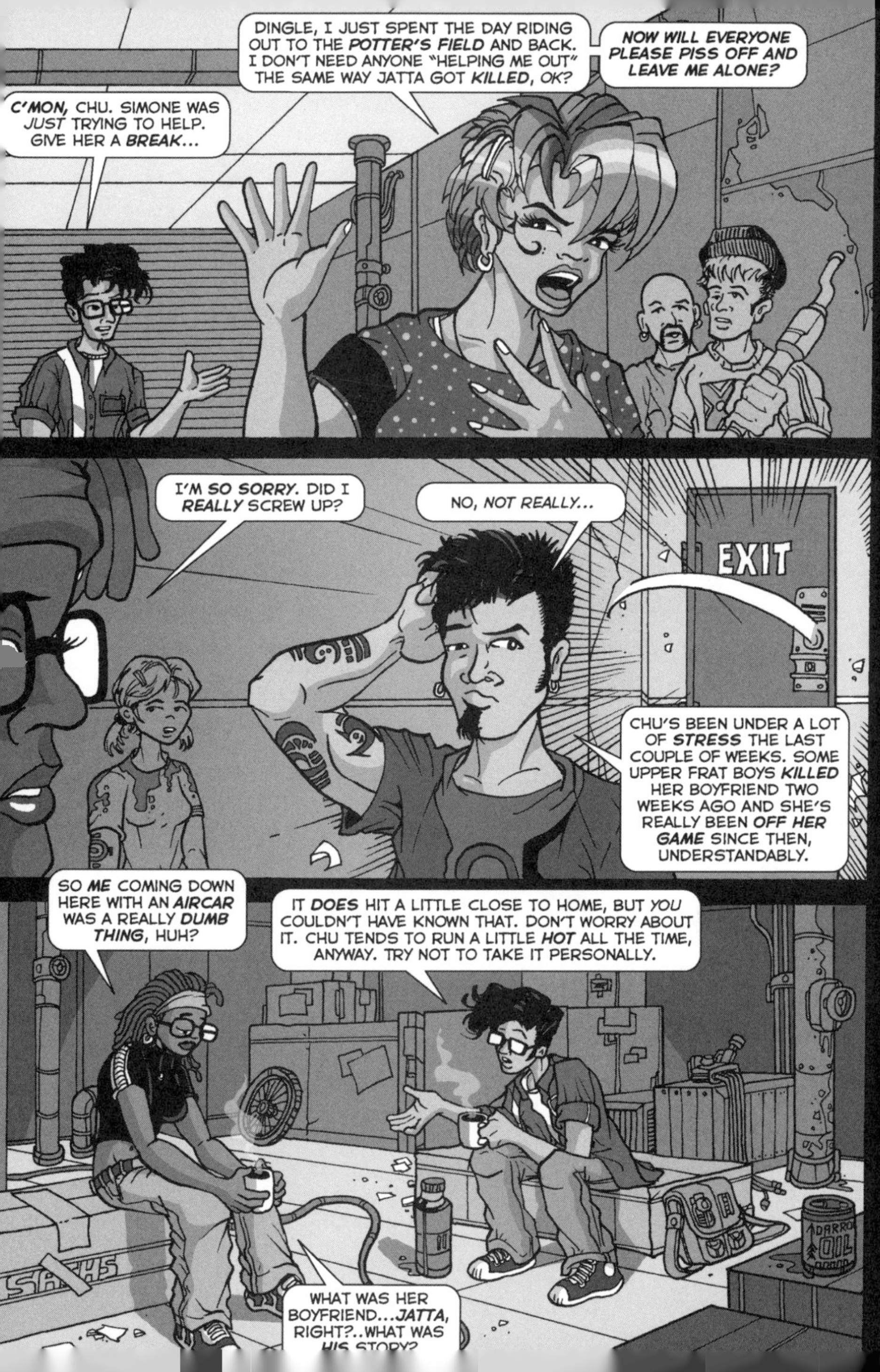
C'MON, CHU. SIMONE WAS JUST TRYING TO HELP. GIVE HER A BREAK...
DINGLE, I JUST SPENT THE DAY RIDING OUT TO THE POTTER'S FIELD AND BACK. I DON'T NEED ANYONE "HELPING ME OUT" THE SAME WAY JATTA GOT KILLED, OK?
NOW WILL EVERYONE PLEASE PISS OFF AND LEAVE ME ALONE?
I'M SO SORRY. DID I REALLY SCREW UP?
NO, NOT REALLY...
EXIT
CHU'S BEEN UNDER A LOT OF STRESS THE LAST COUPLE OF WEEKS. SOME UPPER FRAT BOYS KILLED HER BOYFRIEND TWO WEEKS AGO AND SHE'S REALLY BEEN OFF HER GAME SINCE THEN, UNDERSTANDABLY.
SO ME COMING DOWN HERE WITH AN AIRCAR WAS A REALLY DUMB THING, HUH?
IT DOES HIT A LITTLE CLOSE TO HOME, BUT YOU COULDN'T HAVE KNOWN THAT. DON'T WORRY ABOUT IT. CHU TENDS TO RUN A LITTLE HOT ALL THE TIME, ANYWAY. TRY NOT TO TAKE IT PERSONALLY.
WHAT WAS HER BOYFRIEND...JATTA, RIGHT?..WHAT WAS HIS STORY?

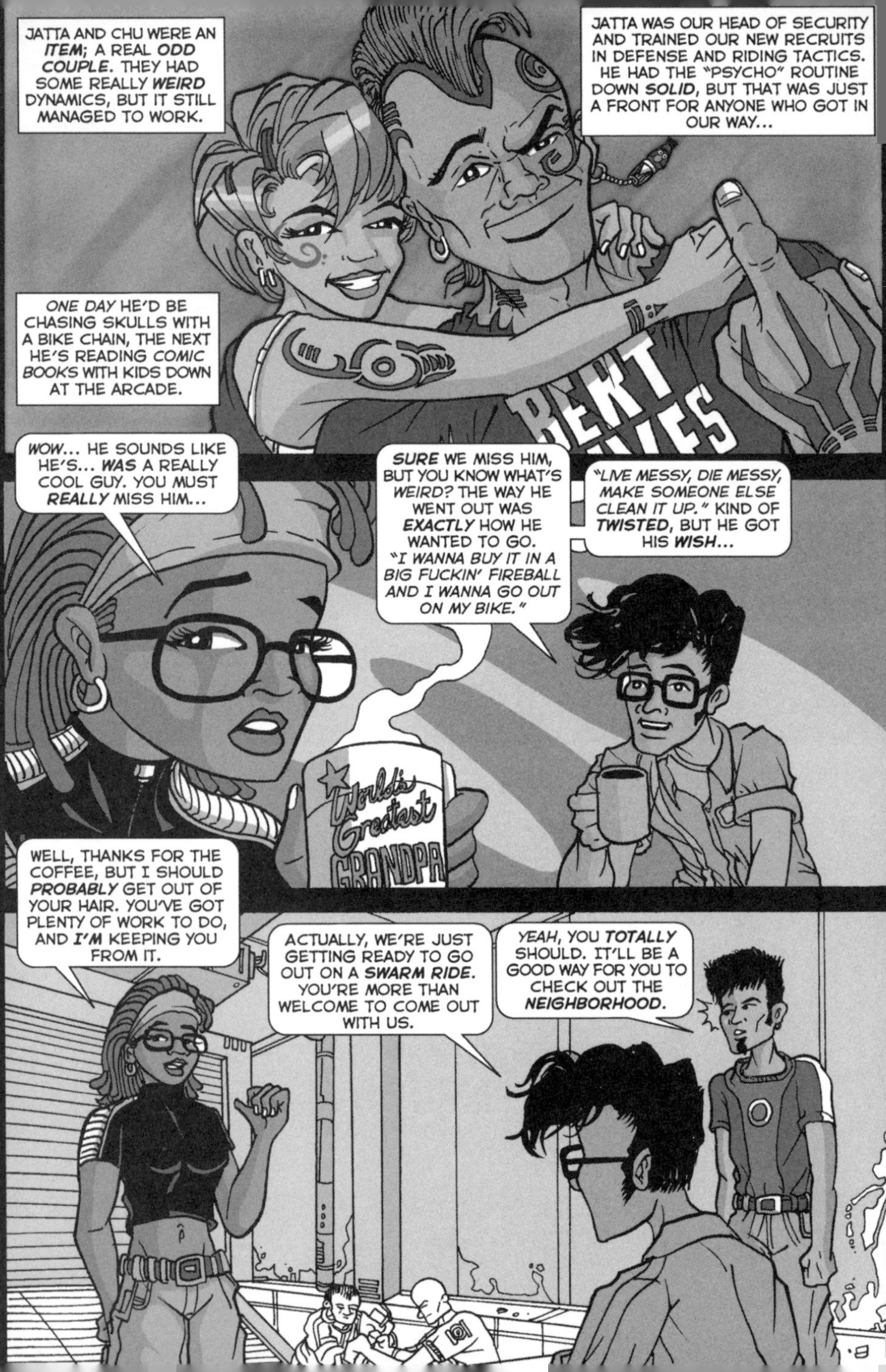
JATTA AND CHU WERE AN ITEM; A REAL ODD COUPLE. THEY HAD SOME REALLY WEIRD DYNAMICS, BUT IT STILL MANAGED TO WORK.
JATTA WAS OUR HEAD OF SECURITY AND TRAINED OUR NEW RECRUITS IN DEFENSE AND RIDING TACTICS. HE HAD THE "PSYCHO" ROUTINE DOWN SOLID, BUT THAT WAS JUST A FRONT FOR ANYONE WHO GOT IN OUR WAY...
ONE DAY HE'D BE CHASING SKULLS WITH A BIKE CHAIN, THE NEXT HE'S READING COMIC BOOKS WITH KIDS DOWN AT THE ARCADE.
WOW... HE SOUNDS LIKE HE'S... WAS A REALLY COOL GUY. YOU MUST REALLY MISS HIM...
SURE WE MISS HIM, BUT YOU KNOW WHAT'S WEIRD? THE WAY HE WENT OUT WAS EXACTLY HOW HE WANTED TO GO. "I WANNA BUY IT IN A BIG FUCKIN' FIREBALL AND I WANNA GO OUT ON MY BIKE."
"LIVE MESSY, DIE MESSY, MAKE SOMEONE ELSE CLEAN IT UP." KIND OF TWISTED, BUT HE GOT HIS WISH...
World's Greatest GRANDPA
WELL, THANKS FOR THE COFFEE, BUT I SHOULD PROBABLY GET OUT OF YOUR HAIR. YOU'VE GOT PLENTY OF WORK TO DO, AND I'M KEEPING YOU FROM IT.
ACTUALLY, WE'RE JUST GETTING READY TO GO OUT ON A SWARM RIDE. YOU'RE MORE THAN WELCOME TO COME OUT WITH US.
YEAH, YOU TOTALLY SHOULD. IT'LL BE A GOOD WAY FOR YOU TO CHECK OUT THE NEIGHBORHOOD.

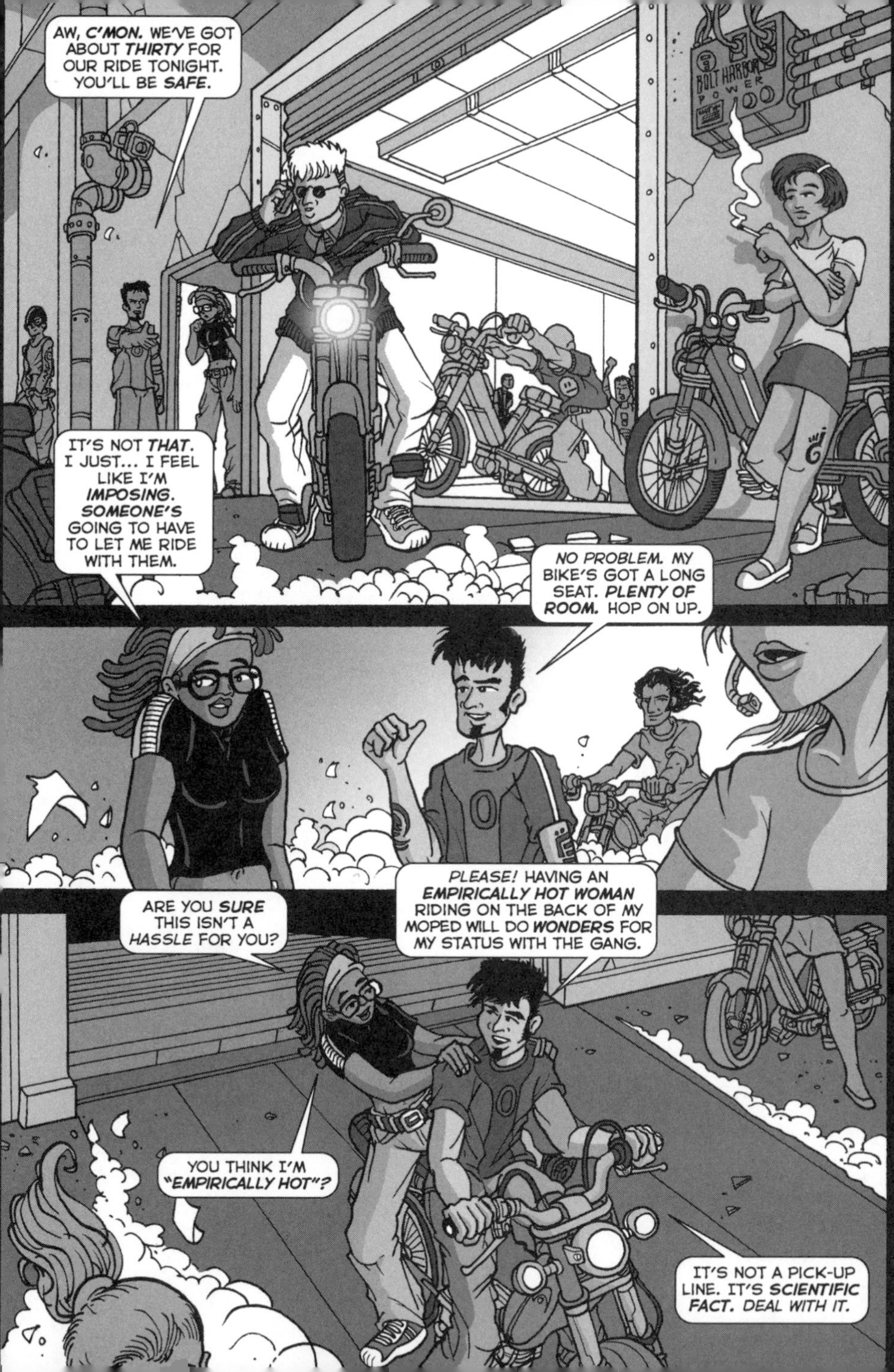
AW, C'MON. WE'VE GOT ABOUT THIRTY FOR OUR RIDE TONIGHT. YOU'LL BE SAFE.
BOLT HARBOR POWER
IT'S NOT THAT. I JUST... I FEEL LIKE I'M IMPOSING. SOMEONE'S GOING TO HAVE TO LET ME RIDE WITH THEM.
NO PROBLEM. MY BIKE'S GOT A LONG SEAT. PLENTY OF ROOM. HOP ON UP.
ARE YOU SURE THIS ISN'T A HASSLE FOR YOU?
PLEASE! HAVING AN EMPIRICALLY HOT WOMAN RIDING ON THE BACK OF MY MOPED WILL DO WONDERS FOR MY STATUS WITH THE GANG.
YOU THINK I'M "EMPIRICALLY HOT"?
IT'S NOT A PICK-UP LINE. IT'S SCIENTIFIC FACT. DEAL WITH IT.

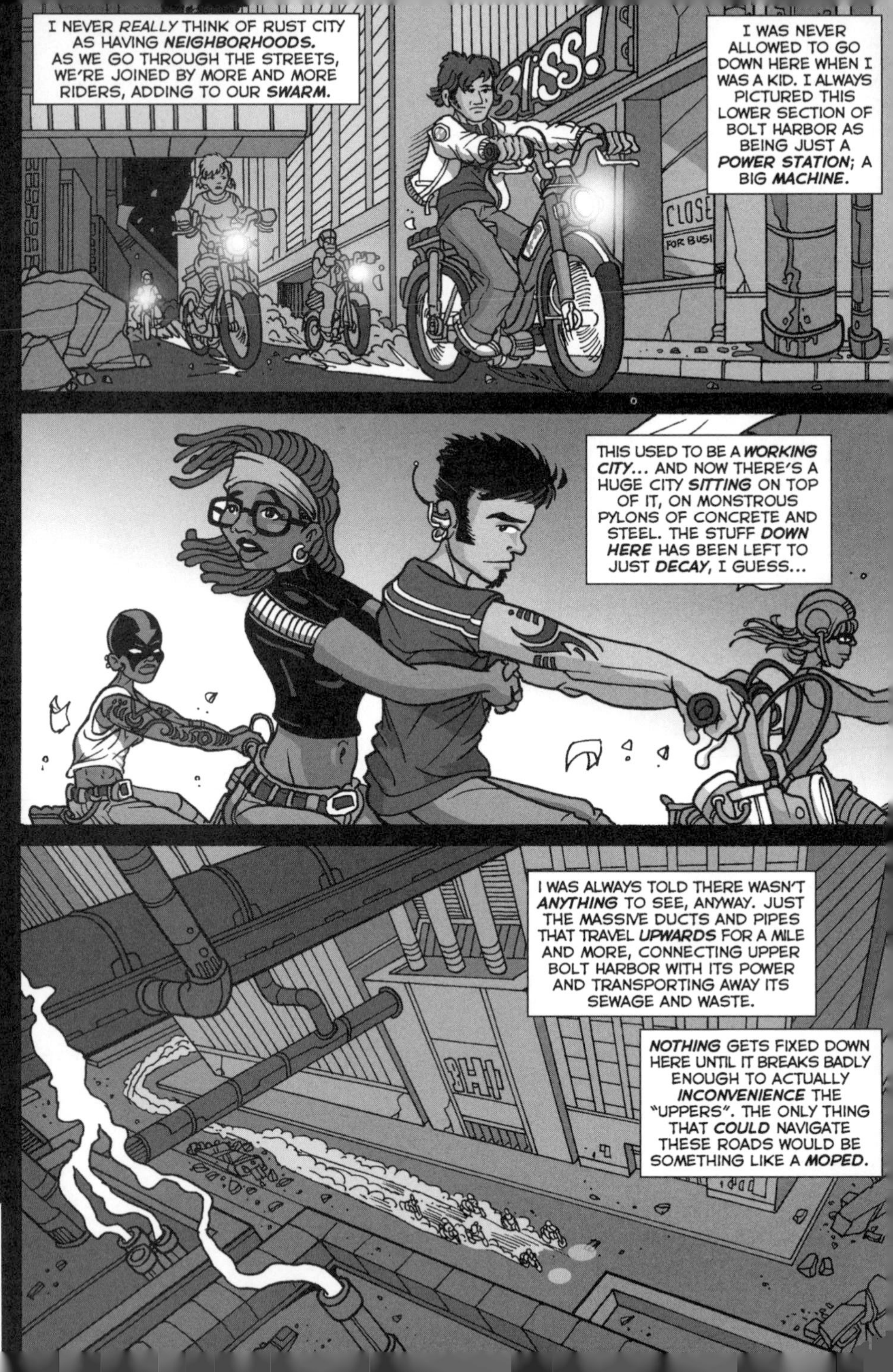
I NEVER *REALLY* THINK OF RUST CITY AS HAVING ***NEIGHBORHOODS.*** AS WE GO THROUGH THE STREETS, WE'RE JOINED BY MORE AND MORE RIDERS, ADDING TO OUR ***SWARM.***
BLISS!
CLOSE
FOR BUSI
I WAS NEVER ALLOWED TO GO DOWN HERE WHEN I WAS A KID. I ALWAYS PICTURED THIS LOWER SECTION OF BOLT HARBOR AS BEING JUST A ***POWER STATION***; A BIG ***MACHINE.***
THIS USED TO BE A ***WORKING CITY...*** AND NOW THERE'S A HUGE CITY ***SITTING*** ON TOP OF IT, ON MONSTROUS PYLONS OF CONCRETE AND STEEL. THE STUFF ***DOWN HERE*** HAS BEEN LEFT TO JUST ***DECAY***, I GUESS...
I WAS ALWAYS TOLD THERE WASN'T ***ANYTHING*** TO SEE, ANYWAY. JUST THE MASSIVE DUCTS AND PIPES THAT TRAVEL ***UPWARDS*** FOR A MILE AND MORE, CONNECTING UPPER BOLT HARBOR WITH ITS POWER AND TRANSPORTING AWAY ITS SEWAGE AND WASTE.
NOTHING GETS FIXED DOWN HERE UNTIL IT BREAKS BADLY ENOUGH TO ACTUALLY ***INCONVENIENCE*** THE "UPPERS". THE ONLY THING THAT ***COULD*** NAVIGATE THESE ROADS WOULD BE SOMETHING LIKE A ***MOPED.***

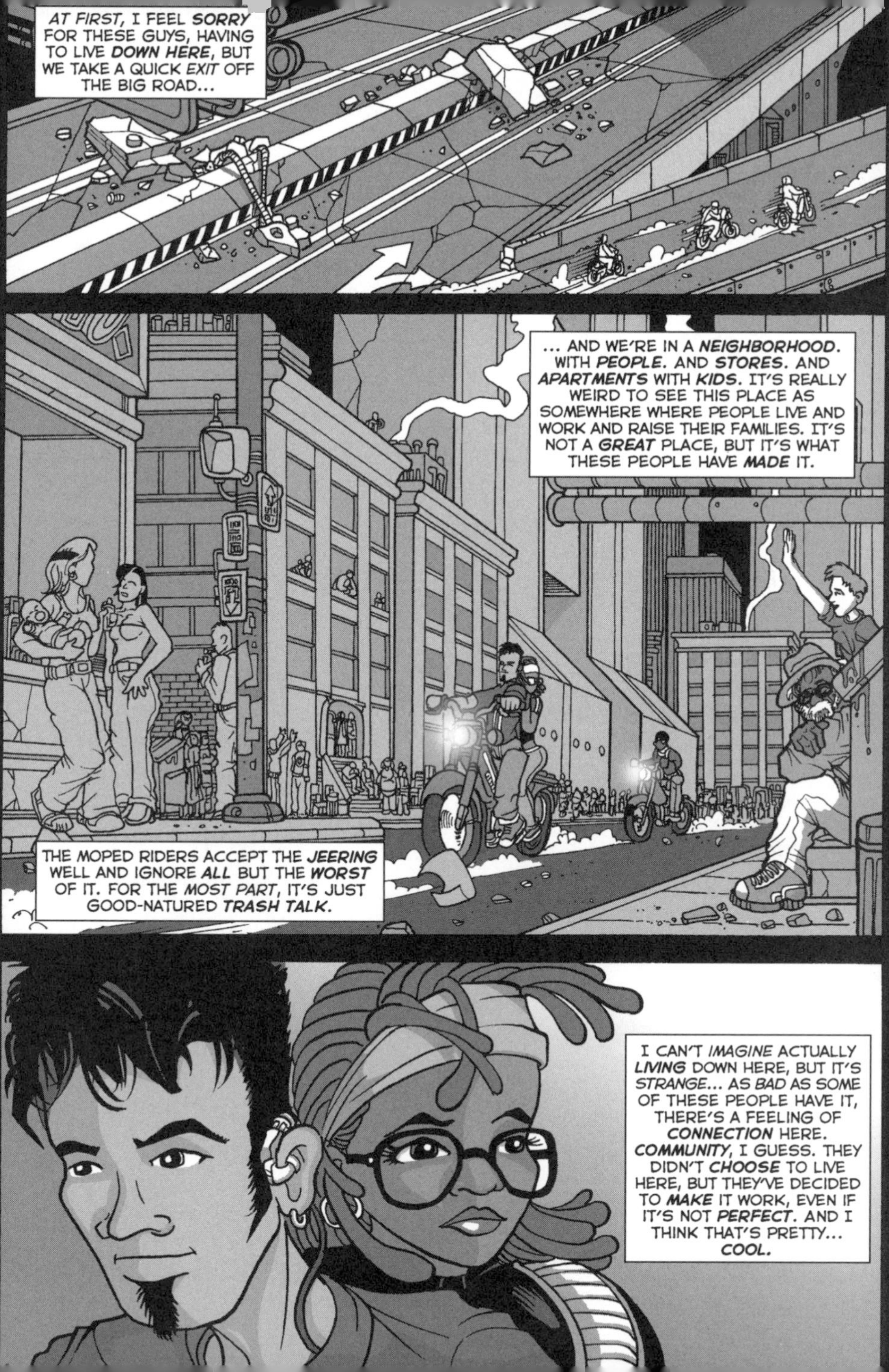
AT FIRST, I FEEL SORRY FOR THESE GUYS, HAVING TO LIVE DOWN HERE, BUT WE TAKE A QUICK EXIT OFF THE BIG ROAD...
... AND WE'RE IN A NEIGHBORHOOD. WITH PEOPLE. AND STORES. AND APARTMENTS WITH KIDS. IT'S REALLY WEIRD TO SEE THIS PLACE AS SOMEWHERE WHERE PEOPLE LIVE AND WORK AND RAISE THEIR FAMILIES. IT'S NOT A GREAT PLACE, BUT IT'S WHAT THESE PEOPLE HAVE MADE IT.
THE MOPED RIDERS ACCEPT THE JEERING WELL AND IGNORE ALL BUT THE WORST OF IT. FOR THE MOST PART, IT'S JUST GOOD-NATURED TRASH TALK.
I CAN'T IMAGINE ACTUALLY LIVING DOWN HERE, BUT IT'S STRANGE... AS BAD AS SOME OF THESE PEOPLE HAVE IT, THERE'S A FEELING OF CONNECTION HERE. COMMUNITY, I GUESS. THEY DIDN'T CHOOSE TO LIVE HERE, BUT THEY'VE DECIDED TO MAKE IT WORK, EVEN IF IT'S NOT PERFECT. AND I THINK THAT'S PRETTY... COOL.

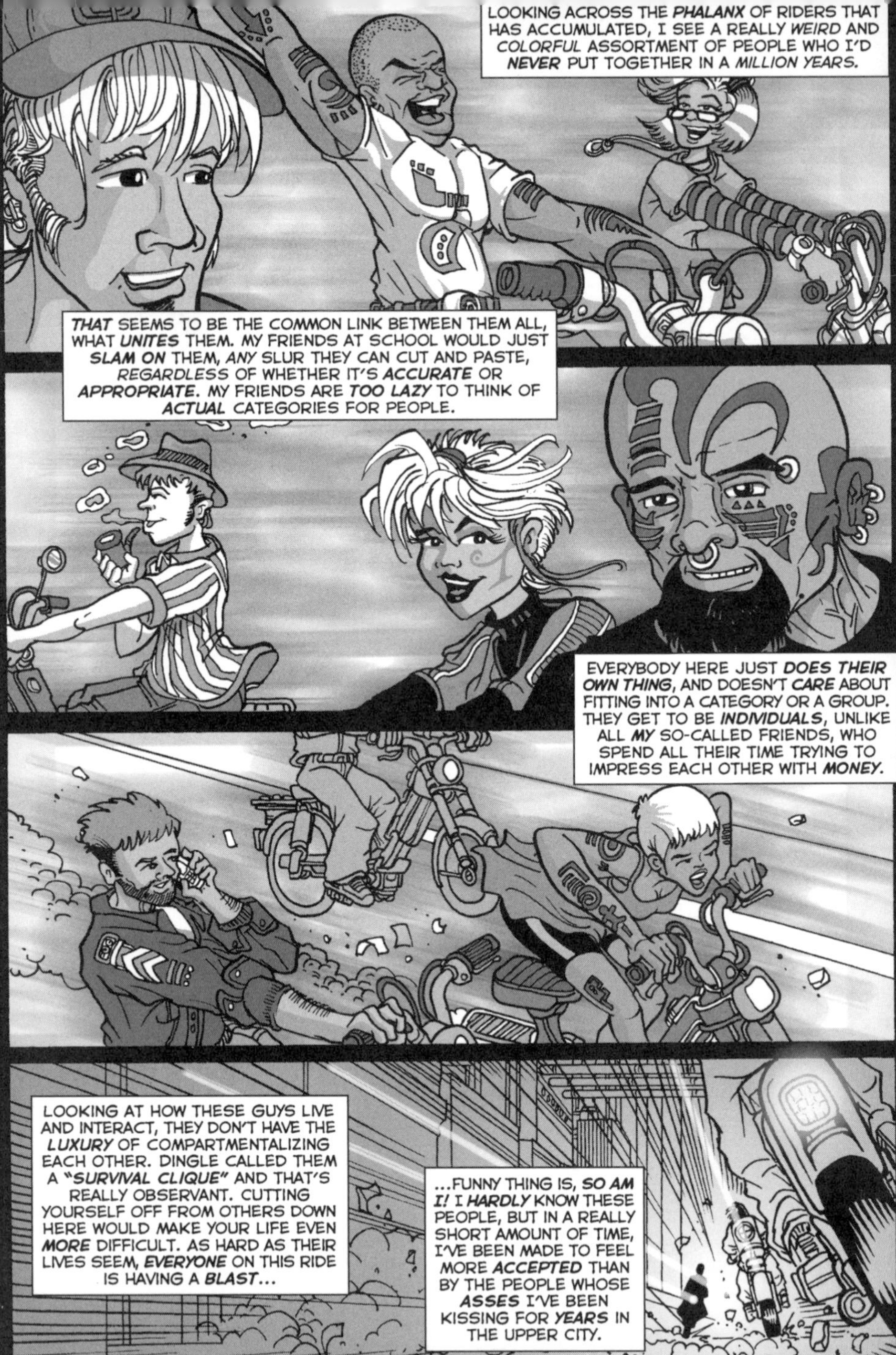
LOOKING ACROSS THE PHALANX OF RIDERS THAT HAS ACCUMULATED, I SEE A REALLY WEIRD AND COLORFUL ASSORTMENT OF PEOPLE WHO I'D NEVER PUT TOGETHER IN A MILLION YEARS.
THAT SEEMS TO BE THE COMMON LINK BETWEEN THEM ALL, WHAT UNITES THEM. MY FRIENDS AT SCHOOL WOULD JUST SLAM ON THEM, ANY SLUR THEY CAN CUT AND PASTE, REGARDLESS OF WHETHER IT'S ACCURATE OR APPROPRIATE. MY FRIENDS ARE TOO LAZY TO THINK OF ACTUAL CATEGORIES FOR PEOPLE.
EVERYBODY HERE JUST DOES THEIR OWN THING, AND DOESN'T CARE ABOUT FITTING INTO A CATEGORY OR A GROUP. THEY GET TO BE INDIVIDUALS, UNLIKE ALL MY SO-CALLED FRIENDS, WHO SPEND ALL THEIR TIME TRYING TO IMPRESS EACH OTHER WITH MONEY.
LOOKING AT HOW THESE GUYS LIVE AND INTERACT, THEY DON'T HAVE THE LUXURY OF COMPARTMENTALIZING EACH OTHER. DINGLE CALLED THEM A "SURVIVAL CLIQUE" AND THAT'S REALLY OBSERVANT. CUTTING YOURSELF OFF FROM OTHERS DOWN HERE WOULD MAKE YOUR LIFE EVEN MORE DIFFICULT. AS HARD AS THEIR LIVES SEEM, EVERYONE ON THIS RIDE IS HAVING A BLAST...
...FUNNY THING IS, SO AM I! I HARDLY KNOW THESE PEOPLE, BUT IN A REALLY SHORT AMOUNT OF TIME, I'VE BEEN MADE TO FEEL MORE ACCEPTED THAN BY THE PEOPLE WHOSE ASSES I'VE BEEN KISSING FOR YEARS IN THE UPPER CITY.

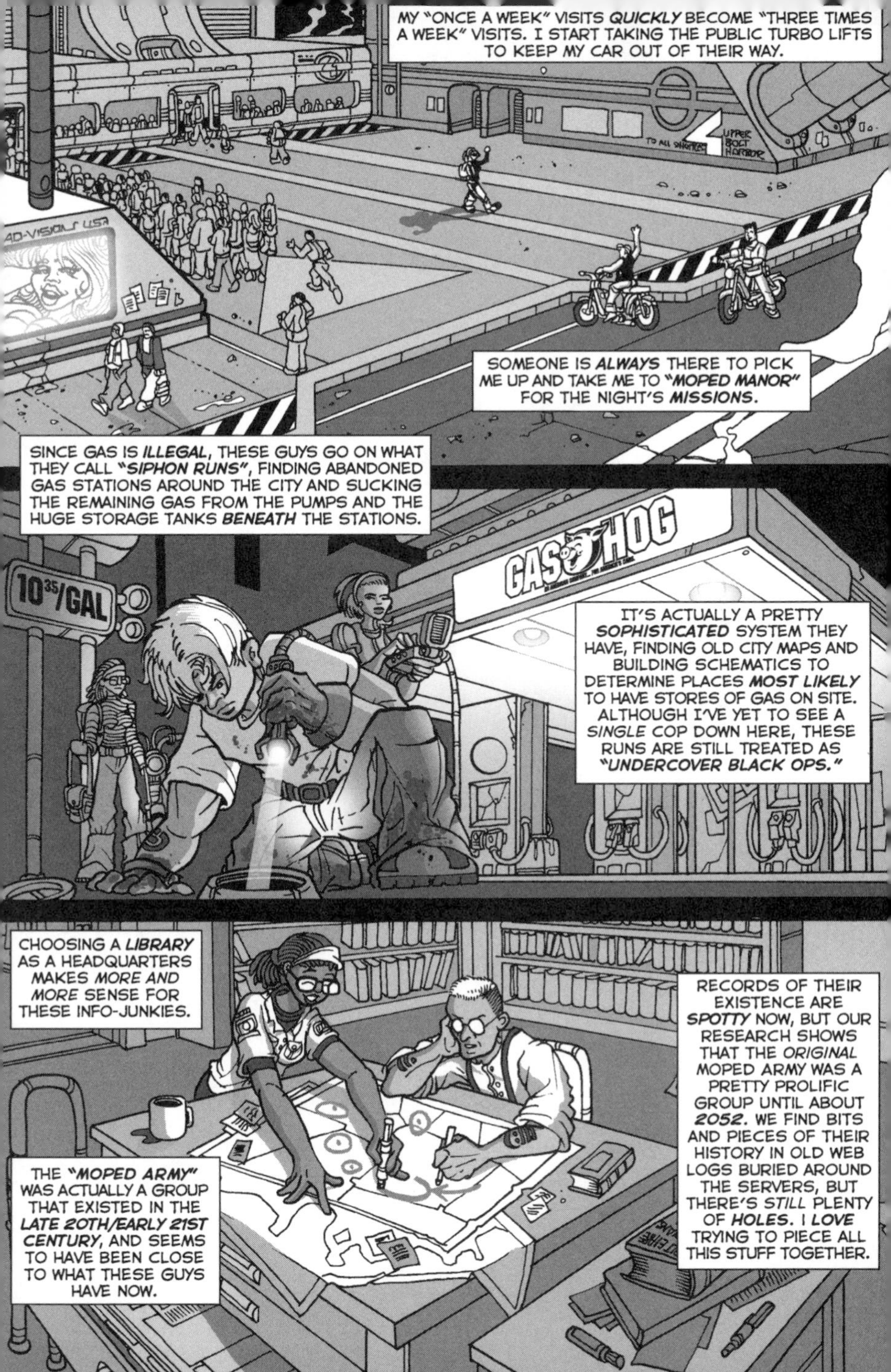
MY "ONCE A WEEK" VISITS *QUICKLY* BECOME "THREE TIMES A WEEK" VISITS. I START TAKING THE PUBLIC TURBO LIFTS TO KEEP MY CAR OUT OF THEIR WAY.
SOMEONE IS *ALWAYS* THERE TO PICK ME UP AND TAKE ME TO *"MOPED MANOR"* FOR THE NIGHT'S *MISSIONS*.
SINCE GAS IS *ILLEGAL*, THESE GUYS GO ON WHAT THEY CALL *"SIPHON RUNS"*, FINDING ABANDONED GAS STATIONS AROUND THE CITY AND SUCKING THE REMAINING GAS FROM THE PUMPS AND THE HUGE STORAGE TANKS *BENEATH* THE STATIONS.
10^{35}/GAL
GAS HOG
IT'S ACTUALLY A PRETTY *SOPHISTICATED* SYSTEM THEY HAVE, FINDING OLD CITY MAPS AND BUILDING SCHEMATICS TO DETERMINE PLACES *MOST LIKELY* TO HAVE STORES OF GAS ON SITE. ALTHOUGH I'VE YET TO SEE A *SINGLE* COP DOWN HERE, THESE RUNS ARE STILL TREATED AS *"UNDERCOVER BLACK OPS."*
CHOOSING A *LIBRARY* AS A HEADQUARTERS MAKES *MORE AND MORE* SENSE FOR THESE INFO-JUNKIES.
RECORDS OF THEIR EXISTENCE ARE *SPOTTY* NOW, BUT OUR RESEARCH SHOWS THAT THE *ORIGINAL* MOPED ARMY WAS A PRETTY PROLIFIC GROUP UNTIL ABOUT *2052*. WE FIND BITS AND PIECES OF THEIR HISTORY IN OLD WEB LOGS BURIED AROUND THE SERVERS, BUT THERE'S *STILL* PLENTY OF *HOLES*. I *LOVE* TRYING TO PIECE ALL THIS STUFF TOGETHER.
THE *"MOPED ARMY"* WAS ACTUALLY A GROUP THAT EXISTED IN THE *LATE 20TH/EARLY 21ST CENTURY*, AND SEEMS TO HAVE BEEN CLOSE TO WHAT THESE GUYS HAVE NOW.

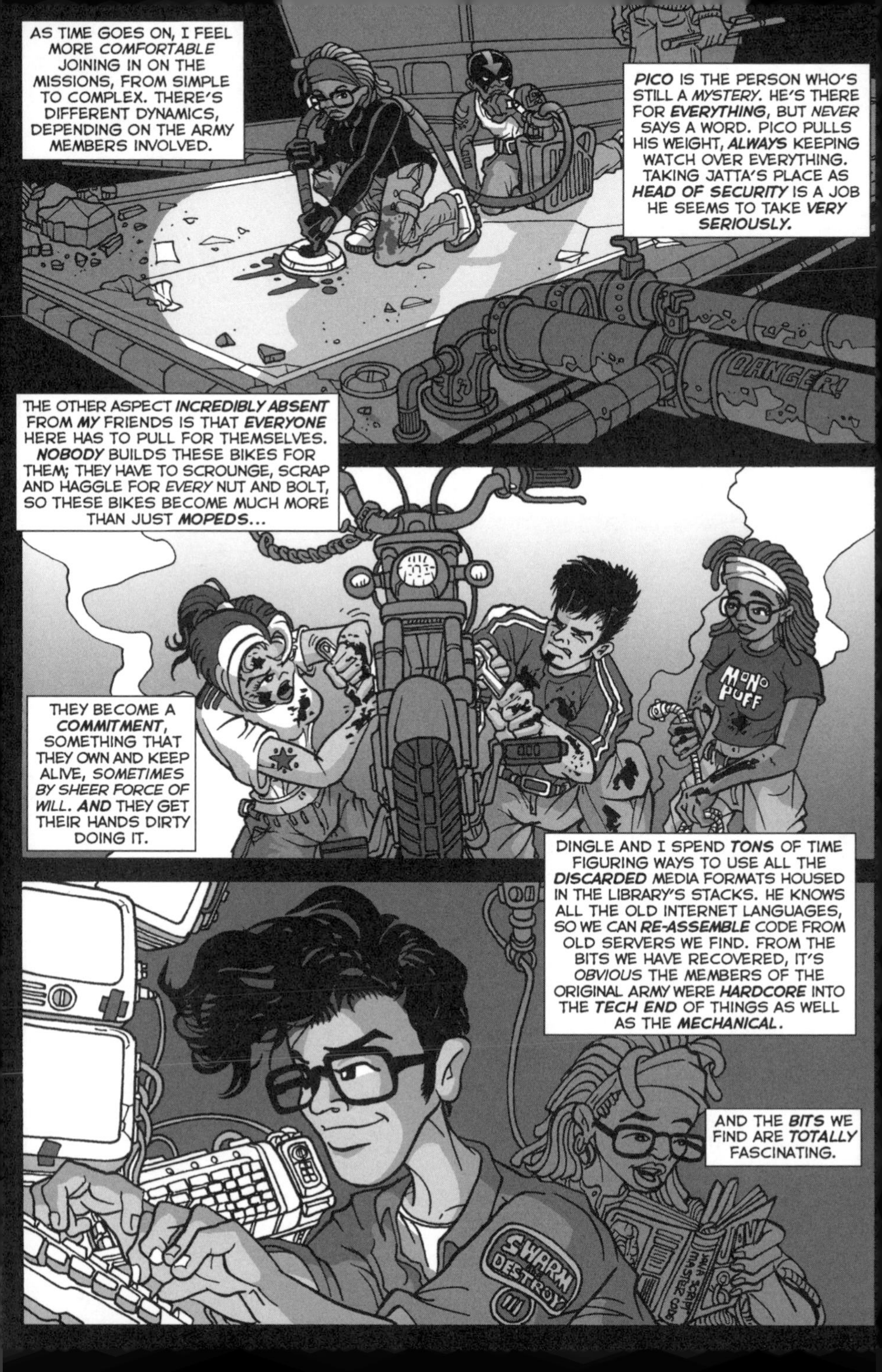
AS TIME GOES ON, I FEEL MORE *COMFORTABLE* JOINING IN ON THE MISSIONS, FROM SIMPLE TO COMPLEX. THERE'S DIFFERENT DYNAMICS, DEPENDING ON THE ARMY MEMBERS INVOLVED.
PICO IS THE PERSON WHO'S STILL A *MYSTERY*. HE'S THERE FOR ***EVERYTHING***, BUT *NEVER* SAYS A WORD. PICO PULLS HIS WEIGHT, ***ALWAYS*** KEEPING WATCH OVER EVERYTHING. TAKING JATTA'S PLACE AS ***HEAD OF SECURITY*** IS A JOB HE SEEMS TO TAKE ***VERY SERIOUSLY.***
DANGER!
THE OTHER ASPECT ***INCREDIBLY ABSENT*** FROM ***MY*** FRIENDS IS THAT ***EVERYONE*** HERE HAS TO PULL FOR THEMSELVES. ***NOBODY*** BUILDS THESE BIKES FOR *THEM*; THEY HAVE TO SCROUNGE, SCRAP AND HAGGLE FOR *EVERY* NUT AND BOLT, SO THESE BIKES BECOME MUCH MORE THAN JUST ***MOPEDS...***
THEY BECOME A ***COMMITMENT***, SOMETHING THAT THEY OWN AND KEEP ALIVE, *SOMETIMES BY SHEER FORCE OF WILL*. ***AND*** THEY GET THEIR HANDS DIRTY DOING IT.
MONO PUFF
DINGLE AND I SPEND ***TONS*** OF TIME FIGURING WAYS TO USE ALL THE ***DISCARDED*** MEDIA FORMATS HOUSED IN THE LIBRARY'S STACKS. HE KNOWS ALL THE OLD INTERNET LANGUAGES, SO WE CAN ***RE-ASSEMBLE*** CODE FROM OLD SERVERS WE FIND. FROM THE BITS WE HAVE RECOVERED, IT'S *OBVIOUS* THE MEMBERS OF THE ORIGINAL ARMY WERE ***HARDCORE*** INTO THE ***TECH END*** OF THINGS AS WELL AS THE ***MECHANICAL***.
SWARM AND DESTROY
AND THE ***BITS*** WE FIND ARE ***TOTALLY*** FASCINATING.
JAVA SCRIPT MASTER CODE

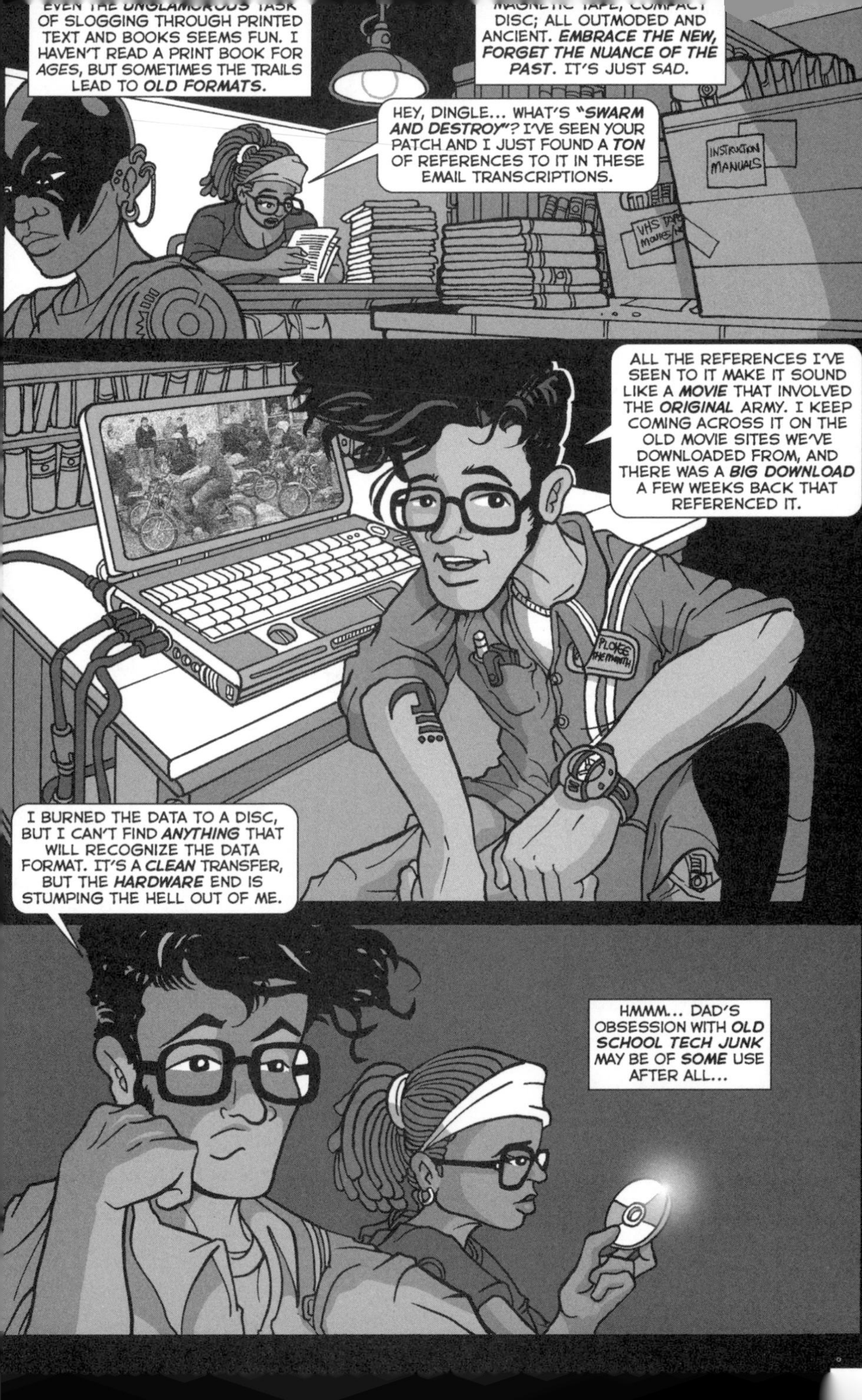
EVEN THE UNGLAMOROUS TASK OF SLOGGING THROUGH PRINTED TEXT AND BOOKS SEEMS FUN. I HAVEN'T READ A PRINT BOOK FOR AGES, BUT SOMETIMES THE TRAILS LEAD TO OLD FORMATS.
MAGNETIC TAPE, COMPACT DISC; ALL OUTMODED AND ANCIENT. EMBRACE THE NEW, FORGET THE NUANCE OF THE PAST. IT'S JUST SAD.
HEY, DINGLE... WHAT'S "SWARM AND DESTROY"? I'VE SEEN YOUR PATCH AND I JUST FOUND A TON OF REFERENCES TO IT IN THESE EMAIL TRANSCRIPTIONS.
INSTRUCTION MANUALS
ALL THE REFERENCES I'VE SEEN TO IT MAKE IT SOUND LIKE A MOVIE THAT INVOLVED THE ORIGINAL ARMY. I KEEP COMING ACROSS IT ON THE OLD MOVIE SITES WE'VE DOWNLOADED FROM, AND THERE WAS A BIG DOWNLOAD A FEW WEEKS BACK THAT REFERENCED IT.
I BURNED THE DATA TO A DISC, BUT I CAN'T FIND ANYTHING THAT WILL RECOGNIZE THE DATA FORMAT. IT'S A CLEAN TRANSFER, BUT THE HARDWARE END IS STUMPING THE HELL OUT OF ME.
HMMM... DAD'S OBSESSION WITH OLD SCHOOL TECH JUNK MAY BE OF SOME USE AFTER ALL...

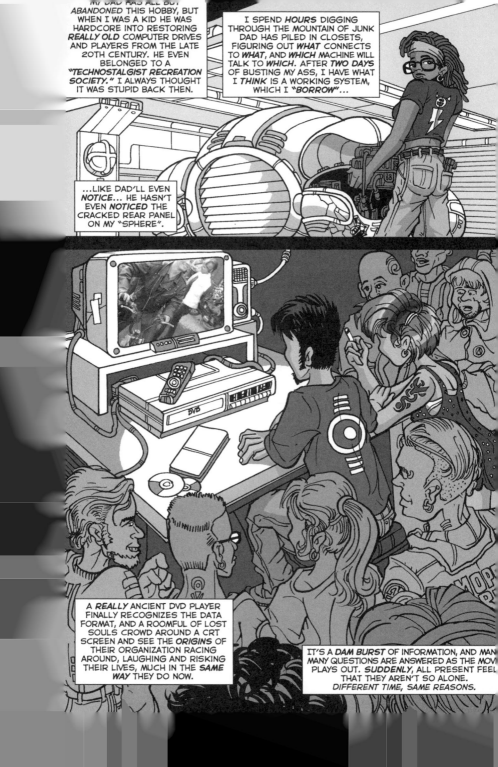

MY DAD HAS ALL BUT *ABANDONED* THIS HOBBY, BUT WHEN I WAS A KID HE WAS HARDCORE INTO RESTORING *REALLY OLD* COMPUTER DRIVES AND PLAYERS FROM THE LATE 20TH CENTURY. HE EVEN BELONGED TO A *"TECHNOSTALGIST RECREATION SOCIETY."* I ALWAYS THOUGHT IT WAS STUPID BACK THEN.

I SPEND *HOURS* DIGGING THROUGH THE MOUNTAIN OF JUNK DAD HAS PILED IN CLOSETS, FIGURING OUT *WHAT* CONNECTS TO *WHAT*, AND *WHICH* MACHINE WILL TALK TO *WHICH*. AFTER *TWO DAYS* OF BUSTING MY ASS, I HAVE WHAT I *THINK* IS A WORKING SYSTEM, WHICH I *"BORROW"*...

...LIKE DAD'LL EVEN *NOTICE*... HE HASN'T EVEN *NOTICED* THE CRACKED REAR PANEL ON MY *"SPHERE".*

A *REALLY* ANCIENT DVD PLAYER FINALLY RECOGNIZES THE DATA FORMAT, AND A ROOMFUL OF LOST SOULS CROWD AROUND A CRT SCREEN AND SEE THE *ORIGINS* OF THEIR ORGANIZATION RACING AROUND, LAUGHING AND RISKING THEIR LIVES, MUCH IN THE *SAME WAY* THEY DO NOW.

IT'S A *DAM BURST* OF INFORMATION, AND MAN[Y] MANY QUESTIONS ARE ANSWERED AS THE MOVI[E] PLAYS OUT. *SUDDENLY*, ALL PRESENT FEEL THAT THEY AREN'T SO ALONE. *DIFFERENT TIME, SAME REASONS.*

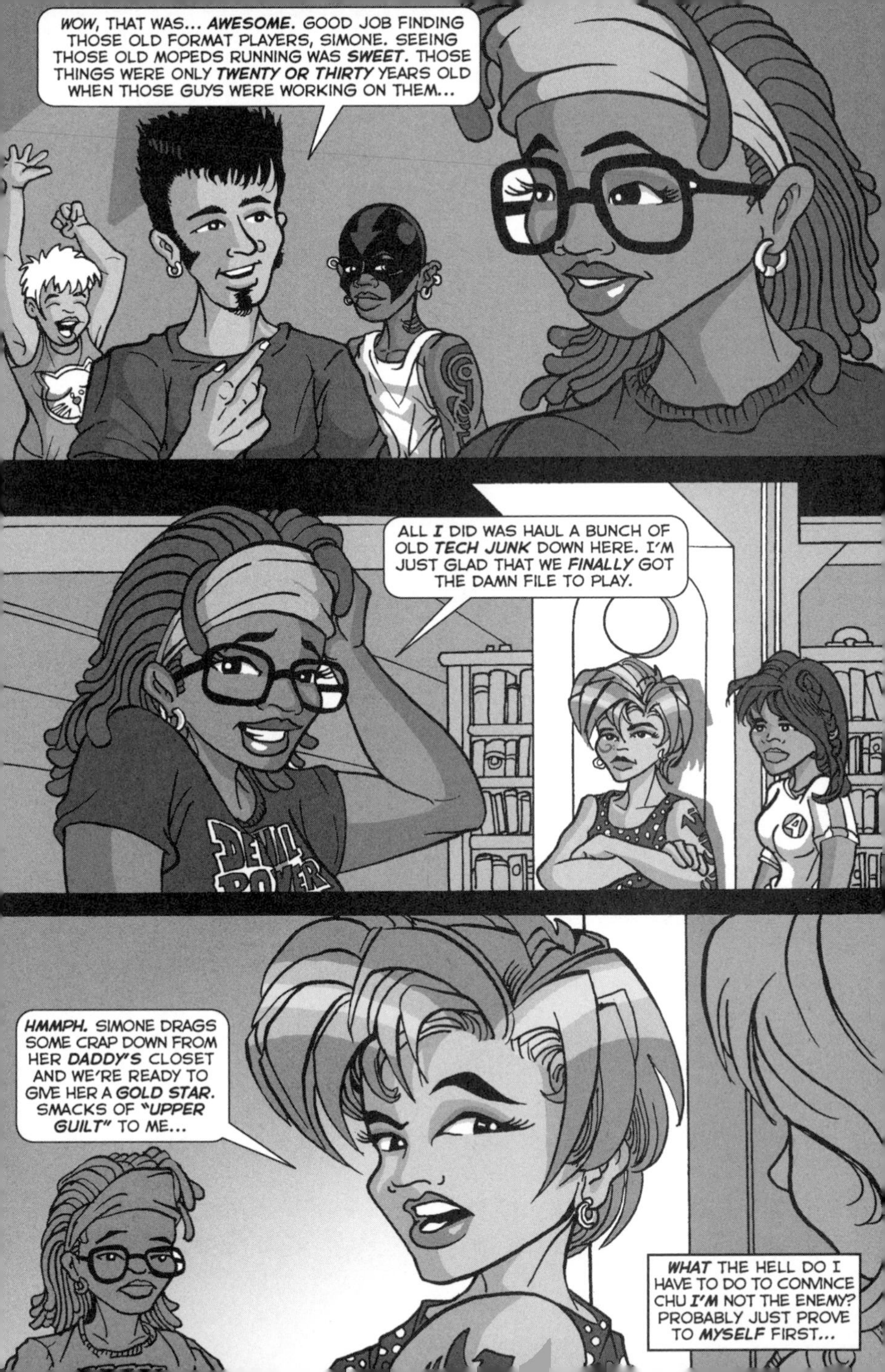
WOW, THAT WAS... AWESOME. GOOD JOB FINDING THOSE OLD FORMAT PLAYERS, SIMONE. SEEING THOSE OLD MOPEDS RUNNING WAS SWEET. THOSE THINGS WERE ONLY TWENTY OR THIRTY YEARS OLD WHEN THOSE GUYS WERE WORKING ON THEM...
ALL I DID WAS HAUL A BUNCH OF OLD TECH JUNK DOWN HERE. I'M JUST GLAD THAT WE FINALLY GOT THE DAMN FILE TO PLAY.
HMMPH. SIMONE DRAGS SOME CRAP DOWN FROM HER DADDY'S CLOSET AND WE'RE READY TO GIVE HER A GOLD STAR. SMACKS OF "UPPER GUILT" TO ME...
WHAT THE HELL DO I HAVE TO DO TO CONVINCE CHU I'M NOT THE ENEMY? PROBABLY JUST PROVE TO MYSELF FIRST...

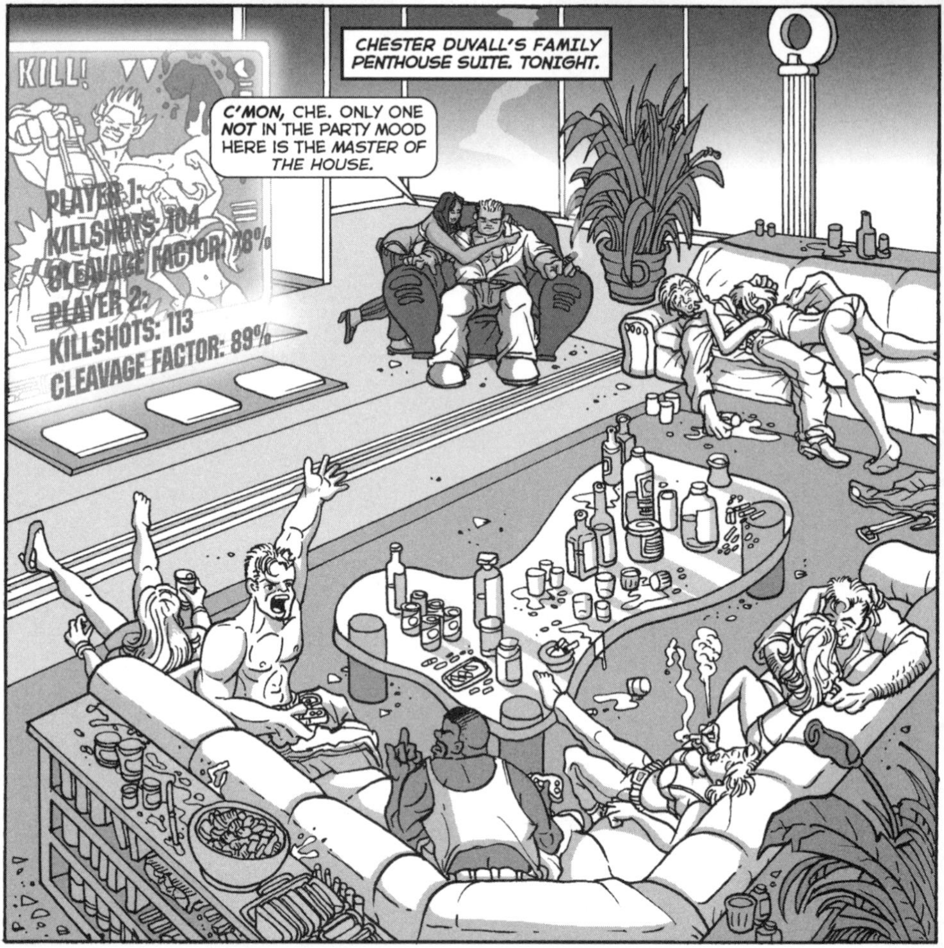
CHESTER DUVALL'S FAMILY PENTHOUSE SUITE. TONIGHT.
KILL!
C'MON, CHE. ONLY ONE NOT IN THE PARTY MOOD HERE IS THE MASTER OF THE HOUSE.
PLAYER 1:
KILLSHOTS: 104
CLEAVAGE FACTOR: 78%
PLAYER 2:
KILLSHOTS: 113
CLEAVAGE FACTOR: 89%

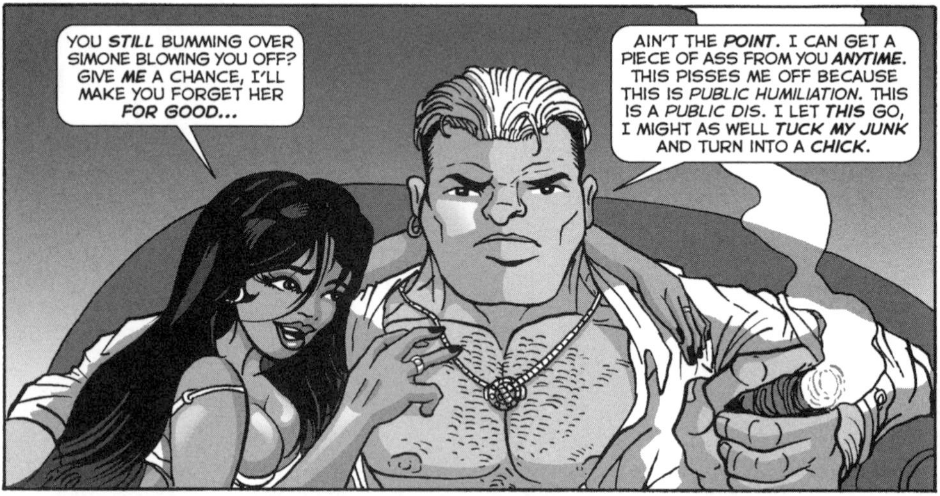
YOU STILL BUMMING OVER SIMONE BLOWING YOU OFF? GIVE ME A CHANCE, I'LL MAKE YOU FORGET HER FOR GOOD...
AIN'T THE POINT. I CAN GET A PIECE OF ASS FROM YOU ANYTIME. THIS PISSES ME OFF BECAUSE THIS IS PUBLIC HUMILIATION. THIS IS A PUBLIC DIS. I LET THIS GO, I MIGHT AS WELL TUCK MY JUNK AND TURN INTO A CHICK.

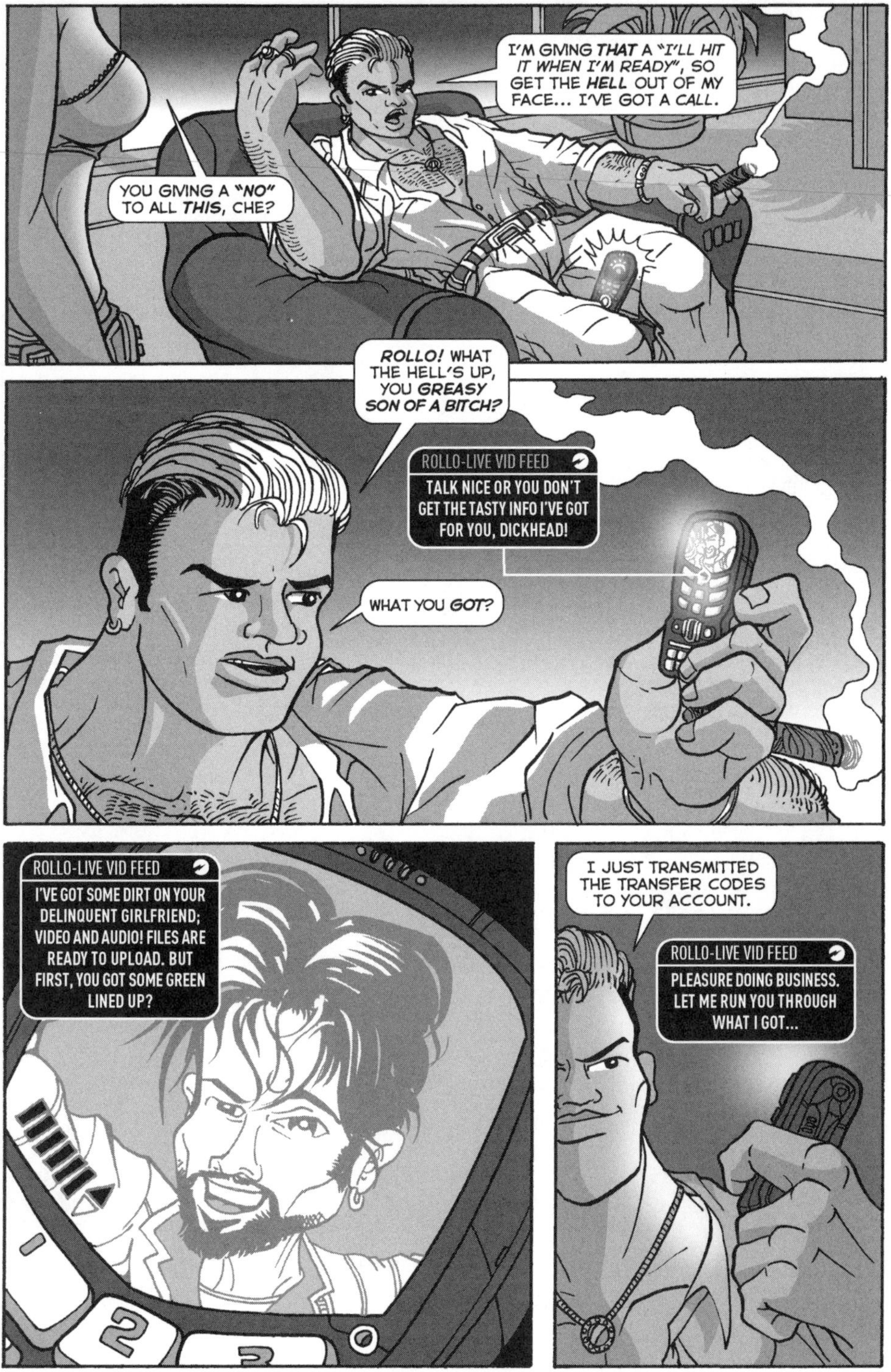

YOU GIVING A "NO" TO ALL THIS, CHE?
I'M GIVING THAT A "I'LL HIT IT WHEN I'M READY", SO GET THE HELL OUT OF MY FACE... I'VE GOT A CALL.
ROLLO! WHAT THE HELL'S UP, YOU GREASY SON OF A BITCH?
ROLLO-LIVE VID FEED
TALK NICE OR YOU DON'T GET THE TASTY INFO I'VE GOT FOR YOU, DICKHEAD!
WHAT YOU GOT?
ROLLO-LIVE VID FEED
I'VE GOT SOME DIRT ON YOUR DELINQUENT GIRLFRIEND; VIDEO AND AUDIO! FILES ARE READY TO UPLOAD. BUT FIRST, YOU GOT SOME GREEN LINED UP?
I JUST TRANSMITTED THE TRANSFER CODES TO YOUR ACCOUNT.
ROLLO-LIVE VID FEED
PLEASURE DOING BUSINESS. LET ME RUN YOU THROUGH WHAT I GOT...

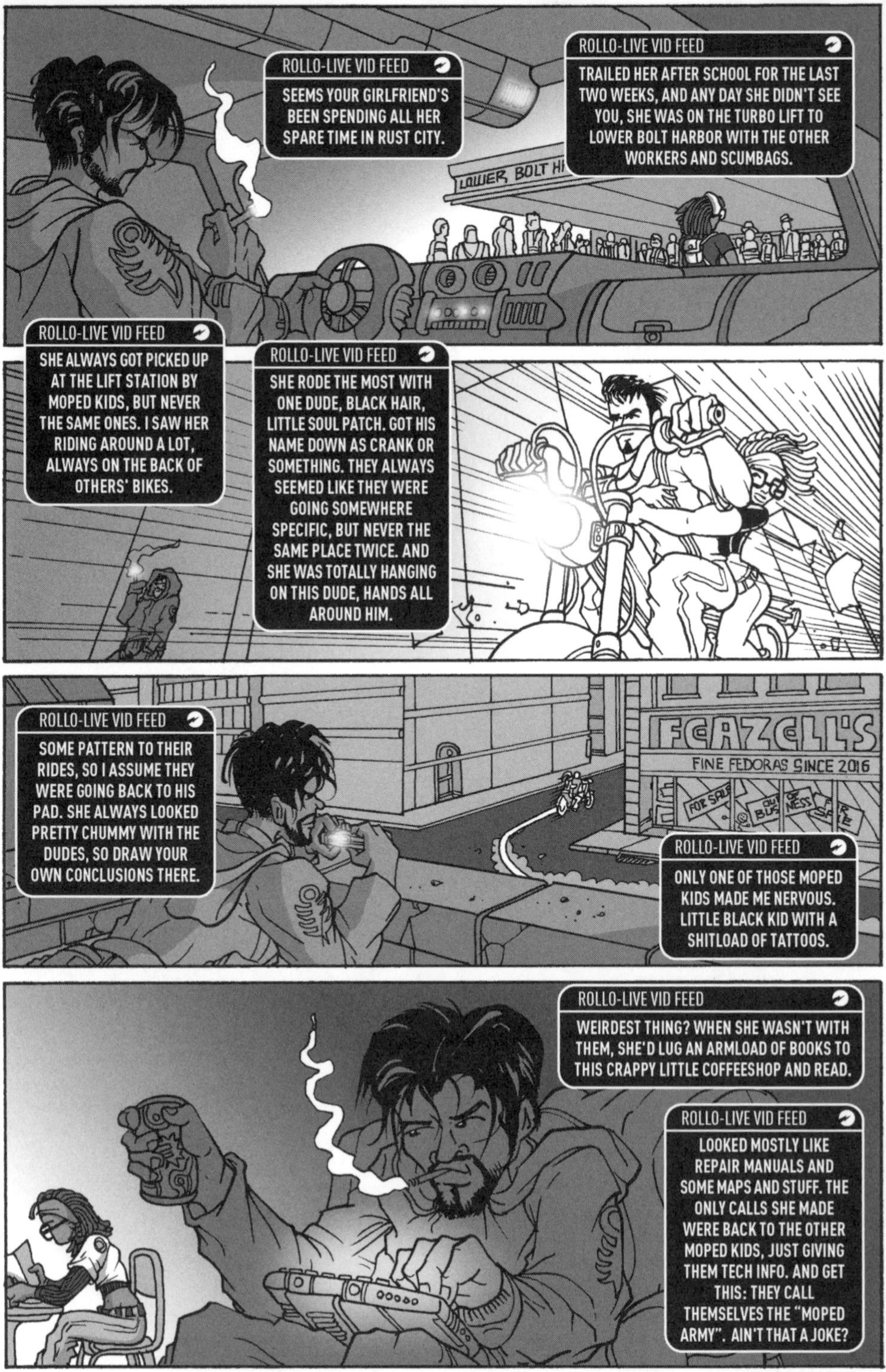
ROLLO-LIVE VID FEED
SEEMS YOUR GIRLFRIEND'S BEEN SPENDING ALL HER SPARE TIME IN RUST CITY.
ROLLO-LIVE VID FEED
TRAILED HER AFTER SCHOOL FOR THE LAST TWO WEEKS, AND ANY DAY SHE DIDN'T SEE YOU, SHE WAS ON THE TURBO LIFT TO LOWER BOLT HARBOR WITH THE OTHER WORKERS AND SCUMBAGS.
ROLLO-LIVE VID FEED
SHE ALWAYS GOT PICKED UP AT THE LIFT STATION BY MOPED KIDS, BUT NEVER THE SAME ONES. I SAW HER RIDING AROUND A LOT, ALWAYS ON THE BACK OF OTHERS' BIKES.
ROLLO-LIVE VID FEED
SHE RODE THE MOST WITH ONE DUDE, BLACK HAIR, LITTLE SOUL PATCH. GOT HIS NAME DOWN AS CRANK OR SOMETHING. THEY ALWAYS SEEMED LIKE THEY WERE GOING SOMEWHERE SPECIFIC, BUT NEVER THE SAME PLACE TWICE. AND SHE WAS TOTALLY HANGING ON THIS DUDE, HANDS ALL AROUND HIM.
ROLLO-LIVE VID FEED
SOME PATTERN TO THEIR RIDES, SO I ASSUME THEY WERE GOING BACK TO HIS PAD. SHE ALWAYS LOOKED PRETTY CHUMMY WITH THE DUDES, SO DRAW YOUR OWN CONCLUSIONS THERE.
FINE FEDORAS SINCE 2016
ROLLO-LIVE VID FEED
ONLY ONE OF THOSE MOPED KIDS MADE ME NERVOUS. LITTLE BLACK KID WITH A SHITLOAD OF TATTOOS.
ROLLO-LIVE VID FEED
WEIRDEST THING? WHEN SHE WASN'T WITH THEM, SHE'D LUG AN ARMLOAD OF BOOKS TO THIS CRAPPY LITTLE COFFEESHOP AND READ.
ROLLO-LIVE VID FEED
LOOKED MOSTLY LIKE REPAIR MANUALS AND SOME MAPS AND STUFF. THE ONLY CALLS SHE MADE WERE BACK TO THE OTHER MOPED KIDS, JUST GIVING THEM TECH INFO. AND GET THIS: THEY CALL THEMSELVES THE "MOPED ARMY". AIN'T THAT A JOKE?

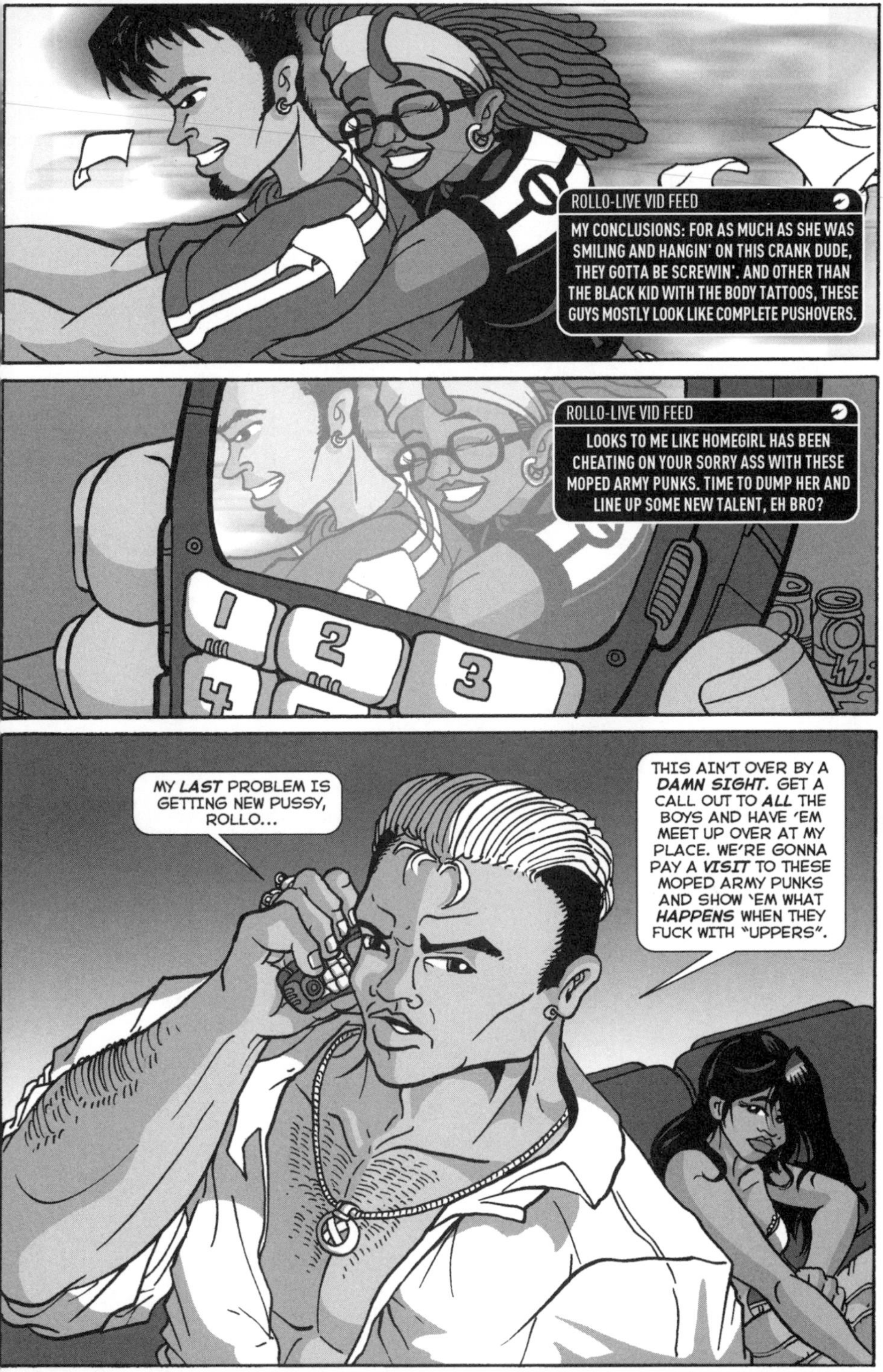
ROLLO-LIVE VID FEED
MY CONCLUSIONS: FOR AS MUCH AS SHE WAS SMILING AND HANGIN' ON THIS CRANK DUDE, THEY GOTTA BE SCREWIN'. AND OTHER THAN THE BLACK KID WITH THE BODY TATTOOS, THESE GUYS MOSTLY LOOK LIKE COMPLETE PUSHOVERS.
ROLLO-LIVE VID FEED
LOOKS TO ME LIKE HOMEGIRL HAS BEEN CHEATING ON YOUR SORRY ASS WITH THESE MOPED ARMY PUNKS. TIME TO DUMP HER AND LINE UP SOME NEW TALENT, EH BRO?
1
2
3
4
MY *LAST* PROBLEM IS GETTING NEW PUSSY, ROLLO...
THIS AIN'T OVER BY A *DAMN SIGHT*. GET A CALL OUT TO *ALL* THE BOYS AND HAVE 'EM MEET UP OVER AT MY PLACE. WE'RE GONNA PAY A *VISIT* TO THESE MOPED ARMY PUNKS AND SHOW 'EM WHAT *HAPPENS* WHEN THEY FUCK WITH "UPPERS".

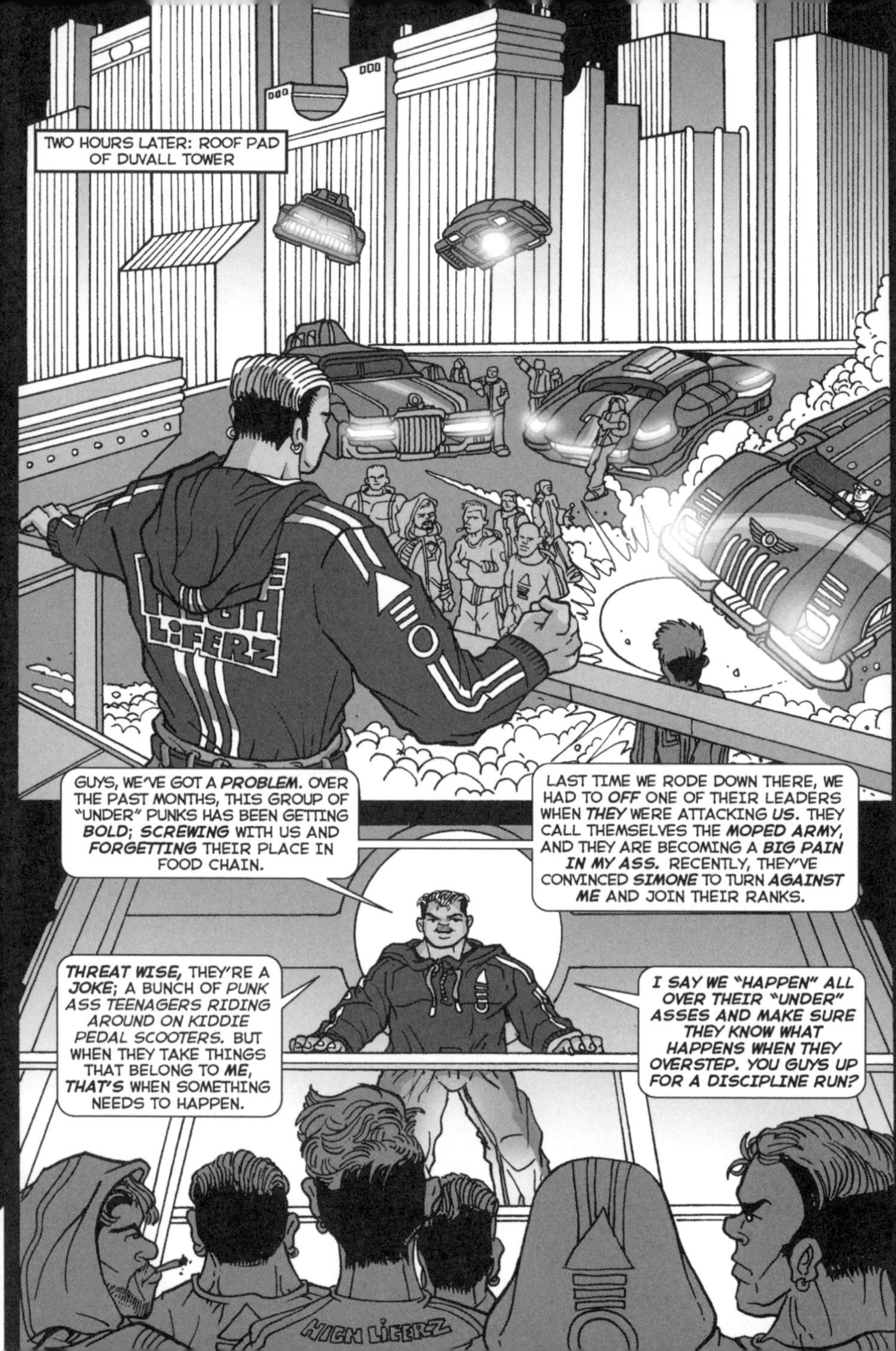
TWO HOURS LATER: ROOF PAD OF DUVALL TOWER
HIGH LiFERZ
GUYS, WE'VE GOT A *PROBLEM*. OVER THE PAST MONTHS, THIS GROUP OF "UNDER" PUNKS HAS BEEN GETTING *BOLD*; *SCREWING* WITH US AND *FORGETTING* THEIR PLACE IN FOOD CHAIN.
LAST TIME WE RODE DOWN THERE, WE HAD TO *OFF* ONE OF THEIR LEADERS WHEN *THEY* WERE ATTACKING *US*. THEY CALL THEMSELVES THE *MOPED ARMY*, AND THEY ARE BECOMING A *BIG PAIN IN MY ASS*. RECENTLY, THEY'VE CONVINCED *SIMONE* TO TURN *AGAINST ME* AND JOIN THEIR RANKS.
THREAT WISE, THEY'RE A *JOKE*; A BUNCH OF *PUNK ASS TEENAGERS RIDING AROUND ON KIDDIE PEDAL SCOOTERS*. BUT WHEN THEY TAKE THINGS THAT BELONG TO *ME*, *THAT'S* WHEN SOMETHING NEEDS TO HAPPEN.
I SAY WE "HAPPEN" ALL OVER THEIR "UNDER" ASSES AND MAKE SURE THEY KNOW WHAT HAPPENS WHEN THEY OVERSTEP. YOU GUYS UP FOR A DISCIPLINE RUN?
HIGH LiFERZ

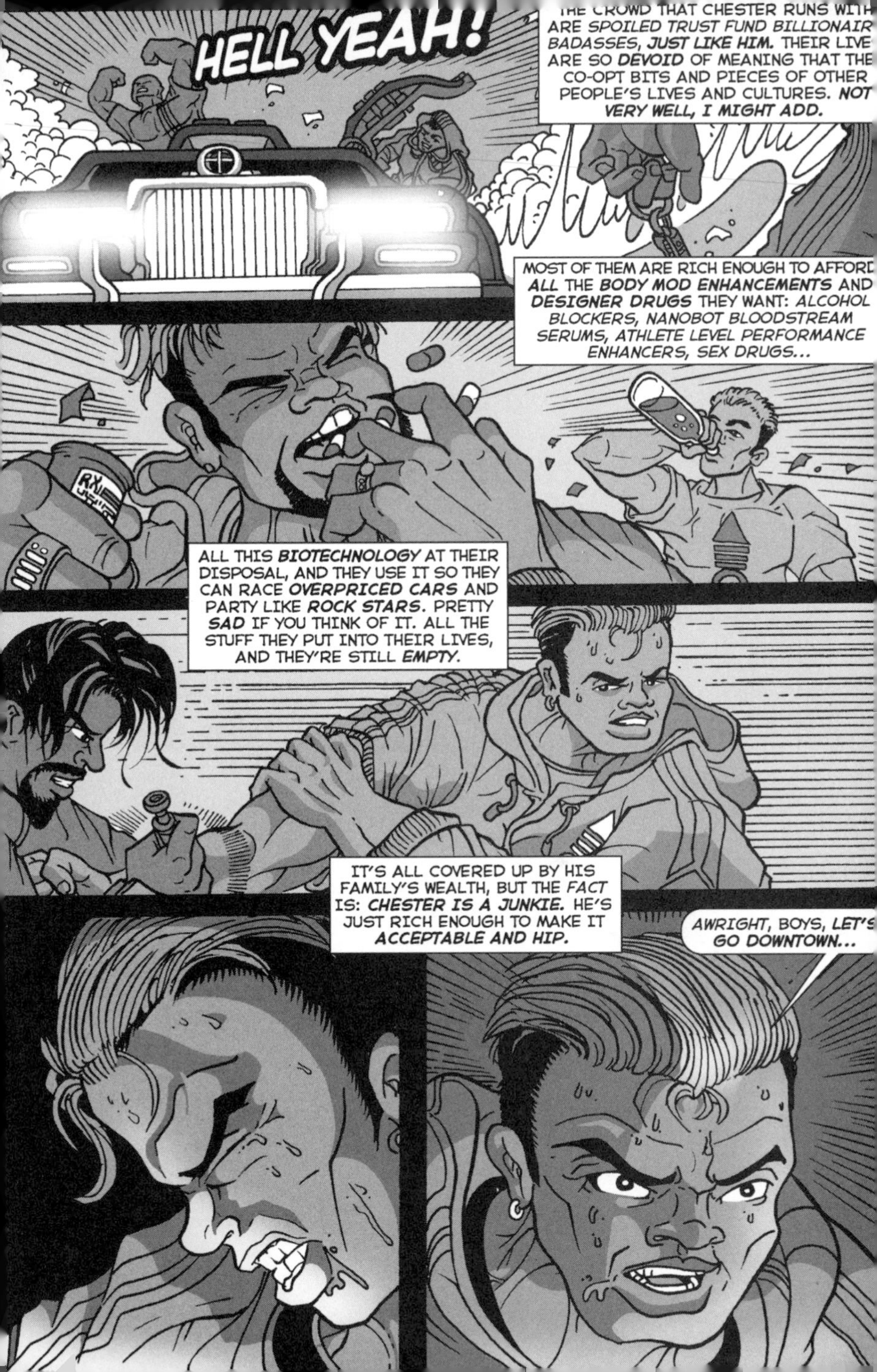
HELL YEAH!
THE CROWD THAT CHESTER RUNS WITH ARE SPOILED TRUST FUND BILLIONAIR BADASSES, JUST LIKE HIM. THEIR LIVE ARE SO DEVOID OF MEANING THAT THE CO-OPT BITS AND PIECES OF OTHER PEOPLE'S LIVES AND CULTURES. NOT VERY WELL, I MIGHT ADD.
MOST OF THEM ARE RICH ENOUGH TO AFFORD ALL THE BODY MOD ENHANCEMENTS AND DESIGNER DRUGS THEY WANT: ALCOHOL BLOCKERS, NANOBOT BLOODSTREAM SERUMS, ATHLETE LEVEL PERFORMANCE ENHANCERS, SEX DRUGS...
ALL THIS BIOTECHNOLOGY AT THEIR DISPOSAL, AND THEY USE IT SO THEY CAN RACE OVERPRICED CARS AND PARTY LIKE ROCK STARS. PRETTY SAD IF YOU THINK OF IT. ALL THE STUFF THEY PUT INTO THEIR LIVES, AND THEY'RE STILL EMPTY.
IT'S ALL COVERED UP BY HIS FAMILY'S WEALTH, BUT THE FACT IS: CHESTER IS A JUNKIE. HE'S JUST RICH ENOUGH TO MAKE IT ACCEPTABLE AND HIP.
AWRIGHT, BOYS, LET'S GO DOWNTOWN...

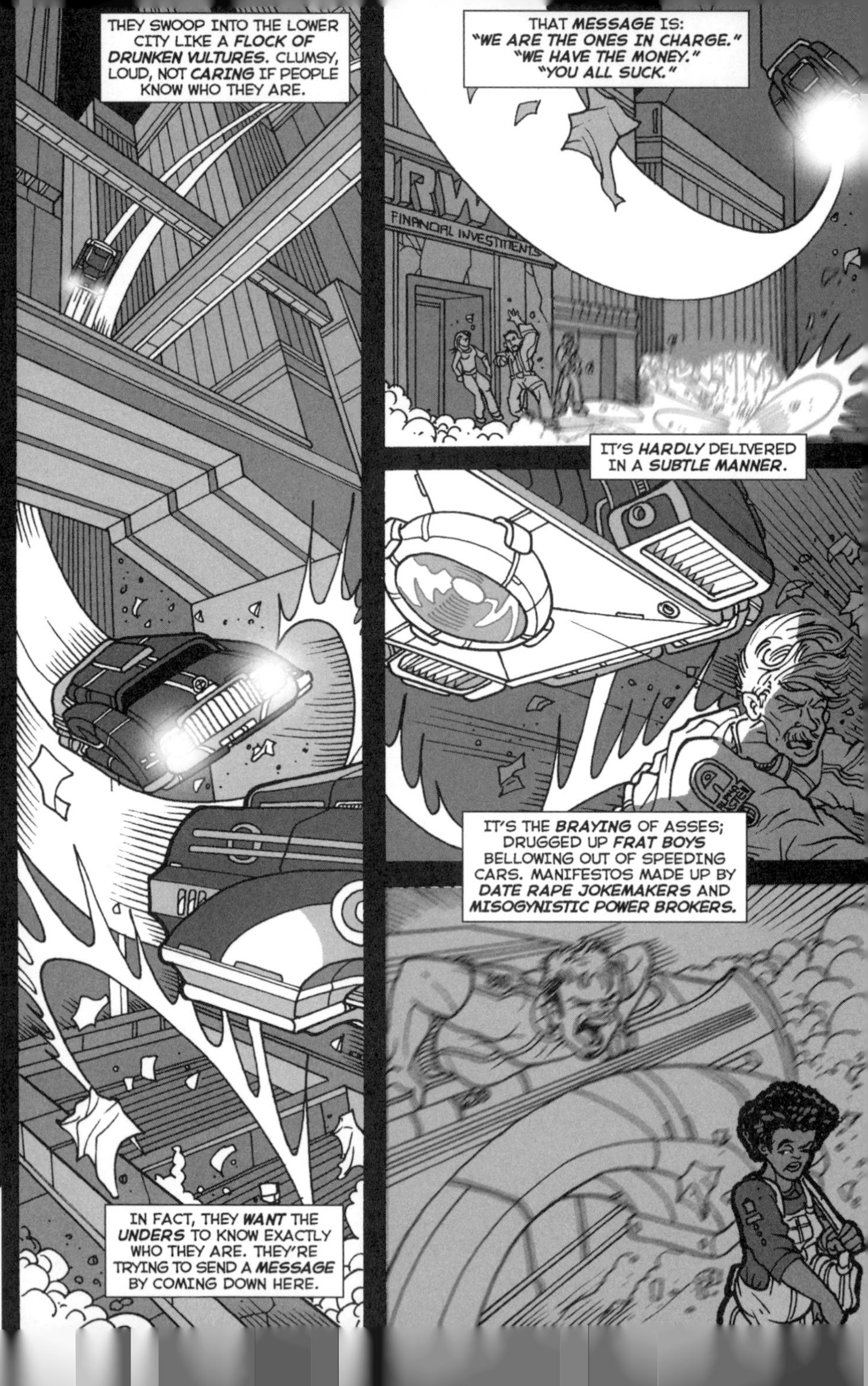
THEY SWOOP INTO THE LOWER CITY LIKE A *FLOCK OF DRUNKEN VULTURES*. CLUMSY, LOUD, NOT *CARING* IF PEOPLE KNOW WHO THEY ARE.
IN FACT, THEY *WANT* THE *UNDERS* TO KNOW EXACTLY WHO THEY ARE. THEY'RE TRYING TO SEND A *MESSAGE* BY COMING DOWN HERE.
THAT *MESSAGE* IS: *"WE ARE THE ONES IN CHARGE." "WE HAVE THE MONEY." "YOU ALL SUCK."*
IT'S *HARDLY* DELIVERED IN A *SUBTLE MANNER*.
IT'S THE *BRAYING* OF ASSES; DRUGGED UP *FRAT BOYS* BELLOWING OUT OF SPEEDING CARS. MANIFESTOS MADE UP BY *DATE RAPE JOKEMAKERS* AND *MISOGYNISTIC POWER BROKERS*.

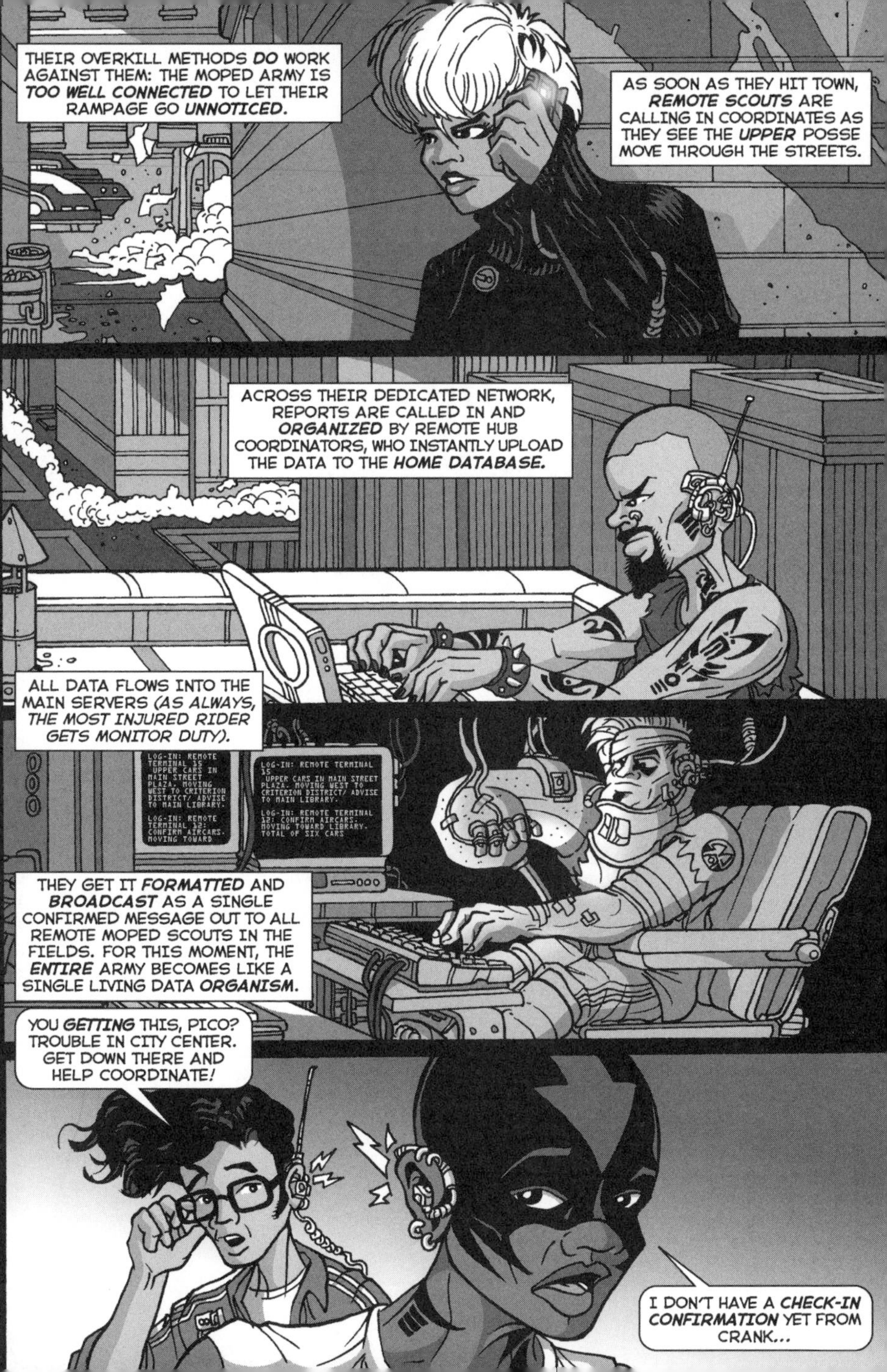
THEIR OVERKILL METHODS DO WORK AGAINST THEM: THE MOPED ARMY IS TOO WELL CONNECTED TO LET THEIR RAMPAGE GO UNNOTICED.
AS SOON AS THEY HIT TOWN, REMOTE SCOUTS ARE CALLING IN COORDINATES AS THEY SEE THE UPPER POSSE MOVE THROUGH THE STREETS.
ACROSS THEIR DEDICATED NETWORK, REPORTS ARE CALLED IN AND ORGANIZED BY REMOTE HUB COORDINATORS, WHO INSTANTLY UPLOAD THE DATA TO THE HOME DATABASE.
ALL DATA FLOWS INTO THE MAIN SERVERS (AS ALWAYS, THE MOST INJURED RIDER GETS MONITOR DUTY).
LOG-IN: REMOTE TERMINAL 15 UPPER CARS IN MAIN STREET PLAZA. MOVING WEST TO CRITERION DISTRICT/ ADVISE TO MAIN LIBRARY.
LOG-IN: REMOTE TERMINAL 12: CONFIRM AIRCARS. MOVING TOWARD
LOG-IN: REMOTE TERMINAL 15 UPPER CARS IN MAIN STREET PLAZA. MOVING WEST TO CRITERION DISTRICT/ ADVISE TO MAIN LIBRARY.
LOG-IN: REMOTE TERMINAL 12: CONFIRM AIRCARS. MOVING TOWARD LIBRARY. TOTAL OF SIX CARS
THEY GET IT FORMATTED AND BROADCAST AS A SINGLE CONFIRMED MESSAGE OUT TO ALL REMOTE MOPED SCOUTS IN THE FIELDS. FOR THIS MOMENT, THE ENTIRE ARMY BECOMES LIKE A SINGLE LIVING DATA ORGANISM.
YOU GETTING THIS, PICO? TROUBLE IN CITY CENTER. GET DOWN THERE AND HELP COORDINATE!
I DON'T HAVE A CHECK-IN CONFIRMATION YET FROM CRANK...

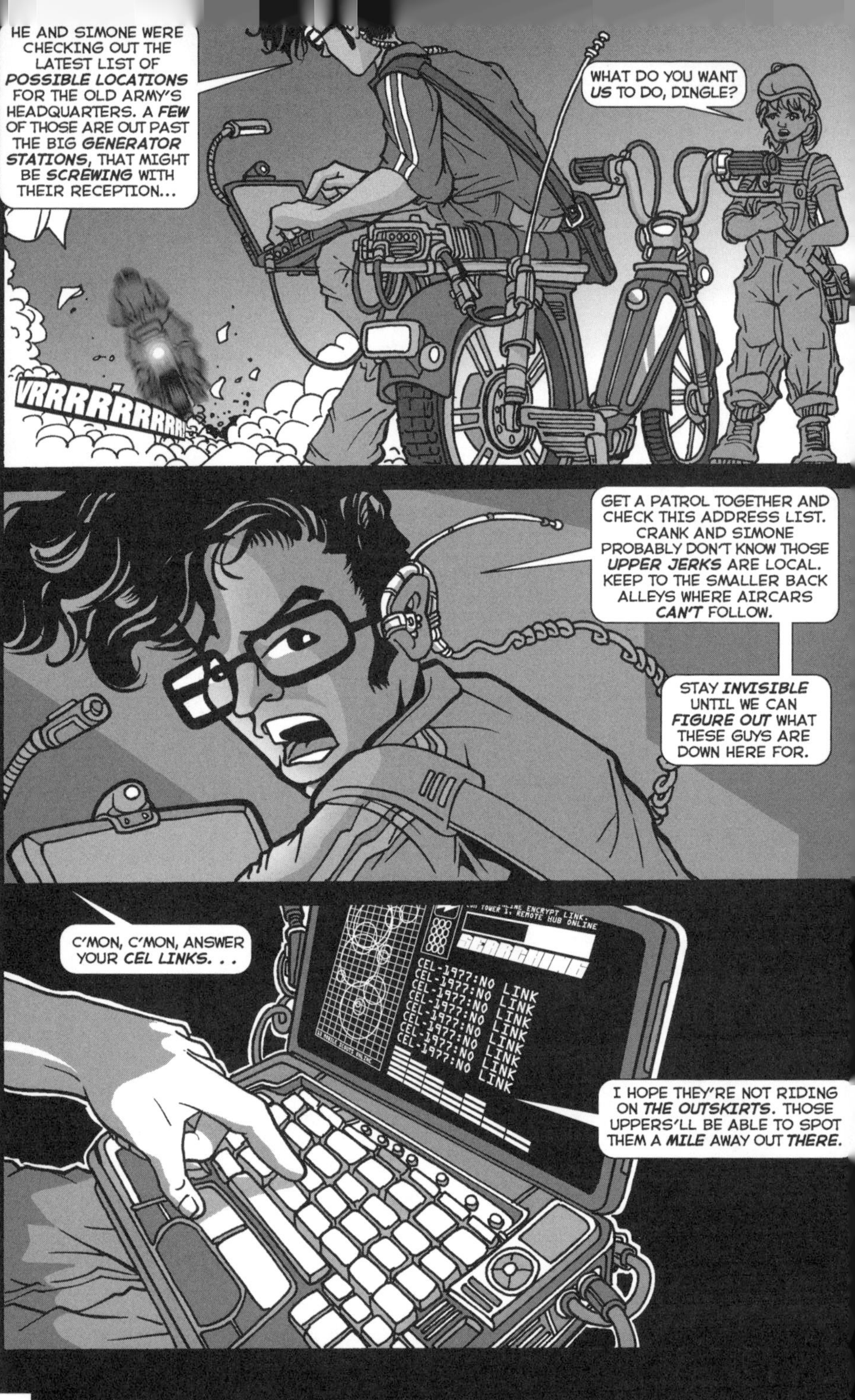
HE AND SIMONE WERE CHECKING OUT THE LATEST LIST OF POSSIBLE LOCATIONS FOR THE OLD ARMY'S HEADQUARTERS. A FEW OF THOSE ARE OUT PAST THE BIG GENERATOR STATIONS, THAT MIGHT BE SCREWING WITH THEIR RECEPTION...
WHAT DO YOU WANT US TO DO, DINGLE?
VRRRRRRRRRR!
GET A PATROL TOGETHER AND CHECK THIS ADDRESS LIST. CRANK AND SIMONE PROBABLY DON'T KNOW THOSE UPPER JERKS ARE LOCAL. KEEP TO THE SMALLER BACK ALLEYS WHERE AIRCARS CAN'T FOLLOW.
STAY INVISIBLE UNTIL WE CAN FIGURE OUT WHAT THESE GUYS ARE DOWN HERE FOR.
C'MON, C'MON, ANSWER YOUR CEL LINKS. . .
CEL-1977:NO LINK
CEL-1977:NO LINK
CEL-1977:NO LINK
CEL-1977:NO LINK
CEL-1977:NO LINK
CEL-1977:NO LINK
CEL-1977:NO LINK
CEL-1977:NO LINK
I HOPE THEY'RE NOT RIDING ON THE OUTSKIRTS. THOSE UPPERS'LL BE ABLE TO SPOT THEM A MILE AWAY OUT THERE.

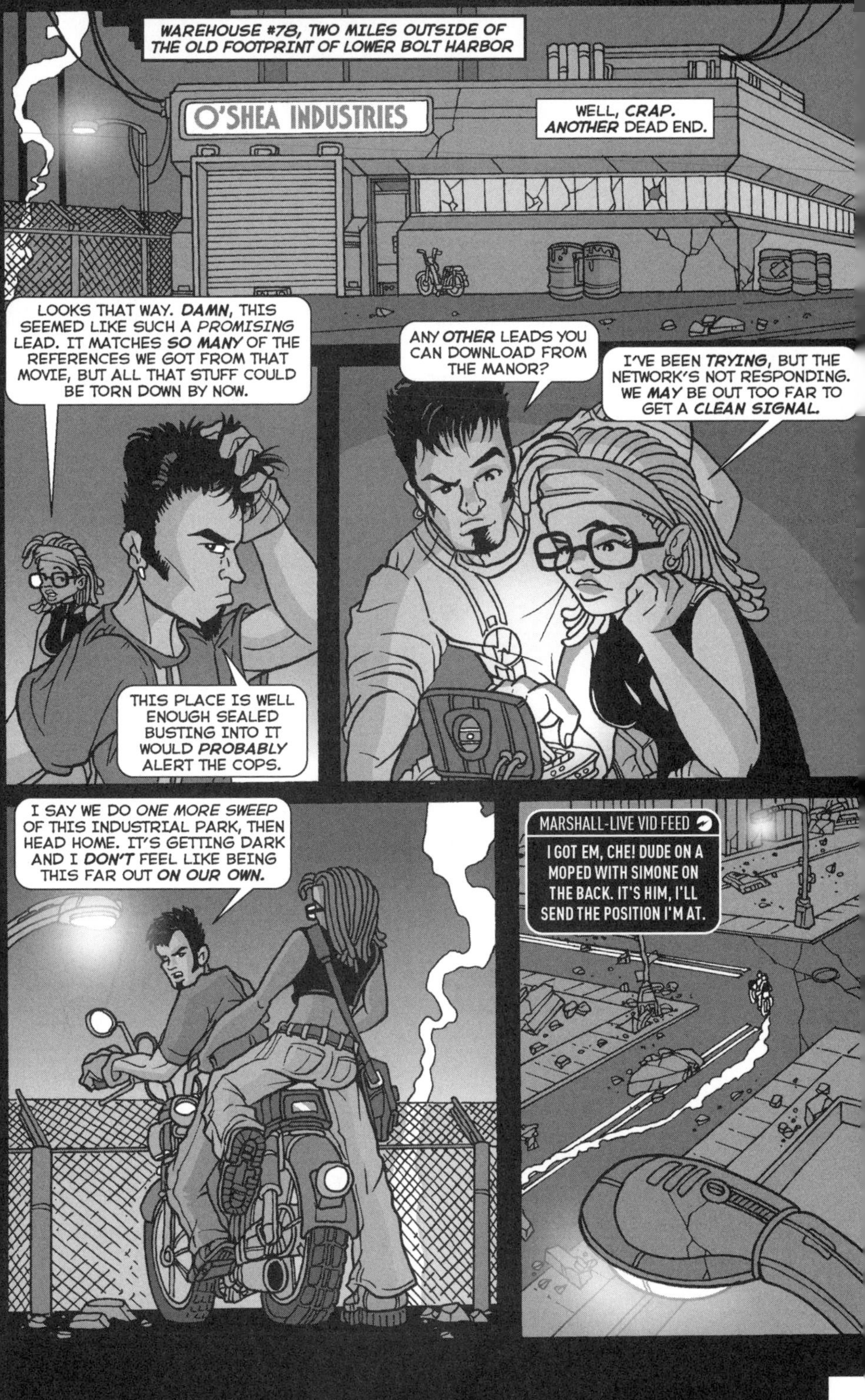
WAREHOUSE #78, TWO MILES OUTSIDE OF THE OLD FOOTPRINT OF LOWER BOLT HARBOR
O'SHEA INDUSTRIES
WELL, CRAP. ANOTHER DEAD END.
LOOKS THAT WAY. DAMN, THIS SEEMED LIKE SUCH A PROMISING LEAD. IT MATCHES SO MANY OF THE REFERENCES WE GOT FROM THAT MOVIE, BUT ALL THAT STUFF COULD BE TORN DOWN BY NOW.
THIS PLACE IS WELL ENOUGH SEALED BUSTING INTO IT WOULD PROBABLY ALERT THE COPS.
ANY OTHER LEADS YOU CAN DOWNLOAD FROM THE MANOR?
I'VE BEEN TRYING, BUT THE NETWORK'S NOT RESPONDING. WE MAY BE OUT TOO FAR TO GET A CLEAN SIGNAL.
I SAY WE DO ONE MORE SWEEP OF THIS INDUSTRIAL PARK, THEN HEAD HOME. IT'S GETTING DARK AND I DON'T FEEL LIKE BEING THIS FAR OUT ON OUR OWN.
MARSHALL-LIVE VID FEED
I GOT EM, CHE! DUDE ON A MOPED WITH SIMONE ON THE BACK. IT'S HIM, I'LL SEND THE POSITION I'M AT.

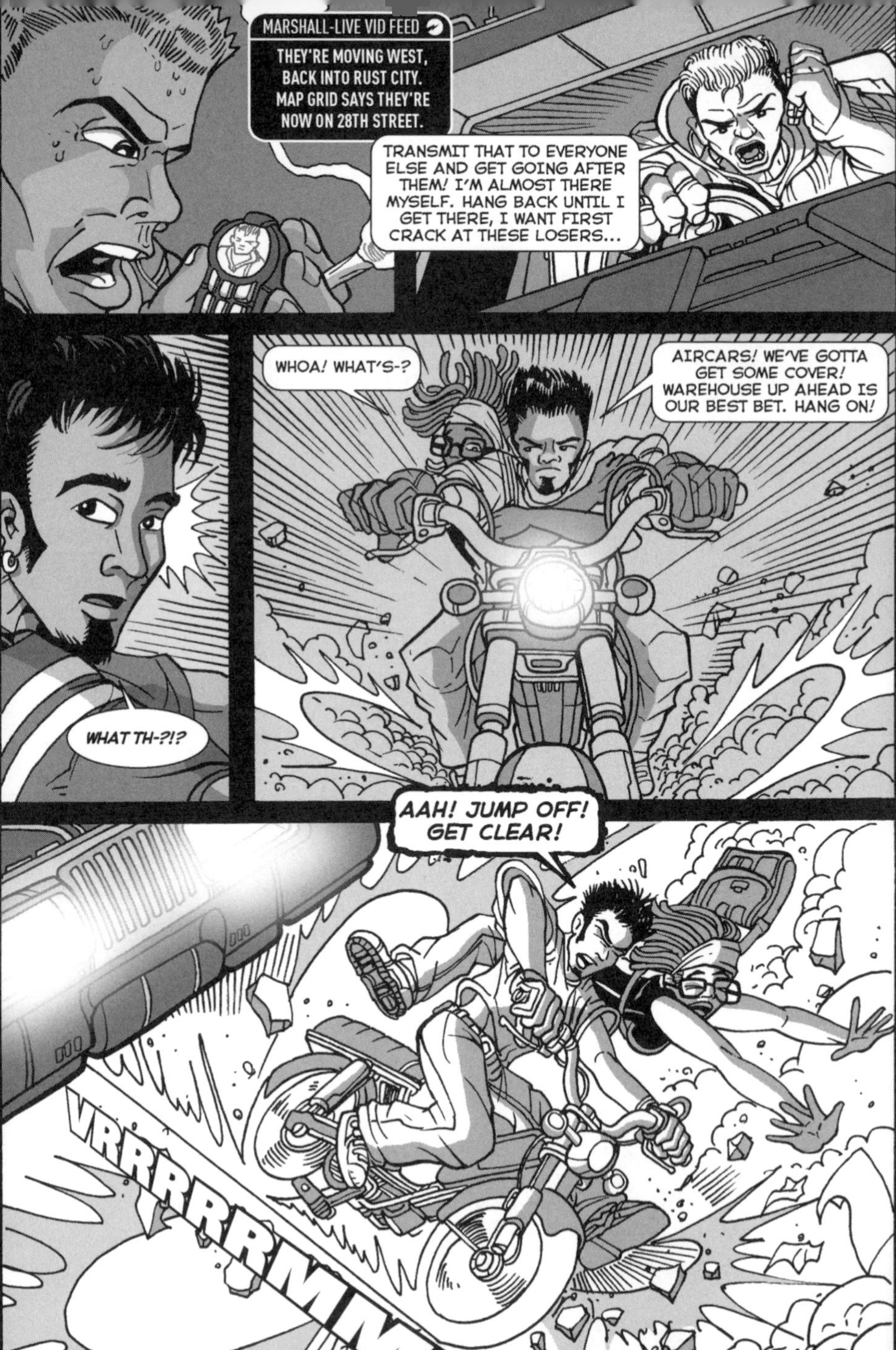
MARSHALL-LIVE VID FEED
THEY'RE MOVING WEST, BACK INTO RUST CITY. MAP GRID SAYS THEY'RE NOW ON 28TH STREET.
TRANSMIT THAT TO EVERYONE ELSE AND GET GOING AFTER THEM! I'M ALMOST THERE MYSELF. HANG BACK UNTIL I GET THERE, I WANT FIRST CRACK AT THESE LOSERS...
WHAT TH-?!?
WHOA! WHAT'S-?
AIRCARS! WE'VE GOTTA GET SOME COVER! WAREHOUSE UP AHEAD IS OUR BEST BET. HANG ON!
AAH! JUMP OFF! GET CLEAR!
VRRRRRMMM

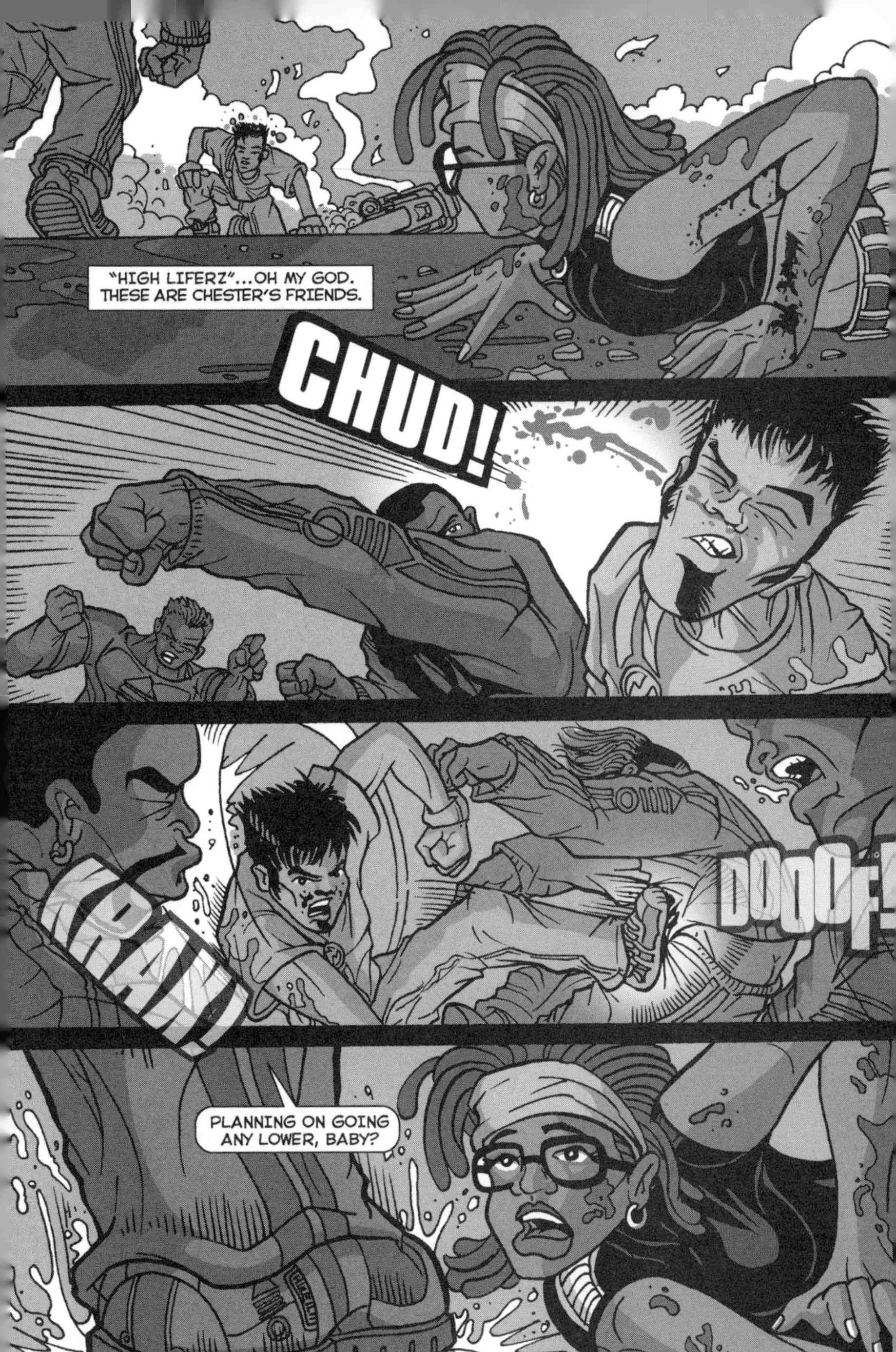
"HIGH LIFERZ"...OH MY GOD. THESE ARE CHESTER'S FRIENDS.
CHUD!
DOOOF
PLANNING ON GOING ANY LOWER, BABY?

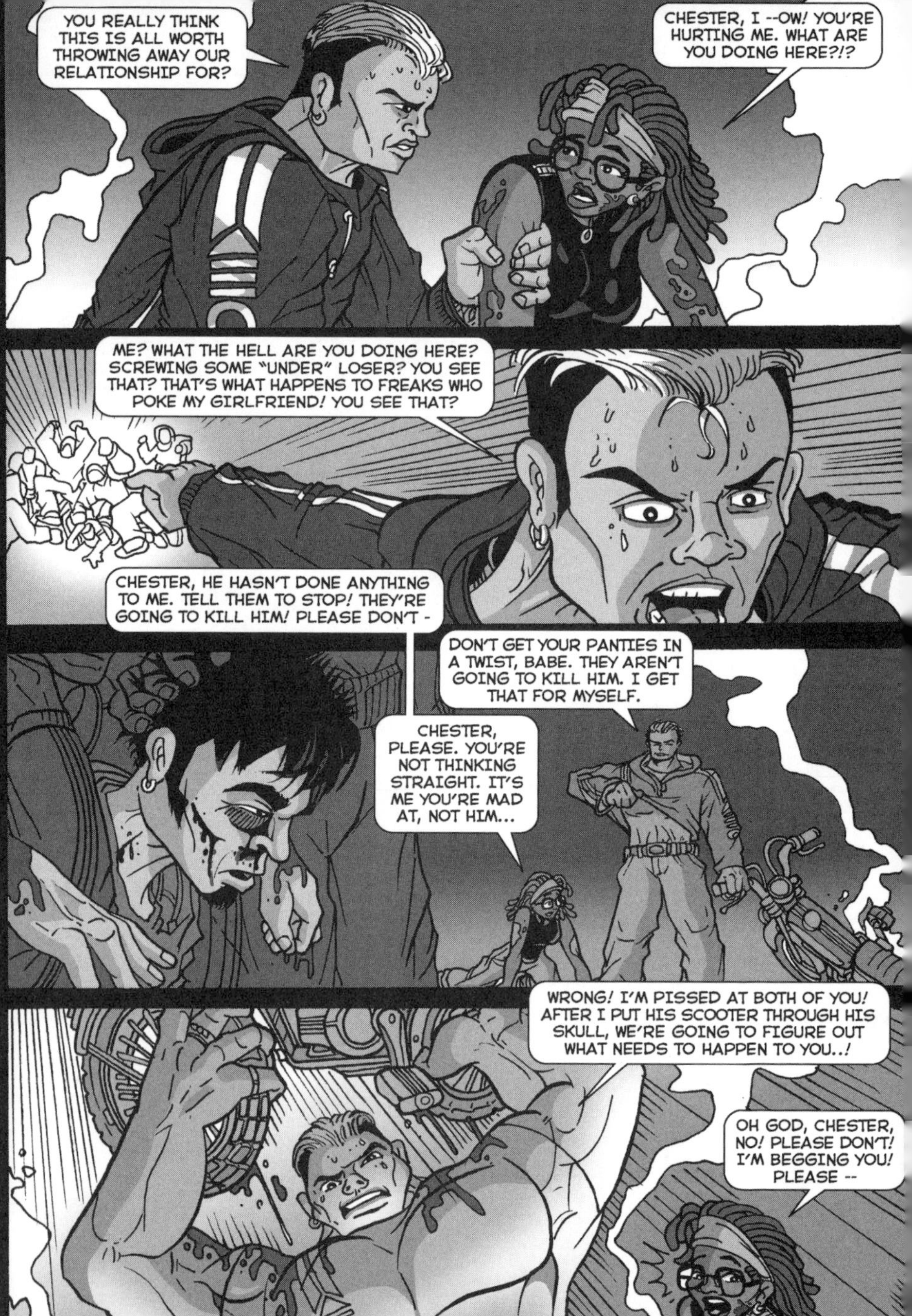
YOU REALLY THINK THIS IS ALL WORTH THROWING AWAY OUR RELATIONSHIP FOR?
CHESTER, I --OW! YOU'RE HURTING ME. WHAT ARE YOU DOING HERE?!?
ME? WHAT THE HELL ARE YOU DOING HERE? SCREWING SOME "UNDER" LOSER? YOU SEE THAT? THAT'S WHAT HAPPENS TO FREAKS WHO POKE MY GIRLFRIEND! YOU SEE THAT?
CHESTER, HE HASN'T DONE ANYTHING TO ME. TELL THEM TO STOP! THEY'RE GOING TO KILL HIM! PLEASE DON'T -
DON'T GET YOUR PANTIES IN A TWIST, BABE. THEY AREN'T GOING TO KILL HIM. I GET THAT FOR MYSELF.
CHESTER, PLEASE. YOU'RE NOT THINKING STRAIGHT. IT'S ME YOU'RE MAD AT, NOT HIM...
WRONG! I'M PISSED AT BOTH OF YOU! AFTER I PUT HIS SCOOTER THROUGH HIS SKULL, WE'RE GOING TO FIGURE OUT WHAT NEEDS TO HAPPEN TO YOU..!
OH GOD, CHESTER, NO! PLEASE DON'T! I'M BEGGING YOU! PLEASE --

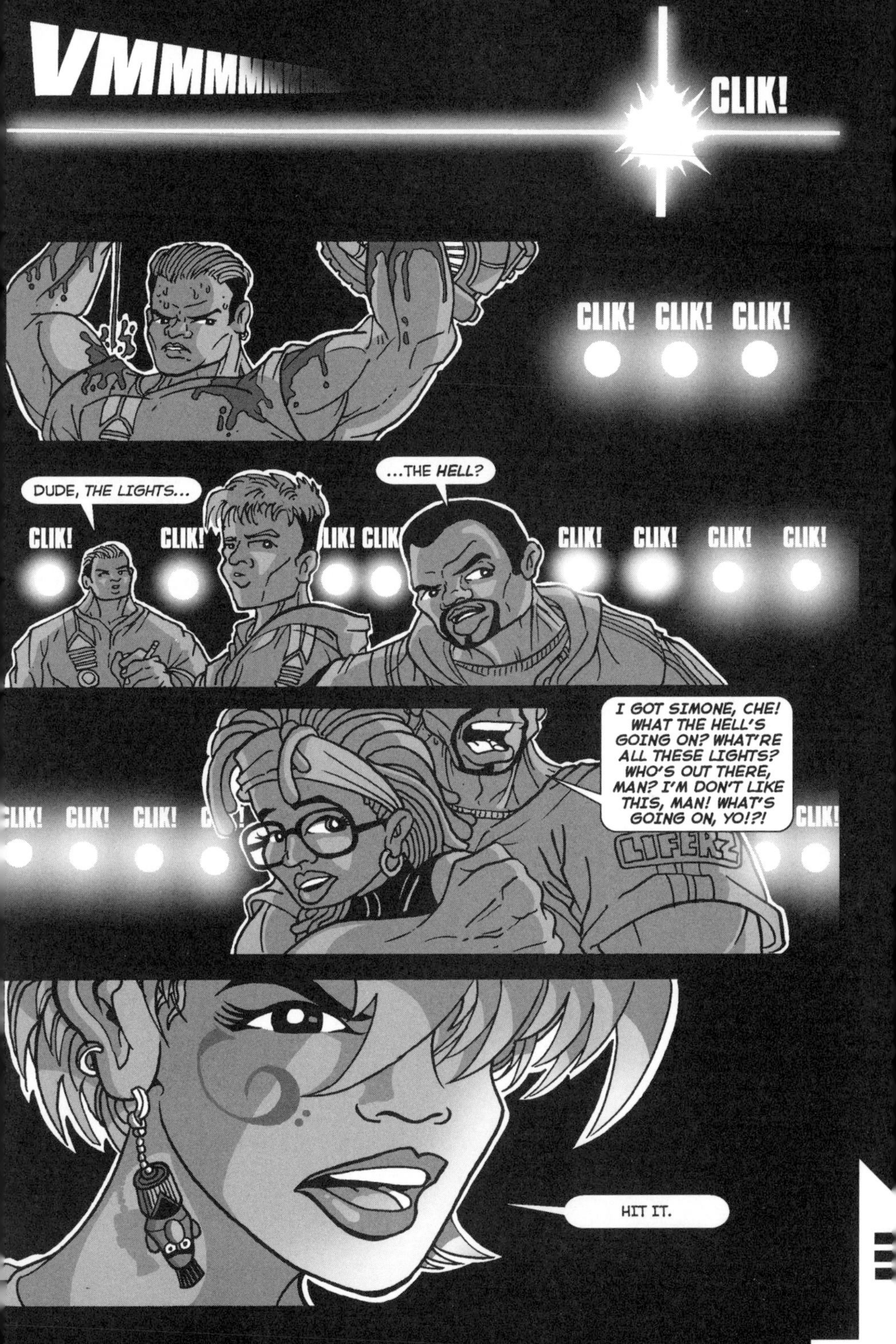
VMMMMMMMM
CLIK!
CLIK! CLIK! CLIK!
DUDE, THE LIGHTS...
CLIK!
CLIK!
...THE HELL?
CLIK! CLIK! CLIK! CLIK!
CLIK! CLIK! CLIK!
I GOT SIMONE, CHE! WHAT THE HELL'S GOING ON? WHAT'RE ALL THESE LIGHTS? WHO'S OUT THERE, MAN? I'M DON'T LIKE THIS, MAN! WHAT'S GOING ON, YO!?!
LIFERZ
CLIK!
HIT IT.

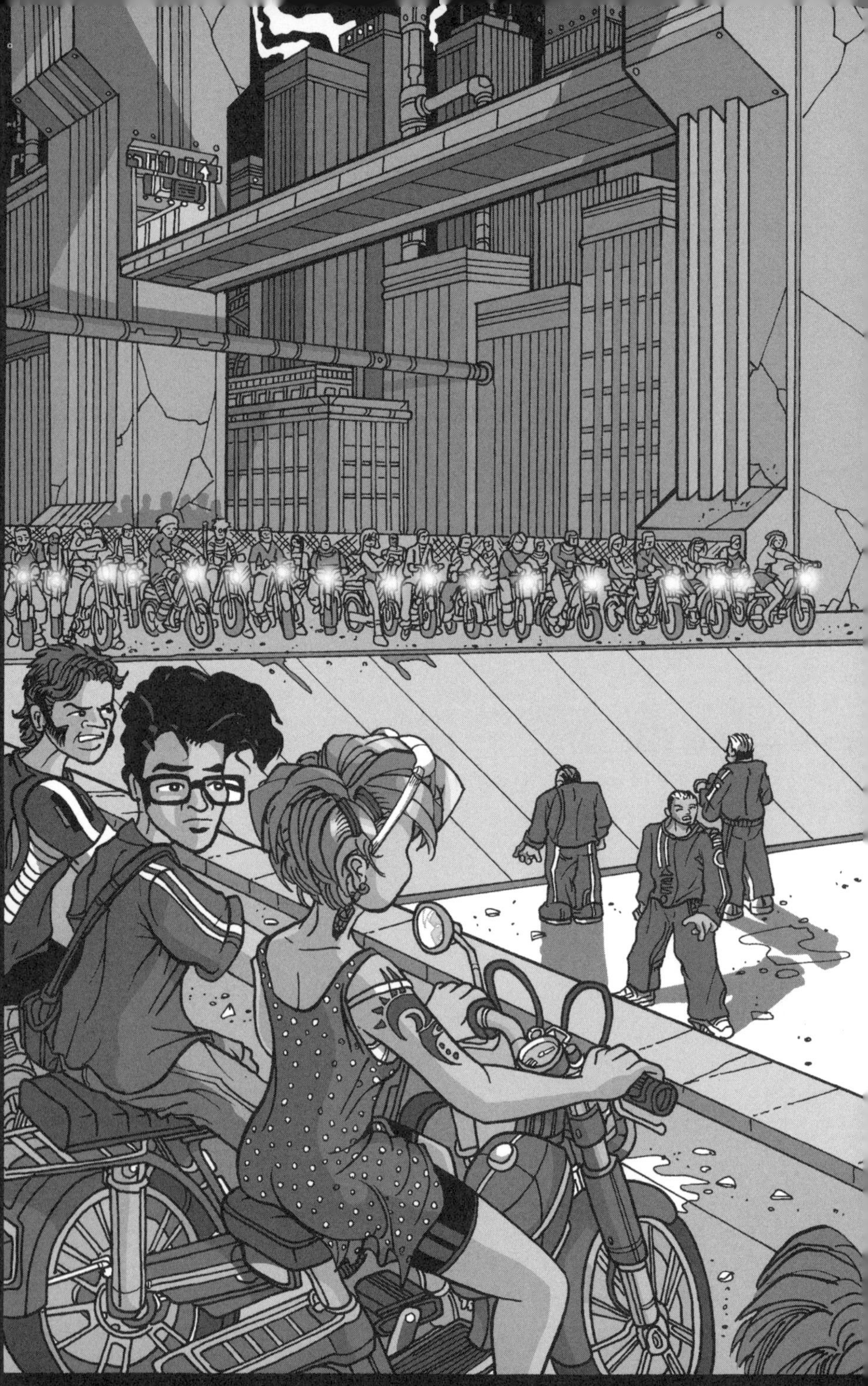

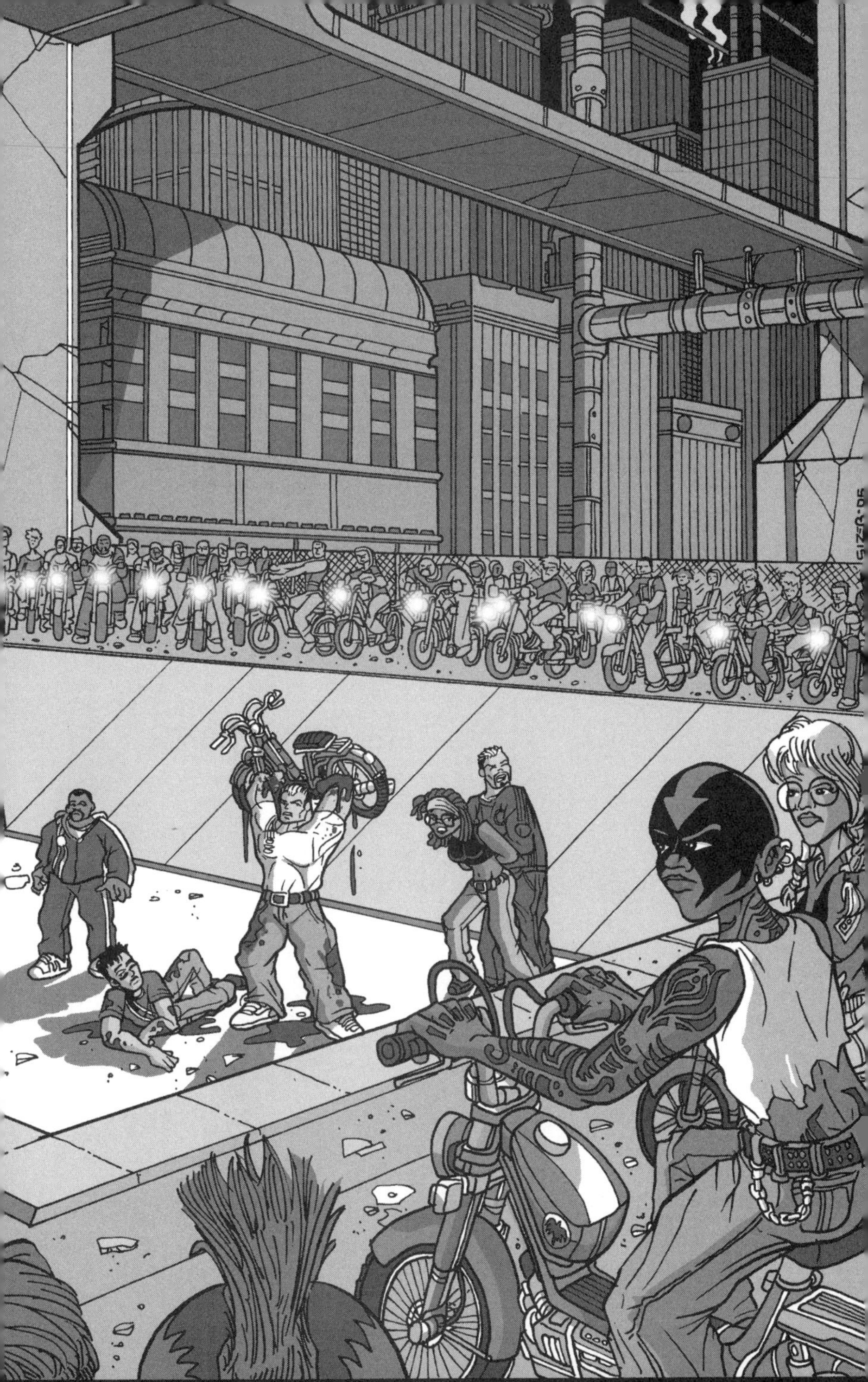

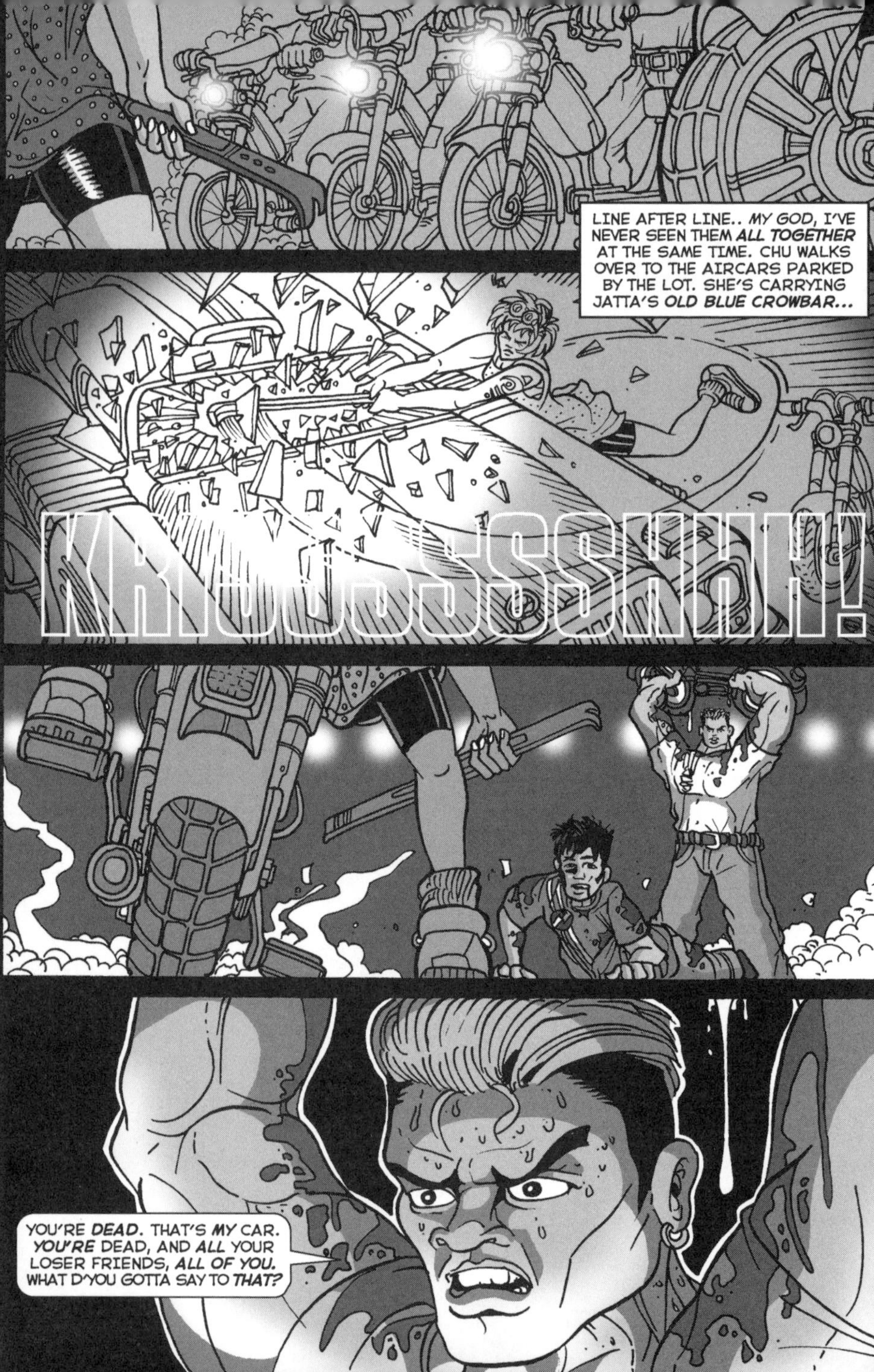

LINE AFTER LINE.. MY GOD, I'VE NEVER SEEN THEM ALL TOGETHER AT THE SAME TIME. CHU WALKS OVER TO THE AIRCARS PARKED BY THE LOT. SHE'S CARRYING JATTA'S OLD BLUE CROWBAR...
KRUSSSHHH!
YOU'RE DEAD. THAT'S MY CAR. YOU'RE DEAD, AND ALL YOUR LOSER FRIENDS, ALL OF YOU. WHAT D'YOU GOTTA SAY TO THAT?

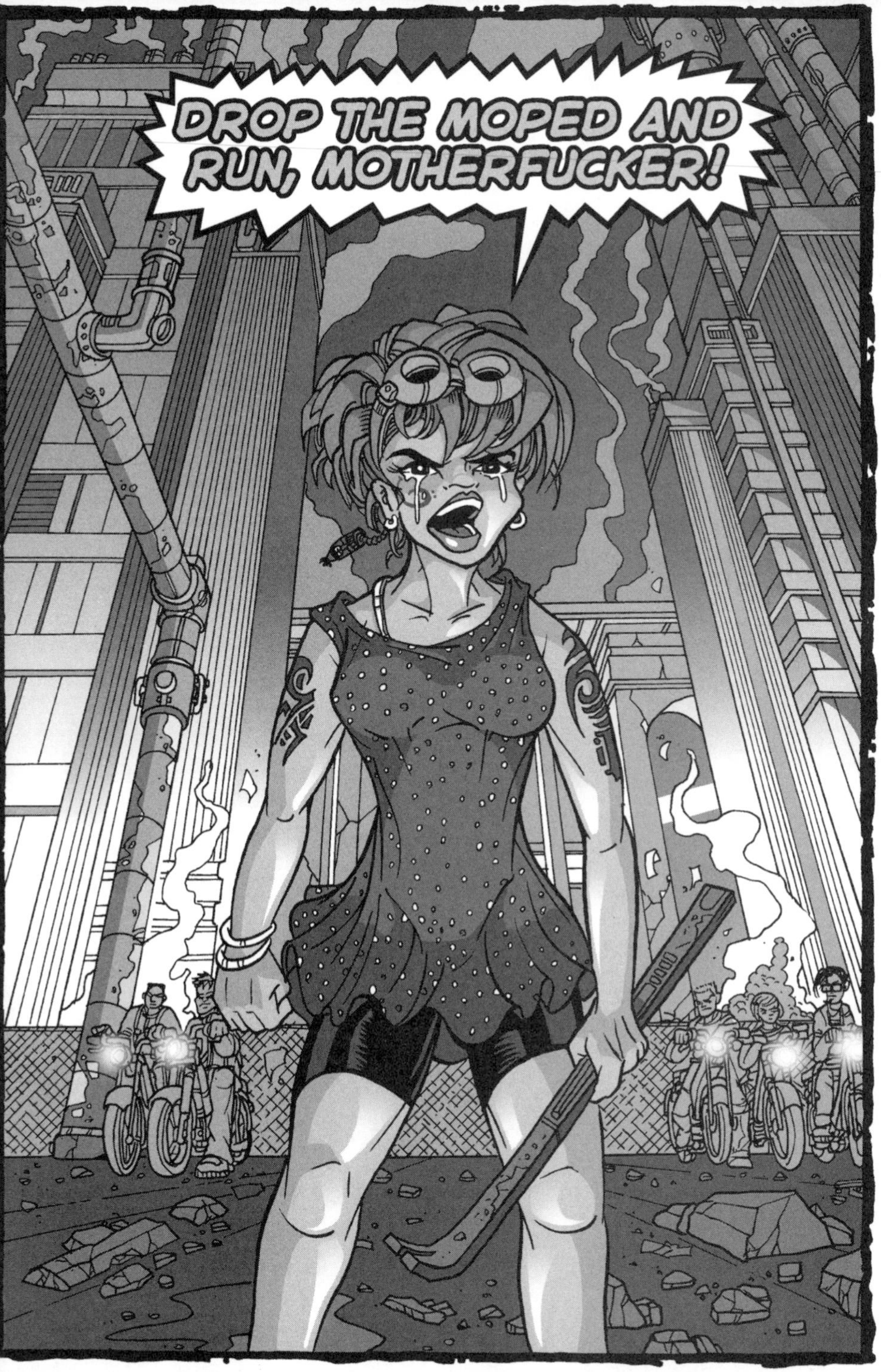
DROP THE MOPED AND RUN, MOTHERFUCKER!

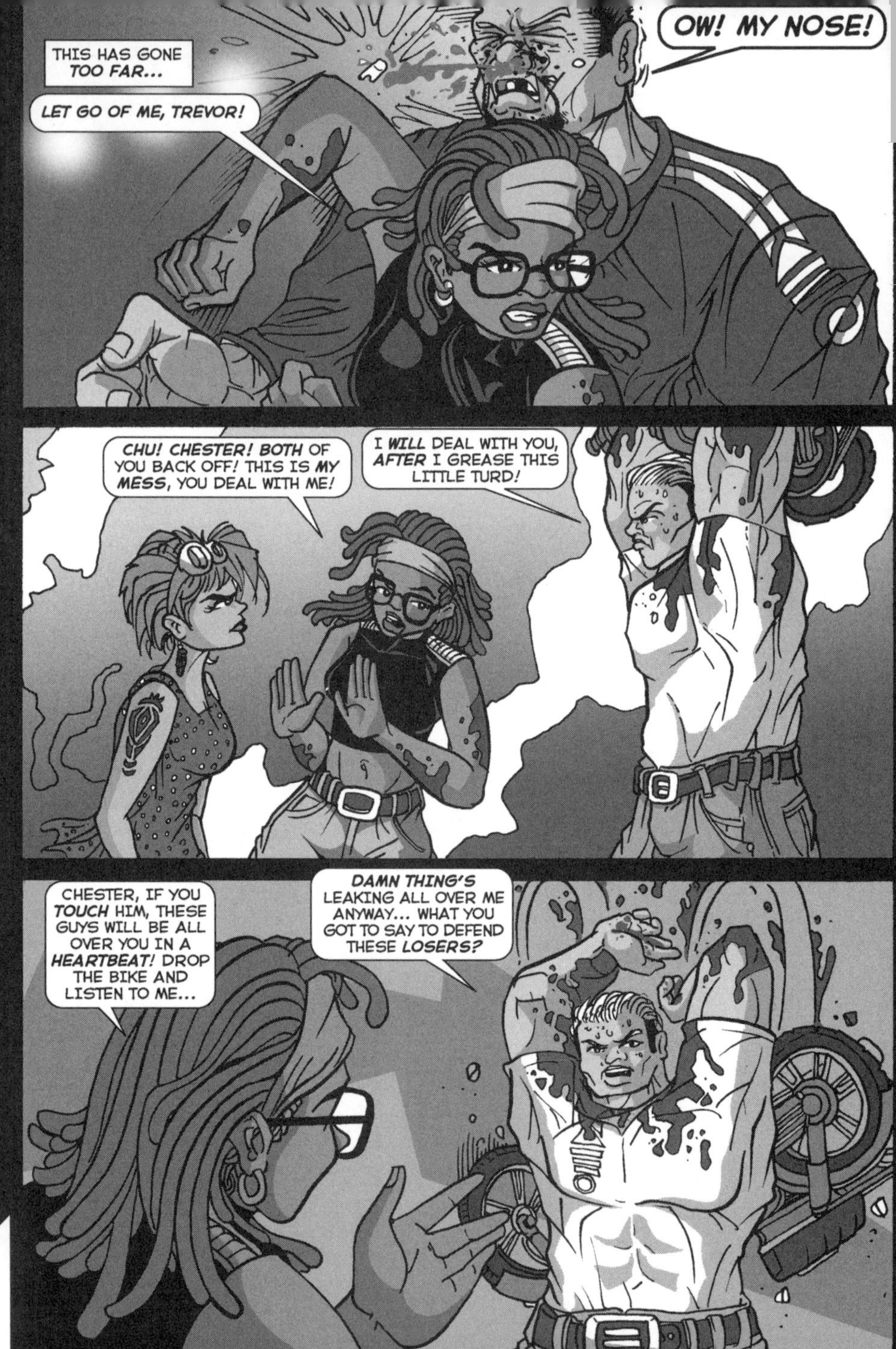

THIS HAS GONE TOO FAR...
LET GO OF ME, TREVOR!
OW! MY NOSE!
CHU! CHESTER! BOTH OF YOU BACK OFF! THIS IS MY MESS, YOU DEAL WITH ME!
I WILL DEAL WITH YOU, AFTER I GREASE THIS LITTLE TURD!
CHESTER, IF YOU TOUCH HIM, THESE GUYS WILL BE ALL OVER YOU IN A HEARTBEAT! DROP THE BIKE AND LISTEN TO ME...
DAMN THING'S LEAKING ALL OVER ME ANYWAY... WHAT YOU GOT TO SAY TO DEFEND THESE LOSERS?

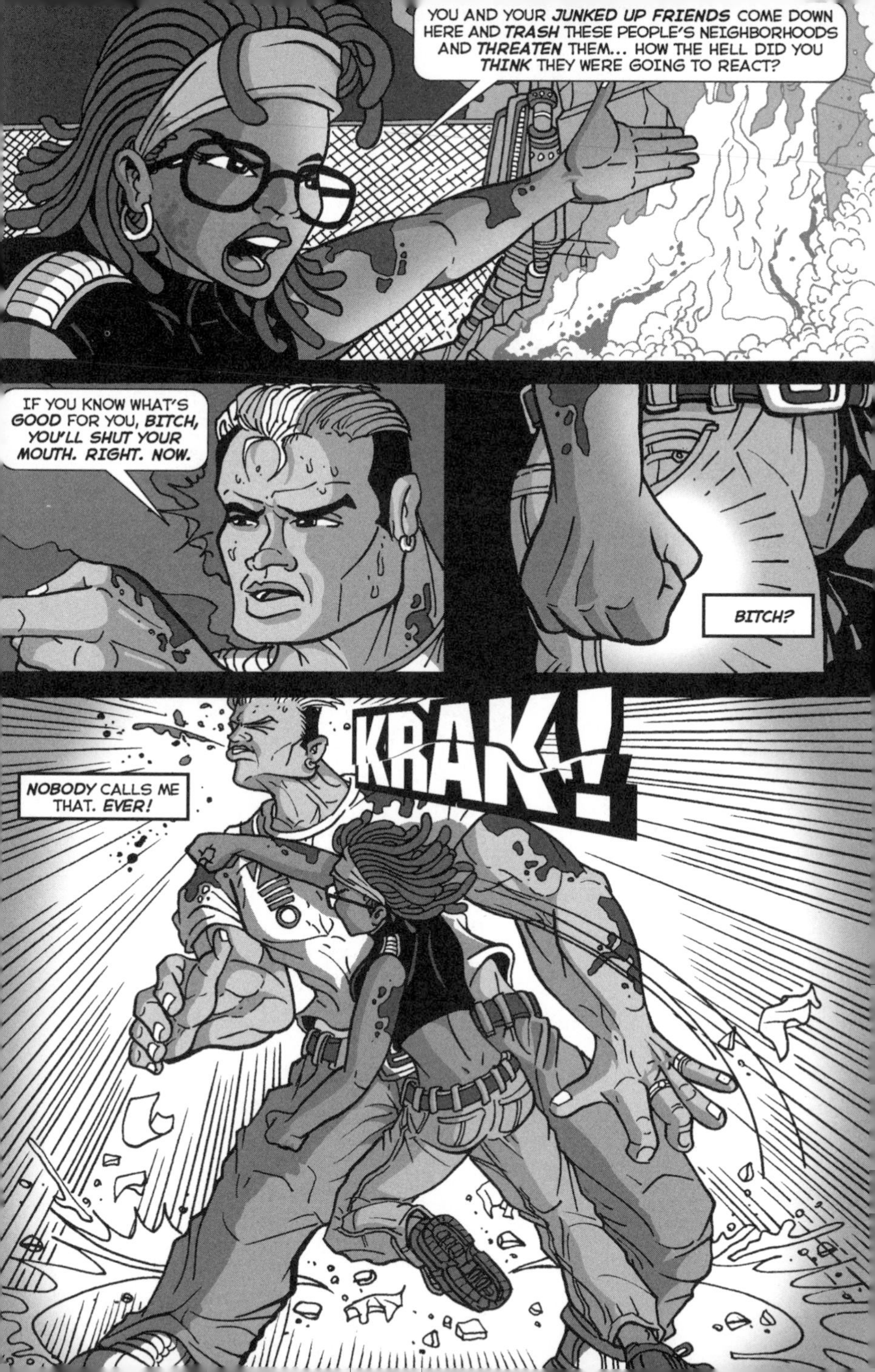
YOU AND YOUR JUNKED UP FRIENDS COME DOWN HERE AND TRASH THESE PEOPLE'S NEIGHBORHOODS AND THREATEN THEM... HOW THE HELL DID YOU THINK THEY WERE GOING TO REACT?
IF YOU KNOW WHAT'S GOOD FOR YOU, BITCH, YOU'LL SHUT YOUR MOUTH. RIGHT. NOW.
BITCH?
KRAK!
NOBODY CALLS ME THAT. EVER!

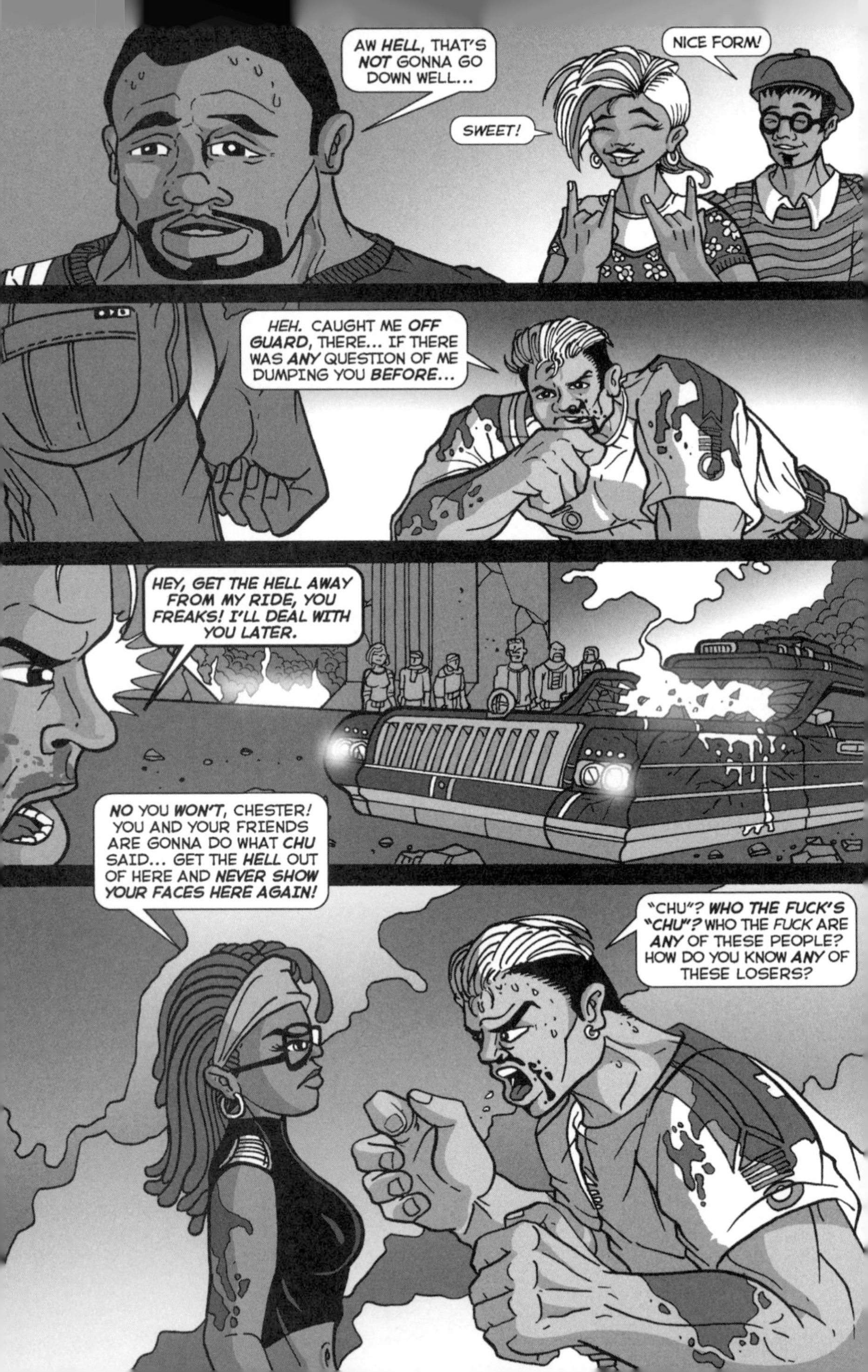
AW HELL, THAT'S NOT GONNA GO DOWN WELL...
SWEET!
NICE FORM!
HEH. CAUGHT ME OFF GUARD, THERE... IF THERE WAS ANY QUESTION OF ME DUMPING YOU BEFORE...
HEY, GET THE HELL AWAY FROM MY RIDE, YOU FREAKS! I'LL DEAL WITH YOU LATER.
NO YOU WON'T, CHESTER! YOU AND YOUR FRIENDS ARE GONNA DO WHAT CHU SAID... GET THE HELL OUT OF HERE AND NEVER SHOW YOUR FACES HERE AGAIN!
"CHU"? WHO THE FUCK'S "CHU"? WHO THE FUCK ARE ANY OF THESE PEOPLE? HOW DO YOU KNOW ANY OF THESE LOSERS?

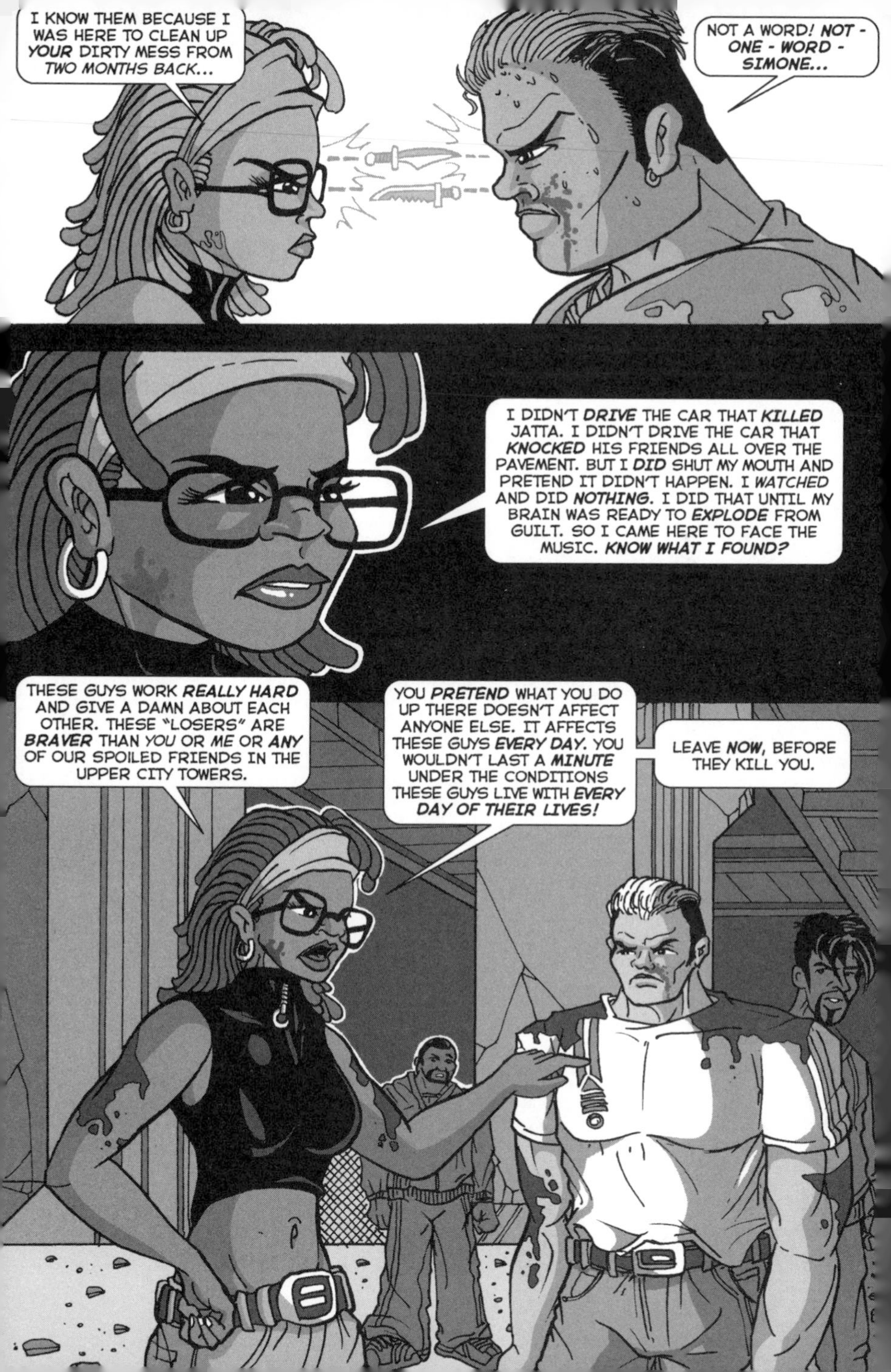
I KNOW THEM BECAUSE I WAS HERE TO CLEAN UP YOUR DIRTY MESS FROM TWO MONTHS BACK...
NOT A WORD! NOT - ONE - WORD - SIMONE...
I DIDN'T DRIVE THE CAR THAT KILLED JATTA. I DIDN'T DRIVE THE CAR THAT KNOCKED HIS FRIENDS ALL OVER THE PAVEMENT. BUT I DID SHUT MY MOUTH AND PRETEND IT DIDN'T HAPPEN. I WATCHED AND DID NOTHING. I DID THAT UNTIL MY BRAIN WAS READY TO EXPLODE FROM GUILT. SO I CAME HERE TO FACE THE MUSIC. KNOW WHAT I FOUND?
THESE GUYS WORK REALLY HARD AND GIVE A DAMN ABOUT EACH OTHER. THESE "LOSERS" ARE BRAVER THAN YOU OR ME OR ANY OF OUR SPOILED FRIENDS IN THE UPPER CITY TOWERS.
YOU PRETEND WHAT YOU DO UP THERE DOESN'T AFFECT ANYONE ELSE. IT AFFECTS THESE GUYS EVERY DAY. YOU WOULDN'T LAST A MINUTE UNDER THE CONDITIONS THESE GUYS LIVE WITH EVERY DAY OF THEIR LIVES!
LEAVE NOW, BEFORE THEY KILL YOU.

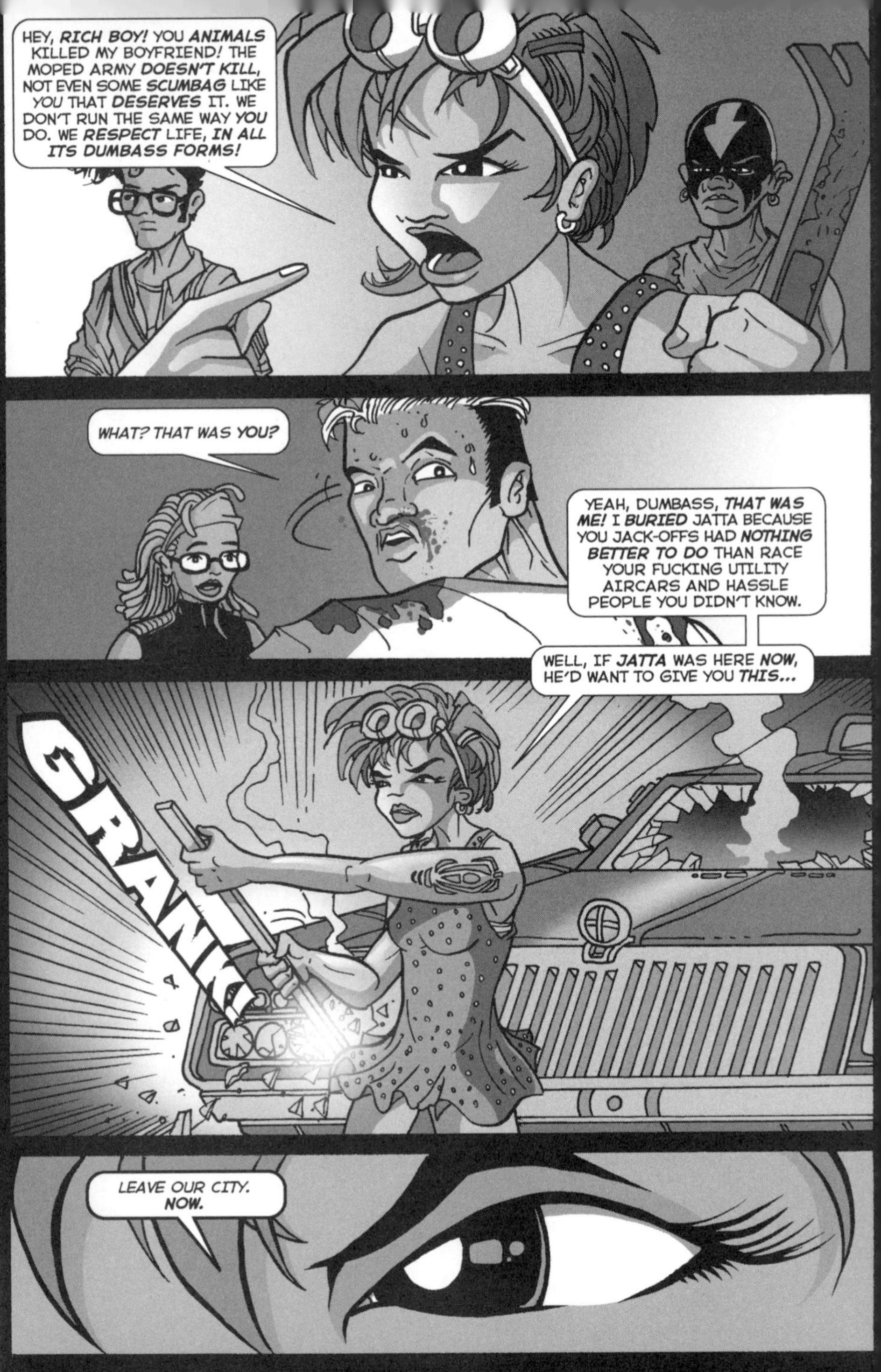
HEY, RICH BOY! YOU ANIMALS KILLED MY BOYFRIEND! THE MOPED ARMY DOESN'T KILL, NOT EVEN SOME SCUMBAG LIKE YOU THAT DESERVES IT. WE DON'T RUN THE SAME WAY YOU DO. WE RESPECT LIFE, IN ALL ITS DUMBASS FORMS!
WHAT? THAT WAS YOU?
YEAH, DUMBASS, THAT WAS ME! I BURIED JATTA BECAUSE YOU JACK-OFFS HAD NOTHING BETTER TO DO THAN RACE YOUR FUCKING UTILITY AIRCARS AND HASSLE PEOPLE YOU DIDN'T KNOW.
WELL, IF JATTA WAS HERE NOW, HE'D WANT TO GIVE YOU THIS...
GRANK
LEAVE OUR CITY. NOW.

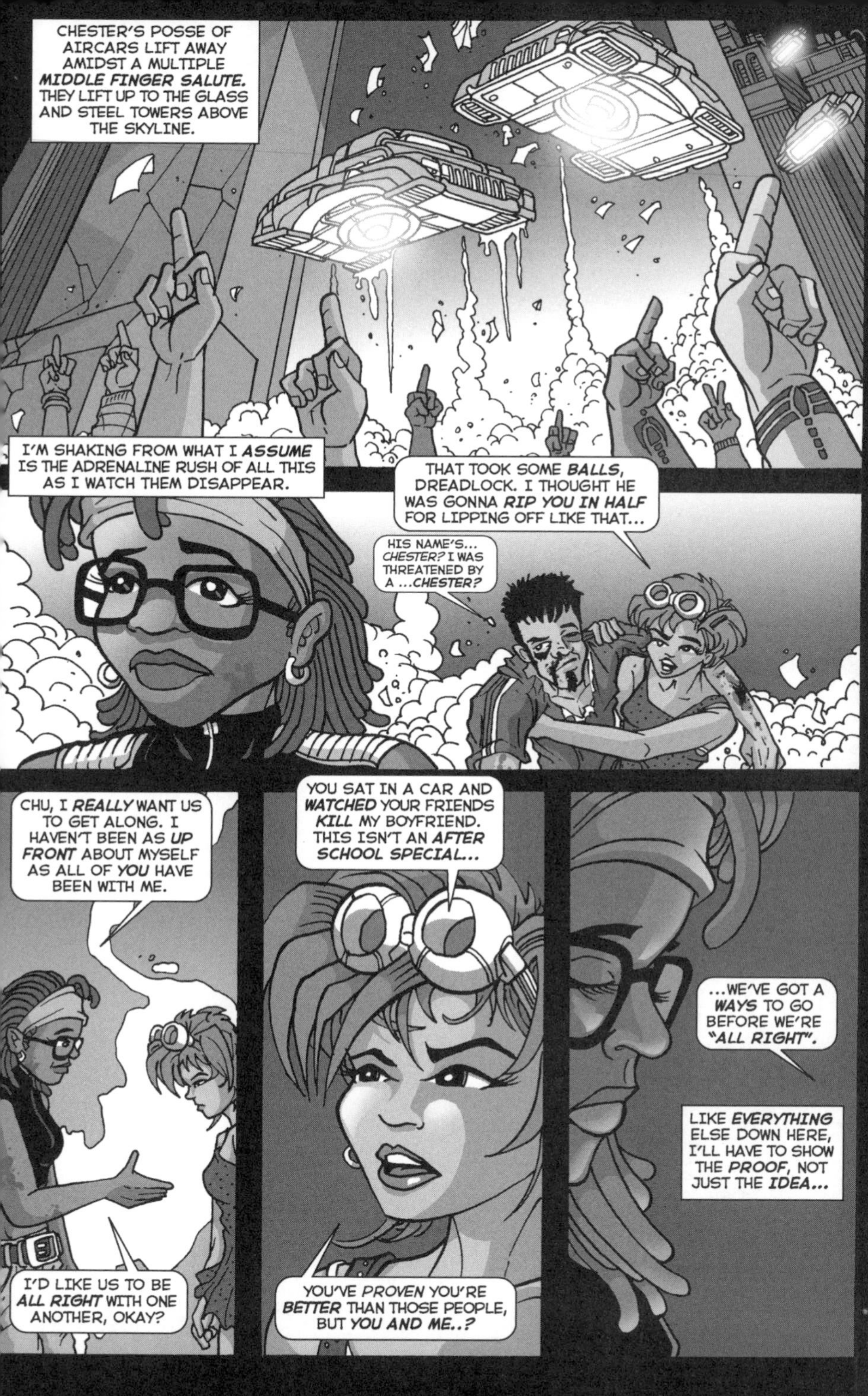
CHESTER'S POSSE OF AIRCARS LIFT AWAY AMIDST A MULTIPLE MIDDLE FINGER SALUTE. THEY LIFT UP TO THE GLASS AND STEEL TOWERS ABOVE THE SKYLINE.
I'M SHAKING FROM WHAT I ASSUME IS THE ADRENALINE RUSH OF ALL THIS AS I WATCH THEM DISAPPEAR.
THAT TOOK SOME BALLS, DREADLOCK. I THOUGHT HE WAS GONNA RIP YOU IN HALF FOR LIPPING OFF LIKE THAT...
HIS NAME'S... CHESTER? I WAS THREATENED BY A ...CHESTER?
CHU, I REALLY WANT US TO GET ALONG. I HAVEN'T BEEN AS UP FRONT ABOUT MYSELF AS ALL OF YOU HAVE BEEN WITH ME.
I'D LIKE US TO BE ALL RIGHT WITH ONE ANOTHER, OKAY?
YOU SAT IN A CAR AND WATCHED YOUR FRIENDS KILL MY BOYFRIEND. THIS ISN'T AN AFTER SCHOOL SPECIAL...
YOU'VE PROVEN YOU'RE BETTER THAN THOSE PEOPLE, BUT YOU AND ME..?
...WE'VE GOT A WAYS TO GO BEFORE WE'RE "ALL RIGHT".
LIKE EVERYTHING ELSE DOWN HERE, I'LL HAVE TO SHOW THE PROOF, NOT JUST THE IDEA...

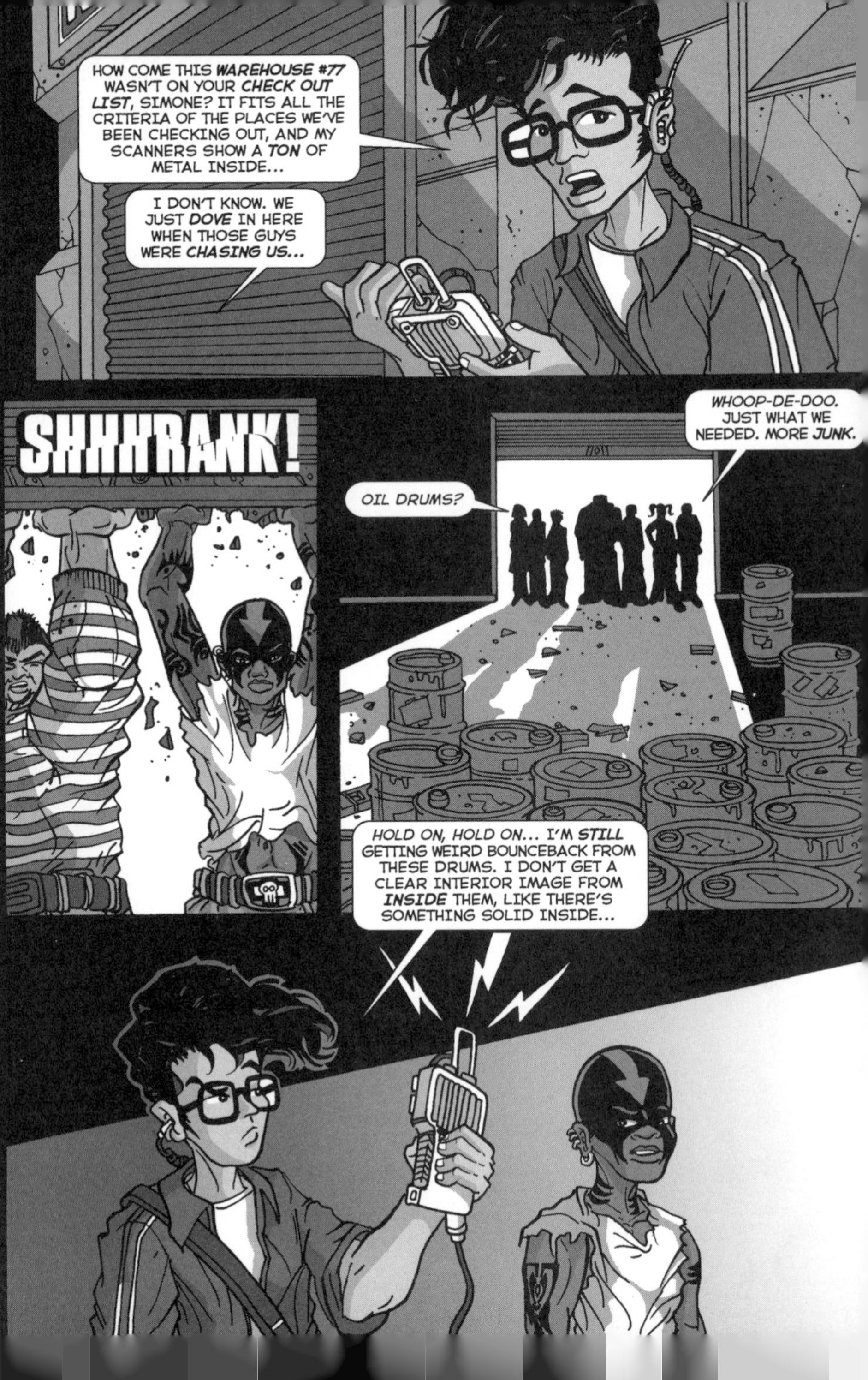
HOW COME THIS WAREHOUSE #77 WASN'T ON YOUR CHECK OUT LIST, SIMONE? IT FITS ALL THE CRITERIA OF THE PLACES WE'VE BEEN CHECKING OUT, AND MY SCANNERS SHOW A TON OF METAL INSIDE...
I DON'T KNOW. WE JUST DOVE IN HERE WHEN THOSE GUYS WERE CHASING US...
SHHHRANK!
OIL DRUMS?
WHOOP-DE-DOO. JUST WHAT WE NEEDED. MORE JUNK.
HOLD ON, HOLD ON... I'M STILL GETTING WEIRD BOUNCEBACK FROM THESE DRUMS. I DON'T GET A CLEAR INTERIOR IMAGE FROM INSIDE THEM, LIKE THERE'S SOMETHING SOLID INSIDE...

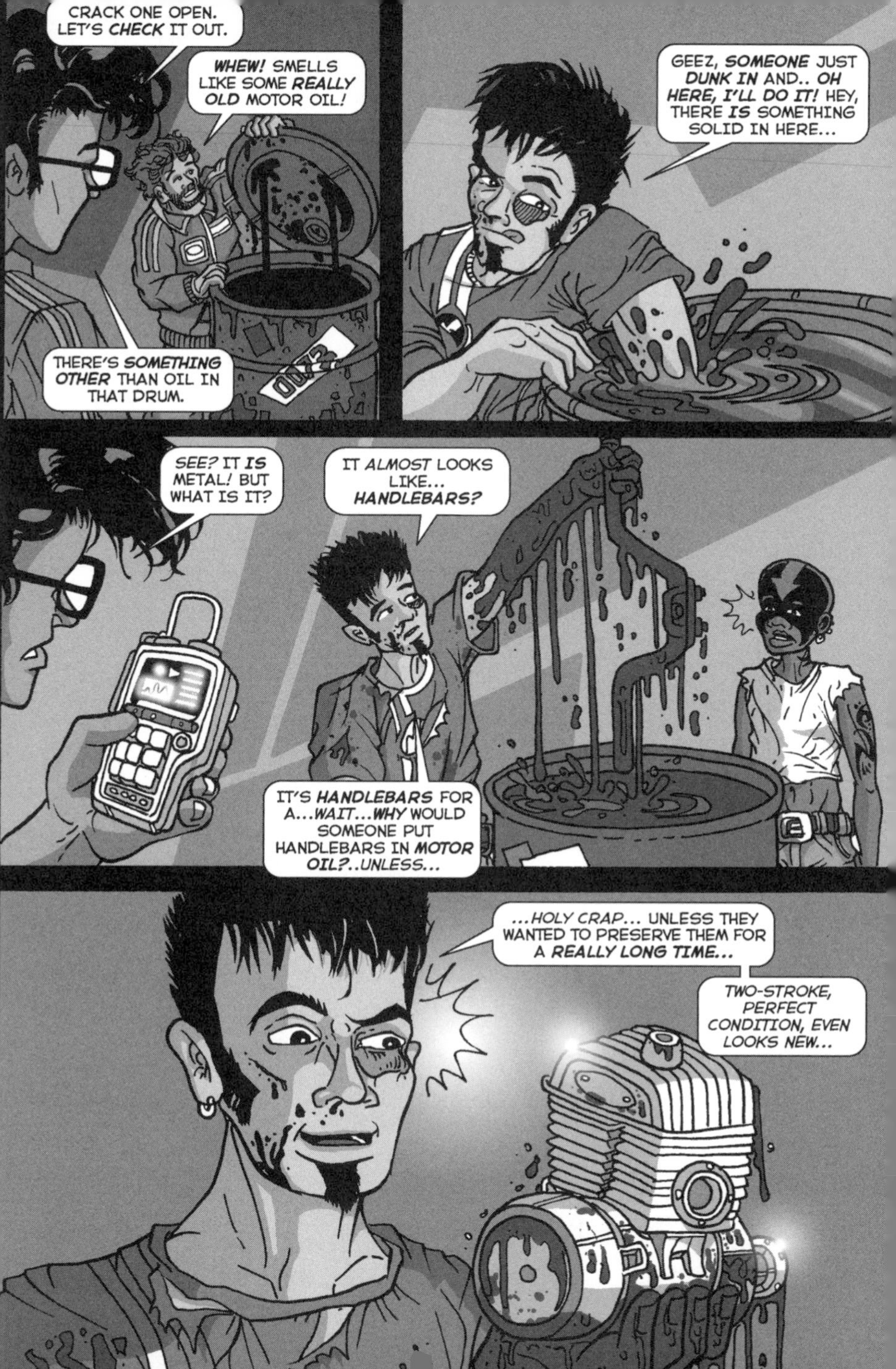
CRACK ONE OPEN. LET'S CHECK IT OUT.
WHEW! SMELLS LIKE SOME REALLY OLD MOTOR OIL!
THERE'S SOMETHING OTHER THAN OIL IN THAT DRUM.
GEEZ, SOMEONE JUST DUNK IN AND.. OH HERE, I'LL DO IT! HEY, THERE IS SOMETHING SOLID IN HERE...
SEE? IT IS METAL! BUT WHAT IS IT?
IT ALMOST LOOKS LIKE... HANDLEBARS?
IT'S HANDLEBARS FOR A...WAIT...WHY WOULD SOMEONE PUT HANDLEBARS IN MOTOR OIL?..UNLESS...
...HOLY CRAP... UNLESS THEY WANTED TO PRESERVE THEM FOR A REALLY LONG TIME...
TWO-STROKE, PERFECT CONDITION, EVEN LOOKS NEW...

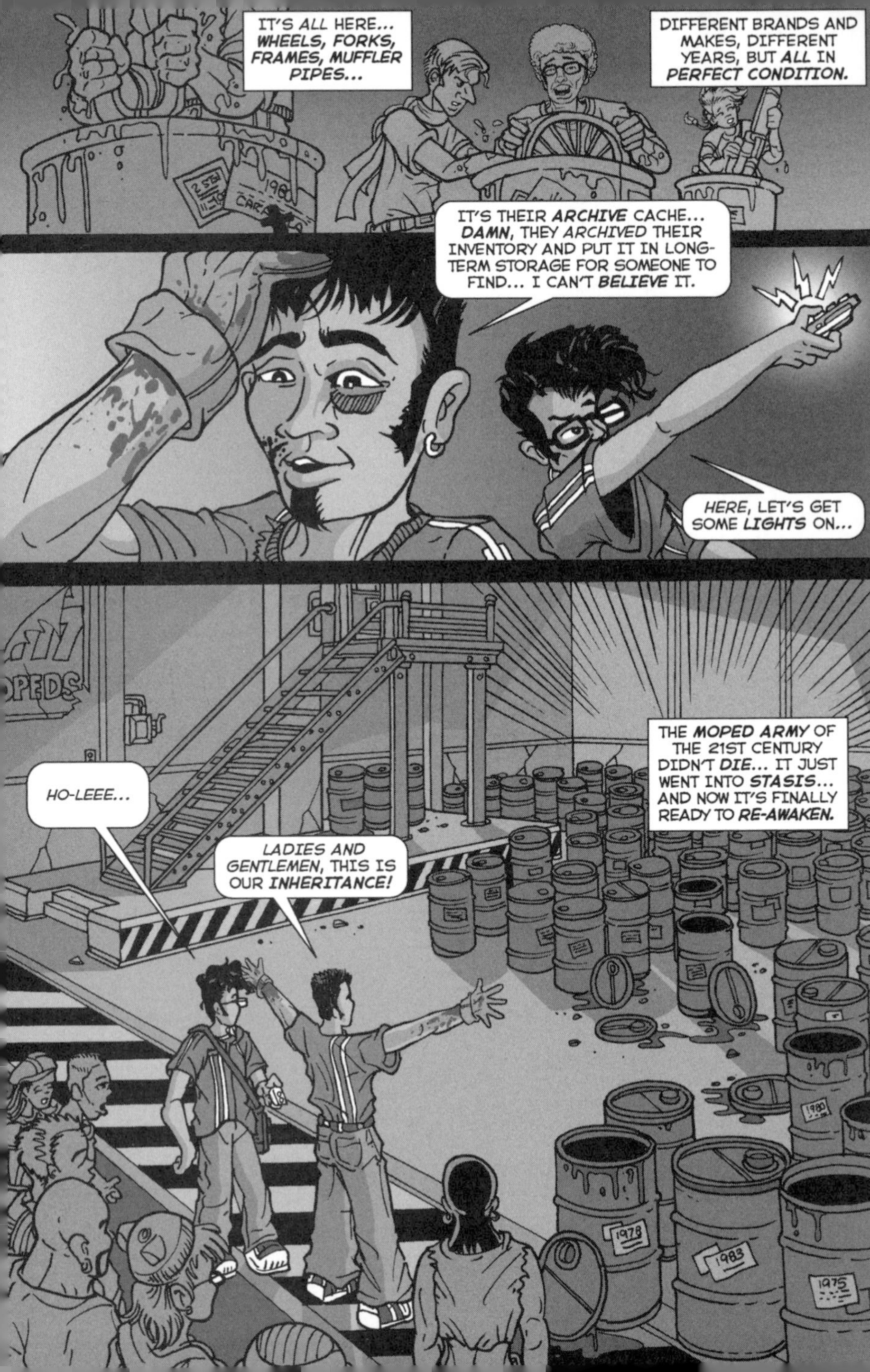
IT'S *ALL* HERE... ***WHEELS, FORKS, FRAMES, MUFFLER PIPES...***
DIFFERENT BRANDS AND MAKES, DIFFERENT YEARS, BUT ***ALL*** IN ***PERFECT CONDITION.***
IT'S THEIR ***ARCHIVE*** CACHE... ***DAMN,*** THEY *ARCHIVED* THEIR INVENTORY AND PUT IT IN LONG-TERM STORAGE FOR SOMEONE TO FIND... I CAN'T ***BELIEVE*** IT.
HERE, LET'S GET SOME ***LIGHTS*** ON...
HO-LEEE...
LADIES AND GENTLEMEN, THIS IS OUR ***INHERITANCE!***
THE ***MOPED ARMY*** OF THE 21ST CENTURY DIDN'T ***DIE***... IT JUST WENT INTO ***STASIS***... AND NOW IT'S FINALLY READY TO ***RE-AWAKEN.***
1978
1983
1975
1980

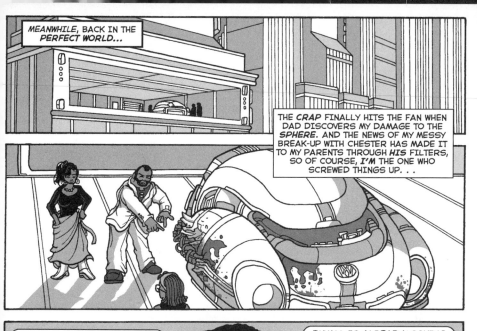

MEANWHILE, BACK IN THE *PERFECT WORLD*...

THE *CRAP* FINALLY HITS THE FAN WHEN DAD DISCOVERS MY DAMAGE TO THE *SPHERE*. AND THE NEWS OF MY MESSY BREAK-UP WITH CHESTER HAS MADE IT TO MY PARENTS THROUGH *HIS* FILTERS, SO OF COURSE, *I'M* THE ONE WHO SCREWED THINGS UP. . .

SIMONE, I CANNOT *BELIEVE* YOU WOULD DO THIS... I *TRUSTED* YOU WITH THIS PROTOTYPE. DO YOU HAVE *ANY* IDEA HOW MUCH GRIEF I WILL GET AT WORK OVER *THIS?!*

DUVALL IS *ALREADY* LOOKING FOR STUFF TO NAIL ME ON, AND THIS JUST PAINTS A *BIG TARGET ON MY BACK*. I *DO NOT* NEED THIS RIGHT NOW, SIMONE! NOT WITH THE NEW LINE ON DEADLINE!

AND LET ME GET THIS STRAIGHT. YOU BROKE UP WITH CHESTER... *IN PUBLIC*... *AFTER DRAGGING HIM ALL THE WAY DOWN TO THE LOWER CITY?* WHAT KIND OF *SICK JOKE* IS THAT? HE LOVED AND PROVIDED FOR YOU, AND YOU DUMP HIM IN FRONT OF A *BIKER GANG?* AND SINCE *WHEN* HAVE YOU BEEN RUNNING WITH A *BIKER GANG?*

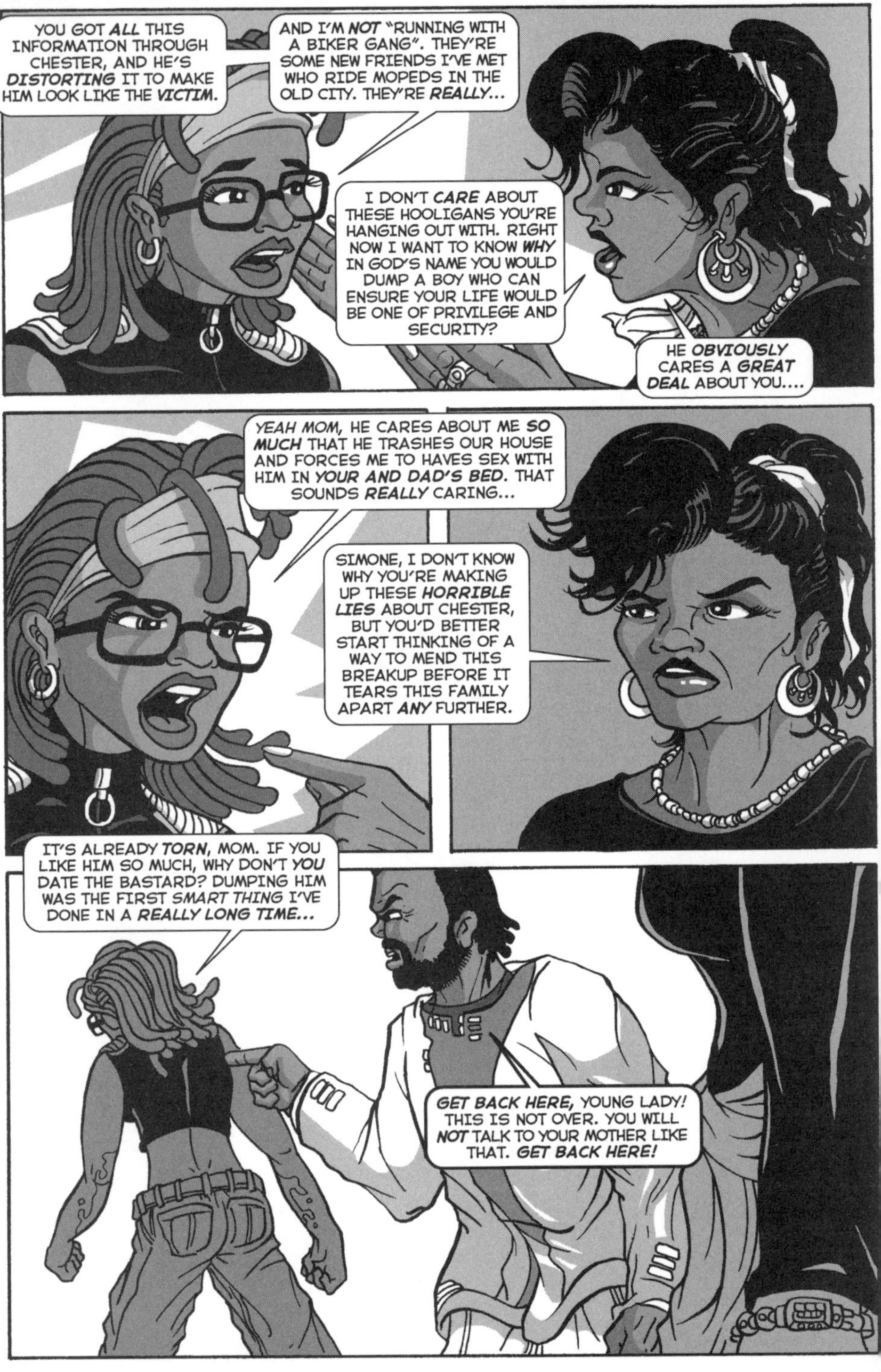
YOU GOT ALL THIS INFORMATION THROUGH CHESTER, AND HE'S DISTORTING IT TO MAKE HIM LOOK LIKE THE VICTIM.
AND I'M NOT "RUNNING WITH A BIKER GANG". THEY'RE SOME NEW FRIENDS I'VE MET WHO RIDE MOPEDS IN THE OLD CITY. THEY'RE REALLY...
I DON'T CARE ABOUT THESE HOOLIGANS YOU'RE HANGING OUT WITH. RIGHT NOW I WANT TO KNOW WHY IN GOD'S NAME YOU WOULD DUMP A BOY WHO CAN ENSURE YOUR LIFE WOULD BE ONE OF PRIVILEGE AND SECURITY?
HE OBVIOUSLY CARES A GREAT DEAL ABOUT YOU....
YEAH MOM, HE CARES ABOUT ME SO MUCH THAT HE TRASHES OUR HOUSE AND FORCES ME TO HAVES SEX WITH HIM IN YOUR AND DAD'S BED. THAT SOUNDS REALLY CARING...
SIMONE, I DON'T KNOW WHY YOU'RE MAKING UP THESE HORRIBLE LIES ABOUT CHESTER, BUT YOU'D BETTER START THINKING OF A WAY TO MEND THIS BREAKUP BEFORE IT TEARS THIS FAMILY APART ANY FURTHER.
IT'S ALREADY TORN, MOM. IF YOU LIKE HIM SO MUCH, WHY DON'T YOU DATE THE BASTARD? DUMPING HIM WAS THE FIRST SMART THING I'VE DONE IN A REALLY LONG TIME...
GET BACK HERE, YOUNG LADY! THIS IS NOT OVER. YOU WILL NOT TALK TO YOUR MOTHER LIKE THAT. GET BACK HERE!

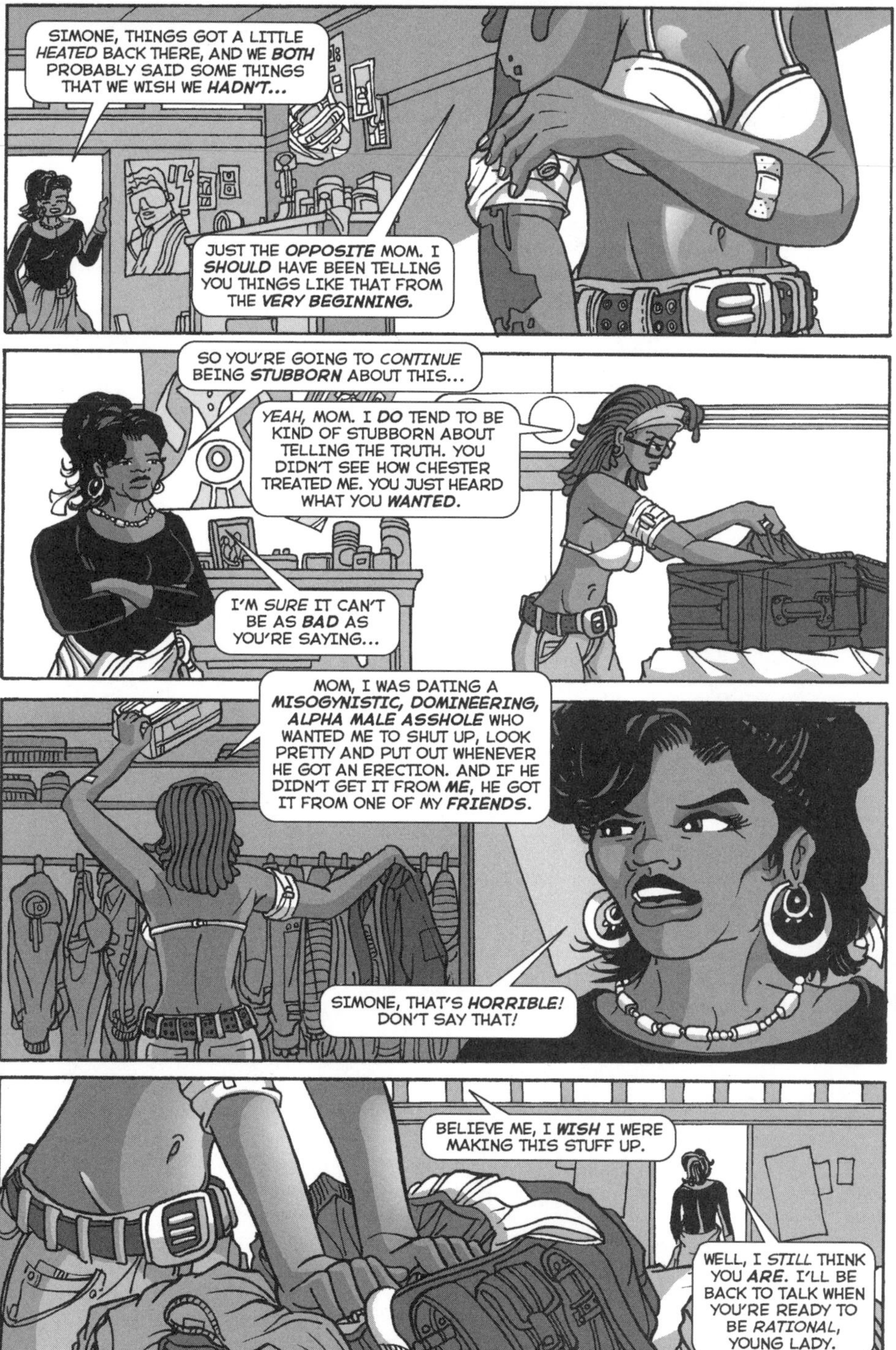
SIMONE, THINGS GOT A LITTLE HEATED BACK THERE, AND WE BOTH PROBABLY SAID SOME THINGS THAT WE WISH WE HADN'T...
JUST THE OPPOSITE MOM. I SHOULD HAVE BEEN TELLING YOU THINGS LIKE THAT FROM THE VERY BEGINNING.
SO YOU'RE GOING TO CONTINUE BEING STUBBORN ABOUT THIS...
YEAH, MOM. I DO TEND TO BE KIND OF STUBBORN ABOUT TELLING THE TRUTH. YOU DIDN'T SEE HOW CHESTER TREATED ME. YOU JUST HEARD WHAT YOU WANTED.
I'M SURE IT CAN'T BE AS BAD AS YOU'RE SAYING...
MOM, I WAS DATING A MISOGYNISTIC, DOMINEERING, ALPHA MALE ASSHOLE WHO WANTED ME TO SHUT UP, LOOK PRETTY AND PUT OUT WHENEVER HE GOT AN ERECTION. AND IF HE DIDN'T GET IT FROM ME, HE GOT IT FROM ONE OF MY FRIENDS.
SIMONE, THAT'S HORRIBLE! DON'T SAY THAT!
BELIEVE ME, I WISH I WERE MAKING THIS STUFF UP.
WELL, I STILL THINK YOU ARE. I'LL BE BACK TO TALK WHEN YOU'RE READY TO BE RATIONAL, YOUNG LADY.

THE DAY YOUR DAD SAYS YOU'RE AN *IRRESPONSIBLE JERK* AND YOUR MOM ALL BUT CALLS YOU A *LIAR*, IT'S TIME FOR A CHANGE IN THE DYNAMIC OF THE LIVING SITUATION.

I WALK OUT THE DOOR WITH WHAT I CAN WEAR AND WHAT I CAN CARRY. PAST THE MARBLE AND CHROME AND ALL THE TRAPPINGS OF A HOME THAT MAKES ME WHAT OTHERS THOUGHT I *SHOULD BE* RATHER THAN *WHO I AM.*

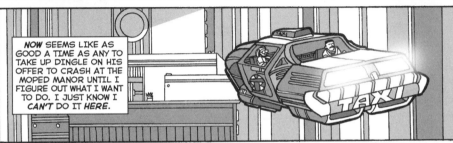

NOW SEEMS LIKE AS GOOD A TIME AS ANY TO TAKE UP DINGLE ON HIS OFFER TO CRASH AT THE MOPED MANOR UNTIL I FIGURE OUT WHAT I WANT TO DO. I JUST KNOW I *CAN'T* DO IT *HERE.*

ALL I LEAVE BEHIND IS A NOTE AND CHESTER'S RING. THEY CAN GIVE THE RING BACK TO CHESTER, OR MOM CAN KEEP IT AS A *REMINDER* OF THE WONDERFUL VISION SHE HAD IN HER HEAD OF OUR RELATIONSHIP.

Dear Mom and Dad,
I've found myself in the last two months, and the real me can't live in the Upper City any more. I'll contact you when I'm ready to explain what my life has become.
—Simone

DAMMIT...

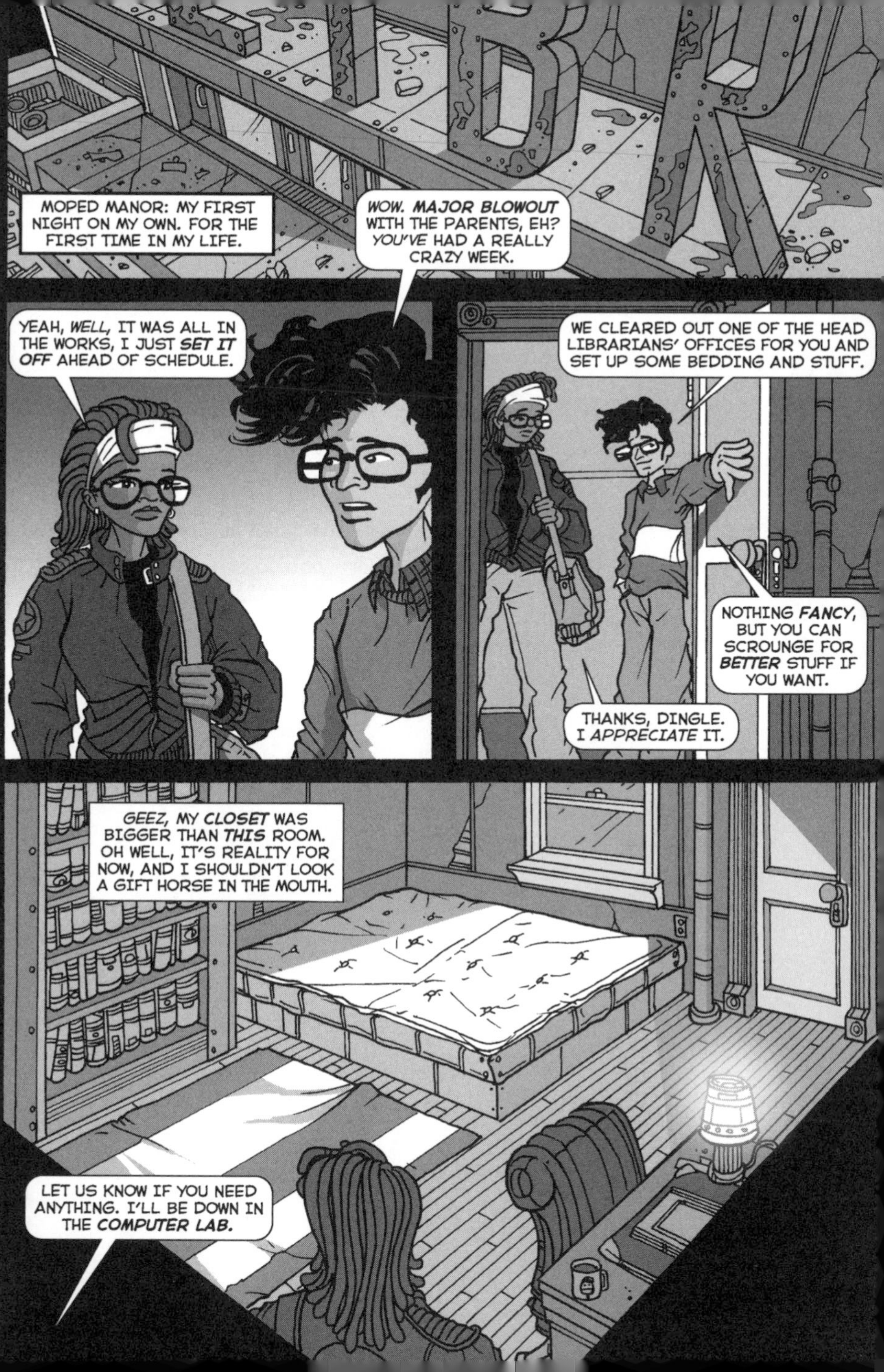
MOPED MANOR: MY FIRST NIGHT ON MY OWN. FOR THE FIRST TIME IN MY LIFE.
WOW. ***MAJOR BLOWOUT*** WITH THE PARENTS, EH? *YOU'VE* HAD A REALLY CRAZY WEEK.
YEAH, *WELL*, IT WAS ALL IN THE WORKS, I JUST ***SET IT OFF*** AHEAD OF SCHEDULE.
WE CLEARED OUT ONE OF THE HEAD LIBRARIANS' OFFICES FOR YOU AND SET UP SOME BEDDING AND STUFF.
NOTHING ***FANCY***, BUT YOU CAN SCROUNGE FOR ***BETTER*** STUFF IF YOU WANT.
THANKS, DINGLE. I *APPRECIATE* IT.
GEEZ, MY ***CLOSET*** WAS BIGGER THAN ***THIS*** ROOM. OH WELL, IT'S REALITY FOR NOW, AND I SHOULDN'T LOOK A GIFT HORSE IN THE MOUTH.
LET US KNOW IF YOU NEED ANYTHING. I'LL BE DOWN IN THE ***COMPUTER LAB.***

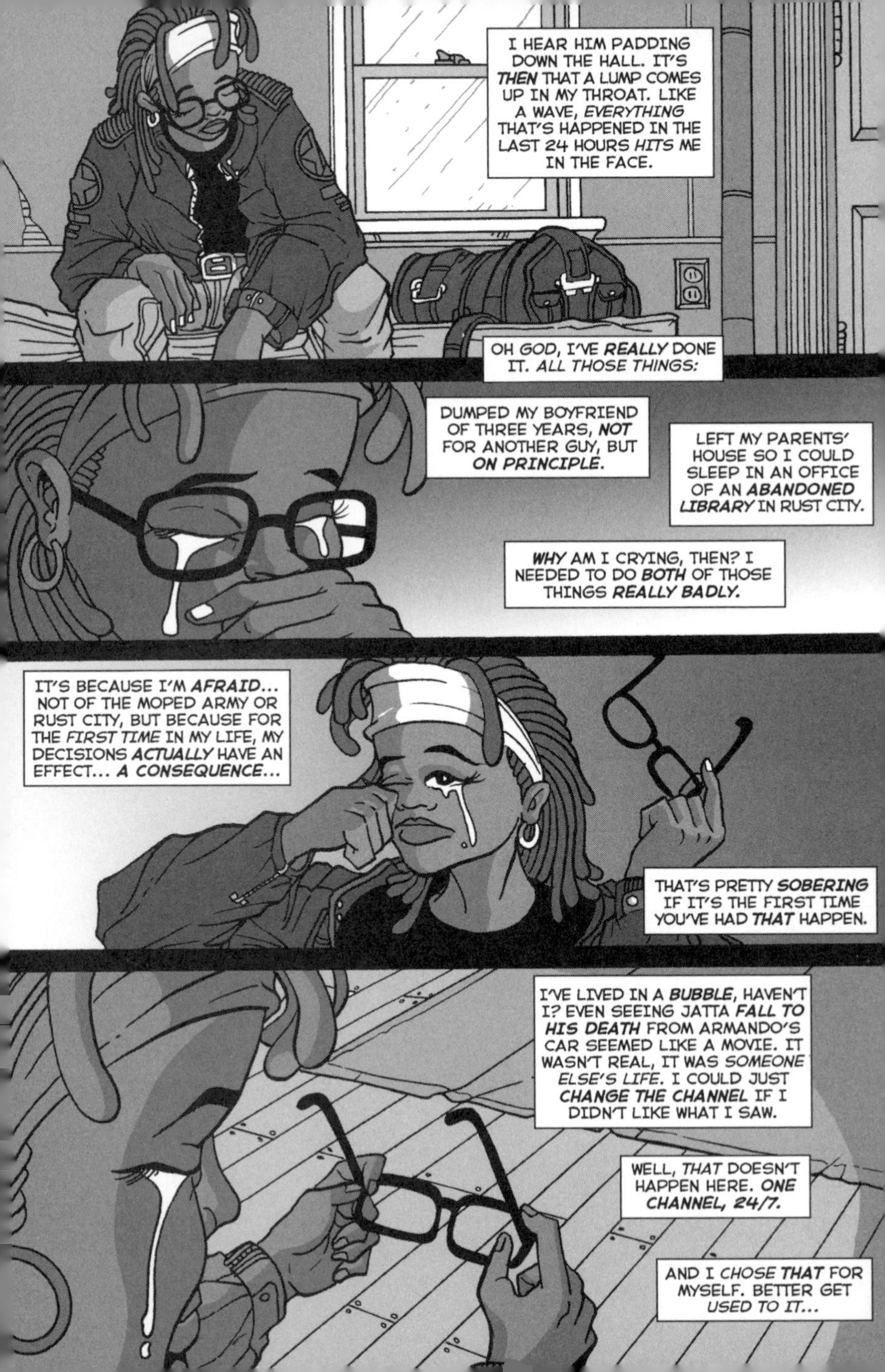
I HEAR HIM PADDING DOWN THE HALL. IT'S *THEN* THAT A LUMP COMES UP IN MY THROAT. LIKE A WAVE, *EVERYTHING* THAT'S HAPPENED IN THE LAST 24 HOURS *HITS* ME IN THE FACE.
OH *GOD*, I'VE ***REALLY*** DONE IT. *ALL THOSE THINGS:*
DUMPED MY BOYFRIEND OF THREE YEARS, ***NOT*** FOR ANOTHER GUY, BUT ***ON PRINCIPLE***.
LEFT MY PARENTS' HOUSE SO I COULD SLEEP IN AN OFFICE OF AN ***ABANDONED LIBRARY*** IN RUST CITY.
WHY AM I CRYING, THEN? I NEEDED TO DO ***BOTH*** OF THOSE THINGS ***REALLY BADLY.***
IT'S BECAUSE I'M ***AFRAID...*** NOT OF THE MOPED ARMY OR RUST CITY, BUT BECAUSE FOR THE *FIRST TIME* IN MY LIFE, MY DECISIONS ***ACTUALLY*** HAVE AN EFFECT... ***A CONSEQUENCE...***
THAT'S PRETTY ***SOBERING*** IF IT'S THE FIRST TIME YOU'VE HAD ***THAT*** HAPPEN.
I'VE LIVED IN A ***BUBBLE***, HAVEN'T I? EVEN SEEING JATTA ***FALL TO HIS DEATH*** FROM ARMANDO'S CAR SEEMED LIKE A MOVIE. IT WASN'T REAL, IT WAS *SOMEONE ELSE'S LIFE*. I COULD JUST ***CHANGE THE CHANNEL*** IF I DIDN'T LIKE WHAT I SAW.
WELL, *THAT* DOESN'T HAPPEN HERE. ***ONE CHANNEL, 24/7.***
AND I *CHOSE* ***THAT*** FOR MYSELF. BETTER GET *USED TO IT...*

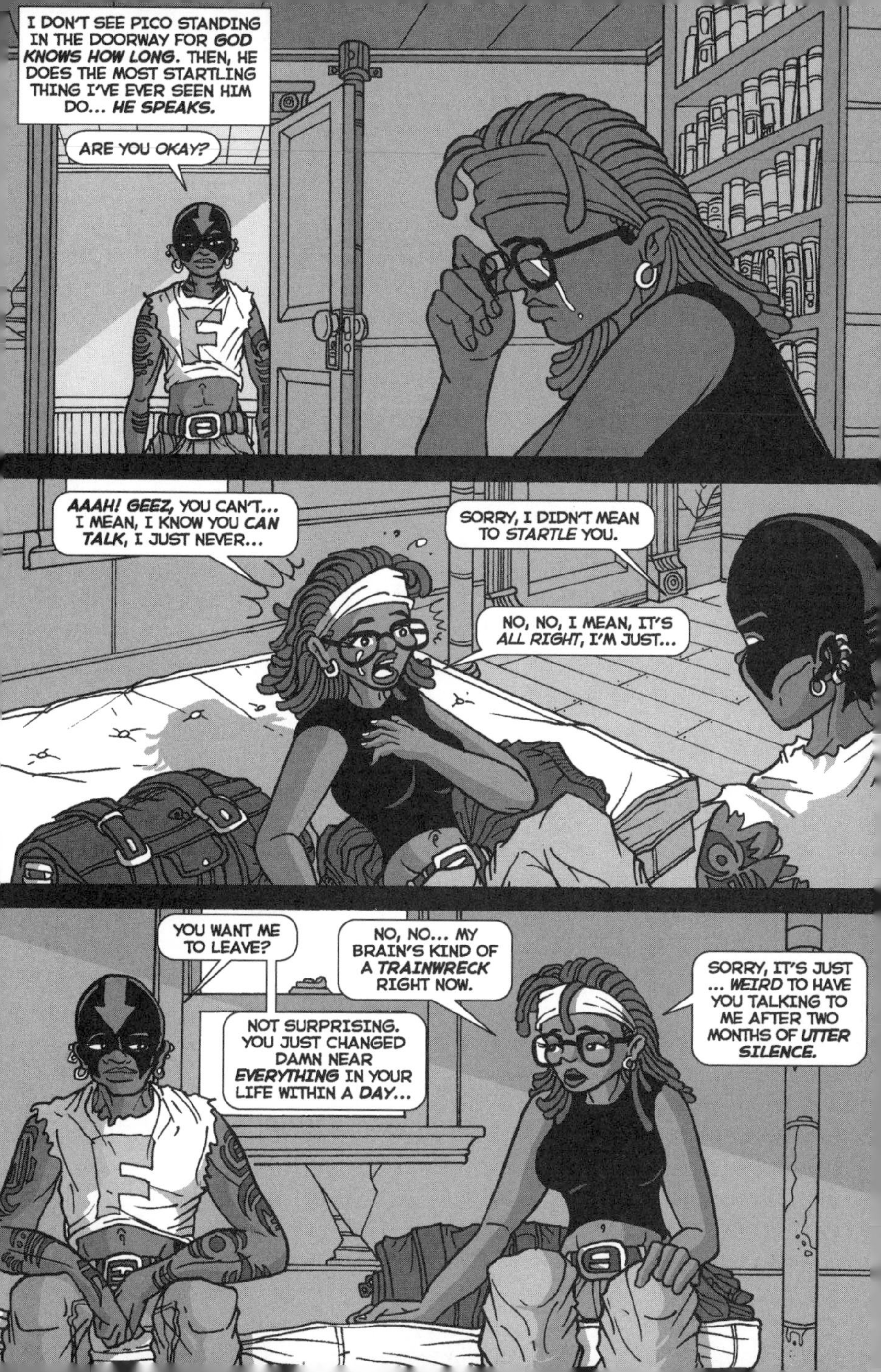
I DON'T SEE PICO STANDING IN THE DOORWAY FOR *GOD KNOWS HOW LONG*. THEN, HE DOES THE MOST STARTLING THING I'VE EVER SEEN HIM DO... *HE SPEAKS.*
ARE YOU *OKAY?*
AAAH! GEEZ, YOU CAN'T... I MEAN, I KNOW YOU *CAN TALK*, I JUST NEVER...
SORRY, I DIDN'T MEAN TO *STARTLE* YOU.
NO, NO, I MEAN, IT'S *ALL RIGHT*, I'M JUST...
YOU WANT ME TO LEAVE?
NOT SURPRISING. YOU JUST CHANGED DAMN NEAR *EVERYTHING* IN YOUR LIFE WITHIN A *DAY*...
NO, NO... MY BRAIN'S KIND OF A *TRAINWRECK* RIGHT NOW.
SORRY, IT'S JUST ... *WEIRD* TO HAVE YOU TALKING TO ME AFTER TWO MONTHS OF *UTTER SILENCE.*

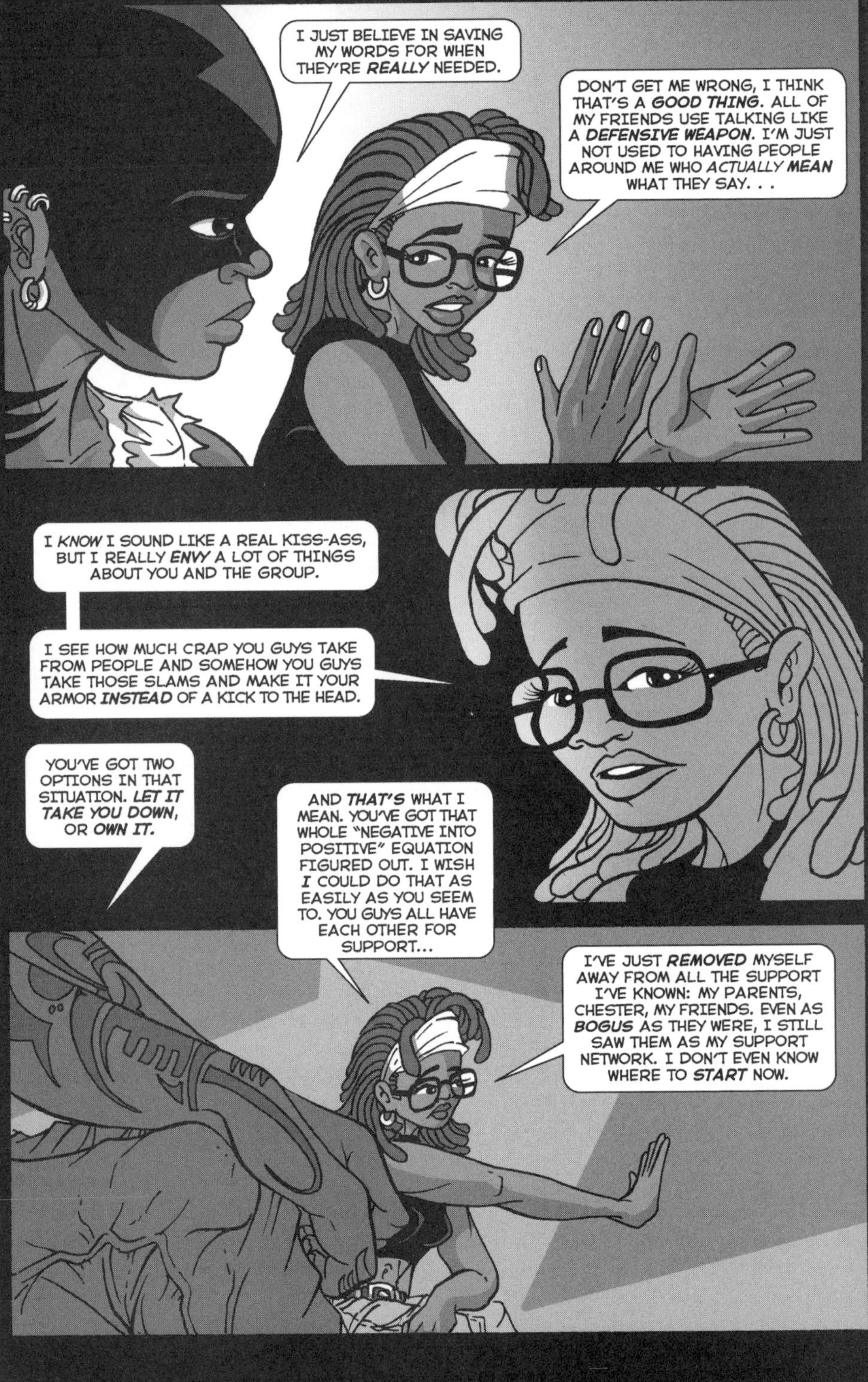
I JUST BELIEVE IN SAVING MY WORDS FOR WHEN THEY'RE *REALLY* NEEDED.
DON'T GET ME WRONG, I THINK THAT'S A ***GOOD THING***. ALL OF MY FRIENDS USE TALKING LIKE A ***DEFENSIVE WEAPON***. I'M JUST NOT USED TO HAVING PEOPLE AROUND ME WHO *ACTUALLY* ***MEAN*** WHAT THEY SAY. . .
I *KNOW* I SOUND LIKE A REAL KISS-ASS, BUT I REALLY ***ENVY*** A LOT OF THINGS ABOUT YOU AND THE GROUP.
I SEE HOW MUCH CRAP YOU GUYS TAKE FROM PEOPLE AND SOMEHOW YOU GUYS TAKE THOSE SLAMS AND MAKE IT YOUR ARMOR ***INSTEAD*** OF A KICK TO THE HEAD.
YOU'VE GOT TWO OPTIONS IN THAT SITUATION. ***LET IT TAKE YOU DOWN***, OR ***OWN IT.***
AND ***THAT'S*** WHAT I MEAN. YOU'VE GOT THAT WHOLE "NEGATIVE INTO POSITIVE" EQUATION FIGURED OUT. I WISH ***I*** COULD DO THAT AS EASILY AS YOU SEEM TO. YOU GUYS ALL HAVE EACH OTHER FOR SUPPORT...
I'VE JUST ***REMOVED*** MYSELF AWAY FROM ALL THE SUPPORT I'VE KNOWN: MY PARENTS, CHESTER, MY FRIENDS. EVEN AS ***BOGUS*** AS THEY WERE, I STILL SAW THEM AS MY SUPPORT NETWORK. I DON'T EVEN KNOW WHERE TO ***START*** NOW.

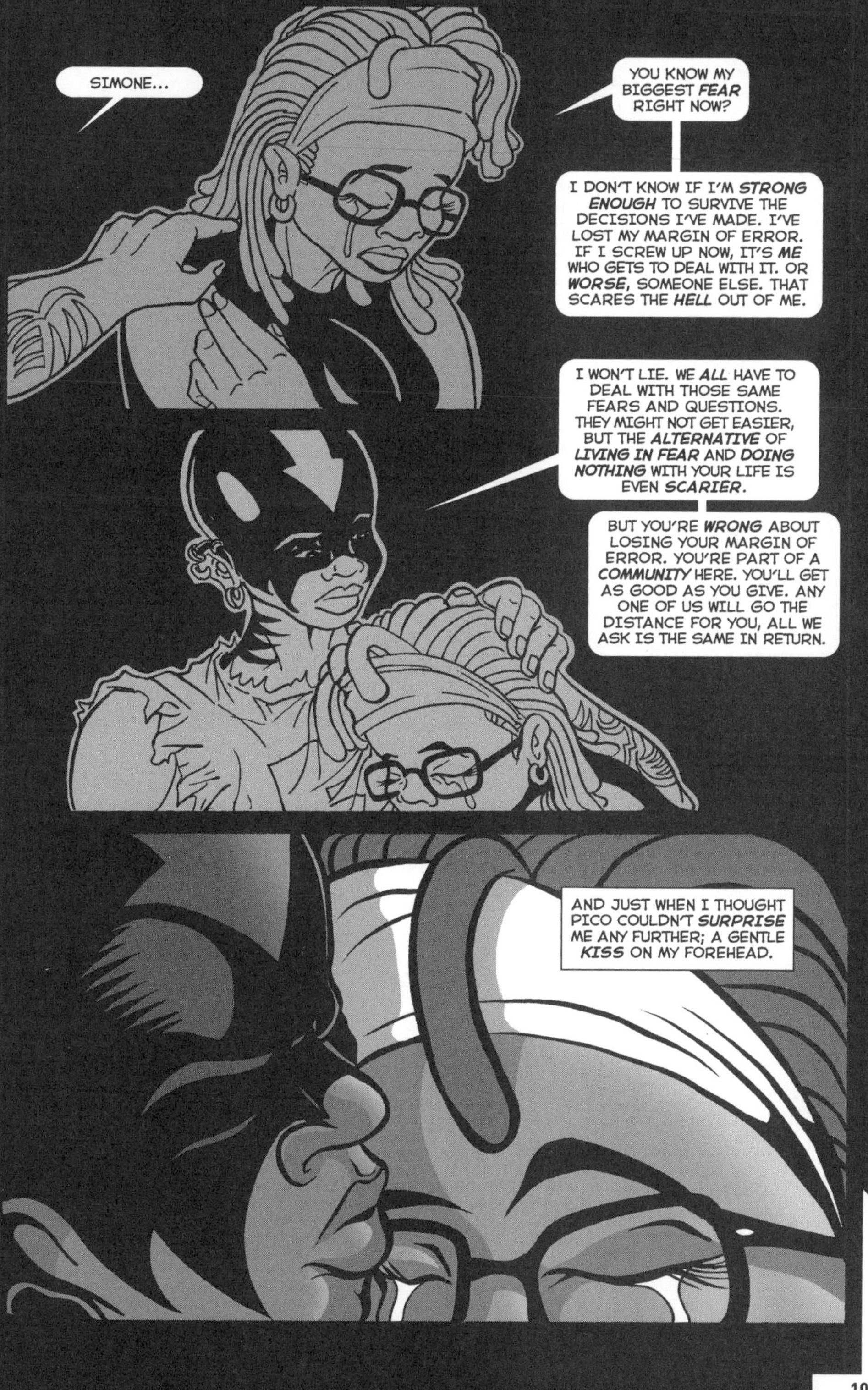
SIMONE...
YOU KNOW MY BIGGEST FEAR RIGHT NOW?
I DON'T KNOW IF I'M STRONG ENOUGH TO SURVIVE THE DECISIONS I'VE MADE. I'VE LOST MY MARGIN OF ERROR. IF I SCREW UP NOW, IT'S ME WHO GETS TO DEAL WITH IT. OR WORSE, SOMEONE ELSE. THAT SCARES THE HELL OUT OF ME.
I WON'T LIE. WE ALL HAVE TO DEAL WITH THOSE SAME FEARS AND QUESTIONS. THEY MIGHT NOT GET EASIER, BUT THE ALTERNATIVE OF LIVING IN FEAR AND DOING NOTHING WITH YOUR LIFE IS EVEN SCARIER.
BUT YOU'RE WRONG ABOUT LOSING YOUR MARGIN OF ERROR. YOU'RE PART OF A COMMUNITY HERE. YOU'LL GET AS GOOD AS YOU GIVE. ANY ONE OF US WILL GO THE DISTANCE FOR YOU, ALL WE ASK IS THE SAME IN RETURN.
AND JUST WHEN I THOUGHT PICO COULDN'T SURPRISE ME ANY FURTHER; A GENTLE KISS ON MY FOREHEAD.

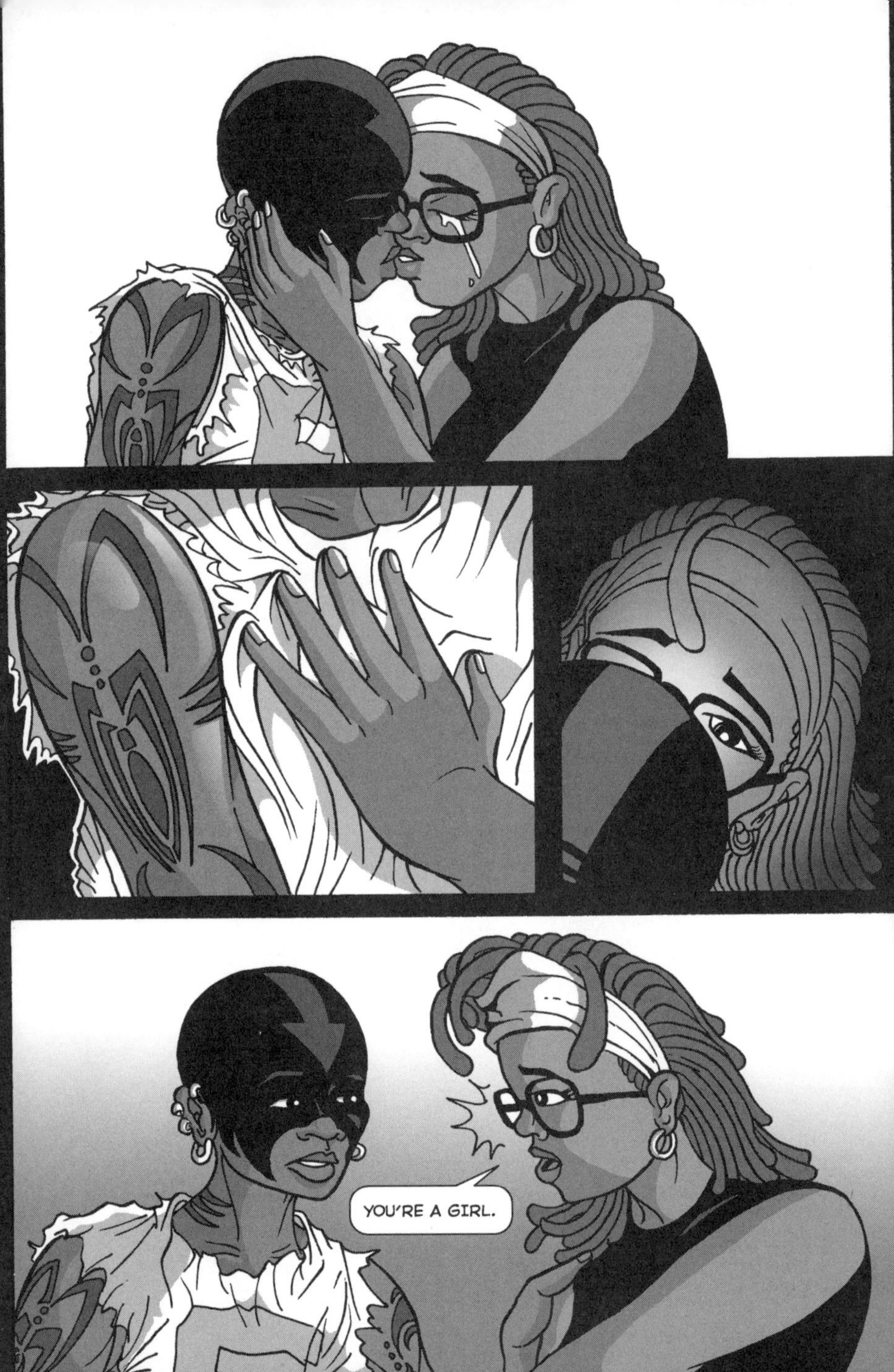YOU'RE A GIRL.

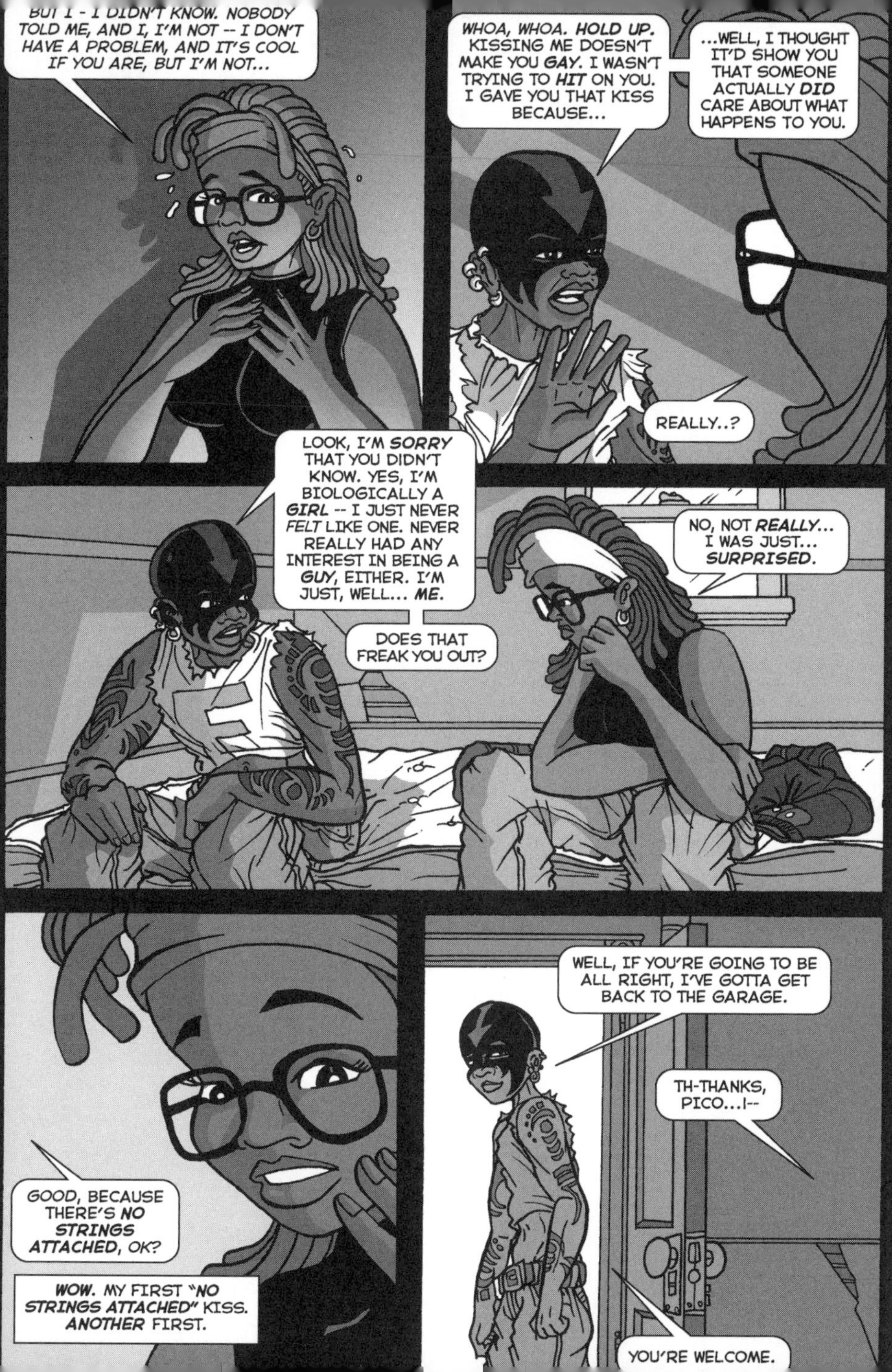
BUT I - I DIDN'T KNOW. NOBODY TOLD ME, AND I, I'M NOT -- I DON'T HAVE A PROBLEM, AND IT'S COOL IF YOU ARE, BUT I'M NOT...
WHOA, WHOA. HOLD UP. KISSING ME DOESN'T MAKE YOU GAY. I WASN'T TRYING TO HIT ON YOU. I GAVE YOU THAT KISS BECAUSE...
...WELL, I THOUGHT IT'D SHOW YOU THAT SOMEONE ACTUALLY DID CARE ABOUT WHAT HAPPENS TO YOU.
REALLY..?
LOOK, I'M SORRY THAT YOU DIDN'T KNOW. YES, I'M BIOLOGICALLY A GIRL -- I JUST NEVER FELT LIKE ONE. NEVER REALLY HAD ANY INTEREST IN BEING A GUY, EITHER. I'M JUST, WELL... ME.
DOES THAT FREAK YOU OUT?
NO, NOT REALLY... I WAS JUST... SURPRISED.
GOOD, BECAUSE THERE'S NO STRINGS ATTACHED, OK?
WOW. MY FIRST "NO STRINGS ATTACHED" KISS. ANOTHER FIRST.
WELL, IF YOU'RE GOING TO BE ALL RIGHT, I'VE GOTTA GET BACK TO THE GARAGE.
TH-THANKS, PICO...I--
YOU'RE WELCOME.

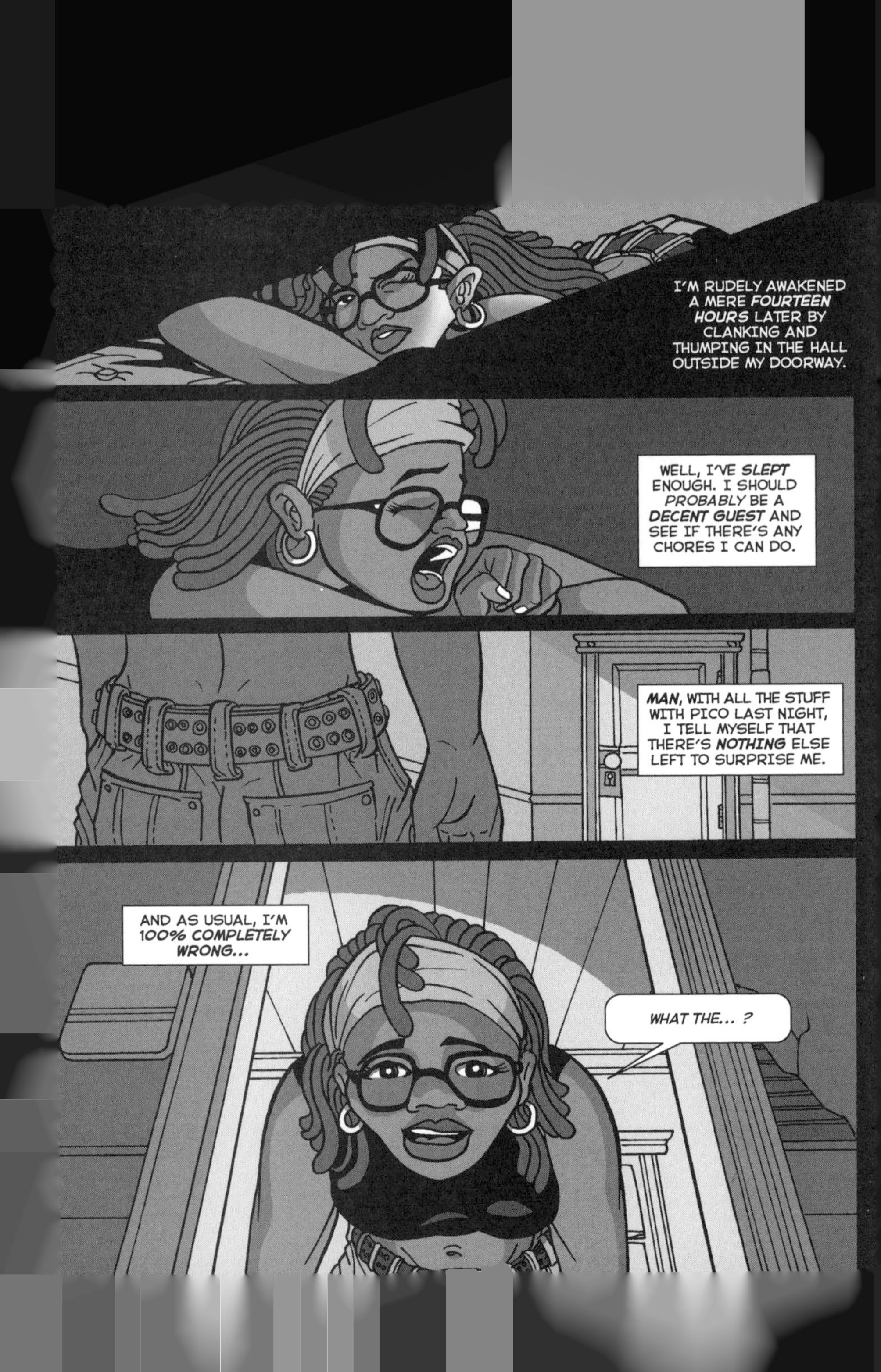
I'M RUDELY AWAKENED A MERE FOURTEEN HOURS LATER BY CLANKING AND THUMPING IN THE HALL OUTSIDE MY DOORWAY.
WELL, I'VE SLEPT ENOUGH. I SHOULD PROBABLY BE A DECENT GUEST AND SEE IF THERE'S ANY CHORES I CAN DO.
MAN, WITH ALL THE STUFF WITH PICO LAST NIGHT, I TELL MYSELF THAT THERE'S NOTHING ELSE LEFT TO SURPRISE ME.
AND AS USUAL, I'M 100% COMPLETELY WRONG...
WHAT THE... ?

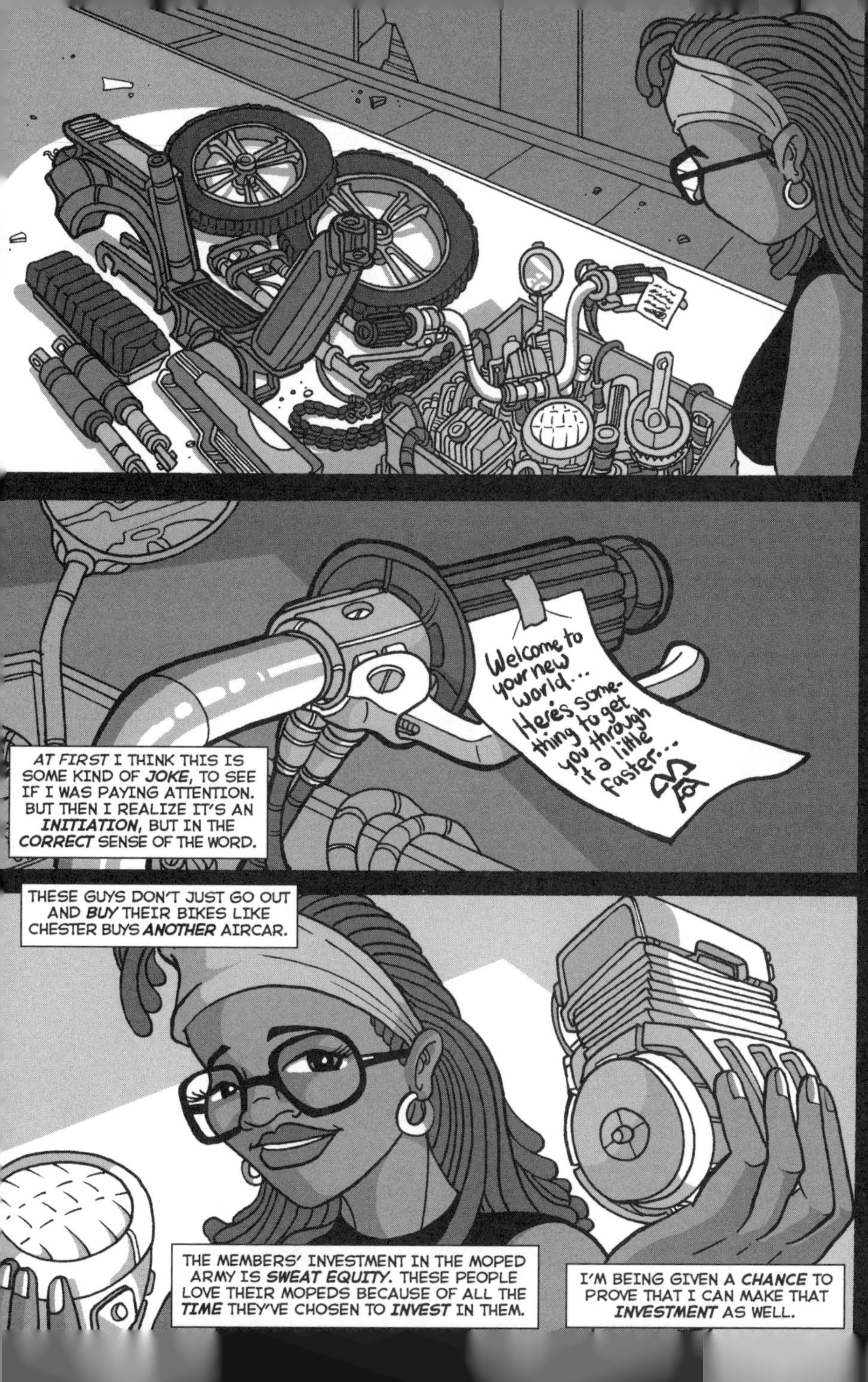
Welcome to your new world... Here's something to get you through it a little faster...
AT FIRST I THINK THIS IS SOME KIND OF JOKE, TO SEE IF I WAS PAYING ATTENTION. BUT THEN I REALIZE IT'S AN INITIATION, BUT IN THE CORRECT SENSE OF THE WORD.
THESE GUYS DON'T JUST GO OUT AND BUY THEIR BIKES LIKE CHESTER BUYS ANOTHER AIRCAR.
THE MEMBERS' INVESTMENT IN THE MOPED ARMY IS SWEAT EQUITY. THESE PEOPLE LOVE THEIR MOPEDS BECAUSE OF ALL THE TIME THEY'VE CHOSEN TO INVEST IN THEM.
I'M BEING GIVEN A CHANCE TO PROVE THAT I CAN MAKE THAT INVESTMENT AS WELL.

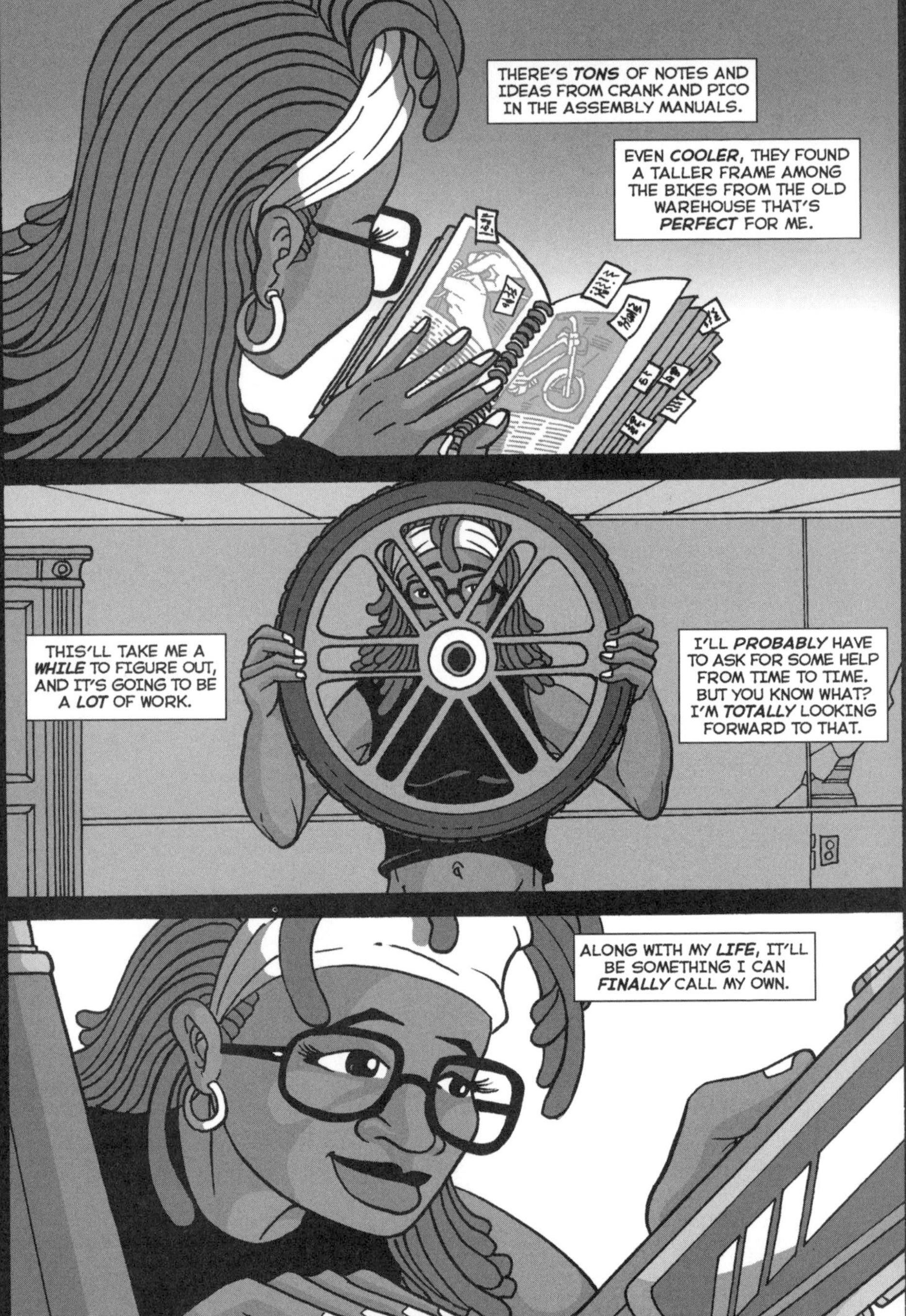
THERE'S *TONS* OF NOTES AND IDEAS FROM CRANK AND PICO IN THE ASSEMBLY MANUALS.
EVEN *COOLER*, THEY FOUND A TALLER FRAME AMONG THE BIKES FROM THE OLD WAREHOUSE THAT'S *PERFECT* FOR ME.
THIS'LL TAKE ME A *WHILE* TO FIGURE OUT, AND IT'S GOING TO BE A *LOT* OF WORK.
I'LL *PROBABLY* HAVE TO ASK FOR SOME HELP FROM TIME TO TIME. BUT YOU KNOW WHAT? I'M *TOTALLY* LOOKING FORWARD TO THAT.
ALONG WITH MY *LIFE*, IT'LL BE SOMETHING I CAN *FINALLY* CALL MY OWN.

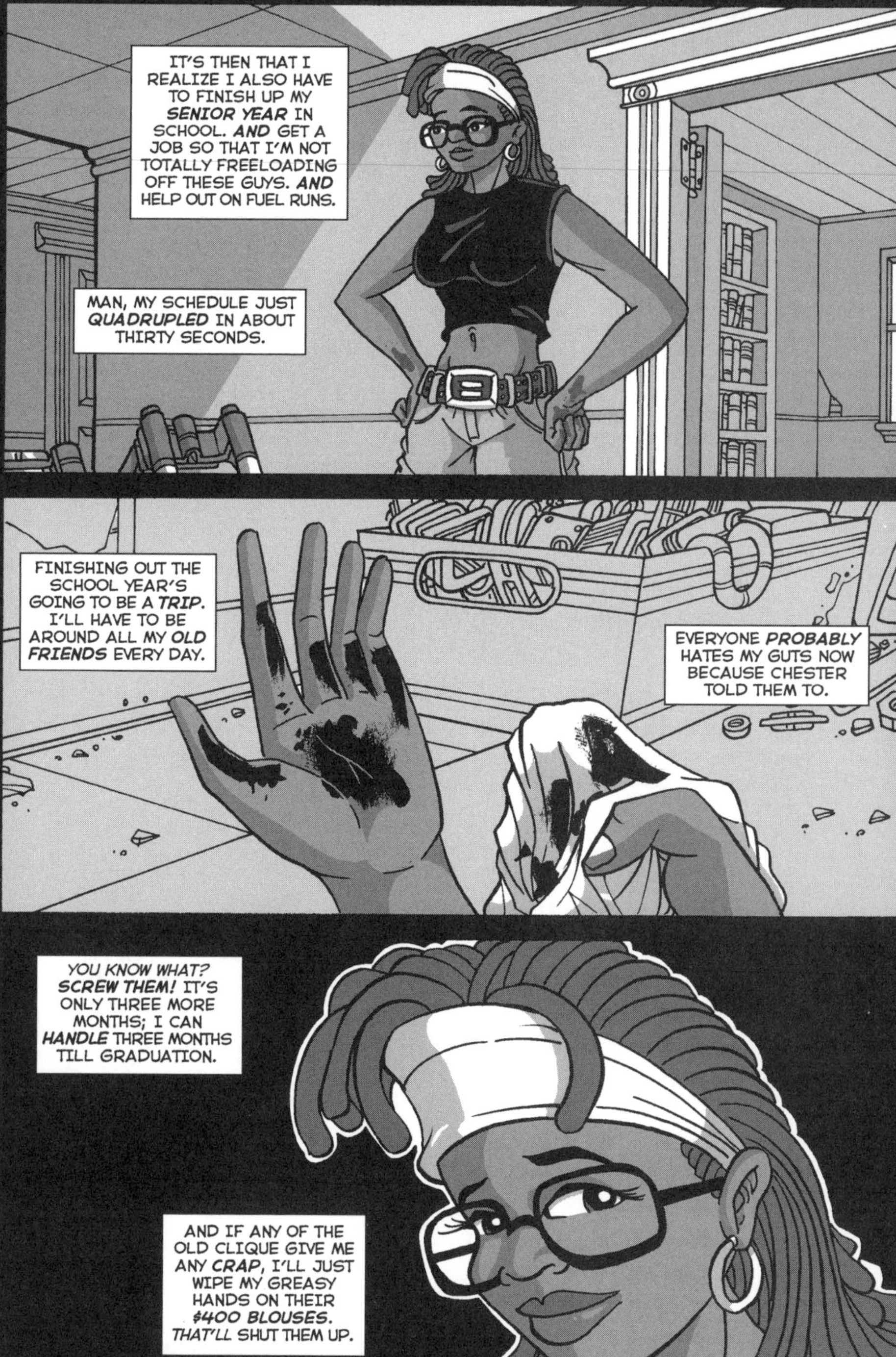
IT'S THEN THAT I REALIZE I ALSO HAVE TO FINISH UP MY **SENIOR YEAR** IN SCHOOL. **AND** GET A JOB SO THAT I'M NOT TOTALLY FREELOADING OFF THESE GUYS. **AND** HELP OUT ON FUEL RUNS.
MAN, MY SCHEDULE JUST **QUADRUPLED** IN ABOUT THIRTY SECONDS.
FINISHING OUT THE SCHOOL YEAR'S GOING TO BE A **TRIP**. I'LL HAVE TO BE AROUND ALL MY **OLD FRIENDS** EVERY DAY.
EVERYONE **PROBABLY** HATES MY GUTS NOW BECAUSE CHESTER TOLD THEM TO.
YOU KNOW WHAT? **SCREW THEM!** IT'S ONLY THREE MORE MONTHS; I CAN **HANDLE** THREE MONTHS TILL GRADUATION.
AND IF ANY OF THE OLD CLIQUE GIVE ME ANY **CRAP**, I'LL JUST WIPE MY GREASY HANDS ON THEIR **$400 BLOUSES**. *THAT'LL* SHUT THEM UP.

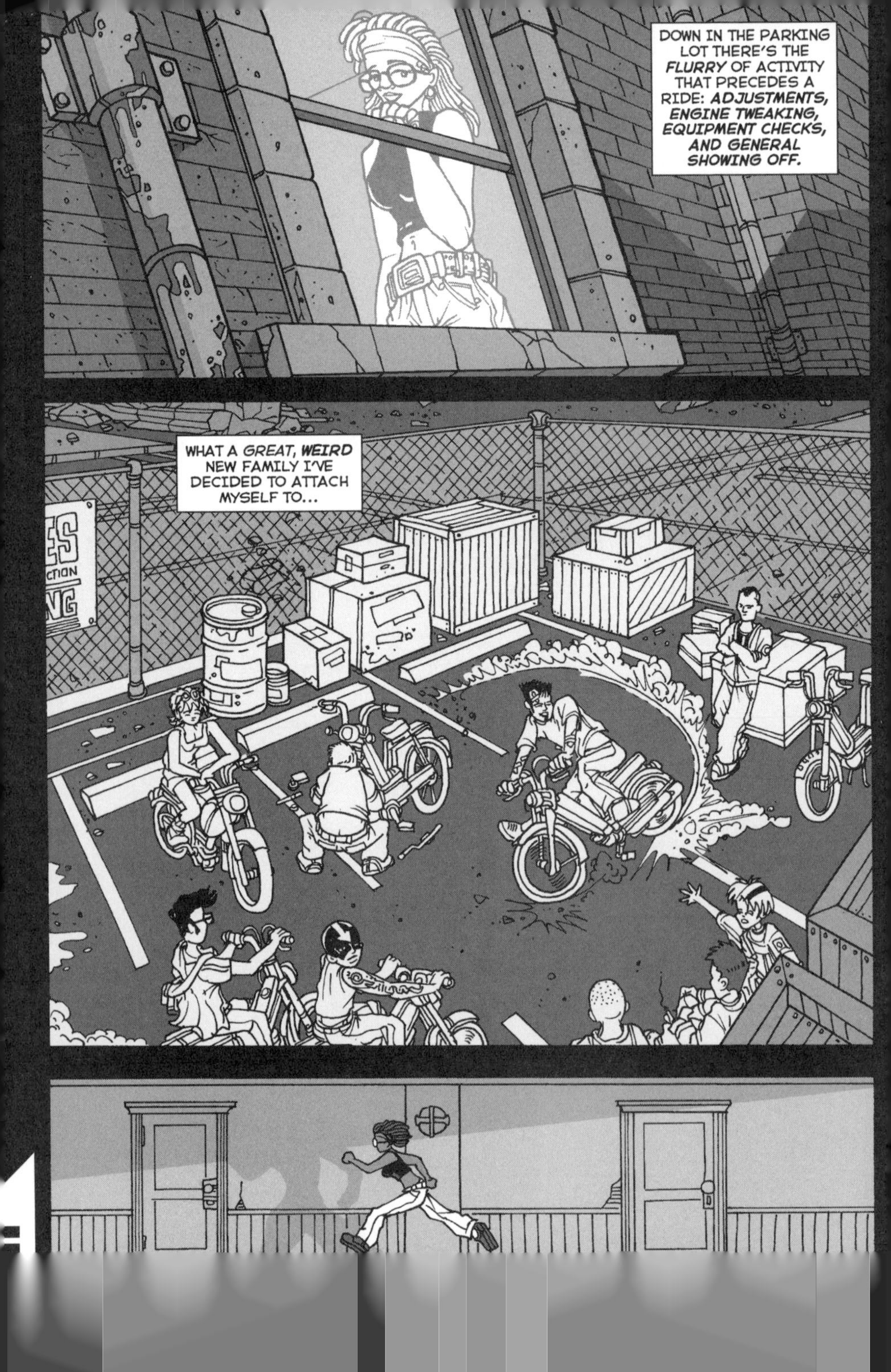
DOWN IN THE PARKING LOT THERE'S THE *FLURRY* OF ACTIVITY THAT PRECEDES A RIDE: ***ADJUSTMENTS, ENGINE TWEAKING, EQUIPMENT CHECKS, AND GENERAL SHOWING OFF.***
WHAT A *GREAT*, **WEIRD** NEW FAMILY I'VE DECIDED TO ATTACH MYSELF TO...

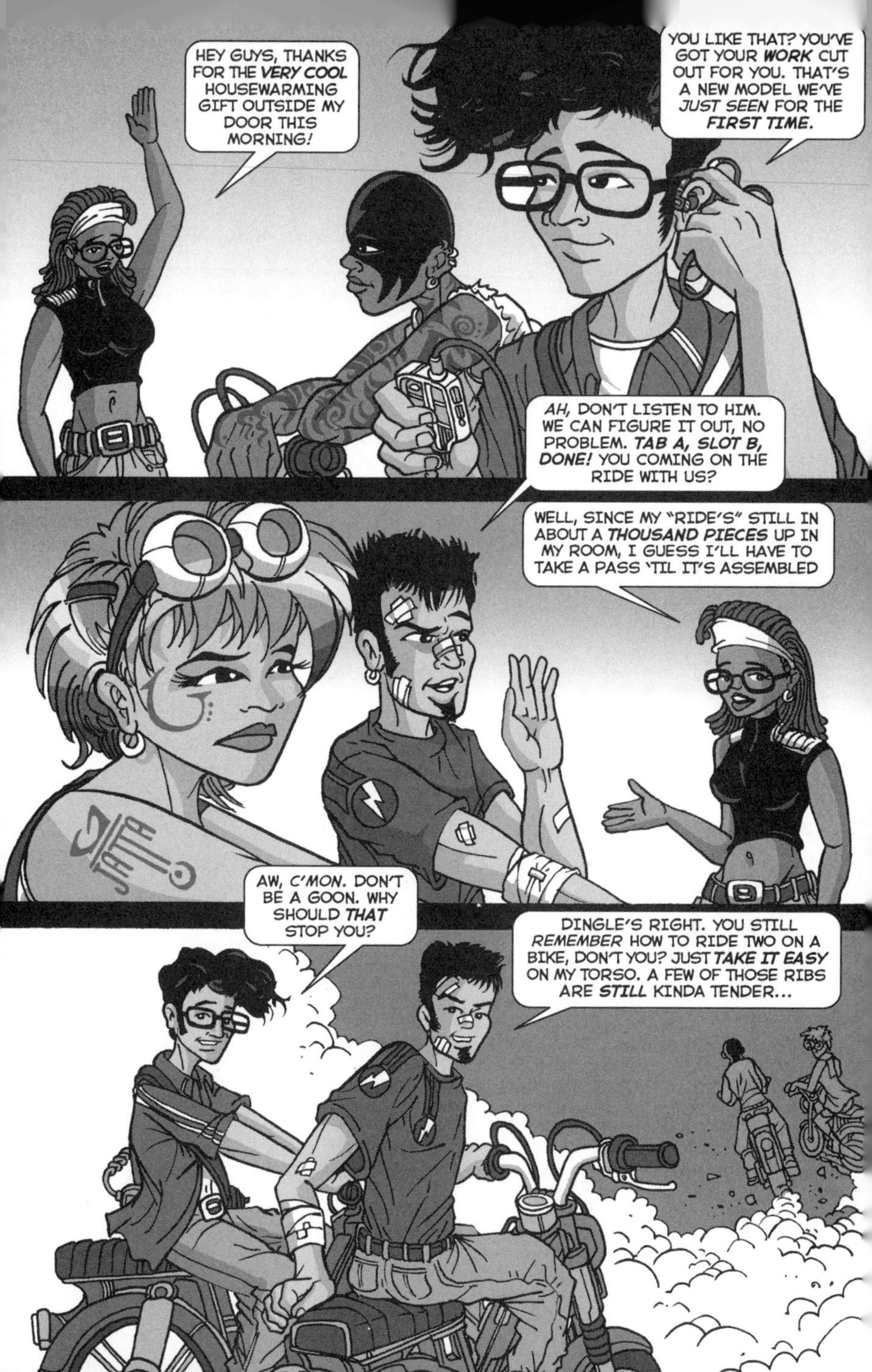
HEY GUYS, THANKS FOR THE VERY COOL HOUSEWARMING GIFT OUTSIDE MY DOOR THIS MORNING!
YOU LIKE THAT? YOU'VE GOT YOUR WORK CUT OUT FOR YOU. THAT'S A NEW MODEL WE'VE JUST SEEN FOR THE FIRST TIME.
AH, DON'T LISTEN TO HIM. WE CAN FIGURE IT OUT, NO PROBLEM. TAB A, SLOT B, DONE! YOU COMING ON THE RIDE WITH US?
WELL, SINCE MY "RIDE'S" STILL IN ABOUT A THOUSAND PIECES UP IN MY ROOM, I GUESS I'LL HAVE TO TAKE A PASS 'TIL IT'S ASSEMBLED
AW, C'MON. DON'T BE A GOON. WHY SHOULD THAT STOP YOU?
DINGLE'S RIGHT. YOU STILL REMEMBER HOW TO RIDE TWO ON A BIKE, DON'T YOU? JUST TAKE IT EASY ON MY TORSO. A FEW OF THOSE RIBS ARE STILL KINDA TENDER...

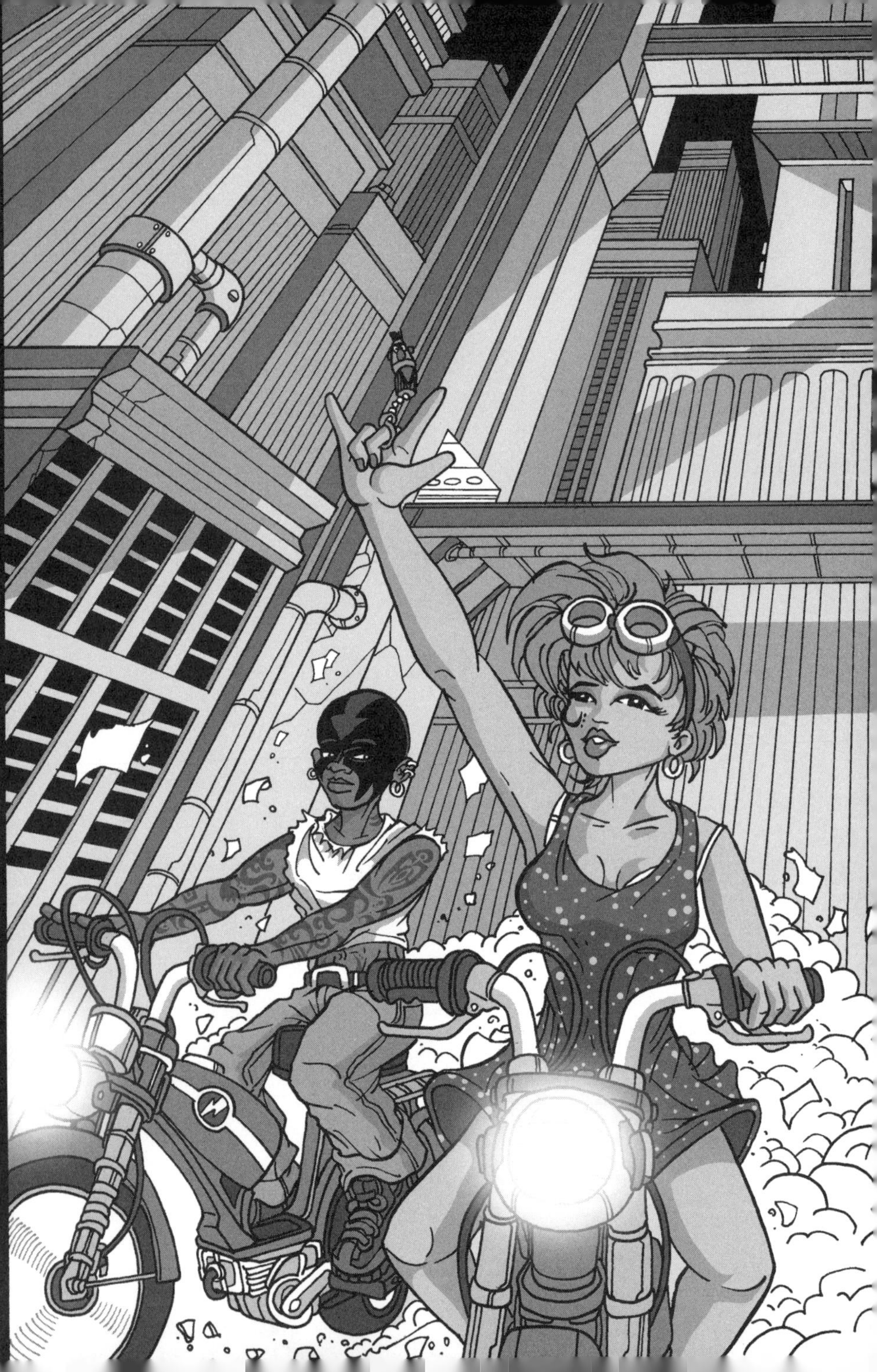

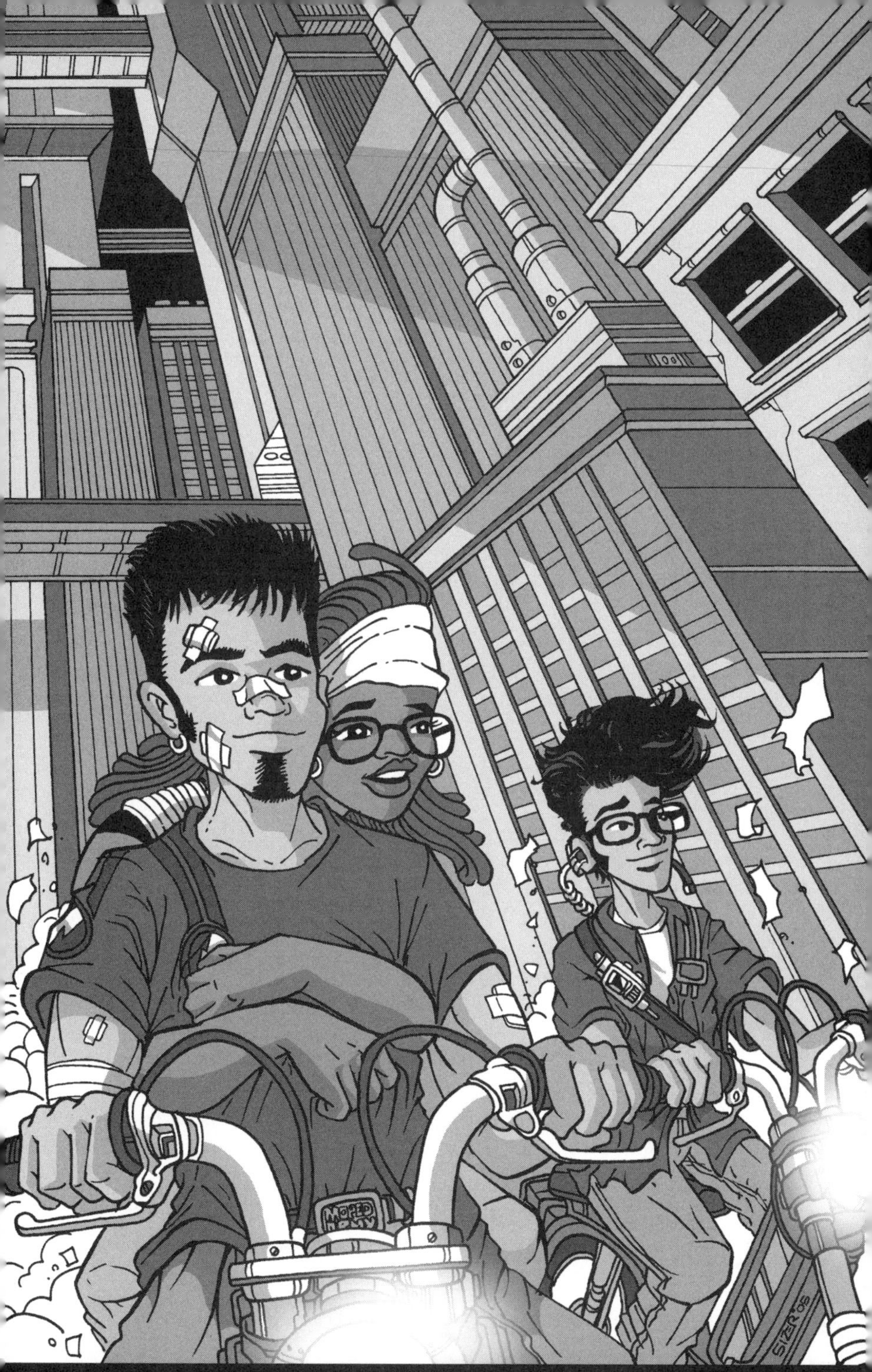
MOPED ARMY
SIZER '05

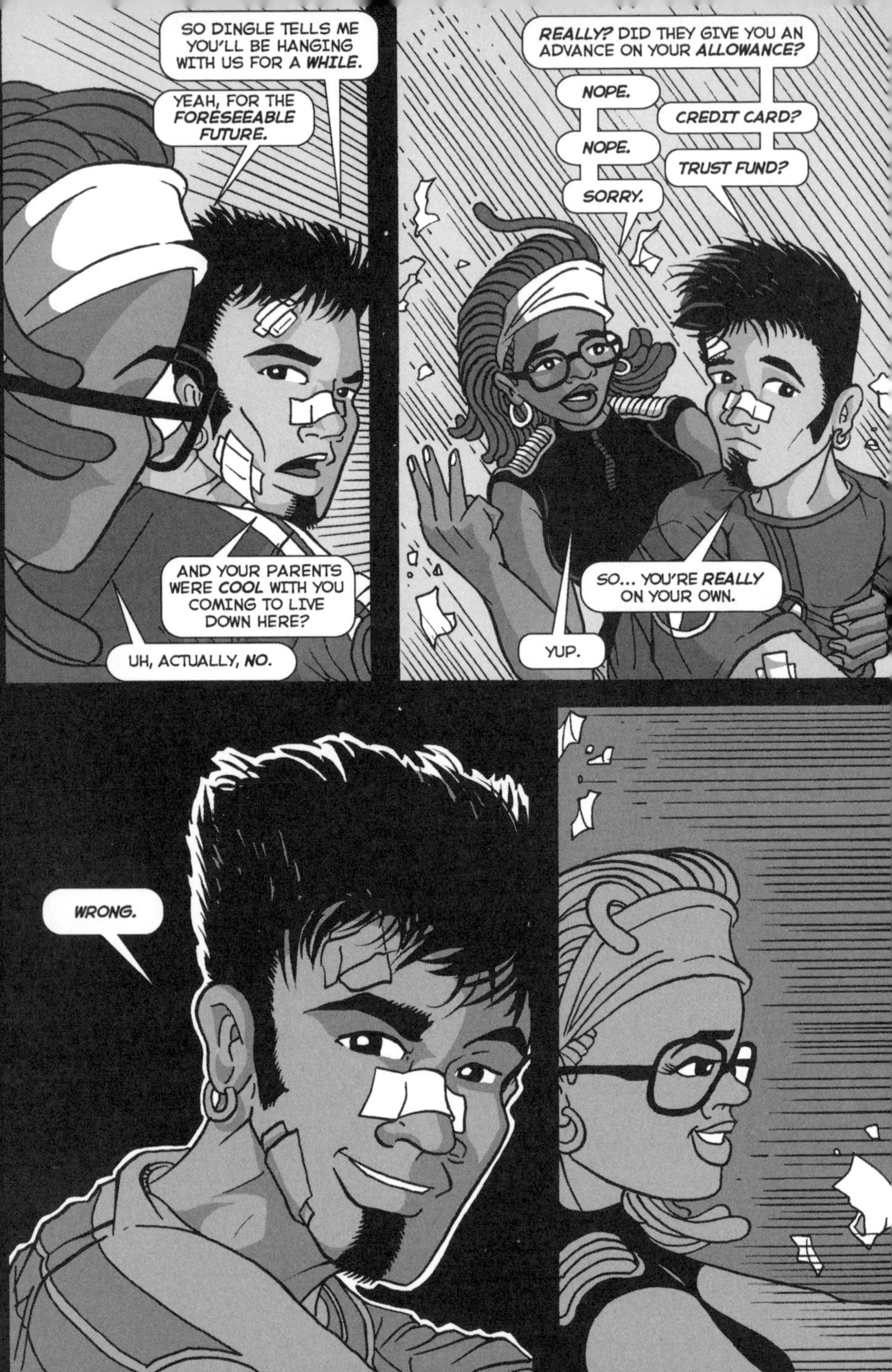
SO DINGLE TELLS ME YOU'LL BE HANGING WITH US FOR A *WHILE*.
YEAH, FOR THE *FORESEEABLE FUTURE*.
AND YOUR PARENTS WERE *COOL* WITH YOU COMING TO LIVE DOWN HERE?
UH, ACTUALLY, *NO*.
REALLY? DID THEY GIVE YOU AN ADVANCE ON YOUR *ALLOWANCE?*
NOPE.
CREDIT CARD?
NOPE.
TRUST FUND?
SORRY.
SO... YOU'RE *REALLY* ON YOUR OWN.
YUP.
WRONG.

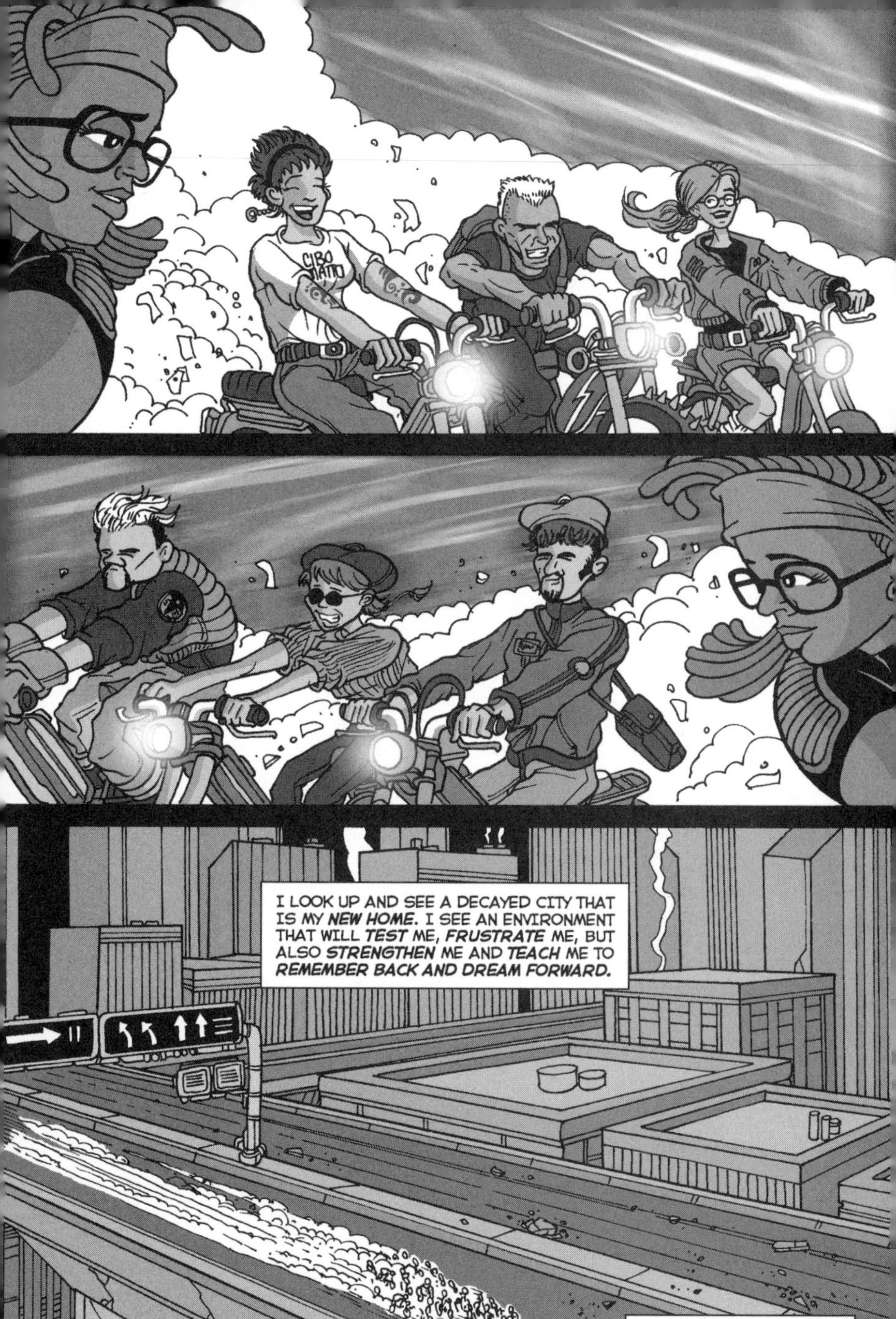
CIBO MATTO
I LOOK UP AND SEE A DECAYED CITY THAT IS MY NEW HOME. I SEE AN ENVIRONMENT THAT WILL TEST ME, FRUSTRATE ME, BUT ALSO STRENGTHEN ME AND TEACH ME TO REMEMBER BACK AND DREAM FORWARD.
FOR THE FIRST TIME IN MY LIFE, I ALLOW MYSELF TO SEE MY FUTURE.

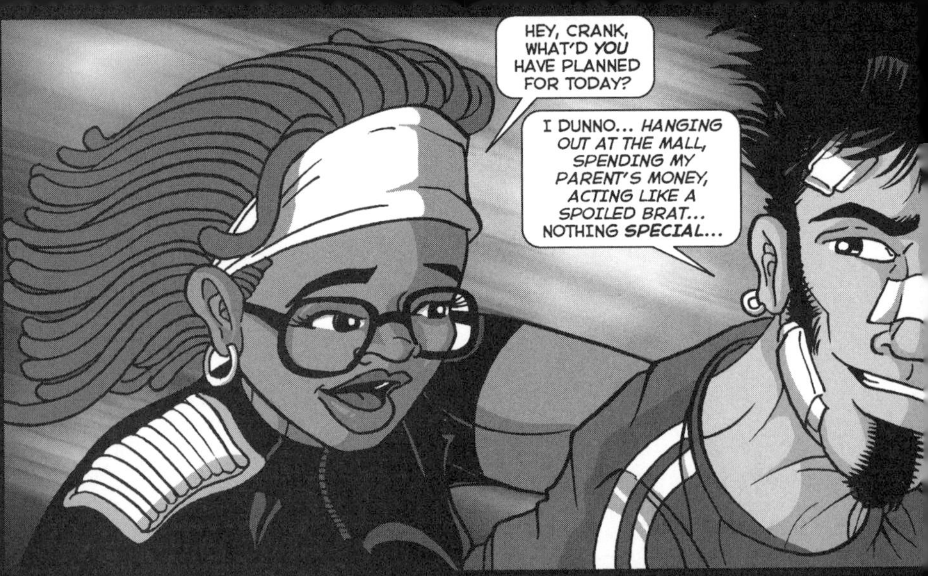
HEY, CRANK, WHAT'D YOU HAVE PLANNED FOR TODAY?
I DUNNO... HANGING OUT AT THE MALL, SPENDING MY PARENT'S MONEY, ACTING LIKE A SPOILED BRAT... NOTHING SPECIAL...

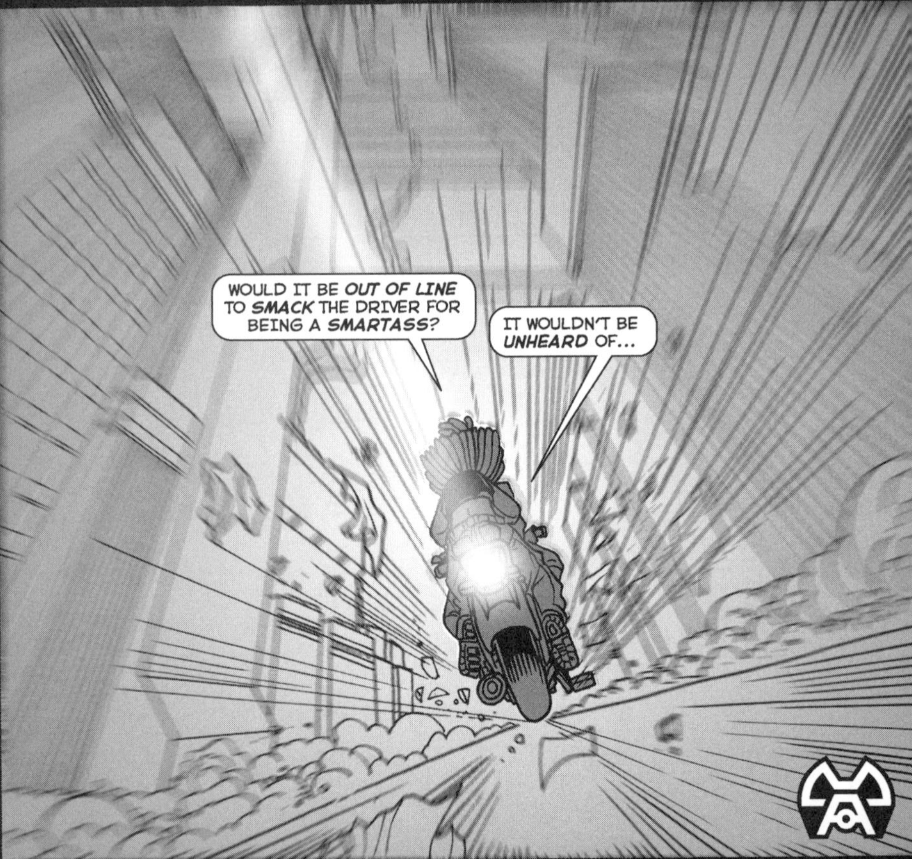
WOULD IT BE OUT OF LINE TO SMACK THE DRIVER FOR BEING A SMARTASS?
IT WOULDN'T BE UNHEARD OF...

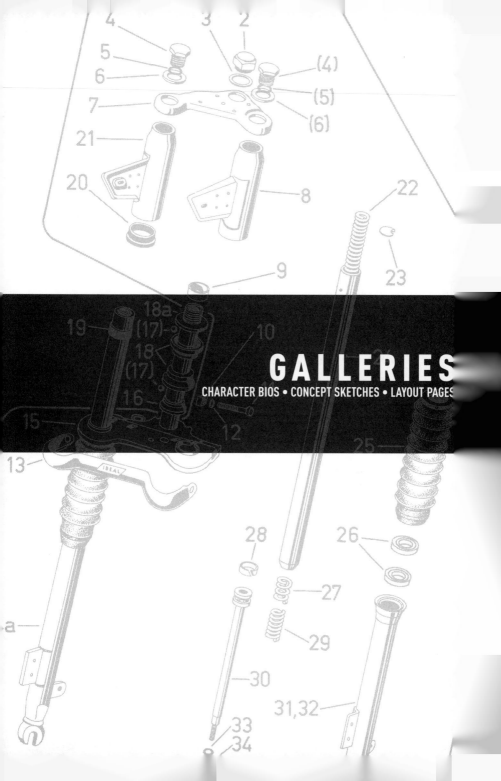

GALLERIES

CHARACTER BIOS • CONCEPT SKETCHES • LAYOUT PAGES

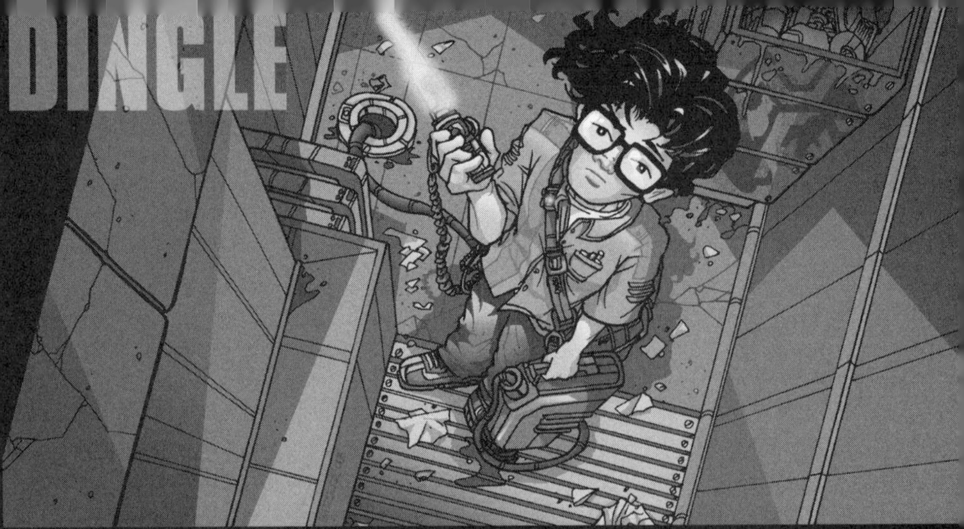
DINGLE

AGE: 22 • MOPED MODEL: MOTOBECANE © 50V (Heavily Modified Version)

INFOBYTE: I HANDLE THE TECH END OF THINGS FOR THE MOPED ARMY. CRANK AND I DISCOVERED THE ARCHIVE FILES FOR THI ORIGINAL MOPED ARMY FROM THE LATE 20TH CENTURY, AND HAVE SPENT THE LAST 5 YEARS TRACING THE DIGITAL REMNANTS OF THI ORGANIZATION. THEIR INFO WAS WELL ENCRYPTED, BUT SERIOUSLY FRAGGED AND HARD TO RECONFIGURE. MOST OF THE TECH FROM BACK THEN DOESN'T EVEN EXIST ANY MORE. THEY SEEMED TO HAVE A TON OF DOCUMENTATION ON THEMSELVES, BUT TIME AND TECH HAS NOT BEEN KIND TO THOSE FILES. I JUST HOPE THERE'S SOMETHING LEFT FOR ME TO FIND...

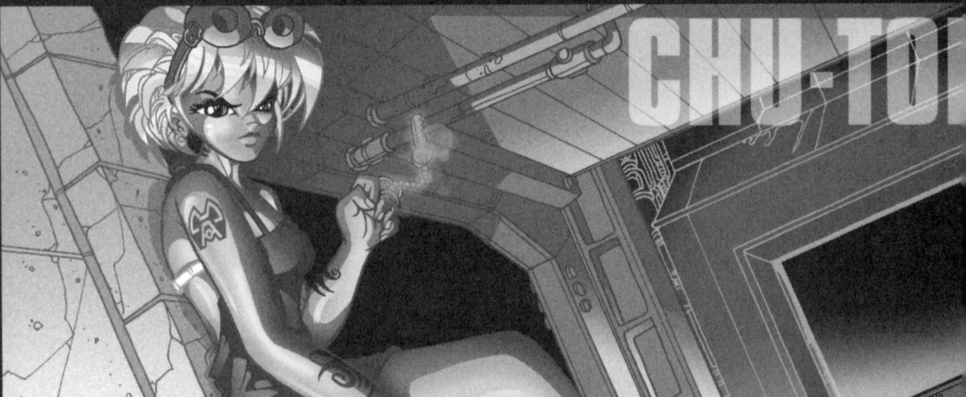
CHU-TOI
SIZER'03

AGE: 19 • MOPED MODEL: SACHS © PRIMA 5 (Heavily Modified Version)

INFOBYTE: THESE BOARDS ARE SO FUCKIN' STUPID, CUZ WE ALL KNOW EACH OTHER, SO WHY DO WE HAVE TO DO THEM IN THE FIRS PLACE? MY NAME IS CHU TOI, WHICH SOUNDS LIKE "CHEW TOY", SO CUT THE CRAP AND GET OVER IT ALREADY. I AM ONE OF THE FEV GIRLS WITH ENOUGH BALLS TO RIDE WITH THESE OTHER DORKS, AND IF ANYONE TELLS YOU THAT I DIDN'T BUILD MY OWN BIKE, THEY'R A DAMN LIAR! JATTA AND I HAVE BEEN GOING OUT FOR TWO YEARS, AND THE ONLY THING HE NEEDS TO CHANGE IS HIS ILLUSION THA I AM NOT FULLY CAPABLE OF KICKING HIS ASS AROUND THE BLOCK IF I HAVE TO. BUT I STILL LOVE THE BIG RETARD, SO I TRY NOT TO EMBARRASS HIM TOO MUCH IN PUBLIC. IS THAT ENOUGH? CAN I GO?

CRANK

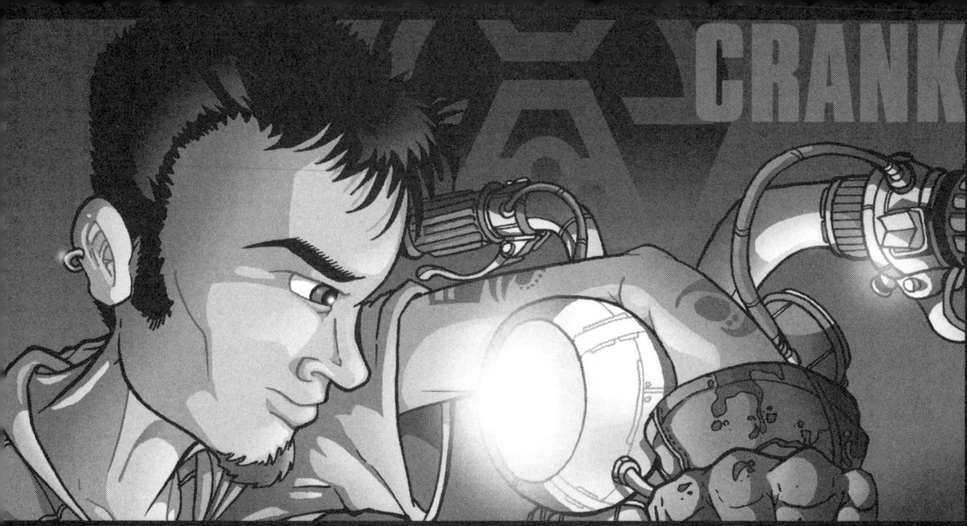

AGE: 23 • MOPED MODEL: CARABELA © SPORT DELUXE (Heavily Modified Version)

INFOBYTE: I LOVE MY BIKES, AND THAT'S REALLY ALL YOU NEED TO KNOW. SOME JOKERS IN THE ARMY CALL ME A MECHANICAL GENIUS, BUT THAT'S REALLY ALL CRAP. I JUST LIKE GETTING MY HANDS DIRTY AND RESURRECTING THESE BEAUTIFUL OLD MACHINES AND MAKING THEM RUN AGAIN. IT'S NOT EASY; SOME OF THESE MOPEDS ARE TOO FAR GONE TO REBUILD, AND NEW PARTS DON'T EXIST. SO I EITHER WORK AROUND IT OR GIVE UP. I'VE SEEN PEOPLE WHO HAVE GIVEN UP DOWN HERE, AND THEY STOP LIVING, EVEN THOUGH THEY'RE STILL TECHNICALLY ALIVE. THAT'S JUST NOT AN OPTION FOR ME, SO IF THAT MAKES ME A GENIUS, THEN THAT'S WHAT I HAVE TO BE.

JATTA

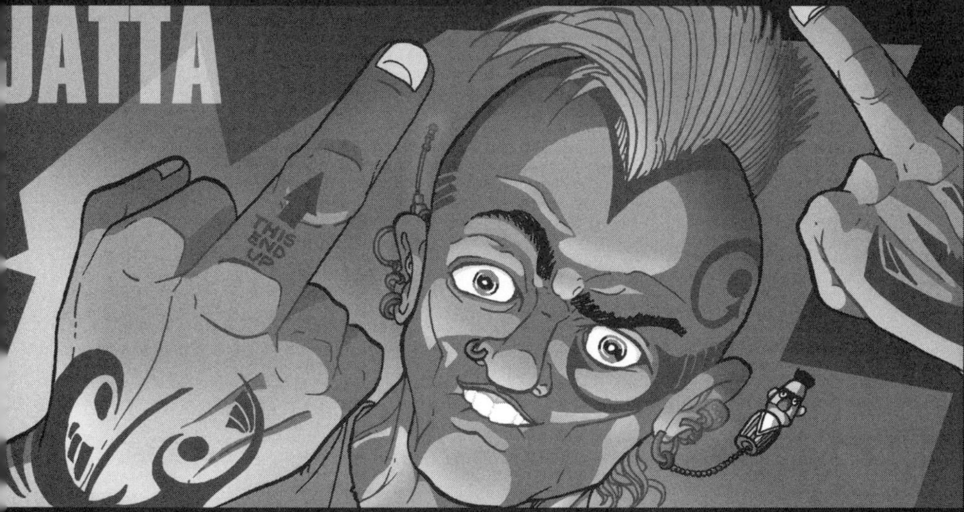
THIS END UP

AGE: 20 • MOPED MODEL: FOXI © GT SPORT (Heavily Modified Version)

INFOBYTE: NOBODY RIDES HARDER THAN I DO IN THIS EXCELLENT ORGANIZATION, AND I'VE GOT THE SKIDMARKS TO PROVE IT. I AM THE ELITE FRONT GUARD SCOUT FOR THE "SWARM AND DESTROY" UNIT OF THE MOPED ARMY. 45 AIRCARS TRASHED. 112 MISSION RIDES IN THE LAST YEAR. ZERO DEATHS FOR MY UNIT, BUT HEAVY LOSSES FOR THE PUDWACKERS WHO SCREW WITH US! I'VE GOT A 10 SQUARE MILE SAFE ZONE PATROLLED AND SECURED AND WE HAVE KEPT "MOPED CENTER" FREE OF JERK-OFFS, CHEMI-KIDS AND CITYCOPS FOR THE LAST 5 YEARS. PLUS, MY 93% RETRIEVAL RECORD FOR STOLEN BIKES IS ONLY GONNA GO UP, SO WATCH OUT ALL YOU LITTLE NANO-BRATS, 'CUZ JATTA'S GONNA DRIVE SOME "BERT" LEVEL JUSTICE UP YOUR BACK FENDER IF I EVER SEE YOU RIDING A BOOSTED MOPED!

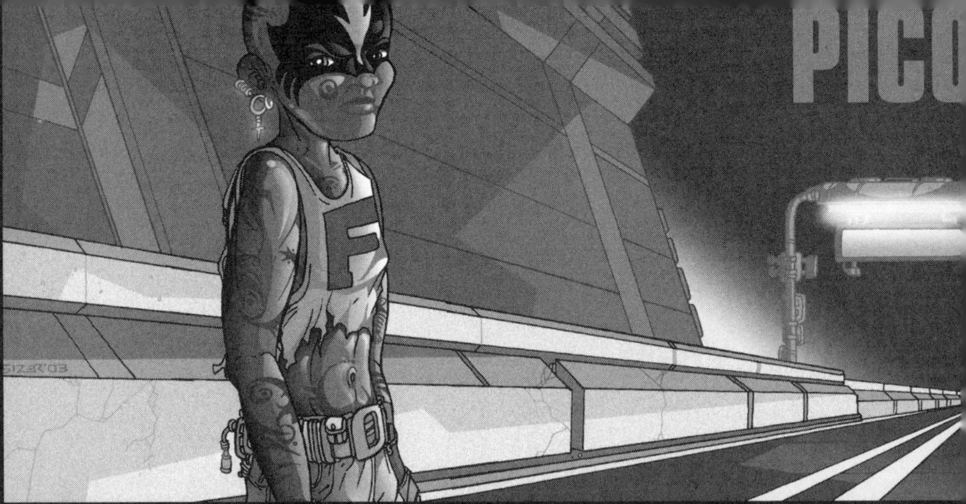
PICO

AGE: 19 • MOPED MODEL: PUCH © KROMAG (Heavily Modified Version)

INFOBYTE: MY NAME IS PICO. I'M 19 YEARS OLD. I RIDE WITH THE MOPED ARMY. PISS OFF.

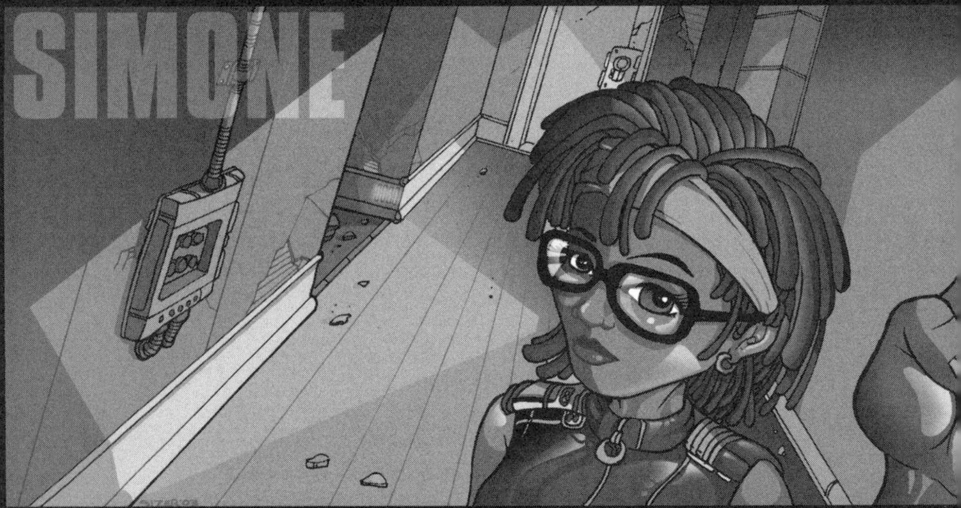
SIMONE

AGE: 18 • MOPED MODEL: NONE

INFOBYTE: I'M KIND OF NEW HERE, SO I DON'T REALLY HAVE MUCH TO ADD. I'M NAMED AFTER NINA SIMONE, AN OLD 20TH CENTUR JAZZ SINGER MY MOM LIKES, AND I'VE LIVED MY ENTIRE LIFE IN THE UPPER SECTION OF BOLT HARBOR. UNTIL A WEEK AGO, I'D NEVE EVEN BEEN DOWN TO "RUST CITY", THE LOWER OLD HALF OF BOLT HARBOR. BUT, SOMETHING... HAPPENED DOWN THERE, AND NOV I FEEL LIKE I NEED TO KNOW MORE ABOUT RUST CITY AND THE PEOPLE WHO LIVE DOWN THERE. I CAN'T EXPLAIN WHY I NEED TO D THIS, BUT I JUST HOPE I CAN FIND WHAT I NEED WITHOUT GETTING KILLED IN THE PROCESS. I DON'T THINK THEY LIKE RICH GIRL

ROUGH EARLY SKETCHES OF THE MAIN CHARACTERS. AT THIS POINT, SIMONE WAS WHITE, PICO WAS MALE, AND JATTA WAS A DREADLOCKED BLACK STRONGMAN. CRANK AND DINGLE WERE PRETTY MUCH FIGURED OUT.

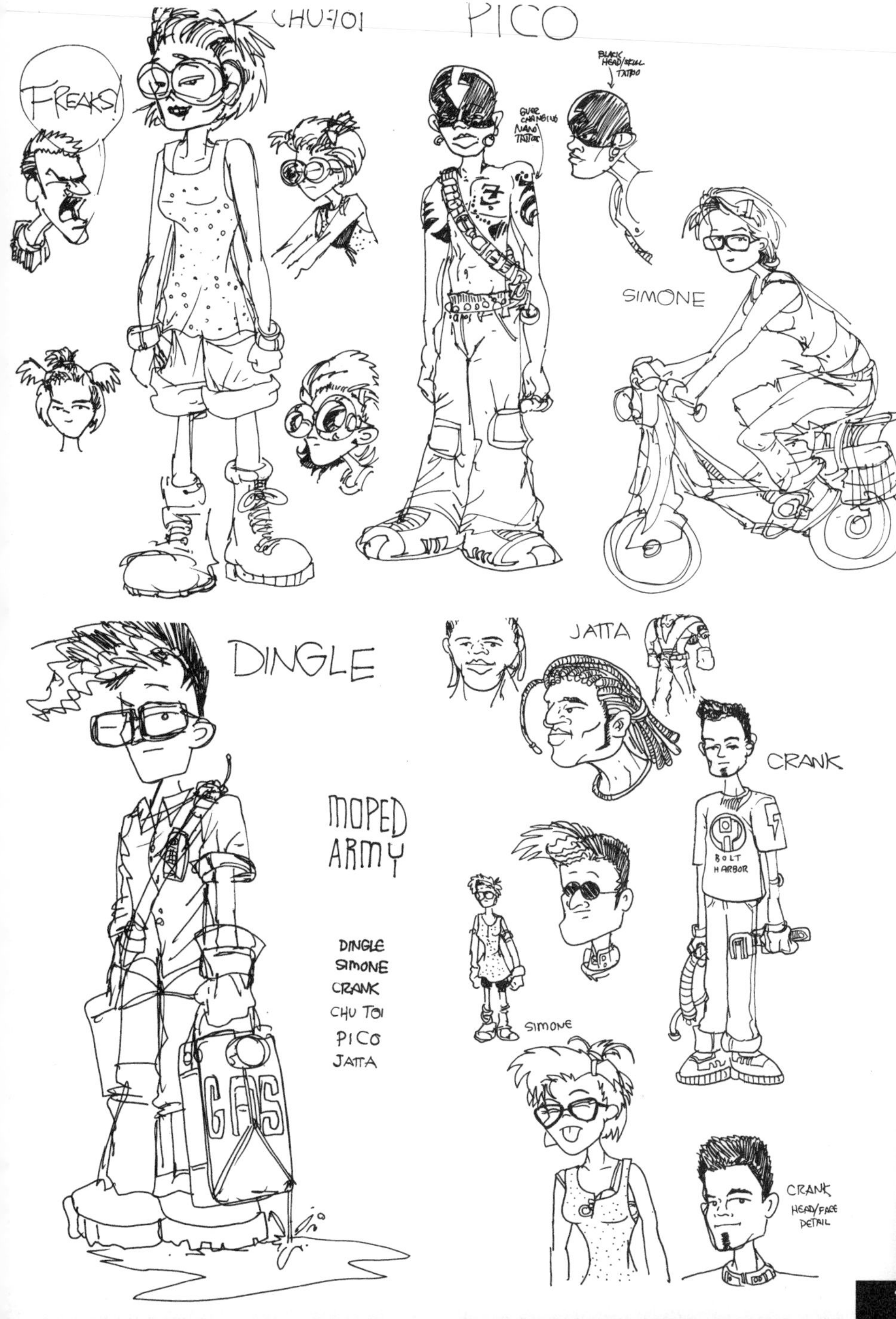

FREAKS!
CHU-TOI
PICO
BLACK HEAD/SKULL TATTOO
EVER CHANGING NANO TATTOO
SIMONE
DINGLE
JATTA
CRANK
MOPED ARMY
BOLT HARBOR
DINGLE
SIMONE
CRANK
CHU TOI
PICO
JATTA
GAS
SIMONE
CRANK
HEAD/FACE DETAIL

REFINED CHARACTER DESIGNS. PICO WAS STILL MALE, BUT THE LOOK WAS PRETTY MUCH FINAL. JATTA WAS A DREADLOCKED GUY UNTIL THE LAST MINUTE. CHU TOI WAS STILL UP IN THE AIR AS TO WHETHER HER REAL NAME WAS SIMONE; EVENTUALLY, I DECIDED TO SPLIT THE TWO AND MAKE SEPARATE CHARACTERS.

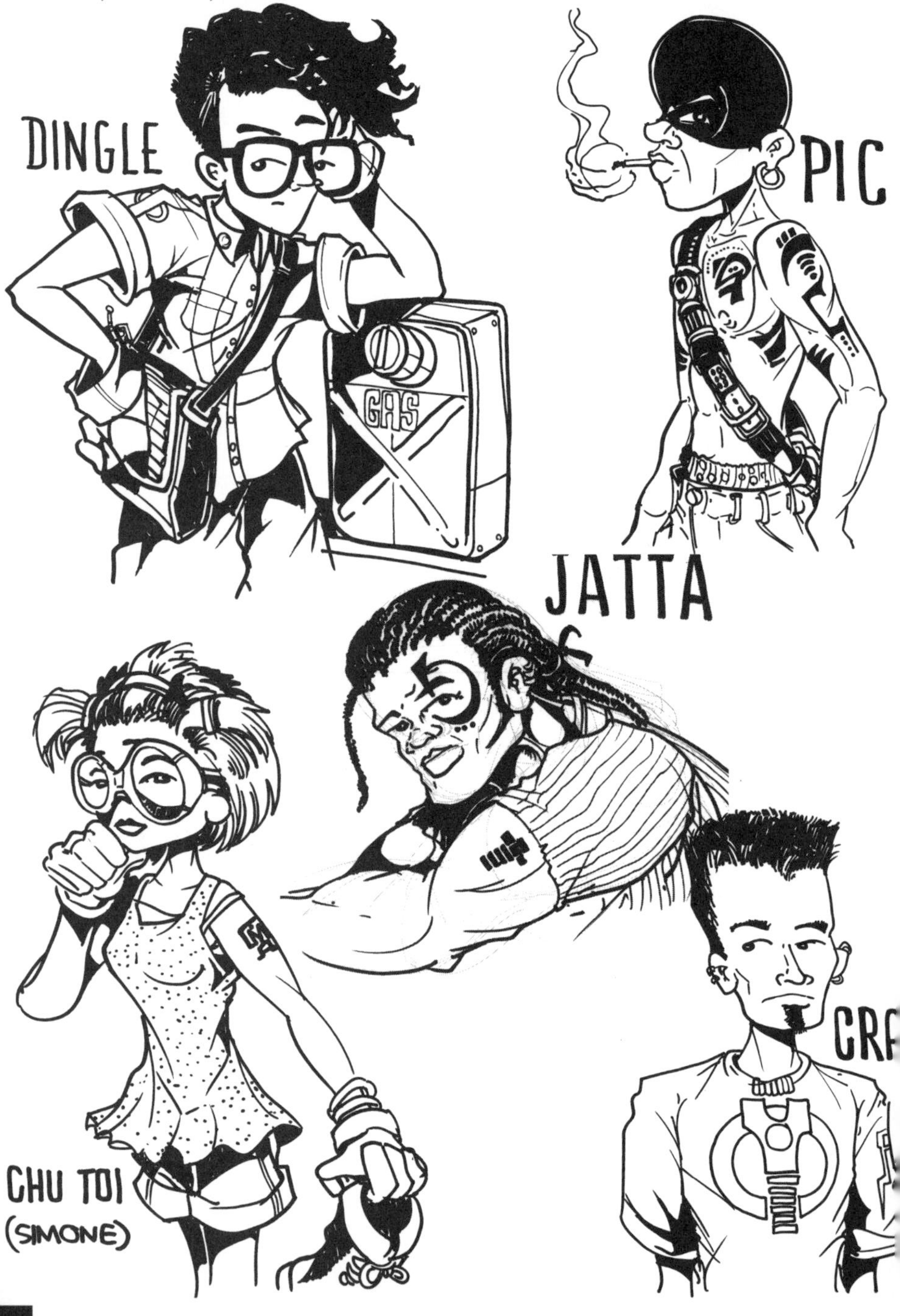
DINGLE
GAS
PIC
JATTA
CHU TOI
(SIMONE)
CR

INITIAL SKETCHES FOR THE BASIC DESIGN AND TECH SPECS FOR AIRCARS.

AIRCAR DESIGNS
AIRCARS ARE LEGAL IN CITIES_ JET & COMBUSTION ENGINES ARE OUTLAWED WITHIN CITYES BECAUSE OF DANGER & POLLUTION TO THE UPPER LEVELS OF THE CITY
FORWARD/REVERSE THRUST TURBINE
SIDE VIEW
AIRCARS MOVE WITH COLUMNS OF FORCED AIR VIA DOWNWARD AND TOP MOUNTED FORWARD AIR-THRUSTERS. A "LOW GRAV" FIELD GENERATOR CREATES AN AREA OF DISRUPTED GRAVITY DIRECTLY UNDER AND AROUND THE CAR WHICH ALLOWS IT TO INITIALLY LIFT AND MAIN-TAIN FLIGHT. THE FORCED AIR ACTUALLY PUSHES THE CAR UP & FORWARD. AIRCARS CAN ONLY FLY 100 FT. ABOVE ANY SURFACE, SO CITIES WITH HIGH BUILDINGS CLOSE TOGETHER WORK VERY WELL WITH AIRCARS.
FRONT HEAD-ON VIEW
THE CARS "POGO" FROM BUILDING TO BUILDING, FORWARD MOMENTUM ALLOWS THEM TO BRIDGE THE GAPS.
BACK
FRONT
TOP VIEW
DOWN TURBINE PODS
BACK
"LOW GRAV" FIELD GENERATORS
MAIN INTAKE TURBINE
FRONT
BOTTOM VIEW

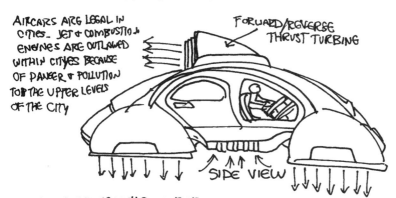

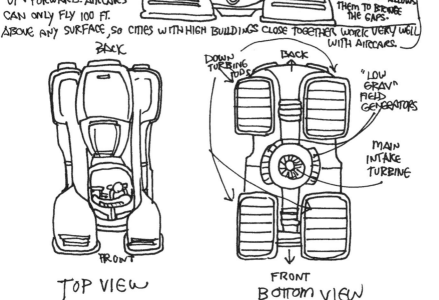

SINCE THE CITY IS SUCH AN INTEGRAL PART OF THE STORY, I DID MANY SKETCHES OF WHAT THE ENVIRONMENT WOULD LOOK LIKE. I ALSO WANTED TO HAVE A SCHEMATIC OF HOW THE CITY WAS STACKED SO I COULD KEEP TRACK OF WHERE THINGS WERE TAKING PLACE. THIS IS AN ROUGH INITIAL CROSS SECTION OF THE CITY.

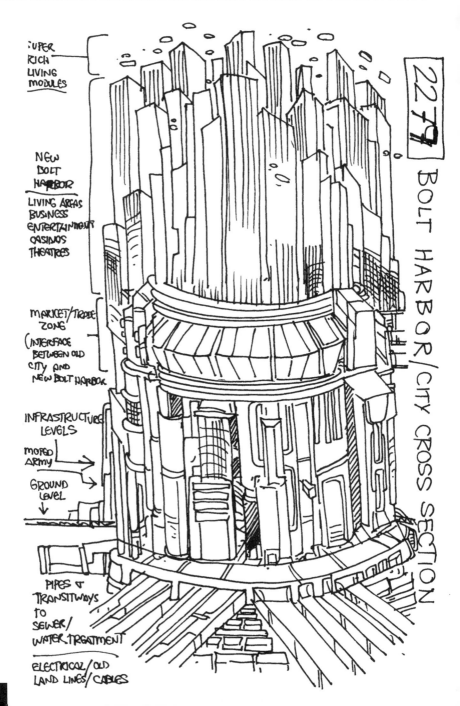

SUPER
RICH
LIVING
MODULES

NEW
BOLT
HARBOR

LIVING AREAS
BUSINESS
ENTERTAINMENT
CASINOS
THEATRES

MARKET/TRADE
ZONE
(INTERFACE
BETWEEN OLD
CITY AND
NEW BOLT HARBOR

INFRASTRUCTURE
LEVELS

MOFED
ARMY

GROUND
LEVEL

PIPES &
TRANSITWAYS
TO
SEWER/
WATER TREATMENT

ELECTRICAL/OLD
LAND LINES/CABLES

2279 BOLT HARBOR/CITY CROSS SECTION

SINCE DINGLE'S SIDE BAG HAD SO MUCH JUNK IN IT, I DECIDED TO TRY AND FIGURE OUT HOW IT ALL MIGHT ACTUALLY FIT IN THERE. HERE'S A ROUGH SKETCH ATTEMPT.

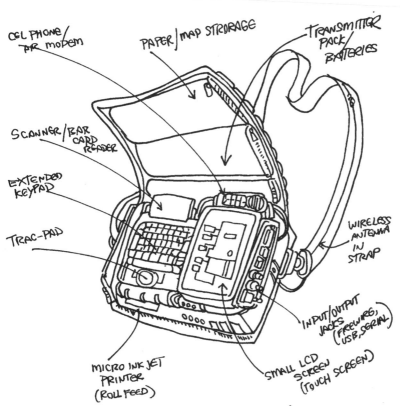

CEL PHONE / AIR MODEM

PAPER / MAP STRORAGE

TRANSMITTER PACK / BATTERIES

SCANNER / BAR CARD READER

EXTENDED KEYPAD

TRAC-PAD

WIRELESS ANTENNA IN STRAP

INPUT/OUTPUT JACKS (FIREWIRE, USB, SERIAL)

MICRO INK JET PRINTER (ROLL FEED)

SMALL LCD SCREEN (TOUCH SCREEN)

CUSTOM BUILT BY DINGLE, MAC + PC HYBRID PLATFORM O.S.

DINGLE'S SIDEBAG

DINGLE'S SIDEBAG IS ESSENTIALLY A REMOTE LAPTOP THAT IS LINKED TO A HARD DRIVE / HUB IN HIS MOPED. ALL MEMBERS OF THE MOPED ARMY ARE MOBILE HUBS, BROADCASTING A BROADBAND SECURED SIGNAL BETWEEN ALL ACTIVE MOPEDS. THEY ALL ACT LIKE THE AIRPORT EXTREME HUBS. THE MORE BIKES OUT AND AROUND AN AREA, THE MORE OF THE ARMY INTERNET / NETWORK EXISTS. THE SIGNALS JUMP FURTHER THE MORE "LINKS" ARE OUT AND AROUND, ALLOWING THE "HOT SPOTS" TO BE MILES AND MILES WIDE.

ONCE I DECIDED TO CREATE SIMONE AS THE LEAD CHARACTER, I WANTED TO MAKE HER PRETTY DIFFERENT LOOKING FROM THE OTHERS. I REALLY VISUALLY WANTED TO HAVE HER BE A DREADLOCKED BLACK WOMAN, SO I DID A TON OF HAIRSTYLE RESEARCH BEFORE FIGURING OUT WHAT LOOK WAS BEST FOR HER. I THEN PROCEEDED TO CURSE MYSELF FOR DESIGNING A COMPLICATED HAIRSTYLE I WOULD HAVE TO DRAW A MILLION TIMES...

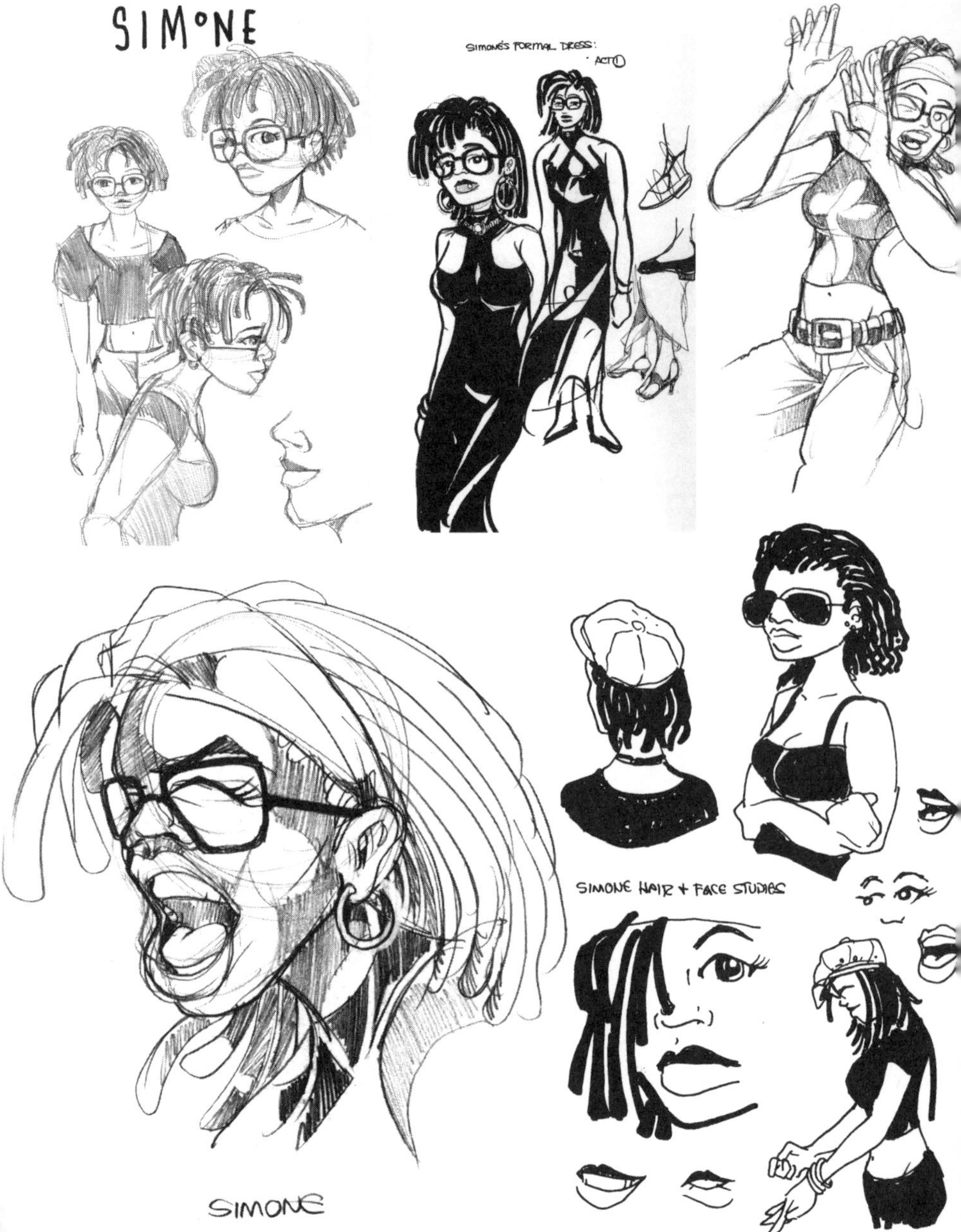
SIMONE
SIMONE'S FORMAL DRESS:
ACT 1
SIMONE HAIR + FACE STUDIES
SIMONE

ONCE THE CAST IS SET, I ALWAYS DO SKETCHES PUTTING THE CHARACTERS TOGETHER TO GET A SENSE OF HOW THEY VISUALLY RELATE, AND ALSO TO FIGURE OUT RELATIVE SCALE, BODY LANGUAGE AND COSTUMING.

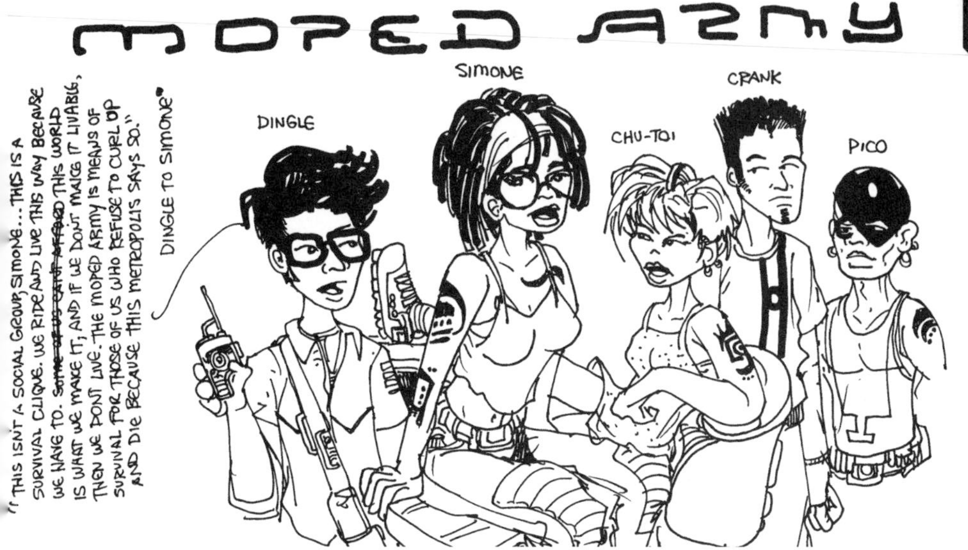
MOPED ARMY
"THIS ISN'T A SOCIAL GROUP, SIMONE... THIS IS A SURVIVAL CLIQUE. WE RIDE AND LIVE THIS WAY BECAUSE WE HAVE TO. THIS WORLD IS WHAT WE MAKE IT, AND IF WE DON'T MAKE IT LIVABLE, THEN WE DON'T LIVE. THE MOPED ARMY IS MEANS OF SURVIVAL FOR THOSE OF US WHO REFUSE TO CURL UP AND DIE BECAUSE THIS METROPOLIS SAYS SO."
DINGLE TO SIMONE"
DINGLE
SIMONE
CHU-TOI
CRANK
PICO

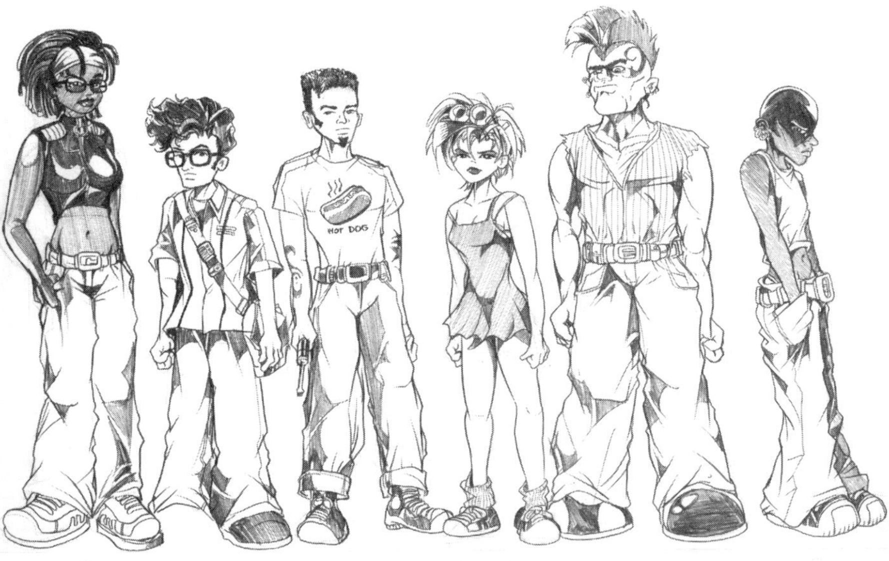
HOT DOG

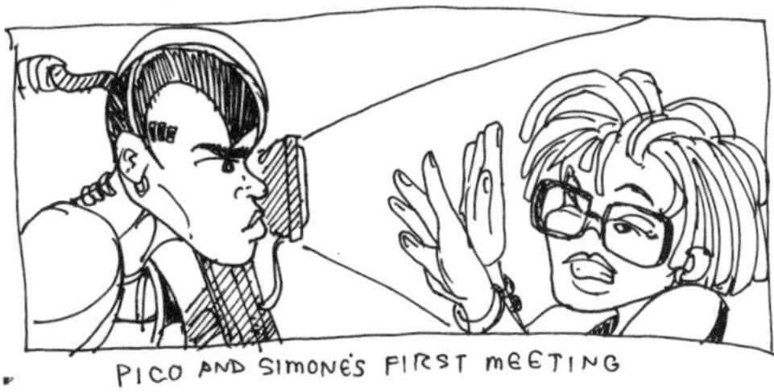

PICO AND SIMONE'S FIRST MEETING

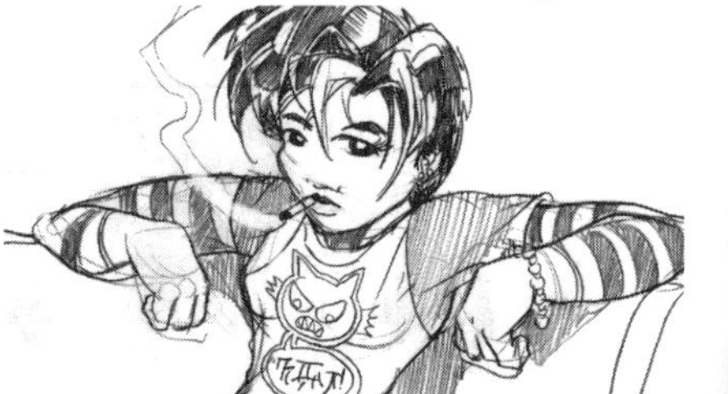

PENCIL SKETCH OF CHU-TOI, A CHARACTER SKETCH OF CRANK'S GIRLFRIEND WHICH NEVER MADE IT INTO THE STORY (SORRY CRANK, MAYBE NEXT TIME!), HEADSHOTS FOR CRANK, AND A SKETCH FOR A CHARACTER NAMED BAY THAT DIDN'T MAKE IT INTO THE BOOK THAT I STILL THOUGHT TURNED OUT PRETTY COOL.

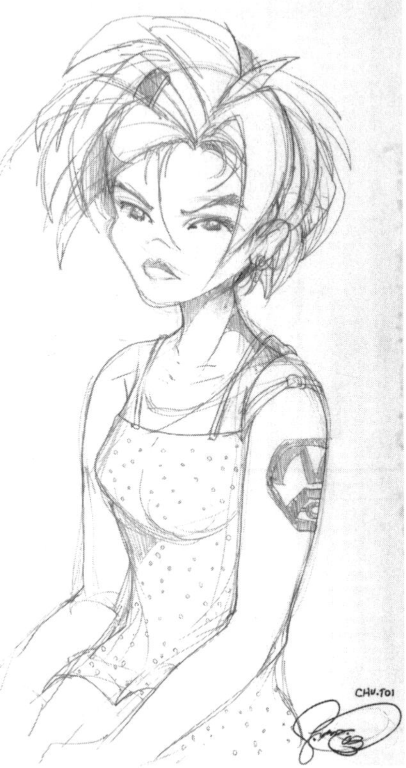
CHU.TOI

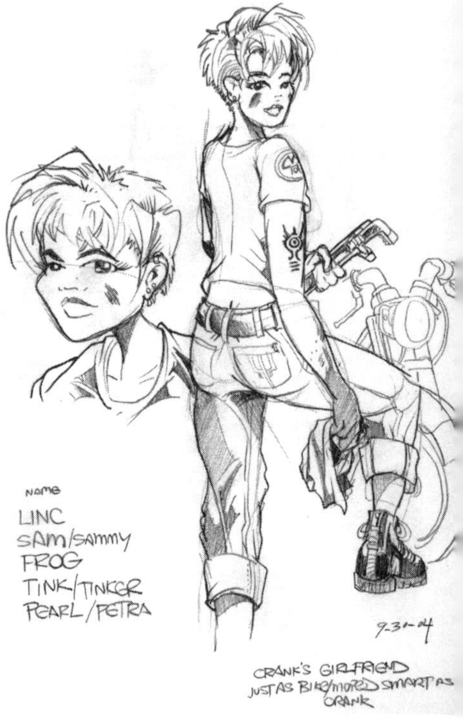
NAME
LINC
SAM/SAMMY
FROG
TINK/TINKER
PEARL/PETRA
9-30-04
CRANK'S GIRLFRIEND
JUST AS BIKE/MORE SMART AS CRANK

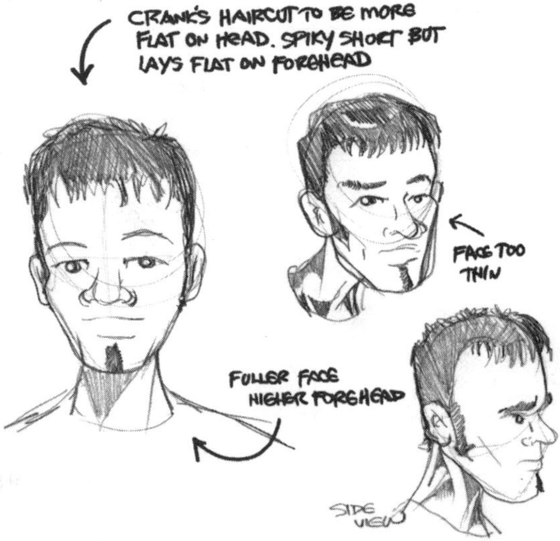
CRANK'S HAIRCUT TO BE MORE FLAT ON HEAD. SPIKY SHORT BUT LAYS FLAT ON FOREHEAD
FACE TOO THIN
FULLER FACE HIGHER FOREHEAD
SIDE VIEW

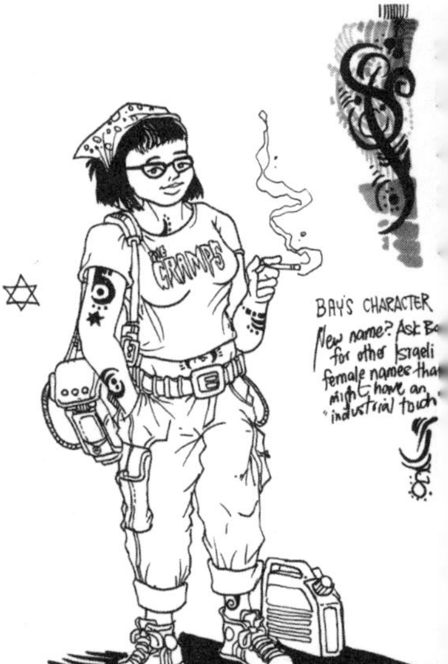
THE CRAMPS
BAY'S CHARACTER
New name? Ask B
for other israeli
female names tha
might have an
"industrial" touch

INITIAL PENCILS FOR THE MASTER CAST SHOT FOR THE SERIES, AND VARIOUS SKETCHES OF MEMBERS ON THEIR MOPEDS AND DURING "SIPHON RUNS" FOR GASOLINE.

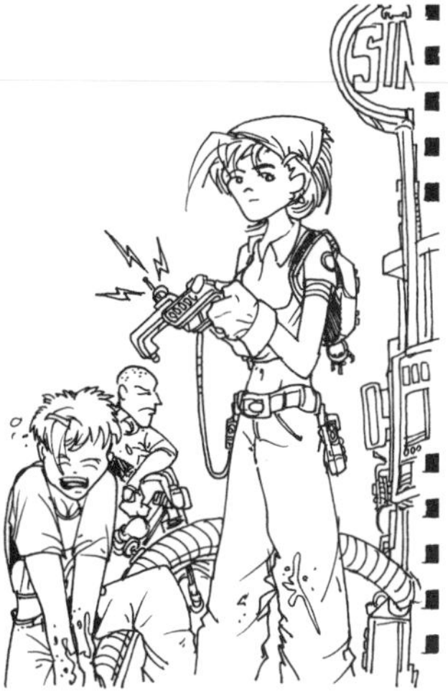

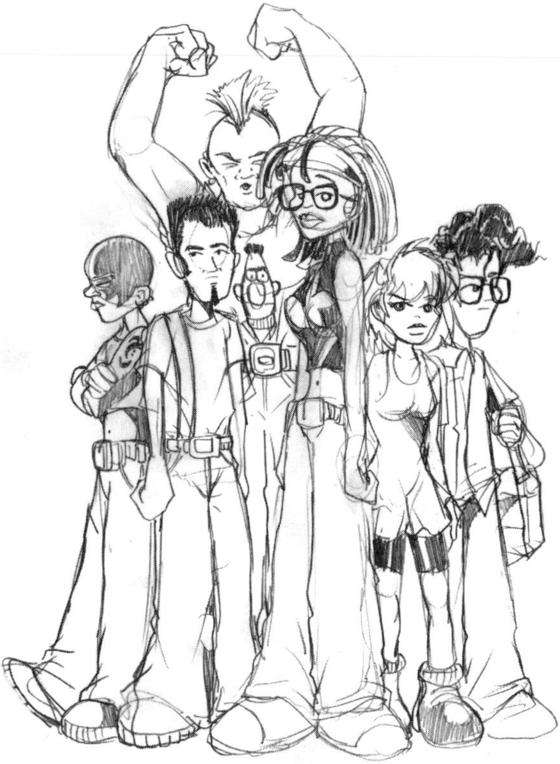

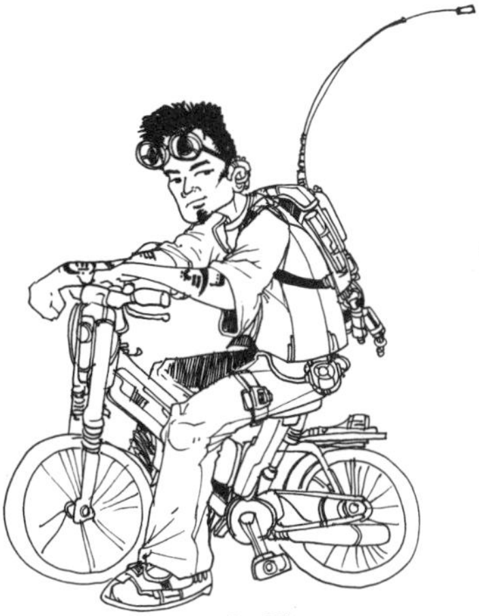

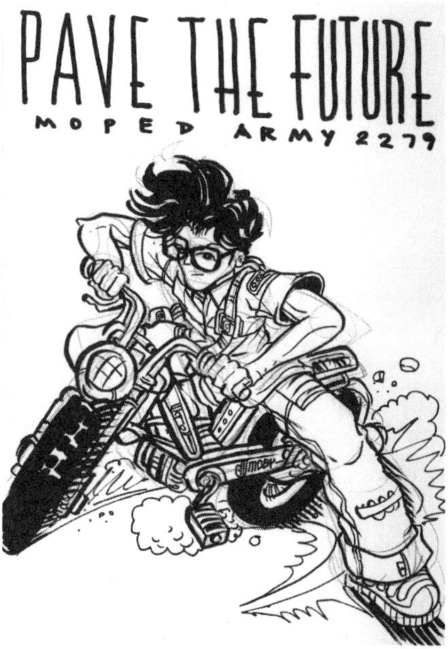
PAVE THE FUTURE
MOPED ARMY 2279

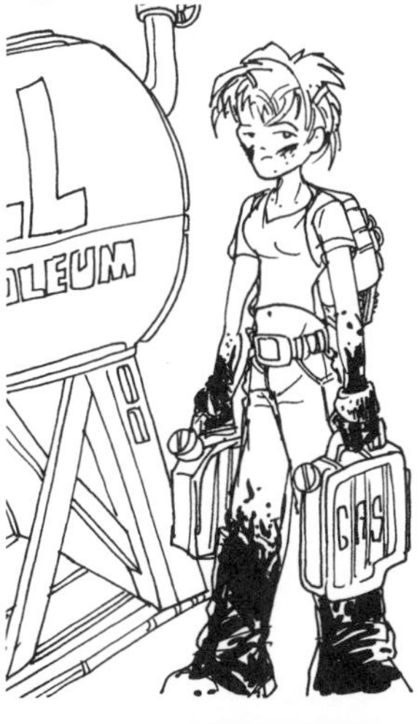
OLEUM
GAS

VARIOUS CONCEPT SKETCHES, INCLUDING THE INITIAL LAYOUT FOR JATTA'S DEATH SCENE, THE FINAL CHARACTER SHEET FOR JATTA, AN UNUSED POLICE UNIT DESIGN, AND A DRAWING DONE FOR A MOPED COUPLE IN THE U.K. WHO USED IT ON THEIR WEDDING INVITES!

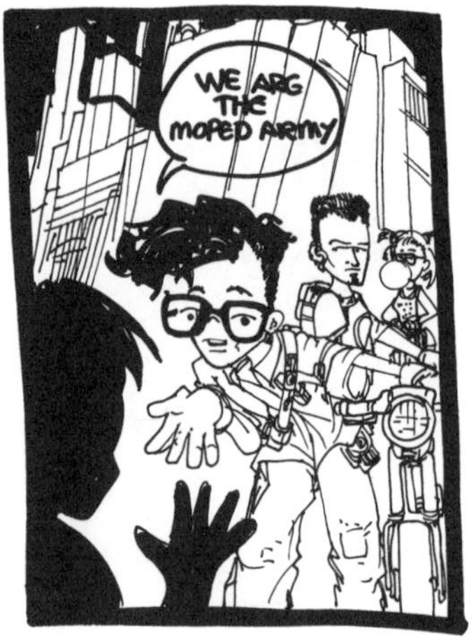
WE ARE THE MOPED ARMY

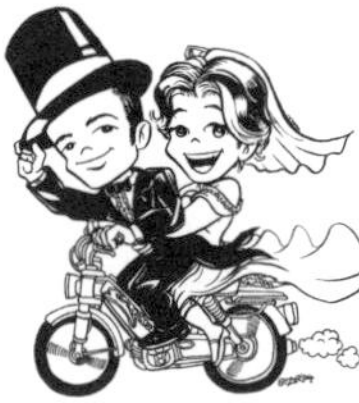

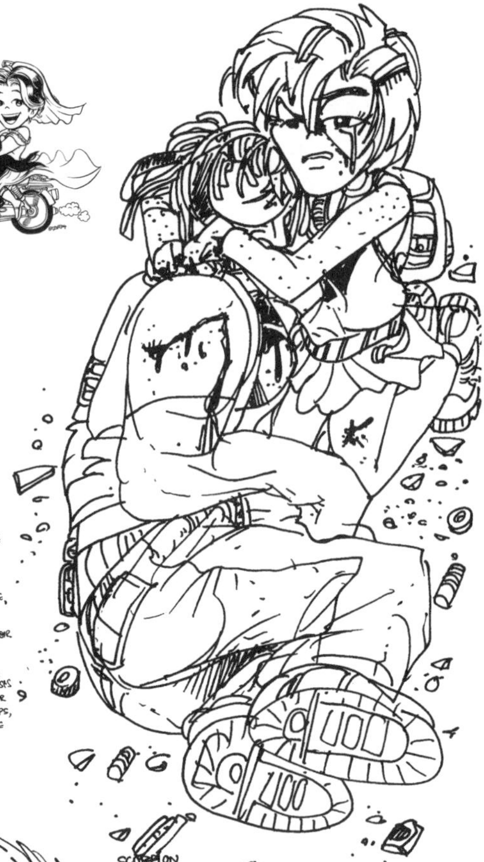

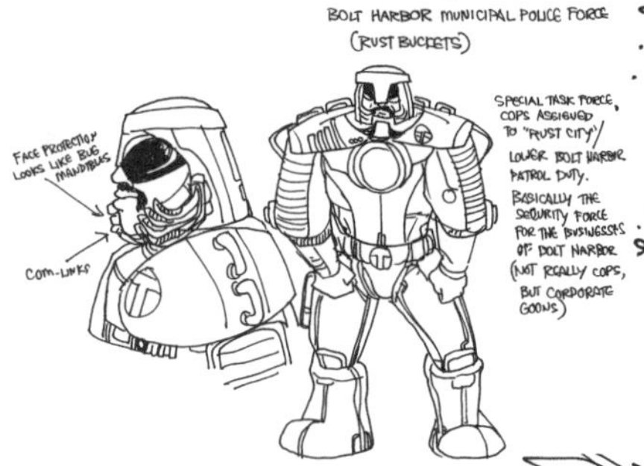
BOLT HARBOR MUNICIPAL POLICE FORCE
(RUST BUCKETS)
FACE PROTECTION LOOKS LIKE BUG MANDIBLES
COM-LINKS
SPECIAL TASK FORCE, COPS ASSIGNED TO "RUST CITY"/ LOWER BOLT HARBOR PATROL DUTY.
BASICALLY THE SECURITY FORCE FOR THE BUSINESSES OF BOLT HARBOR
(NOT REALLY COPS, BUT CORPORATE GOONS)

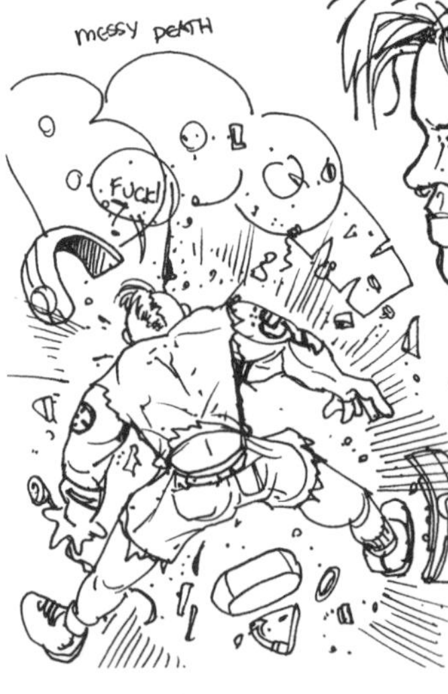
messy death
Fuck!

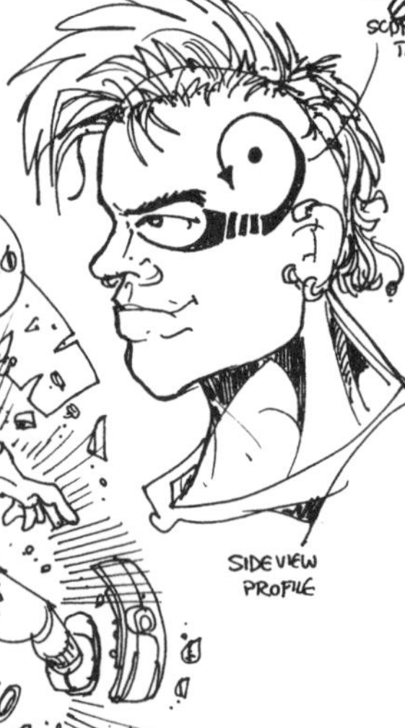
SCORPION TATTOO
SIDE VIEW PROFILE

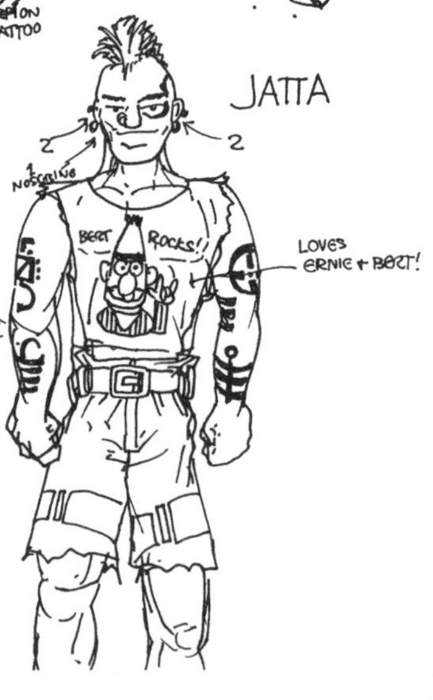
JATTA
2
2
1 NOSE RING
BERT ROCKS!
LOVES ERNIE + BERT!

ACTUAL SCANS OF THE SKETCHBOOK PAGES WITH MY ROUGH PAGE LAYOUTS. AS YOU CAN SEE, THESE THUMBNAIL DRAWINGS SOMETIMES ARE FOLLOWED VERY CLOSELY, AND SOMETIMES CHANGED PRETTY SIGNIFICANTLY WHEN I FINALLY PENCIL THE PAGE. I ALWAYS TRY TO KEEP THESE VERY LOOSE AND ENERGETIC, THEN WORK TO CAPTURE THAT ENERGY WHEN I PENCIL AND INK. (NOTE: THE PAGE SEQUENCE IN MY SKETCHBOOKS IS ALWAYS RIGHT TO LEFT BECAUSE I'M LEFT HANDED.)

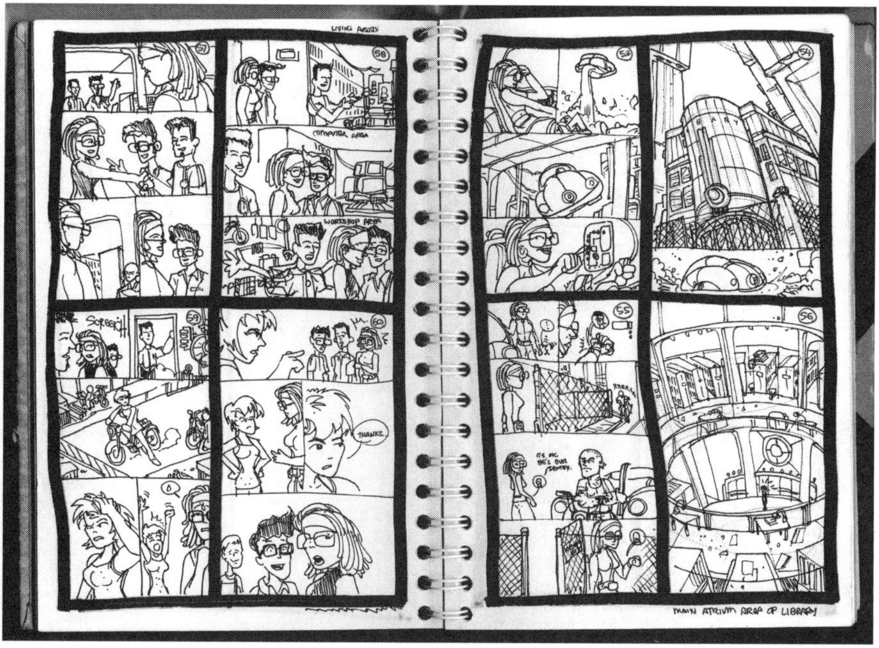
COMPUTER AREA
WORKSHOP AREA
THANKS.
IT'S OK. HE'S OUR SENTRY.
MAIN ATRIUM AREA OF LIBRARY

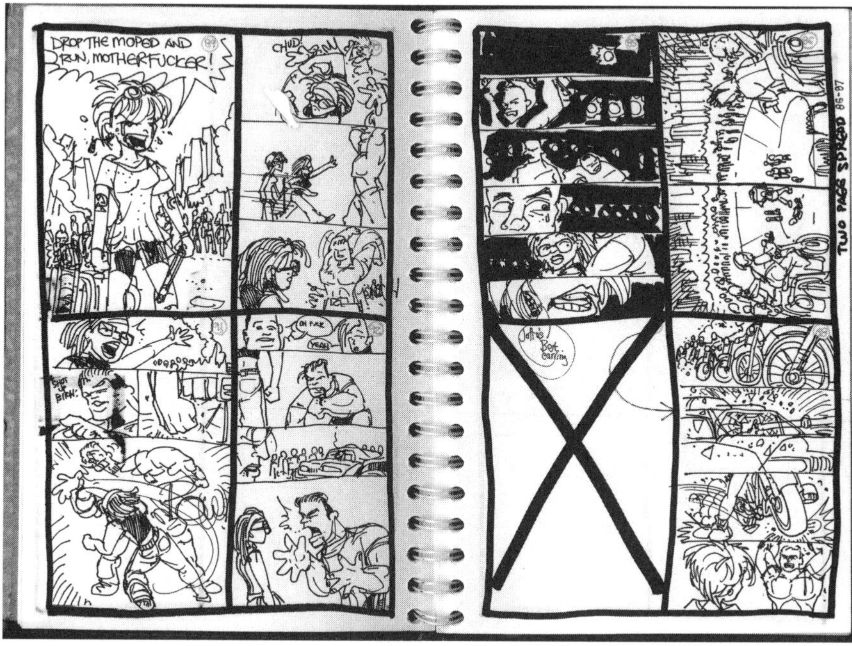
DROP THE MOPED AND RUN, MOTHERFUCKER!
TWO PAGE SPREAD 86-87

AN AWESOME PIN-UP FROM "SWARM AND DESTROY" DVD ARTIST **ZACK PAGE-WOOD**. TO SEE THE FULL COLOR VERSION OF THIS ART, ALONG WITH A TON OF OTHER FULL COLOR CHARACTER SKETCHES, COLOR TEST GALLERIES, AND PROMOTIONAL ARTWORK, CHECK OUT **WWW.PAULSIZER.COM** AND GO TO THE "MOPED ARMY" SECTION FOR MORE ART, OFFICIAL PATCHES AND MOPED ARMY INFORMATION!

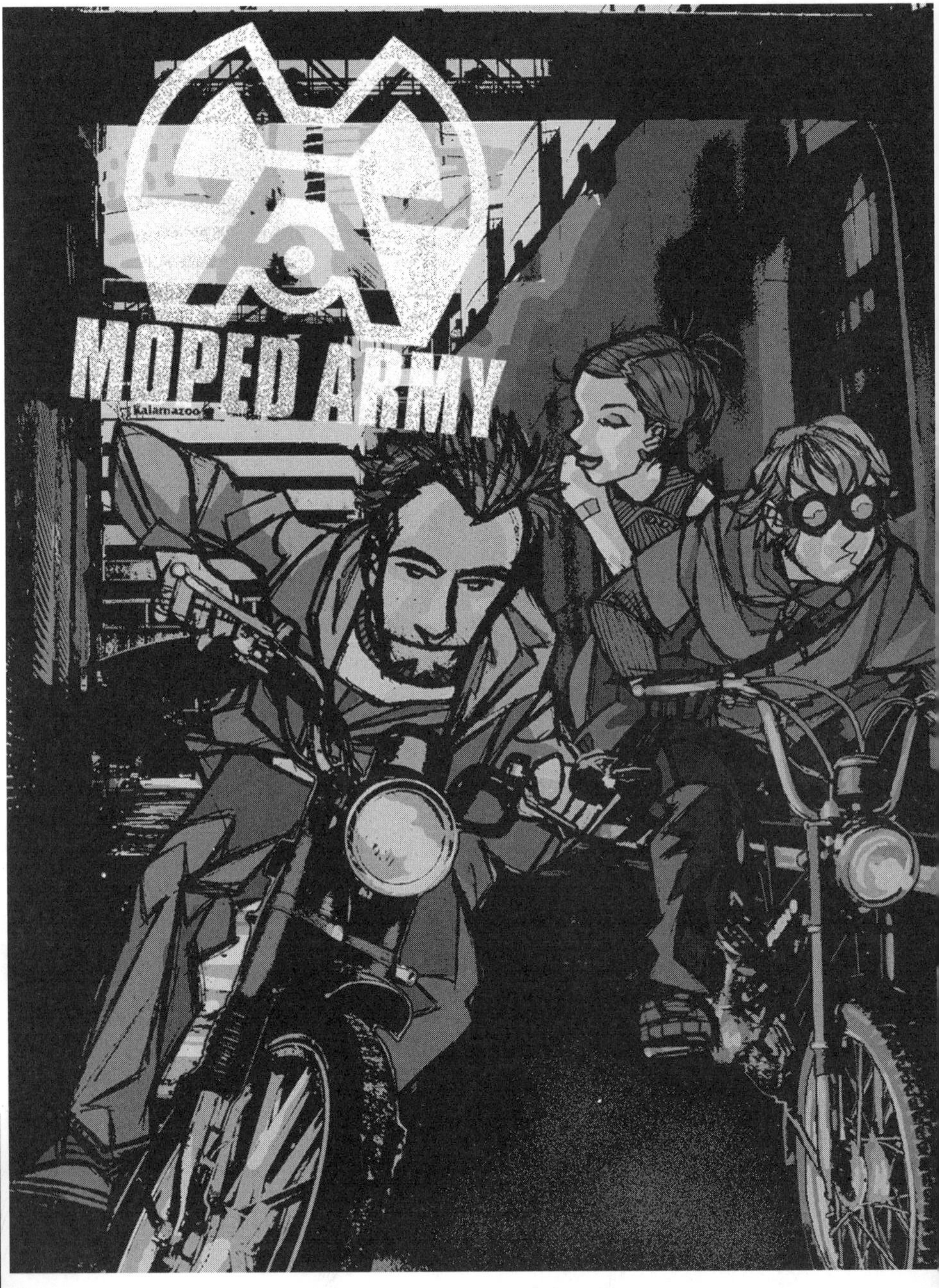
MOPED ARMY
Kalamazoo

ABOUT THE ARTIST

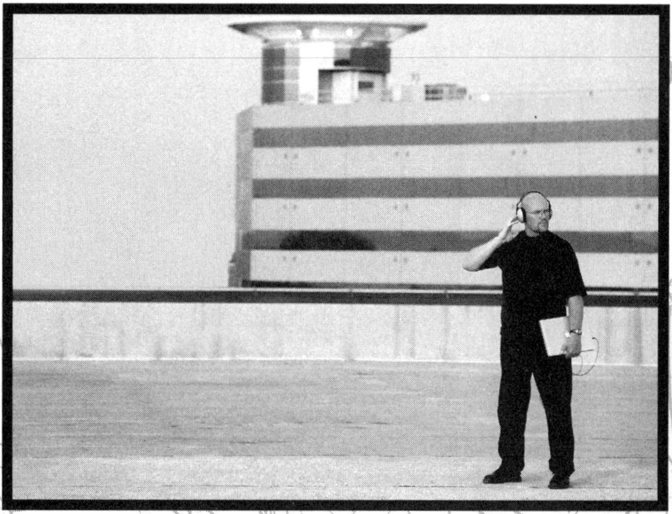

PHOTO: DOUG NEAL

PAUL SIZER has spent two years crafting this tale of moped culture, despite the fact that he doesn't actually own a moped and looks like a circus bear on a tricycle when he does ride one.

Sizer's art career began at age five and has been steadily improving ever since. He began his comics career drawing pictures of the Peanuts characters blowing each other up, then moved to destroying his own creations. At Western Michigan University he produced the national award-winning comic strip **BILL THE RABBIT** for four years. After college, he worked on numerous small press titles, finally releasing his first solo series **LITTLE WHITE MOUSE** in 1997 through Caliber Comics, and then through Blue Line Pro Comics. **LITTLE WHITE MOUSE** was critically praised by fans and professionals alike and produced four series of comics. In 2005, Sizer decided to self-publish all his comic work and started **CAFE DIGITAL STUDIOS** as a publishing venture to produce **LITTLE WHITE MOUSE** and **MOPED ARMY** as graphic novels. Paul's next graphic novel project, **B.P.M.**, will be released in the second half of 2008.

Sizer lives and works in Kalamazoo, Michigan with his wife and fellow comic creator Jane Irwin (Vogelein). For more information on Paul's comic and graphic design work, visit his website at www.paulsizer.com

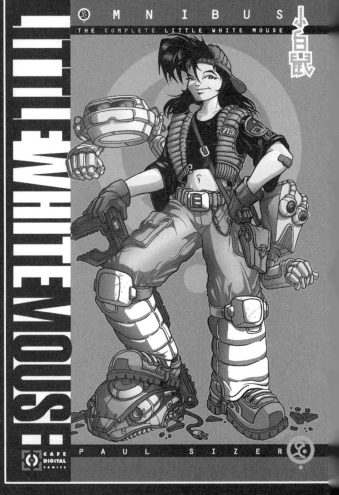